Sensor Technologies

Healthcare, Wellness, and Environmental Applications

Michael J. McGrath

Cliodhna Ní Scanaill

Apress open

Sensor Technologies: Healthcare, Wellness, and Environmental Applications

Michael J. McGrath and Cliodhna Ní Scanaill

President and Publisher: Paul Manning
Lead Editors: Jeffrey Pepper (Apress); Stuart Douglas (Intel)
Coordinating Editor: Kevin Shea
Cover Designer: Anna Ishchenko

Distributed to the book trade worldwide by Springer Science+Business Media New York, 233 Spring Street, 6th Floor, New York, NY 10013. Phone 1-800-SPRINGER, fax (201) 348-4505, e-mail orders-ny@springer-sbm.com, or visit www.springeronline.com.

For information on translations, please e-mail rights@apress.com, or visit www.apress.com.

About ApressOpen

What Is ApressOpen?

- ApressOpen is an open-access book program that publishes high-quality technical and business information.

- ApressOpen eBooks are available for global, free, noncommercial use.

- ApressOpen eBooks are available in PDF, ePub, and Mobi formats.

- The user-friendly ApressOpen free eBook license is presented on the copyright page of this book.

For my girls, Aisling, Aoise, and Doireann—I love you dearly.

—Michael J. McGrath

Nige and Sophie—this would not have been possible without your love and support.

—Cliodhna Ní Scanaill

Contents at a Glance

Contents

About the Authors

Dr. Michael J. McGrath is a senior researcher at Intel Labs Europe. He has been with Intel for 14 years, holding a variety of operational and research roles. His areas of interest include ambient and body-worn sensor applications, networking technologies, mobile technologies, and data management techniques. Michael was previously a principle investigator at the TRIL Centre, where his research focused on the development of technologies to support independent living. Michael coauthored the book *Wireless Sensor Networks for Healthcare Applications* (Artech House, 2009). He received his B.Sc. in Analytical Science from Dublin City University in 1992 and a Ph.D. in sensors and instrumentation from Dublin City University in 1995. In 1999, Michael received a graduate diploma in information technology from Dublin City University, a graduate diploma in computing from ITB in 2004, and a master's degree in computing from ITB in 2007. Michael is a chartered chemist and a chartered scientist.

Dr. Cliodhna Ní Scanaill is a senior sensor applications engineer with Intel Labs Europe, where she develops and deploys large-scale sensor-based systems for environmental monitoring. Before joining Intel Labs in 2006, Cliodhna worked on the falls prevention strand at the TRIL Centre for over five years, as a software engineer, researcher, and principal investigator. Her research interests include falls and aging, sports and fitness sensing, and sensor network design and manageability. Cliodhna holds a B.Eng. in computer engineering and a Ph.D. in biomedical electronics from the University of Limerick. Her dissertation is titled "Remote Mobility Monitoring of the Elderly Using SMS Messaging."

Dr. Dawn Nafus is a senior research scientist at Intel Labs, where she conducts anthropological research to inspire new products and strategies. She holds a Ph.D. in anthropology from the University of Cambridge and was previously a research fellow at the University of Essex. She has published widely on technology and society in academic journals, and has worked with public policy makers and industry leaders on issues such as widening participation in open source communities. Her research interests include experiences of time, beliefs about technology and modernity, the politics of measuring global technology adoption, and the anthropology of numbers.

About the Technical Reviewers

Dermot Diamond received his Ph.D. and D.Sc. from Queen's University Belfast (chemical sensors, 1987, Internet scale sensing, 2002), and was vice-president for research at Dublin City University (2002-2004). He has published 300 peer-reviewed papers in international journals, is a named inventor in 18 patents, and is coauthor and editor of four books. Dermot is a director and founding member of the National Centre for Sensor Research (www.ncsr.ie) at Dublin City University, a principal investigator at the SFI-funded CLARITY Centre for Sensor Web Technologies (www.clarity-centre.com/), and an SFI-funded investigator in the INSIGHT Centre (www.insight-centre.org). In 2002, he was awarded the inaugural silver medal for sensor research by the Royal Society of Chemistry, London, and in 2006 he received the DCU President's Award for research excellence. His research focuses on the fundamental science of stimuli-responsive polymers, the development of futuristic autonomous chemical sensing platforms, and the use of analytical devices and sensors as information providers for wireless networked systems; that is, building a continuum between the digital and molecular worlds. Details of his research can be found at www.dcu.ie/chemistry/asg.

Chris Nugent received a bachelor of engineering in electronic systems and Ph.D. in biomedical engineering, both from the University of Ulster. He is now professor of biomedical engineering at the University of Ulster.

Chris's research addresses the design, development, and evaluation of mobile and pervasive technologies in smart environments. The main application of this work to date has been in the domain of ambient assisted living. He has published extensively in these areas, with work that spans theoretical, clinical, and biomedical engineering domains.

Currently Chris is group leader of the Smart Environments Research Group. The group's aim is to, using an integrated and multidisciplinary approach, advance research to support and monitor people within their homes and beyond.

Acknowledgments

The authors would like to thank their colleagues for their support, thoughts, and discussions that contributed to shaping this book. We are particularly grateful to Dawn Nafus of Intel Labs, who wrote Chapter 7. Dawn's anthropological insights into how sensors are being used and how their use will evolve in the future brings a unique and stimulating perspective to the technical content of this book.

We want to especially thank Niamh Scannell for her continuous support and for giving us the confidence to take on such a large challenge. And we very much appreciate the support of Professor Martin Curley, VP Intel Labs, without which this book project would not have been possible. Cliodhna would also like to thank Charlie Sheridan, Director of the Sustainable Intelligent Cities Lab, for his encouragement throughout the book-writing process.

We also want to express our gratitude to David Gordon and Stephen Whalley from Intel's Platform Engineering Group for their sponsorship and industry insights. They helped us tie the potential of sensors in the health and wellness domains to the real world—a world that is full of exciting opportunities for sensing, where sensing can making a meaningful impact on the quality of people's lives.

We would like to recognize the contribution of Gabriel Mullarkey in helping his graphically challenged colleagues with the preparation of various figures in the book. That help was very much appreciated. Additionally, we would like to acknowledge the contributions and input of our colleagues Barry Greene and Emer Doheny. Their work in falls research added greatly to the book. Finally, we would like to recognize Adrian Burns, who played a key role in the development of the SHIMMER platform, which was instrumental in many of the TRIL Centre research projects and provided us with many of the insights shared in this book.

It is also important to recognize the efforts of the TRIL Centre and its researchers. Many of the insights gained with respect to sensor applications were made possible by the center's unique multidisciplinary research program. TRIL gave us the opportunity to understand, develop, and deploy sensor technologies across a spectrum of applications and environments with real users.

Michael McGrath would like to thank his wife, Aisling, and daughters, Aoise and Doireann, for their love, support, and patience through the working holidays, lost weekends, and late evenings during the course of writing this book. He is also grateful to Aisling for proofreading the chapters and for helping to break up the long-winded essays.

Cliodhna Ní Scanaill would like to thank her husband, Nigel, her daughter, Sophie, and her family and friends for their love, support, and encouragement. Cliodhna would particularly like to thank Nigel for everything he's done to help her get through this crazy, busy year.

We would like thank our technical reviewers Professors Dermot Diamond and Chris Nugent for their dedication, rigor, and insightful suggestions that helped us improve the relevance, quality, and accuracy of the subject matter.

Special thanks go to Patrick Haulke, our program manager at Intel, for his calm and assured guidance during the course of this book project, as well as to our editors, Jeff Pepper, Kevin O'Shea, Corbin Collins, and the rest of the team at Apress for seamlessly guiding us through the writing and publication process. They took our raw text and images and produced a great-looking book, which we hope people will enjoy.

Michael J. McGrath
Cliodhna Ní Scanaill

Foreword

The Arithmetic of Life

Have you ever dived among the molecular landscapes of a rock sample through the "lens" of an electron microscope? Seen into the pitch darkness with an infrared camera? Traveled down your intestine with a miniature pill camera? Examined the toe of a baby scheduled to be born in five months? The world is full of mystery and wonder that's beyond the reach of our traditional five senses.

Now the time has come for us all to see and feel the magic beyond, inside, and outside of ourselves. Sensing in and around humans is the story of uncovering, discovering, and recovering, whether we're capturing the signal of our heart beat, measuring oxygen levels in our blood flow, detecting the electrical impulses that bring life to our muscles and nerves, or letting our breath and bodily fluids tell happy and sad stories about our present and future. We can sense and make sense of all this and put it all to enormously good use.

Biosensors that sense our health and well-being are on the way, and they are coming to our everyday life. I use the definition of "biosensors" quite broadly, as sensors that detect and measure attributes of our bodies and the environment in which we live. So here's the plan: we all will employ biosensors to expose the invisible, measure the exposed, intensify these measurements, make sense of the intensity, and trigger actions and alerts based on this sensing on an unprecedented scale.

Why, and why now? Because we are ready, and because we must. We are ready, as major technological trends are converging: the information revolution is upon us with global networking, popular computing, and computer programs ("apps") as commodities; and nano-technological advances are paving the way to put the right sensors into many hands. We must, because there are major problems to solve and needs to satisfy in many aspects of life.

We are very fortunate to be living in a day and age where military, medical, and industrial advancements are standing in line to join the smartphone revolution. This is made possible by the promise of global popularity and an adaptation of requirements relevant to daily life rather than to rocket science or open heart surgery.

Living by Numbers

To me, all of this is very personal. I'm a diabetic, and technology is keeping me alive—and thankful for the development of the glucose biosensor more than 30 years ago. The role of sensing in my daily life has helped to mold my approach to biosensing as a strategic thinker in a global, technologically pioneering company.

Diabetes is the prime example of a condition managed by information technology. Essentially, the condition is an interplay between carbs consumed, medication taken, and physical activity—as monitored by a personal biosensor. By interplay, I mean doing the arithmetic: if my ice-cream cone boasts 28 grams of carbohydrates, I divide by 4 (my own specific coefficient) and inject seven units of Insulin. If my biosensor, also known as a glucometer, reads 100 units too high, I divide by 50 and inject 2 units. And if it reads below 70, I gobble some 25 grams of sugar. A bit complex, but this is how it works, and it really does work.

Today, there are tens of millions of glucometers out there. The recent introduction of the next big thing in healthcare systems, continuous blood monitoring, is absolutely revolutionary—for those with the condition, for doctors, and for payers. Not only will we be able to manage blood sugar with a higher resolution that better mimics our impaired metabolism, the increased visibility into the full daily routine will provide exciting new insights and practices, easing the burden of daily management. We will be able to recognize the immediate cause and effect of our actions, and eventually improve our quality of life and lower healthcare costs. Today, many experts will admit, this is still a world of mystery to the caregivers and sufferers alike.

The opinionated information technologist will readily generate expectations for the final frontier—the "artificial pancreas." This is not an implanted organ but rather a piece of software that inputs continuous glucose measurements and calculates instructions to forward to a connected insulin pump. The eager medical technologist will readily come up with several other conditions that could follow a similar development path with much associated promise.

Magical Transitions of Power

You have the right to be amazed: diabetics today are living through a major transition in medical systems, a transition to an era of self-service medicine. Yes, in effect we prescribe our own dosages of a dangerous drug, a relatively small overdose of insulin could be deadly.

The expectation is that the story of biosensing is also the story of a magical transition of power. The 21st century is offering us opportunities to look inside ourselves, see the invisible, look beyond our legacy frames of perception, and shatter the power of the few that operated huge and expensive machines to do all this before. Remember what the digital camera and the camera phone did to the world of photography? We are headed toward an era of such disruptions across a wide array of domains—medicine and wellness, food and diet, water, electricity, environmental monitoring, and home care. Sensing will play a key role in the quality of healthcare delivery by providing on-demand access to current health status. Sensors will also enable service innovation by enabling access to new personal modes of care and services that until now have been the preserve of the privileged few.

Uncovering the Mysteries of Life

The mysteries of life are right under our noses and biosensors will provide new ways to look around and feel reality. In the era of "biosensing in everyday life," we'll be exposed to new data every day, lots of it; it will be ours to own, and ours to utilize and share in whatever manner we deem fit. Our sensors will be always on and always connected; they will work in unison with other biosensors and other crowdsourced data to generate new meanings and extract new patterns of occurrence and reoccurrence in time, space, and among various populations. This will enable increased introspection and greater learning about ourselves; it will also allow for more intimate interaction with loved ones and increase our awareness of the world around us.

Heart rate and steps taken, UV exposure from sunlight, ambient pollution, brain activity, bacteria— all will be available to a new generation of sensing consumers, one that will surpass the mobile generation in its race to exploit emerging capabilities.

As technology shrinks and becomes more mobile and accessible, the price of generating these signals will decrease even further. Data will become much easier to acquire. No longer will it be necessary for us to invade our bodies to extract blood or other bodily fluids; instead, we will employ noninvasive methods—sound, light, electricity, breath-sniffing, and clothing that senses our tiniest motions. The ancients contemplated an aura surrounding our bodies; biosensors will prove they were right, albeit in a different and much more useful sense.

This book is an introduction to sensors and to their applications that allow us to take greater personal ownership in monitoring our own health, wellness and the environments we live in. We are introduced to a future that will let each of us peer with unprecedented clarity into the complexities of the human body, to see our own aura and tap into it for data that can be processed into personal or public knowledge bases. The authors provide exciting insights into the pipeline of capabilities and usages, while looking beyond the hype and calibrating expectations.

Biosensors are upon us—welcome to the definitive technology handbook of yet another age of wonder, empowerment, and mysteries unfolded.

David Gordon
Strategic Planning Director,
Intel Corporation

Preface

The groundwork of all happiness is health.

Leigh Hunt, 19th-century English poet

When we first decided to write a book on sensors and their applications, we had little doubt about the theme or type of book we wanted to write. Though there are some excellent books on sensors and how they function, we felt this could be an opportunity to provide some practical insights into sensor application development, deployment, and evaluation. Having worked together in Intel's Digital Health Group and the Technology Research for Independent Living (TRIL) Centre for over six years, we were involved in developing and deploying healthcare technology to the homes of hundreds of older Irish adults. During that time, we worked in various multidisciplinary teams and collected insights from patients and clinical professionals, learning many valuable lessons along the way. These experiences have hopefully allowed us to gain a greater understanding of how sensor technology can be successfully applied and how external factors influence real-world sensor applications. In this book, we share much of what we've learned in a practical and easy-to-understand manner. We cover topics such as device regulation, managing sensor deployments, data visualization, and societal considerations, which are fundamental to all modern sensor-based applications, but are rarely described in sensor- or domain-specific books. We also examine how recent technology trends, such as mass adoption of smartphones and tablets, are affecting the proliferation of sensors applications into the consumer market.

We focus on the domains of healthcare, wellness, and environmental monitoring as they present some of the largest global challenges affecting us in the 21st century. Sensing plays an important role in these domains to help us to learn about the factors that influence our well-being, including our health status, our lifestyles, the food and water we consume, the air we breathe, and the quality of the environments in which we live. In a world that is becoming increasingly sensorized, we wanted to write an accessible book for anyone who wants to understand sensors and the technical and non-technical challenges in developing sensor applications, including clinical and technical researchers, engineers, students, and those who are simply curious about sensors. We hope this book will also help domain experts, such as clinicians or engineers, to understand the sensor applications in a more holistic manner.

This book is split into three sections: Chapters 2 to 5 describe sensors and the various hardware and software components required to create an end-to-end smart-sensor application; Chapters 6 to 8 describe the non-technical factors that must be considered for a successful sensor application; Chapters 9 to 11 describe sensor applications for health, wellness, and environmental monitoring. The chapters can be read sequentially or readers can dip in and out of the chapters that interest them. Throughout the book, we were mindful to reference links between chapters or to external material, to allow the reader to get more in-depth information on a topic, if they wish. Although we discuss sensing from a health, wellness, and environmental monitoring perspective, we believe that the core content of this book is applicable to any sensing domain.

We encourage people to download a copy of the ebook and to share it among their colleagues, friends, and families. We only ask that you follow the license on the copyright page.

We hope after reading this book, you will not only share our knowledge of sensing and sensor applications, you will also share our curiosity and wonder at the rapid evolution of sensor-applications and how these tiny devices will impact our lives for the better.

Michael J McGrath
Cliodhna Ní Scanaill
Intel Labs Europe
November 2013

CHAPTER 1

■ ■ ■

Introduction

For a successful technology, reality must take precedence over public relations, for Nature cannot be fooled.

—Richard P. Feynman, Physicist

We live in an age of relentless and accelerating change, driven by demographic, social, and economic evolution. Each day, there are more of us consuming the finite natural resources of the planet. Our impact on the planet is increasing through urbanization, energy utilization, waste production, and so on, and this impact is not without consequences. Levels of pollution are increasing in our environment, with corresponding effects on our health and well-being. From smog clouds in cities and pollution of our drinking water to simply being denied sufficient peace to sleep soundly at night, human activity has enormous impact on us and on our planet. Major changes in the way we work and live during the last century mean we are also living much more sedentary lifestyles. This has resulted in growing public health issues, such as obesity, arteriosclerosis, cancer, chronic liver disease, and other lifestyle diseases. Increased life expectancy places greater pressures on our healthcare systems as the world's population continues to grow older. Governments are being forced to cut programs such as home healthcare assistance to reduce burgeoning costs. The current model simply does not scale into the future.

We also need to move our fundamental approach to healthcare from a reactive model to a wellness-oriented model. Here, the focus is on keeping people healthy for as long as possible with the least cost to the system. Providing people with actionable information about their health and the factors influencing it, either positively or negatively, is important. Systems that provide easy access to data on exercise, diet, ambient environment, and so forth, along with intelligent processing and presentation of the data, are critical to supporting sustainable behavior change. It is a world full of challenges and in need of solutions to address key global issues. Technologies such as sensors can give us the tools to help address many of the significant global challenges of the 21st century.

Sensors play an integral role in numerous modern industrial applications, including food processing and everyday monitoring of activities such as transport, air quality, medical therapeutics, and many more. While sensors have been with us for more than a century, modern sensors with integrated information and communications technology (ICT) capabilities—*smart sensors*—have been around for little more than three decades. Remarkable progress has been made in computational capabilities, storage, energy management, and a variety of form factors, connectivity options, and software development environments. These advances have occurred in parallel to a significant evolution in sensing capabilities. We have witnessed the emergence of biosensors that are now found in a variety of consumer products, such as tests for pregnancy, cholesterol, allergies, and fertility.

The development and rapid commercialization of low-cost microelectromechanical systems (MEMS) sensors, such as 3D accelerometers, has led to their integration into a diverse range of devices extending from cars to smartphones. Affordable semiconductor sensors have catalyzed new areas of ambient sensing platforms, such as those for home air-quality monitoring. The diverse range of low-cost sensors fostered the emergence of pervasive sensing. Sensors and sensor networks can now be worn or integrated into our living environment or even into our clothing with minimal effect on our daily lives. Data from these sensors promises to support new proactive healthcare paradigms with early detection of potential issues, for example, heart disease risk (elevated cholesterols levels) liver

1

disease (elevated bilirubin levels in urine), anemia (ferritin levels in blood) and so forth. Sensors are increasingly used to monitor daily activities, such as exercise with instant access to our performance through smartphones. The relationship between our well-being and our ambient environment is undergoing significant change. Sensor technologies now empower ordinary citizens with information about air and water quality and other environmental issues, such as noise pollution. Sharing and socializing this data online supports the evolving concepts of citizen-led sensing. As people contribute their data online, crowdsourced maps of parameters such air quality over large geographical areas can be generated and shared.

Although all these advances are noteworthy and contribute meaningfully and positively to many people's lives, a note of caution is also in order. As Richard Feynman points out, reality must take precedence over public relations. Sensors should not be regarded as a panacea for all our problems. Instead, they should be treated as highly useful tools. As always, the right tool is required for the right job and, like any complex tool, sensors and sensor systems have their strengths and weaknesses. Careful matching of the sensor and its operational characteristics to the use case of interest is critical. The data must be of the required accuracy with appropriate stability for the lifetime of the required application. Highly sensitive and accurate sensors are generally more expensive, however, and therefore the cost of the sensor should be weighed carefully against an application's data quality requirement. Sensor technologies, particularly wireless sensor networks (WSNs) (see Chapter 4), offer a wide variety of capabilities. However, they can sometimes lack meaningful use cases grounded in real-world needs that have either a clear social or economic benefit. These technologies do not have a meaningful value unless they address a problem of real interest in an innovative manner, with performance equal or superior to existing solutions. Real and committed consumers of the data must also exist. Finally, any discussion of the potential cost benefits of using sensors, particularly WSNs, is usually relevant only after the necessary operational performance criteria for an application can be met.

Many challenges remain for sensor technologies, particularly in the consumer domain. However, we are confident that the range of opportunities that are emerging will ensure rapid evolution of their capabilities to address any gaps that currently exist. The 20th century heralded the wide-scale emergence of sensors based on a diverse range of sensing approaches. The 21st will be the century of their application—driven by the convergence of sensing and ICT that will influence many aspects of our lives, especially the domains discussed in this book.

What This Book Covers

In this book we explore a wide range of topics related to sensing, sensor systems, and applications for monitoring health, wellness, and the environment. The book targets clinical and technical researchers, engineers, students, and members of the general public who want to understand the current state of sensor applications in the highlighted domains. The reader should gain a full awareness of the key challenges, both technical and non-technical, that need to be addressed in the development of successful end-to-end sensor applications. We provide real-world examples to give the reader practical insights into the successful development, deployment, and management of sensor applications. The reader will also develop an understanding of the personal, social, and ethical impact of sensor applications, now and in the future. The book provides an application-based approach to illustrate the application of sensor technologies in a practical and experiential manner. It guides the reader from the formulation of the research question, through the design and validation process, to the deployment and management phases of a sensor application. The processes and examples used in the book are primarily based on research carried out by Intel or by joint academic research programs.

The subject of sensing has grown enormously over the last 30 years. Therefore, we focus our treatment of basic sensing principles primarily on the chosen application domains described in Chapter 2. Key topics include electrochemical, optical biosensors, and MEMS sensor technologies. The influence of ICT technologies over the same period has been significant and has fundamentally changed the way in which we use sensors in our lives. Chapter 3 deals with the key technologies that have influenced the evolution of the smart sensor and sensor systems. Chapter 4 covers the use of sensors from an architectural perspective. Architectures range from discrete sensors to wireless sensor networks covering large geographic areas to the Internet of Things, in which vast numbers of sensors are connected to the Internet contributing to the creation of "big data". We review the entire spectrum, from discrete sensors that might be used by an individual to sensor networks that are deployed over wide geographical areas. We also discuss the growing role of sensors in machine-to-machine applications.

A sensor is only as valuable as the data it can produce—so, ensuring quality is key for any sensor application. The way we present and consume sensor data can significantly influence its value, too. Processing, visualizing, and adding vibrancy to sensor data is discussed in Chapter 5. Regulatory considerations are dealt with in Chapter 6, particularly in the context of the application domains covered in this book. The ability to sense key aspects of our health and well-being is having a growing influence on society with both positive and in sometimes case negative consequences. Chapter 7 is primarily concerned with these influences and potential impacts from a social science perspective. A key challenge with sensor technologies is translating promising laboratory prototypes into real-world deployments. Chapter 8 looks at important aspects of planning and deploying sensors in real-world settings. Chapters 9, 10, and 11 outline the current applications of sensor technologies in monitoring the health, wellness, and environmental domains, analyzing the key drivers and inhibitors in the respective domains. We focus on the main emerging-technology practices, such as the role of mobile platforms like smartphones and tablets. Examples of practical solutions and innovative products appear throughout these chapters together with a view of how solutions in these domains will evolve in the future. Chapter 12 looks at how the early pioneers are building a vision of a new model of medicine in the 21st century. This vision is based on use of sensor technologies to provide continuous monitoring of the human body to provide a better understanding of its complexities and the influence of factors such as lifestyle, genetic make-up, the quality of the environment, and so on. It is a future where a visit to the doctor will no longer automatically result in a prescription for drugs to treat an aliment but rather one where doctors will prescribe patients with sensors and apps to diagnose the root cause of their health problems. We also look at the key trends that will influence the evolution of sensor applications in the future, such as the evolving use of crowdsourcing approaches, particularly in environmental applications.

A Brief History of Sensors

The emergence of the first thermostat in 1883 is considered by some to be the first modern sensor. Innumerable forms of sensors have since emerged, based on a variety of principles. Early sensors were simple devices, measuring a quantity of interest and producing some form of mechanical, electrical, or optical output signal. In just the last decade or so, computing, pervasive communications, connectivity to the Web, mobile smart devices, and cloud integration have added immensely to the capabilities of sensors, as shown in Figure 1-1.

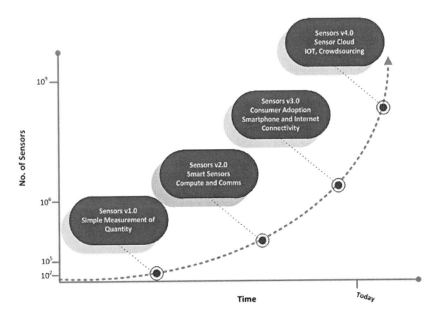

Figure 1-1. Evolution of sensors reflecting the integration of ICT capabilities and consumer adoption

Sensing in the healthcare domain has been, until recently, restricted primarily to use in hospitals, with limited adoption outside this environment. Developments in both technology and care models are supporting adoption by patients, in-home care providers, public authorities, and individuals who want to proactively manage their health and wellness. For example, the concept of biosensing was first proposed by Clarke and Lyons in 1962. The concept of the glucose biosensor was brought to commercial reality in 1975 by the Yellow Springs Instrument Company. Biosensors have rapidly evolved in the intervening years to the point where they are a multi-billion dollar industry. They are now found in a wide variety of over-the-counter health-related applications, such as those for home testing AIDS or pregnancy, and for allergy detection, to mention just a few. More recently, biosensors are being used in the environmental domain for applications that, for example, detect bacteria, pesticides, and heavy metals in water samples.

The development of MEMS-based sensors led to the availability of small, accurate sensors at a price point that made it feasible to integrate them into a wide variety of devices ranging from sports watches to consumer electronics to cars. MEMS have become a key building block for many of the application domains discussed in this book. In 1959, Richard Feynman gave an insightful lecture at the California Institute of Technology called "There is Plenty of Room at the Bottom." In this lecture he outlined the basic concepts and techniques for MEMS devices. However, it wasn't until the early 1990s that U.S. government agencies started large programs that drove rapid acceleration in the development of MEMS sensors. Using semiconductor manufacturing techniques, the first surface micromachined accelerometer (ADXL50) was sold commercially by Analog Devices in 1992. This was followed in 1998 with MEMS-based gyroscopes from Bosch for commercial applications in the automotive sector (Marek et al., 2012). The availability of low cost, accurate, and reliable motion sensors has spawned a variety of applications, including those targeted at the health and wellness domains.

In recent decades the evolution of sensors has been strongly influenced by ICT technologies, with integration of microcontrollers, wireless communications modules, and permanent data storage. These technologies have supported the development of sensor systems with common architectures. Computing, storage, and communications features are used to serve multiple sensors with common connectivity. Collectively these enhancements have produced smart sensors that allow the delivery of intelligent sensor solutions with key features such as digital signal processing and wireless data streaming. In the health and wellness domain, wireless body-worn networks appeared around 1995. These networks—commonly referred to as wireless body area networks (WBAN)—comprise several sensors that measure physiological signals of interest and make that data available wirelessly to a computing device.

How will sensors continue to evolve? A number of key trends are emerging. First, we are starting to see the consumerization of sensors. There is a clear transition from limited, specialized use of sensors to greater general use among the public. Commercial sensor products can be found with greater frequency in pharmacies, sports stores, supermarket chains, and, of course, online. Adoption is rapidly growing in sports and wellness applications, with significant brands staking claims on the market and fueling its growth. The first personal environmental monitoring products have also emerged, with a focus on improving well-being. Crowdsourcing of data, though still in its infancy, is being driven by sensors either connected to smartphones or tablets or integrated into them, and by apps, and by connectivity to the Web or cloud. Continuous miniaturization of sensors and low-cost systems on chips (SOCs) will continue to fuel future development of the Internet of Things (IOT). Sensors will fade into the background of everyday life, and interaction with them will become passive and routine. The nexus of health, wellness, and environmental monitoring will continue to evolve and drive changes in human behaviors. Monitoring enabled by sensors will raise our awareness of how lifestyle choices and external influences impact our personal health and well-being. The adoption of data mining, particularly pattern-matching and machine-learning techniques, will help unlock the hidden patterns and associations in sensor data. These trends could give us the first glimpses of collective intelligence in which epidemiological insights may be possible with customizations for personalized health.

Drivers for Sensor Applications

As mentioned, a variety of social, economic, and environmental challenges are having a global impact. Changes in worldwide demographics have sparked significant debate on how to deliver effective healthcare in the 21st century that is affordable and sustainable. Technology, including sensing, has been an integral part of these discussions. Public health challenges due to the increase in lifestyle-related diseases such as obesity, once the preserve of Western nations, are gaining a foothold across the world. The industrialization of the planet over the last two centuries has had a profound effect on the quality of our environment. In the same period, the capacity of human activities such as transport to impact our environmental has grown substantially. There is a growing realization that the integral nature of our environment can significantly influence health and well-being. Solutions using sensor technologies allow people to be better informed by empowering them with information about the quality of the environment and its influence on them. Let us now look at some of these key drivers in more detail.

Health and Fitness

Lifestyle-related illnesses, resulting from lack of exercise, poor diet, smoking, and excessive alcohol consumption, are on the rise globally. A recent publication in the Lancet medical journal estimates that as many as 5.3 million of the 57 million deaths worldwide in 2008 could be a result of physical inactivity, and that increasing physical activity could increase the life expectancy across the globe by 0.68 years (Lee et al., 2013). Analysis of the Framingham heart study also provides evidence that physical activity conveys long-term beneficial effects by providing a protective effect against incidences of cardiovascular disease (Shortreed et al., 2013). Current guidelines recommend about 150 minutes of physical activity each week for adults. However, almost one-third of adults do not get enough physical activity, leading to greater risk of diseases such as heart disease and diabetes (Park, 2012).

Our diets have also changed significantly over the last century. With each passing decade, the consumption of processed foods and fast foods continues to rise globally, resulting in an increased intake of fat, salt, sweeteners, and simple sugars. There has also been significant growth in the consumption of meat and a decrease in the consumption of non-citrus fruits, vegetables, and whole-grain foods. Collectively these changes significantly increase the number of calories we consume, leading to rising obesity levels, among other issues. Patterns of alcohol consumption also changed in this period. The World Health Organization (WHO) has estimated that 2.5 million people die annually from the harmful consumption of alcohol (WHO_a, 2011). Although average per capita consumption of alcohol in many countries of the Western world has either stabilized or fallen over the last few decades, it has risen significantly in other countries, such as India. The distribution of alcohol consumption within populations has become a major societal issue. For example, it has been found that 20 percent of the United States population is responsible for 90 percent of the alcohol consumption. Similar patterns exist in other countries, such as the Netherlands, China, and Canada. Binge drinking (consumption of five or more drinks), especially on weekends, has become common. This type of drinking can cause acute health problems, such as induced coma, respiratory depression, neurological damage, and more. (Babor, 2010). Smoking remains the single biggest cause of preventable disease (American Lung Association, 2013). Rates of smoking have remained largely unchanged over the last couple of decades. It is estimated that smoking will result in 450 million deaths between 2000–2050 (Jha, 2009). These lifestyle choices result in significant disease burdens and economic impact on our healthcare systems (Al-Maskari, 2010).

Illnesses such as cancer, cardiovascular disease, and diabetes have become the leading causes of death and disability globally (UN_a, 2010). The Global Burden of Disease Study points out that growing numbers of young and middle-aged adults are developing noncommunicable diseases, such as cancer, that are driven by smoking, alcohol use, and obesity. For example, the prevalence of obesity in the Western world is 20–30 percent and increasing. As Asian countries adopt Western lifestyles and diets, obesity is increasing in countries such as China and India. Obesity is associated with elevated blood glucose levels, increased blood lipids (hyperlipidemia), high blood pressure, and decreased sensitivity to insulin. The WHO estimates that being overweight or obese is globally the fifth leading risk for death, resulting in at least 2.8 million adult deaths annually. It estimates that more than 500 million people are obese around the world (WHO_b, 2013). For individuals who are already obese, regular monitoring of key factors such as blood pressure, blood glucose levels, heart rate, and blood lipids, helps to improve management of the disease. Sensor technologies can play a role in supporting the monitoring of these parameters either in community settings or in the home.

A more significant driver for sensor technology utilization is the growing trend in fitness. People are becoming more aware of how lifestyle can affect their health, thanks especially to high visibility public health campaigns. Individuals are motivated by a desire to manage their weight and maintain a sufficient level of fitness for a healthy lifestyle. Other individuals who are already overweight may want to take corrective actions to reduce their weight and improve their fitness levels. Insurance companies are also playing a role by offering premium discounts to individuals who adopt and maintain healthier lifestyles. And some employers have put programs in place to encourage employees to live more active lifestyles, with the benefit of reduced sick days and health insurance premium savings.

A variety of fitness technologies are now available to consumers, ranging from standalone sensing devices, such as pedometers, to apps for use with smartphones, to sports watches with integrated sensors. Also, computer game platforms, such as the Nintendo Wii, Microsoft Kinect, and PlayStation Move, now feature fitness games that use sensing. Many consumer electronics devices such as smartphones and MP3 players have integrated sensors and other features such as a GPS that can be used for fitness applications. The combination of sensing and other technologies can let people monitor and either maintain or improve their fitness levels on a day-to-day basis. There are also fitness developments among older adults, with a growing focus on encouraging participation in sports and similar physical activities. Improvements in muscle strength, balance, endurance, and so forth play a key role in allowing older adults to maintain their independence longer and slow or prevent the onset of frailty. Currently, this group is not among those adopting sports-sensing technologies; however, this is likely to change in the future. Greater convergence between health and wellness monitoring will play a significant role in adoption.

Aging Demographics

Global aging and the associated impact on healthcare systems have been well-documented. As a result of medical advances, better management of communicable diseases, and improved diet, people are living longer. The U.S. Census Bureau predicts an average increase in life expectancy between 1970 and 2020 of 12.2% (70.8 to 79.5 years). Conservative estimates place the increase in life expectancy during the course of the 21st century at 13 years (Fogel, 2011). The UN estimates that, globally, life expectancy will increase from 68 years in 2005–2010 to 81 in 2095–2100 (UN$_b$, 2011). Others argue that the increase could actually be much larger. While there is debate over the exact increase in life expectancy during the 21st century, everyone agrees that we will live longer and that the increase in life span will have significant implications for our society.

Many countries, particularly Western ones, are suffering from an aging population. In this process, older adults become a proportionally larger share of the total population. The number of people aged 65 or older is projected to grow from an estimated 524 million in 2010 to nearly 1.5 billion in 2050. One interesting consequence of this growth is that by 2020 the number of people over 65 will outnumber children aged 5 or younger. This will be a first for humankind (WHO$_c$, 2011). This demographic transition results in rising demands for health services and higher expenditures because older people are normally more vulnerable to health issues, including chronic diseases. This increased expenditure on public healthcare services is a growing concern for many governments.

Various efforts to address the increased level of expenditure have been tried and evaluated. Central to many efforts has been the use of ICT technologies, including sensors to deliver new, more affordable models of care in community and home locations. Sensors can monitor the key health indicators of a person directly or indirectly through ambient monitoring of daily patterns. In many respects, at-home healthcare is becoming part of the IOT. Initial deployments of technologies have been somewhat static and tied to the physical location of the person under observation. The near future will see small, wearable sensors that can monitor a person's vital signs 24/7. An alert can be sent to a clinician when a certain limit is exceeded or when an abnormal event, such as someone collapsing and being unable to get up, is detected. These types of sensor technologies are fundamental to making health affordable and scalable to address the transition in global demographics.

Personalized Healthcare

As we have pointed out, the economics of healthcare is already under considerable strain due to changes in global demographics. Costs continue to climb, with a consequent need to shift the focus away from reactive treatment and toward proactive healthcare. This model encompasses prediction, diagnosing, and monitoring using various data sources. A cornerstone of this shift is the development of personalized medicine. In this model we move away from a population-level epidemiological approach to small groups or individuals defined by their biochemistry and genetics. Currently this information is beginning to be used to select the most appropriate drugs to treat diseases such as cancer. As the next generation of drug therapies emerge that target specific disease pathways, it is important to know the genetic profile of a patient to see whether he or she will respond to a particular drug therapy. This in turn is generating a growing demand for diagnostic tests that provide clinicians with specific information about the biology of the patient as well as disease-specific information, such as the cellular profile of a tumor. The need for a companion diagnostic test to accompany a therapy has already emerged in cancer treatments. For example, Genentech's Herceptin targets breast tumor cells that exhibit significant amounts of the Her2/neu protein on their cell membranes. Testing for this protein in all new breast cancer tumors to determine if they can be treated by Herceptin has been specified by the National Comprehensive Cancer Network in the U.S. These tests represent both diagnostics and subsequent treatment monitoring opportunities for the biosensor industry.

These targeted treatments are a significant step forward in disease treatment but they are still reactive in nature. The future of personalized healthcare will be about using sensor technologies to establish and monitor biological norms and quickly identify deviations from them. We are starting to see the emergence of health maps constructed by proactive individuals that capture and document their health metrics on a longitudinal basis. Wired magazine, in an article entitled "Know Thyself: Tracking Every Facet of Life, from Sleep to Mood to Pain, 24/7/365," discusses the utility of health-related metrics. The article describes how data can be used to create a personal macroscope to link a variety of data into a larger, readable pattern (Wolf, 2009). In this way we may be able to intervene to prevent a disease from occurring or to begin treatment at the earliest possible juncture to maximize efficacy, minimize long-term impact, and keep costs to a minimum. The combination of sensor and ICT technologies will cause medicine to morph. The tools to start this monitoring process for the motivated few already exist. This form of monitoring will become the norm, representing a major driver both for the development and adoption of sensor technologies into our everyday lives.

We should be cautious not forget the role sustainable behavior change has to play in the area of personalized healthcare. Aside from clinical diagnostic applications, it is ultimately the decision of individuals how they use the data provided by sensor technologies and what steps if any they take in modifying their behaviors and lifestyles. The ICT software tools provided with sensors can play a vital enabling role in supporting individuals. As individuals move along the path of behavior change, the manner in which the sensor data is visualized, information is personalized, goals are set, and on-line community supports are structured needs to continuously re-engage the individual over the long term. Behavior change of this nature is not a sprint but a marathon that for some will go on over a lifetime. ICT technologies that are static may have short-term impact but will suffer failure in the longer term. Successful solutions will place the sensing and supporting technologies around the needs of individuals in a manner that is highly personalized and supportive and evolves with the individual and their needs.

Public Health

Healthcare spending is regularly near the top of the political agenda in most countries. It will account for 20–30 percent of GDP in some economies by 2050, a figure that is economically unsustainable (McKinsey, 2010). We have seen that this rapid increase in expenditure is driven by multiple factors, such as aging demographics, increasing prevalence of lifestyle illnesses, environmental factors, and so on. Public health policies are shifting away from reactive models of healthcare to preventative ones with a focus on wellness. Authorities see smarter healthcare as a means of maintaining quality while reducing delivery costs. Health and well-being are increasingly being positioned by public health authorities as an integral part of improving quality of life. More and more, public health bodies are becoming consumers of sensor technologies. At present, the most common applications of interest are home management of chronic disease patients and monitoring the well-being of older adults in their own homes.

There is also growing interest in the deployment of rehabilitation applications such as those required by patients recovering from surgery, for example joint replacements or stroke sufferers. Commercial applications targeting these patient groups are already available from companies like Telefonica and Philips. Additionally, systems are supporting the delivery of in-home exercise programs to improve strength and balance in older adults as a preventative measure against health concerns such as falls. Initial trials of telehealth solutions have had mixed results to date. A recent publication in the Lancet that analyzed the effectiveness of the whole systems demonstrator program for telehealthcare in the UK, one of the largest studies of its kind, found it to be ineffective based on the cost of outcomes when compared to care-as-usual models (Henderson et al., 2013). Most issues identified in these trials are not technology related, however. Structural reform of medicine will be required to fully embrace the value of these technologies in treatment and care options. Although many studies into telehealth deployments indicate that the lack of acceptance of this new way of working is a key barrier to adoption, little progress has been made to date in developing solutions that can be implemented by front-line staff (Brewster et al., 2013).

This focus on health and well-being in our personal lives by the public health domain has also generated opportunities for companies not in the clinical sensing-technologies domain. Companies are considering public health opportunities by strengthening their brand value and repositioning their products. Opportunities include activity monitoring, calorie-intake tracking, fitness evaluation through vital-signs monitoring, and so on. Many product offerings intersect with key public health messages on exercise and activity, managing diet, and detecting early signs of health-related issues. These messages will be amplified as governments struggle with healthcare budgets in the future, creating more opportunities for sensor-related products.

Another key challenge facing healthcare services in the future will be a shortage of physicians to meet growing demands. The Association of American Colleges has estimated a potential shortfall of up to 124,000 physicians in the U.S. by 2025 (Dill et al., 2008). This shortage will inevitably require changes to the way healthcare is delivered. There will likely be a greater emphasis on the roles of nurse practitioners and physician assistants to deliver standardized protocols through the use of technology. Sensors will play a key role in such clinical tools, with intelligent software applications providing a layer of interpretation to support these practitioners. Examples of this approach are presented in Chapter 8.

Technology Nexus

As we will see throughout this book, sensors have evolved beyond being just "dumb" sensing devices to become smart sensors or sensor systems through the integration of ICT technologies. These capabilities have allowed sensors to participate in the larger technology ecosystem. We have now reached a technology nexus that is driving the rapid adoption of sensors technologies. Over one billion smartphones have been sold (Reisinger, 2012) and smartphone purchases exceeded that of standard mobile phones for the first time in 2013 (Svensson, 2013). 3G mobile broadband connectivity is widely available, particularly in urban areas, with faster 4G broadband services being rolled out. Connectivity, whether 3G or 4G, General Packet Radio Service (GPRS), Wi-Fi, or Bluetooth, is becoming pervasive. Cloud-based technologies are providing ever-increasing data storage, processing, aggregation, visualization, and sharing capabilities. Social media gives us a mechanism to crowdsource (sensor) data, to share this data, and to derive information from the data among Internet communities. Visionary technologist evangelists are already defining and creating a new future for medicine and healthcare by using sensors and ICT technologies to provide insights into the human body that were not previously possible. In his book *The Creative Destruction of Medicine: How the Digital Revolution Will Create Better Health Care*, Eric Topol describes how we are in the midst of a perfect digital storm. Super-convergence in the form of sensors and ICT technologies is the *"start of illuminating the human black box"* (Topol, 2012*)*. Clinicians now have access to tools that will allow them to move toward a model of patient care based on predictive, preventive, and personalized medicine. The convergence of sensor and ICT technologies will give consumers an incredible capacity to generate information about their health and well-being and to participate in the management of their own healthcare with their clinicians. It will also allow them to control and exploit that information in a manner that would not have been previously possible. Sensing, social networking, smartphones, and connectivity will have a profound effect on medicine.

It is important to acknowledge the rapid advancements made in sensor technologies over the last thirty years. Biosensors and MEMS-based sensors have developed from essentially nothing in that timeframe to pervasive availability in a vast array of products. Biosensors have been a key cornerstone in the development of the consumer sensor market, driven by their relative low cost and reasonable accuracy. This market will continue to grow significantly as people take greater personal ownership of their health, driven by many of the factors discussed in this chapter. As the cost of MEMs-based sensors continues to fall, they can be found with ever-greater frequency in consumer electronics. This has led to the rapid growth of health- and wellness-related applications based around these sensing capabilities. As we embrace the data-driven society in our daily lives, demand for personal health metrics will continue to grow.

National Security

The threat of terrorism remains a constant source of concern for government and security agencies. Threats from terrorism have now evolved to include potential attacks from chemical, biological, radiological, and nuclear (CBRN) sources. Chemical threats involve the potential use of highly toxic industrial chemicals (for example, methyl isocyanate) or poisonous nerve agents (such as Sarin). Biological threats include the airborne release or introduction into water supplies of weaponized biological agents such as anthrax. Nuclear and radiological attacks pose a significant threat, particularly in urban areas. Large numbers of people could be exposed to radioactive contamination from so-called dirty bombs—non-fissile explosions of radioactive material released into the atmosphere.

Constant monitoring and vigilance is therefore required to prevent these forms of attack from occurring. Laboratory-based detection of agents offers excellent sensitivity and selectivity. However, national analytical laboratories are normally geographically removed from the threat location, resulting in significant delays in detection. Flexible in-field detection in the form of sensors is vital to continually provide information about a potential CBRN situation. Sensing capabilities that are available any time, any place to support the detection, identification, and quantification of CBRN hazards are a key requirement. Sensors are necessary to detect threats in air and water, and on land, personnel, equipment, or facilities. They are also required to detect these threats in their various physical states, whether solid, liquid, or gas. Ongoing threats will continue to drive the development of sensing technologies in the chemical and biological domains to improve the sensitivity and flexibility of detection of known agents. New sensor technologies will also be required as new forms of threat emerge in the future. For example, in the environmental domain, sensor technologies will be required to provide continuous monitoring of water sources and air quality to ensure their integrity and to immediately identify possible releases of chemical and biological agents. A variety of new biosensing and optical sensor technologies are in development that hopefully will be able to identify of the many current threats. This will allow authorities to react with greater speed than is currently possible.

The Internet of Things

The IOT is rapidly becoming a reality that surrounds us and intersects with many aspects of our lives. Pervasive connectivity and advances in ICT technologies have made possible the connection of more and more devices to the Internet. This is leading to a new wave of applications that have the potential to dramatically improve the way people live, learn, work, and entertain themselves. Sensors play a key role in connecting the physical world (temperature, CO_2, light, noise, moisture) with the digital world of IOT. Availability of this data can make us more proactive and less reactive in our interaction with the world around us (Evans, 2011).

The IOT is the next evolution of the Internet. The success of IOT will be driven by applications that deliver tangible improvements to people's everyday lives. Sensors are likely to play a central role in providing the data streams upon which these applications can be built. For example, mobile and home-based environmental monitors allow people to track ambient air quality. They can use this data to either modify their environment or alter their behavior in order to maintain their health and wellness. As the value and impact of these applications reach widespread public visibility, the need for both improved and new sensor technologies is likely to grow rapidly.

Water and Food

The pressure on water and food resources will grow during the course of this century. A new lexicon has emerged around water. Terms such as water scarcity, water stress, water shortage, water deficits, and water crisis have now entered public consciousness in many parts of the world. Various estimates put the number of people affected by water shortages as 3.1 to 4.3 billion people by 2050 (Gosling et al., 2013). A recent article in the *Guardian* newspaper paints an even more dramatic picture by suggesting that within two generations, most people on the planet will experience water shortages (Harvey, 2013). In the U.S., the Southwest states of Arizona and Texas and the Midwest states of Kansas and Nebraska in particular are facing severe freshwater shortages (Stockdale et al., 2010)(Koch, 2010). Countries such as China (Economist, 2013) and India (Duxfield, 2013) and regions of Africa, the Middle East, and Asia are already experiencing water shortages that are likely to lead to local and regional tensions (Waslekar, 2012, Connor, 2013). The UN has estimated that the world's population will grow to 8.1 billion by 2025 (Lederer, 2013), driven by high birth rates in the developing world and increased life expectancy. These population changes will further increase pressure on dwindling water resources in many areas.

Stewart Patrick, in his article "The Coming Global Water Crisis," identifies a number of other key contributors to the water crisis in addition to climate change. The global population is becoming increasingly urbanized, leading to rises in personal consumption, sanitation needs, and public infrastructure expenditures. Changes in dietary preferences as the global middle class expands will have a significant impact on the amount of meat consumed. This will result in increased livestock rearing, which is a water-intensive activity (Patrick, 2102). Water management is extremely poor in most parts of the world. Even where it does exist, particularly in the Western world, the infrastructure is antiquated with as much as 50 percent of water being lost through leakage. The development of smart water grids with integrated sensing capabilities is gaining prominence among utilities and government organizations. Sensors will provide detection of leakages, as well as the identification of water quality issues such as treatment problems or pollution. Sensors have the potential to help improve the sustainability of water resources through better management and protection. This will require continued evolution of sensors to deliver laboratory analytical capabilities in-situ on a 24/7 monitoring basis to protect this valuable resource. We will also see innovations in how we produce our fresh drinking water, such as chemical-free production and waste-water treatments. These innovations will require sensor technologies to provide continuous monitoring in order to ensure water quality from both human health and environmental perspectives.

In the agricultural domain, water use is enormously inefficient, particularly with respect to irrigation practices. The UN has identified that use of water for irrigation represents almost 70 percent of the total withdrawn for human uses. In comparison, industry represents 20 percent and municipal use about 10 percent (UN_c, 2013). Currently, irrigation regimes are typically schedule-based, with no system intelligence. The use of sensors to provide soil moisture measurements, combined with ambient environmental monitoring and crop-specific parameter monitoring, will enable intelligent crop irrigation. This will help to reduce water consumption while maintaining or improving crop yields.

Consumers driven by health concerns adopting sensor technologies to test the quality of their drinking water and food will become a growing trend. People are becoming more aware of the types and sources of their food. Health-conscious consumers have embraced, among other things, organic foods. Sensors to identify whether a food is organic are now commercially available. Consumer-oriented sensors that measure common aspects of water quality are also emerging. The sensor data can be easily shared online to support crowdsourced knowledge-sharing. This will allow people to make informed decisions and to advocate for change or improvements in their water and food supplies as necessary.

Environmental Challenges

There are many potential factors surrounding us on a daily basis that can affect our wellness or directly influence the development of illness. The effects of poor water and air quality, pathogens in the food supply, and noise and light pollution will continue to have significant health impacts. Increased urbanization, growing use of motor vehicles and other forms of transport, increased waste production (human, animal, and industrial), and other factors will increase pressure on our natural environment. The effects of these are clearly visible in many large cities in the form of poor air quality. Smog clouds, common in many large cities, can have a dramatic effect on people suffering from respiratory issues, such as chronic obstructive pulmonary disease (COPD) and asthma. Exposure to fumes, gases, or dust in the workplace is estimated to be responsible for 11 percent of asthma cases globally (WHO_d, 2007). The number of asthma sufferers continues to grow on a global basis. In the U.S., about 1 in 14 had asthma in 2001; that number had increased to 1 in 12 by 2009 (AAAAI, 2013). People are now turning to sensor technologies to better understand the relationship between parameters such as air quality and their health.

Institutional environmental monitoring, particularly of air quality, does provide us with insight into the quality of the environment. However, this form of monitoring can lack geographical granularity and a level of interactivity that people expect or require. Commercial sensor technologies now starting to emerge that empower people to track the air quality of their home environments and other areas they frequent. Other sensor-based applications are emerging that can be used to identify and track areas of high pollen and dust that affect people suffering from asthma and other respiratory conditions. This information allows suffers to make decision such as adjusting their route to work or school to avoid areas that might affect their condition. Although many of these applications are in development or are relatively new to the market, interest is already significant. Development of these of technologies and products will see strong growth over the next decade. Growth will be driven by changes in attitude toward environmental awareness as sensor technologies make it much more tangible. Personal perspectives will move from general awareness to a more personal outlook. This personal perspective will encourage greater interactivity with sensor data and modification of living environments to improve levels of wellness. Data will be shared and analyzed via the Web and the cloud as individuals endeavor to understand what the data is telling them, by using the collective intelligence of online communities and engaging in informed speculation on what the data is inferring about potential future impacts. These activities will mirror in many ways what is already happening in the health and wellness domains. It is also likely that over time greater overlap in these domains will occur as individuals and groups endeavor to build an understanding of how the quality of their environment such as their home impacts on their personal health and wellbeing.

Challenges for Sensor Applications

The drivers for sensor applications are significant and will continue to grow. Evolution of existing sensor technologies and development of new ones will continue to deliver new, innovative applications. The demand is there and growing—but can sensor technologies deliver on the promise? We must be careful to not equate demand with delivery without evidence. It has been pointed out that scanning the Internet, literature, and popular commentary can give the impression that fully functional sensor solutions are available to meet our needs (McAdams et al., 2012). We must be careful not to conclude that sensors are a panacea for all our needs. The truth is more complicated.

It is important to disaggregate sensors into their respective architectures: standalone, body-worn wireless networks, and more general wireless sensor networks. Each configuration presents its own unique set of challenges, some of which are more significant than others. Across the three configurations, sensor data quality is a universal requirement. For body-worn applications, the sensor-human interface is typically challenging, with issues such as compliance, comfort, artifact introduction, and hygiene being some of the key issues that must be dealt with. For diagnostic applications, considerable regulatory hurdles may have to be addressed. Questions need to be asked about the accuracy of products that are focused on in-home testing without regulatory approval or independent certification.

With standalone sensors, ensuring the measurement of a representative sample can be challenging. The actual technology used in the sensor can also have significant influence on the quality and accuracy of the data. Whereas inexpensive sensors can increase affordability and access to data, this may come at the cost of data quality. In such cases, no sensor data may be better than inaccurate measurements, which can create a false sense of security or result in an unnecessary false alarm.

For wireless sensor networks, communications, power, cost of deployment, and remote manageability are a few of the key factors that influence the viability of WSN applications. The deployment of WSNs at scale (thousands of nodes) is a challenge that has not yet been addressed properly. Throughout this book we present the technical, social, and organizational challenges that accompany the adoption, deployment, and utilization of sensors. Although we acknowledge the fantastic capabilities of sensors, a sprinkling of reality must also apply. Armed with a balanced view of sensors, we can better set realistic expectations, utilize them appropriately, and set achievable evolutionary demands.

Sensors Enabling Innovation

Over the last decade there has been a growing emphasis on adding embedded intelligence to the world around us in order to make it smarter. This vision of smart encompasses cities, transport, energy, health, homes, and public buildings, among other areas. The goal of smarter environments and activities is driven by the complex mixture of challenges outlined in this chapter. We increasingly need creative solutions that can do more with less to meet these growing challenges. Innovation should be about bringing a great idea to market. For example, 60 percent of the world population will live in cities by 2020, creating enormous challenges in delivering sustainable living environments for those city dwellers.

Sensors are playing and will continue to play a key role in enabling innovative solutions. Smart technologies—such as smart sensors, data acquisition systems, ubiquitous data connectivity, and big data analytics—provide key technology building blocks. Integrated appropriately, they provide efficiencies, scalability, and cost reduction. They also act as an innovation platform for long-term solutions to enable meaningful citizen engagement or "stickiness." The potential of these systems will continue to evolve, particularly as the trajectory and merging of technologies increases. You will see throughout this book how smartphones and tablets are acting as one such catalyst for innovation through the fusion of technologies. Sensing, geo-positioning, imaging, software, and ubiquitous connectivity in this single form factor presents fascinating scenarios. In healthcare, the use of sensors will be integrated into daily routine to provide both diagnostic capabilities and routine wellness monitoring. Figure 1-2 shows how the various technologies can be combined to deliver a smart healthcare sensing solution.

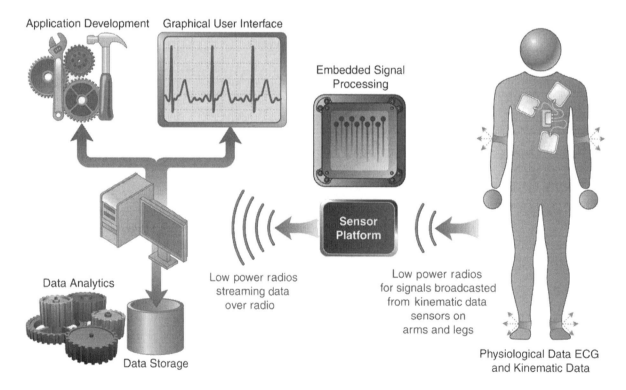

Figure 1-2. *A smart health scenario using body-worn sensors*

It is interesting to note that the proliferation of these devices and services may well be driven by real-world virality. Social media and other forms on online engagement will spark conversations leading to public engagement. This type of engagement is already playing a greater role in shaping products and services. The smart aspects of our lives will contain a greater element of pull, rather than the push that has been the de facto approach to date. Smart sensors and services need to be insight-driven, prototype-powered, and foresight-inspired, particularly in the domains discussed in this book, as they have direct and tangible connection to human end users. It is important to maintain the balance requirements between the creative and analytical processes. We must ensure that needs are identified and appropriate insights collected to realize the opportunities in a way that makes sense from the perspectives of customers, science, engineering, and economics.

The continued technological evolution of sensors will see increasing levels of miniaturization. This is critical for embedded applications where limited form factor space (such as in a smartphone) is a constraint. Commercially viable sensor materials that can be integrated into items such as clothing will likely emerge. In the research domain, we see many interesting demonstrations of these materials. Innovative application of these materials will be central to bridging the gap between interesting research and commercial reality. Sensors will continue to become smarter, driven by ever- closer integration with ICT capabilities. This combination will provide an exciting platform for future innovation product and services.

References

Marek, Jiri and Udo-Martin Gómez, "MEMS (Micro-Electro-Mechanical Systems) for Automotive and Consumer" in *Chips 2020: A Guide to the Future of Nanoelectronics*, Höfflinger, Bernd, Ed., Heidelberg, Springer-Verlag, 2012, pp. 293–314.

Lee, I-Min, *et al.*, "Effect of physical inactivity on major non-communicable diseases worldwide: an analysis of burden of disease and life expectancy," *The Lancet,* vol. 380 (9838), pp. 219–229, 2013.

Shortreed, Susan M, Anna Peeters, and Andrew B Forbes, "Estimating the effect of long-term physical activity on cardiovascular disease and mortality: evidence from the Framingham Heart Study," *Heart,* vol. 99 (9), pp. 649–654, 2013.

Park, Alice. *"Lack of Exercise as Deadly as Smoking, Study Finds"*, Last Update: July 18th 2012, http://healthland.time.com/2012/07/18/lack-of-exercise-as-deadly-as-smoking-study-finds/

WHO_a. *"Alcohol"*, Last Update: February, 2011, http://www.who.int/mediacentre/factsheets/fs349/en/index.html

Babor, Thomas F., "Alcohol comsumption trends and patterns of drinking," in *Alcohol: No Ordinary Commodity: Research and Public Policy*, Babor, Thomas, Ed., Oxford, UK, Oxford Press, 2010, pp. 23–42.

American Lung Association, "Smoking", http://www.lung.org/stop-smoking/about-smoking/health-effects/smoking.html, 2013.

Jha, Prabhat, "Avoidable global cancer deaths and total deaths from smoking," *Nature Reviews Cancer,* vol. 9 pp. 655–664, 2009.

Al-Maskari, Fatma, "Lifestyle Disease: An Economic Burden on the Health Services", *UN Chronicle - Achieving Global Health*, vol. XLVII (2), 2010.

United Nations_c, "Global status report on noncommunicable disease", http://www.who.int/nmh/publications/ncd_report_full_en.pdf, 2010.

WHO_b. *"Obesity and Overweight"*, Last Update: March, 2013, http://www.who.int/mediacentre/factsheets/fs311/en/index.html

Fogel, Robert W. *"Longer Lives and Lower Health Costs in 2040: Business Class"*, Last Update: July 21st 2011, http://www.bloomberg.com/news/2011-07-21/business-class-longer-lives-and-lower-health-costs.html

United Nations_a, "World Population to reach 10 billion by 2100 if Fertility in all Countries Converges to Replacement Level", http://esa.un.org/unpd/wpp/Other-Information/Press_Release_WPP2010.pdf, 2011.

WHO_c, "Global Health and Aging", http://www.who.int/ageing/publications/global_health.pdf, 2011.

Wolf, Gary, "Know Thyself: Tracking Every Facet of Life, from Sleep to Mood to Pain, 24/7/365", *Wired*, vol., 2009, http://www.wired.com/medtech/health/magazine/17-07/lbnp_knowthyself?currentPage=2

McKinsey & Company, "mHealth: A new vision for healthcare",
 http://www.mckinsey.com/Search.aspx?q=mHealth&l=Insights%20%26%20Publications, 2010.

Henderson, Catherine, *et al.*, "Cost effectiveness of telehealth for patients with long term conditions (Whole Systems Demonstrator telehealth questionnaire study): nested economic evaluation in a pragmatic, cluster randomised controlled trial," *BMJ*, vol. 346, 2013.

Brewster, Liz, Gail Mountain, Bridgette Wessels, Ciara Kelly, and Mark Hawley, "Factors affecting front line staff acceptance of telehealth technologies: a mixed-method systematic review," *Journal of Advanced Nursing*, 2013.

Dill, Michael J. and Edward S. Salsberg, "The Complexities of Physician Supply and Demand: Projects Through 2025", Association of American Medical Colleges (AAMC), 2008.

Reisinger, Don. "*Worldwide smartphone user base hits 1 billion*", Last Update: October 17th 2012,
 http://news.cnet.com/8301-1035_3-57534132-94/worldwide-smartphone-user-base-hits-1-billion/

Svensson, Peter. "*Smartphone now outsell 'dumb' phones*", Last Update: April 29th 2013,
 http://www.3news.co.nz/Smartphones-now-outsell-dumb-phones/tabid/412/articleID/295878/Default.aspx

Topol, Eric, *The Creative Destruction of Medicine: How the Digital Revolution Will Create Better Health Care.* New York: Basic Books, 2012.

Evans, Dave, "The Internet of Things - How the Next Evolution of the Internet Is Changing Everything", Cisco, 2011.

Gosling, Simon N. and Nigel W. Arnell, "A global assessment of the impact of climate change on water scarcity," *Climatic Change,* pp. 1–15, 2013.

Harvey, Fiona. *Global majority faces water shortages 'within two generations'*, The Guardian,
 http://www.theguardian.com/environment/2013/may/24/global-majority-water-shortages-two-generations, 2013.

Stockdale, Charles B., Michael B. Sauter, and Douglas A. McIntyre. "*The Ten Biggest American Cities That Are Running Out Of Water*", Last Update: October 29th 2010,
 http://247wallst.com/investing/2010/10/29/the-ten-great-american-cities-that-are-dying-of-thirst/

Koch, Wendy. *Global warming raises water shortage risks in one-third of U.S. counties*, USA Today, 2010.

The Econmist, "All dried up - Northern China is running out of water, but the government's remedies are potentially disastrous", http://www.economist.com/news/china/21587813-northern-china-running-out-water-govern-ments-remedies-are-potentially-disastrous-all, 2013.

Duxfield, Flint. "*Irrigation depleting global water stores*", Last Update: July 10th 2013,
 http://www.abc.net.au/news/2013-07-10/nrn-dist-global-water-shortages/4811140

Waslekar, Sundeep. "*Will Water Scarcity Increase Tensions Across Asia*", Last Update: October 1st, 2012,
 http://www.forbes.com/2012/01/09/forbes-india-water-wars-across-asia.html

Connor, Steve. *Water shortage in Dead Sea could increase tensions in Middle East*, The Independent,
 http://www.independent.co.uk/news/science/water-shortages-in-dead-sea-could-increase-tensions-in-middle-east-6273289.html, 2013.

Lederer, Edith M. "*UN: Global population to reach 8.1 billion by 2025*", Last Update: June 13th 2013,
 http://www.businessweek.com/ap/2013-06-13/un-world-population-to-reach-8-dot-1-billion-in-2025

Patrick, Stewart M. "*The Coming Global Water Crisis*", Last Update: May 9th 2102,
 http://www.theatlantic.com/international/archive/2012/05/the-coming-global-water-crisis/256896/

UN Water$_b$, "Water Use", http://www.unwater.org/statistics_use.html, 2013.

WHO$_d$, "Global surveillance, prevention and control of chronic respiratory diseases: a comprehensive approach",
 http://www.who.int/gard/publications/GARD_Manual/en/index.html, 2007.

American Academy of Allergy Asthma & Immunology, "Asthma Statistics",
 http://www.aaaai.org/about-the-aaaai/newsroom/asthma-statistics.aspx, 2013.

McAdams, Eric, Claudine Gehin, Bertrand Massot, and James McLaughlin, "The Challenges Facing Wearable Sensor Systems," in *9th International Conference on Wearable Micro and Nano Technologies for Personalized Health*, Porto, 2012, pp. 196–202.

CHAPTER 2

■ ■ ■

Sensing and Sensor Fundamentals

Sensors utilize a wide spectrum of transducer and signal transformation approaches with corresponding variations in technical complexity. These range from relatively simple temperature measurement based on a bimetallic thermocouple, to the detection of specific bacteria species using sophisticated optical systems. Within the healthcare, wellness, and environmental domains, there are a variety of sensing approaches, including microelectromechanical systems (MEMS), optical, mechanical, electrochemical, semiconductor, and biosensing. As outlined in Chapter 1, the proliferation of sensor-based applications is growing across a range of sensing targets such as air, water, bacteria, movement, and physiology. As with any form of technology, sensors have both strengths and weaknesses. Operational performance may be a function of the transduction method, the deployment environment, or the system components. In this chapter, we review the common sensing mechanisms that are used in the application domains of interest within the scope of this book, along with their respective strengths and weaknesses. Finally, we describe the process of selecting and specifying sensors for an application.

What Is a Sensor and What Is Sensing?

There are no uniform descriptions of sensors or the process of sensing. In many cases, the definitions available are driven by application perspectives. Taking a general perspective, a sensor can be defined as:

> *A device that receives a stimulus and responds with an electrical signal.*

> (Fraden, 2010)

Sensor definitions from a scientific or biomedical engineering perspective broaden the potential types of output signals to include, for example, an optical signal:

> *A device that responds to a physical input of interest with a recordable, functionally related output that is usually electrical or optical.*

> (Jones, 2010)

Another common variation, which takes into account the observational element of the measurement, describes a sensor as follows:

> *A sensor generally refers to a device that converts a physical measure into a signal that is read by an observer or by an instrument.*

> (Chen, et al., 2012)

Therefore, setting aside the various nuances of domain and application, a sensor simply measures something of interest and provides an output you can do something useful with.

The words sensor and transducer are both commonly used in the context of measurement systems, and often in an interchangeable manner. Transducer is used more in the United States while sensor has greater popularity in Europe (Sutherland, 2004). The blurring of the lines between the exact meaning of sensors and transducers leads to a degree of confusion.

ANSI (The American National Standards Institute) created a standard for Electrical Transducer Nomenclature and Terminology (ANSI, 1975), which defines a transducer as:

> *A device which provides a usable output in response to a specific measurand.*

An output is defined as an "electrical quantity," and a measurand is "A physical quantity, property, or condition which is measured".

The National Research Council (NRC, 1995) found, however, that the scientific literature had not generally adopted the ANSI definition (AALIANCE, 2010). Instead, descriptions of transducers focusing on the process of converting a physical quality into a measurable output, electrical or optical, for example, have emerged. One such definition is:

> *A converter of any one type of energy into another [as opposed to a sensor, which] converts any type of energy into electrical energy.*

> (Fraden, 2010)

An alternative description is:

> *A sensor differs from a transducer in that a sensor converts the received signal into electrical form only. A sensor collects information from the real world. A transducer only converts energy from one form to another.*

> (Khanna 2012)

However, it is difficult to find consensus on the distinction between sensors and transducers. This problem is exacerbated when the sensor becomes more sophisticated. For example, chemical sensors can be transducers that have been modified to become a sensor e.g. through the use of a sensitive coating covering the sample interface of the transducer. It is clear that strict definitions will always be contentious and driven in part by philosophical differences between engineers and scientists. These differences only hold academic interest when it comes to application development. So while there may be differences in the definitions of sensors and transducers, this has little impact on the ability to utilize sensors in applications. Within this book we use the simple and broad definition that a sensor measures something of interest using a variety of mechanisms, and a transducer converts the output of the sensing processing into a measurable signal. Sensor application developers simply focus on delivering a sensor system that can measure a quantity of interest with the required accuracy. A sensor system usually consists of sensors, measuring and processing circuits, and an output system (Wang, et al., 2011). The key hardware components of a sensor system are described in Chapter 3.

Introduction to the Key Sensing Modalities

Sensors can be used to measure or detect a vast variety of physical, chemical, and biological quantities, including proteins, bacteria, chemicals, gases, light intensity, motion, position, sound and many others, as shown in Figure 2-1. Sensor measurements are converted by a transducer into a signal that represents the quantity of interest to an observer or to the external world. In this section, we will review the most commonly used sensing techniques for our target domains.

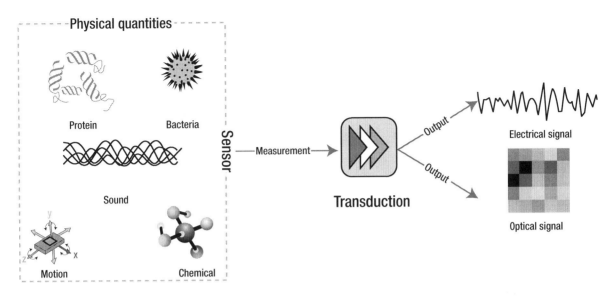

Figure 2-1. *The sensing process*

For any given quantity, there is usually more than one form of sensor that can be used to take a measurement. Each sensor type offers different levels of accuracy, sensitivity, specificity, or ability to operate in different environmental conditions. There are also cost considerations. More expensive sensors typically have more sophisticated features that generally offer better performance characteristics. Sensors can be used to measure quantities of interest in three ways:

- *Contact:* This approach requires physical contact with the quantity of interest. There are many classes to sense in this way—liquids, gases, objects such as the human body, and more. Deployment of such sensors obviously perturbs the state of the sample or subject to some degree. The type and the extent of this impact is application-specific. Let us look at the example of human body-related applications in more detail.

  Comfort and biocompatibility are important considerations for on-body contact sensing. For example, sensors can cause issues such as skin irritation when left in contact for extended periods of time. Fouling of the sensor may also be an issue, and methods to minimize these effects are critical for sensors that have to remain in place for long durations. Contact sensors may have restrictions on size and enclosure design. Contact sensing is commonly used in healthcare- and wellness-oriented applications, particularly where physiological measurements are required, such as in electrocardiography (ECG), electromyography (EMG), and electroencephalography (EEG). The response time of contact sensors is determined by the speed at which the quantity of interest is transported to the measurement site. For example, sensors such as ECGs that measure an electrical signal have a very fast response time. In comparison, the response time of galvanic skin response (GSR) is lower as it requires the transport of sweat to an electrode, a slower process. Contact surface effects, such as the quality of the electrical contact between an electrode and subject's skin, also play a role. Poor contact can result in signal noise and the introduction of signal artifacts.

On-body contact sensing can be further categorized in terms of the degree of "invasion" or impact. Invasive sensors are those, for example, introduced into human organs through small incisions or into blood vessels, perhaps for in vivo glucose sensing or blood pressure monitoring. Minimally invasive sensing includes patch-type devices on the skin that monitor interstitial fluids. Non-invasive sensors simply have contact with the body without effect, as with pulse oximetery.

- *Noncontact:* This form of sensing does not require direct contact with the quantity of interest. This approach has the advantage of minimum perturbation of the subject or sample. It is commonly used in ambient sensing applications—applications based on sensors that are ideally hidden from view and, for example, track daily activities and behaviors of individuals in their own homes. Such applications must have minimum impact on the environment or subject of interest in order to preserve state. Sensors that are used in non-contact modes, passive infrared (PIR) , for example, generally have fast response times.

- *Sample removal:* This approach involves an invasive collection of a representative sample by a human or automated sampling system. Sample removal commonly occurs in healthcare and environmental applications, to monitor E. coli in water or glucose levels in blood, for example. Such samples may be analyzed using either sensors or laboratory-based analytical instrumentation.

With sensor-based approaches, small, hand-held, perhaps disposable sensors are commonly used, particularly where rapid measurements are required. The sensor is typically in close proximity to the sample collection site, as is the case with a blood glucose sensor. Such sensors are increasingly being integrated with computing capabilities to provide sophisticated features, such as data processing, presentation, storage, and remote connectivity.

Analytical instrumentations, in contrast, generally have no size limitations and typically contain a variety of sophisticated features, such as autocalibration or inter-sample auto-cleaning and regeneration. Sample preparation is normally required before analysis. Some instruments include sample preparation as an integrated capability. Results for nonbiological samples are generally fast and very accurate. Biological analysis, such bacteria detection, is usually slower taking hours or days.

Mechanical Sensors

Mechanical sensors are based on the principle of measuring changes in a device or material as the result of an input that causes the mechanical deformation of that device or material (Fink, 2012). Inputs, such as such motion, velocity, acceleration, and displacement that result in mechanical deformation that can be measured. When this input is converted directly into an electrical output, the sensor is described as being electromechanical. Other possible output signals include magnetic, optical, and thermal (Patranabis, 2004).

The common mechanical and electromechanical sensing approaches as described by the IEEE Sensors Council are shown in Table 2-1.

Table 2-1. *Common Mechanical and Electromechanical Sensors*

Sensor	Type	Sensor	Type
Strain Gauge	Metallic Thin film Thick film Foil Bulk Resistance	Displacement	Resistive Capacitive Inductive
Pressure	Piezoelectric Strain gauge Potentiometric Inductive Capacitive	Force	Hydraulic load cell Pneumatic load cell Magneto-elastic Piezoelectric Plastic deformation
Accelerometer	Piezoelectric Piezoresistive Capacitive MEMS Quantum tunneling Hall effect	Acoustic Wave	Bulk Surface
Gyroscope	Vibrating structure Dynamically tuned MEMS London moment	Ultrasonic	Piezoelectric Magnetostrictive
Potentiometer	String Linear taper Linear slider Logarithmic Membrane	Flow	Gas Fluid Controller

Strain gauges are one of the most common mechanical sensors and come in many forms and types. They have been used for many years, and are the key sensing element in a variety of sensors types, including pressure sensors, load cells, torque sensors, and position sensors. Measurement is based on a change in resistance due to strain on a material or combination of materials. A common strain gauge implementation uses a grid-shaped sensing element, which comprises a thin metallic resistive foil (3 to 6 μm thick) bonded onto a thin plastic film backing (15 to 16 μm thick). The entire structure is encapsulated within a protective polyimide film. Strain gauges generally have nominal resistance values ranging from tens of ohms to thousands of ohms, with 120, 350, and 1,000Ω being the most common. An excitation voltage (typically 5V or 12V) is applied to the input leads of the gauge network and a voltage reading is taken from the output leads. The output readings in millivolts are measured by a measurement circuit normally in the form of a Wheatstone bridge, as shown in Figure 2-2 (Kyowa, 2013). As stress is applied to the strain gauge, a change in resistance unbalances the Wheatstone bridge. This results in a signal output, related to the magnitude of the applied stress. Both strain gauge elements and bridge resistors can usually be purchased in an encapsulated housing. This form of package is commonly called a load cell.

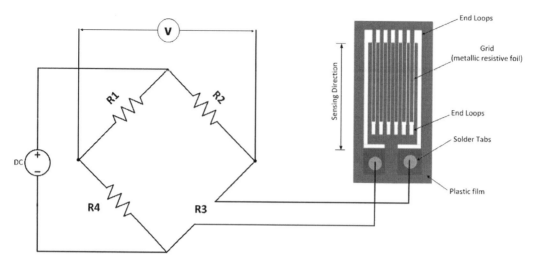

Figure 2-2. *Foil strain gauge attached to a wheatstone bridge*

Another common form of strain gauge is based on the piezoelectric (production of electricity when certain materials are subjected to mechanical stress) properties of some semiconductor materials, such as silicon or germanium. These were first used in the car industry during the 1970s, before being applied in other domains, including sports. This form of strain gauge is smaller, has higher unit resistance and sensitivity, and is lower in cost than grid-style strain gauges.

A key problem with strain measurements is that of thermal effects. Changes in temperature cause expansion or contraction of the sensing element, resulting in thermally induced strain. Temperature compensation is required to address the problem and this can be built into the Wheatstone bridge. Piezoelectric strain gauges have even greater sensitivity to temperature variation and greater drift characteristics, which must be compensated for during use by regular recalibration. Strain gauges are used in a variety of sporting and healthcare applications, including clinical dynamometers that measure grip strength (Kasukawa, et al., 2010, Bohannon, 2011).

MEMS Sensors

The name MEMS is often used to describe both a type of sensor and the manufacturing process that fabricates the sensor. MEMS are three-dimensional, miniaturized mechanical and electrical structures, typically ranging from 1 to 100 μm, that are manufactured using standard semiconductor manufacturing techniques. MEMS consist of mechanical microstructures, microsensors, microactuators, and microelectronics, all integrated onto the same silicon chip.

MEMS sensors are widely used in the car industry and, since the early 1990s, accelerometers have been used in airbag restraint systems, electronic stability programs (ESPs), and antilock braking systems (ABS). The recent availability of inexpensive, ultra-compact, low-power multi-axis MEMS sensors has led to rapid growth into customer electronics (CE) devices; MEMS can be found in smartphones, tablets, game console controllers, portable gaming devices, digital cameras, and camcorders. They have also found application in the healthcare domain in devices such as blood pressure monitors, pacemakers, ventilators, and respirators. While there are many forms of MEMS sensors, two of the most important and widely used forms are accelerometers and gyroscopes, which are produced by companies such as Analog Devices and Freescale Semiconductor.

Accelerometers

There are five modes of motion sensing: acceleration, vibration (periodic acceleration), shock (instantaneous acceleration), tilt (static acceleration), and rotation. All of these, except rotation, can be measured using accelerometers. It is unsurprising, therefore, that accelerometers have a wide range of applications, from triggering a hard disk protection system as a device is falling, to gesture recognition for gaming. MEMS accelerometers are typically either capacitive or piezoresistive. Capacitive accelerometers are composed of fixed plates attached to a substrate and moveable plates attached to the frame. Displacement of the frame, due to acceleration, changes the differential capacitance, which is measured by the on-board circuitry. Capacitive accelerometers offer high sensitivities and are utilized for low-amplitude, low-frequency devices. Piezoresistive accelerometers contain resistive material bonded to a cantilever beam that bends under the influence of acceleration. This bending causes deformation of the resistor, leading to a change in its resistance relative to the acceleration applied. Piezoresistive accelerometers tend to be more rugged and are used for accelerometers that achieve higher amplitudes and higher frequency response (Piezotronics[1], 2013, Piezotronics[2], 2013, Nanogloss, 2009).

Gyroscopes

MEMS gyroscopes measure the angular rate of rotation of one or more axes, as shown in Figure 2-3. Gyroscopes can measure intricate motions accurately in free space. They have no rotating parts that require bearings, and therefore lend themselves to miniaturization and batch fabrication using semiconductor manufacturing processes. Almost all MEMS gyroscopes use vibrating mechanical elements (proof-mass) to sense rotation based on the transfer of energy between two vibration modes of a structure caused by Coriolis acceleration. The most popular form of MEMS gyroscope is a tuning fork gyroscope, which contains a pair of masses that are driven to oscillate with equal amplitude but in opposite directions. When rotated, the Coriolis force creates an orthogonal vibration that can be sensed by a variety of mechanisms (Nasiri, 2013). Other forms of MEMS design include vibrating wheel, wine glass resonator (hemispherical resonator gyro), cylindrical vibratory, and piezoelectric. Major manufacturers of MEMS gyroscopes include Robert Bosch GmbH, InvenSense, STMicroelectronics, and Analog Devices. MEMS gyroscopes can be found in smartphones, fall detectors, and games consoles.

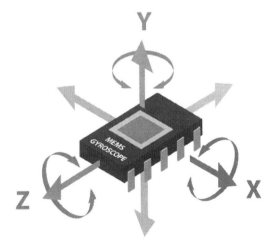

Figure 2-3. *3D Angular rotation measurements with a MEMS gyroscope*

Optical Sensors

Optical sensors work by detecting waves or photons of light, including light in the visible, infrared, and ultraviolet (UV) spectral regions. They operate by measuring a change in light intensity related to light emission or absorption by a quantity of interest. They can also measure phase changes occurring in light beams due to interaction or interference effects. Measuring the absence or interruption of a light source is another common approach. Sensors based on this principle are commonly used in automated doors and gates to ensure no obstacles are present in their opening path. They are widely used in industrial applications for measuring liquids and material levels in tanks or in factory production lines to detect the presence or absence of objects. Optical sensors are also used with stepper motors in applications that require position sensing and encoding, for example, in automated lighting systems in the entertainment industry (Cadena, 2013). Let us now look at the most common types of optical sensors.

Photodetectors

Photodetector sensors are based on the principle of photoconductivity, where the target material changes its conductivity in the presence or absence of light. Sensors are sensitive for a given spectral region (range of optical wavelengths) from ultra-violet to infrared. Examples include:

- Active pixel sensors, such as those found in smartphone cameras and web cams.

- Charged-coupled devices (CCD), such as those found in digital cameras.

- Light-dependent resistors (LDRs), such as those found in street lighting systems.

- Photodiodes, such as those used in room lighting-level control systems or in UV measurement systems.

- Phototransistors, such as those used in optoisolators for a variety of applications, including healthcare equipment, to provide electrical isolation between the patient and equipment.

- Photomultipliers such as those found in spectrophotometers detectors. Photomultipliers are also used in flow cytometers (a laser-based technology used for cell counting and sorting and biomarker detection) for blood analysis applications.

Infrared (IR)

IR sensors come in both active and passive forms, as shown in Figure 2-4. In the active form, the sensor employs an infrared light source, such as a light-emitting diode (LED) or laser diode, which projects a beam of light that is detected at a separate detector (photoelectric cells, photodiodes, or phototransistors). An object that passes through the beam disrupts the received signal at the detector. An alternative configuration is reflectance-based detection, where the source and detector are located in the same enclosure. Light from the IR source is reflected from an object as it moves into the sensor's field of detection. The amount of light received at the detector depends upon the reflectivity of the object surface. Infrared sensors can be used as counters, proximity sensors (as with automatic doors), or to identify the presence of people or other mobile objects under day or night conditions.

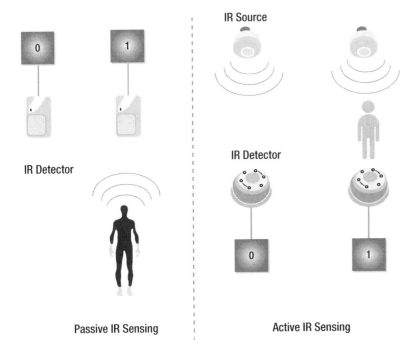

Figure 2-4. *Passive and active infrared sensing modes*

Unlike active sensors, passive sensors do not generate or radiate energy for the purposes of detection. They rely on detected heat from objects, such as human bodies in their detection field. They are commonly used in security lighting around homes and in home security systems to detect intruders (Fried, 2012). They can also be used for ambient sensing applications, an example of which is presented in Chapter 8.

Infrared sensors generally have low power requirements, relatively high immunity to noise, and do not require complex signal processing circuitry. They do, however, have a number of key disadvantages, including the need to be in line-of-sight of the object of interest, a relatively short detection range, and being subject to interference from environmental sources such as sunlight, fog, rain, and dust (EngineersGarage, 2012).

Fiber Optic

This form of optical sensor uses an optical glass fiber as the sensing element. Multimode fibers with large core diameters (>10 μm) are used for sensor applications. Optical fibers can be coated with materials that respond to changes in strain, temperature, or humidity. The most commonly used fiber-optic sensor types include:

- *Strain sensing:* Mechanical strain in the fiber changes the geometric properties of the fiber, which changes the refraction of the light passing through it. These changes can be correlated to the applied strain.

- *Temperature sensing:* Strain in the fiber is caused by thermal expansion or contraction of the fiber. A strain measurement can be correlated directly with changes in temperature.

- *Pressure sensing:* Fiber-optic pressure sensors can be of two types—intensity and interferometric. In intensity-sensing fiber-optic sensors, the magnitude of light intensity reflected from a thin diaphragm changes with applied pressure (Udd, 2011). Interferometric pressure sensors work on the principle that pressure changes introduce perturbations into the sensor, which generate path-length changes in a fiber. This in turn causes the light/dark bands of an interference pattern to shift. By measuring the shift of the wavelength spectrum, the pressure applied on it can be quantitatively obtained (Lee, et al., 2012).

- *Humidity sensing:* A broad range of principles have been applied to optical fiber-based humidity sensors, including (i) luminescent systems with fluorescent dyes that are humidity-sensitive (ii) refractive index changes due to absorption in a hygroscopic (moisture absorbing) fiber coating such as polyimide; and (iii) reflective thin film-coated fibers made from tin dioxide (SiO_2) and titanium dioxide (TiO_2), which change the refractive index, resulting in a shift in resonance frequency (Morendo-Bondi, et al., 2004).

Interferometers

An interferometer is a device used to measure changes in a propagating light beam, such as path length or wavelength along the path of propagation. Generally, the sensor uses a light source such as a laser LED and two single fibers. The light is split and coupled into both of the fibers. The quantity being measured modulates the phase of the optical signal, which can be detected by comparison with a reference optical signal. There are four types of interferometric configuration: Fabry-Perot, Mach-Zehnder, Michelson, and Sagnac. This form of sensor is commonly used for measuring physical quantities, such as temperature, velocity, vibration, pressure, and displacement (Baldini, et al., 2002).

Because optical sensors use light either directly or indirectly for measurements, they have a number of advantages over other forms of sensing. However, these advantages are application-specific, as are the associated disadvantages. Table 2-2 presents the general advantages and disadvantages of optical sensors.

Table 2-2. *Advantages and Disadvantages of Optical Sensors*

Advantages	Disadvantages
High sensitivity	Susceptible to interference from environmental effects
Chemically inert	Can be costly
Small and lightweight	Susceptible to physical damage
Suitable for remote sensing	
Immunity to electromagnetic interference	
Wide dynamic range	
Capable of monitoring a wide range of chemical and physical parameters	
Reliable operation	

Semiconductor Sensors

Semiconductor sensors have grown in popularity due to their low cost, reliability, low power consumption, long operational lifespan, and small form factor. They can be found in a wide range applications including:

- Gas monitoring

  - Pollution monitoring, for example CO, NO_2, SO_2, and O_3 (Nihal, et al., 2008, Wetchakun, et al., 2011)

  - Breath analyzers, for breath-alcohol content (BAC) measurements (Knott, 2010)

  - Domestic gas monitoring, such as propane(Gómez-Pozos, et al., 2013)

- Temperature, as in integrated electronic equipment (Fraden, 2010)

- Magnetism, for example, magnetometers for six degrees of freedom applications (Coey, 2010, Sze, et al., 2007)

- Optical sensing, such as in charge-coupled device detectors in cameras (`EUROPE.COM`, 2013)

Gas Sensors

Semiconductor sensors are commonly used to detect hydrogen, oxygen (O_2), alcohol, and harmful gases, such as carbon monoxide (CO). Domestic CO detectors are one of the most popular applications of gas-monitoring semiconductors. A typical gas sensor has a sensing layer and a sensor base, and is housed in a porous enclosure. The sensing layer is composed of a porous, thick-film metal oxide semiconductor (MOS) layer, such as SnO_2 or tungsten trioxide (WO_3). This is deposited onto a micro-sensor layer containing electrodes that measure the resistance of the sensing layer and a heater that heats the sensing layer to 200°C to 400°C. When the metal oxide is heated to a high temperature in air, oxygen is absorbed on the crystal surface with a negative charge, and donor electrons in the crystal surface are transferred to the absorbed oxygen, leaving positive charges in a space-charge layer. This creates a potential barrier against electron flow. In the presence of reducing gases, such as CO or (Hydrogen) H_2, catalytic reduction at the pre-absorbed oxygen layer decreases the resistance of the sensor. Oxidizing gases, such as nitrogen dioxide (NO_2) and ozone (O_3), have the opposite effect, resulting in an increase in resistance. The magnitude of resistance change can be correlated to the concentration of the gas species. The magnitude of the change depends on the microstructure and composition/doping of the base material; on the morphology and geometrical characteristics of the sensing layer and substrate; as well as on the temperature at which the sensing takes place (AppliedSensor, 2008). These parameters can be altered to tune the sensitivity toward different gases or classes of gases.

Despite many advantages, including low cost, relatively low maintenance, and long operational lifespan, semiconductor gas sensors can lack specificity in mixed gas environments. Thus, gases that are not of interest contribute to the overall signal response, resulting in an inaccurate elevated reading or false positives. To increase the selectivity of the gas sensors, chemical filters can be placed before the sensing material to remove the interfering components in the sample. These filters can be either passive or active, depending on whether a physical (passive) or chemical (active) mechanism is used. Filters can also be classified according to their location in the sensor, that is, internal (directly on the sensing element) or external (in a separate block). External filters such as charcoal are commonly used in commercial gas sensors.

Temperature Sensors

Semiconductor temperature sensors are based on the change of voltage across a p-n junction, which exhibits strong thermal dependence. The simplest form of temperature sensor is a silicon diode where the forward bias across the diode has a temperature coefficient of approximately 2.0–2.3mV/°C. Measurements are made by holding the bias current constant and measuring voltage changes. For accurate readings, the sensor needs to be calibrated (two-point calibration is sufficient due to good linearity) as significant inter-device variations can occur in the ±30 °C range. For more accurate measurements, diode-connected bipolar transistors are used. Again, a constant current is applied through the base-emitter junction, generating a voltage that is a linear function of the temperature. An offset may be applied to convert the signal from absolute temperature to Celsius or Fahrenheit. Typically, operating ranges are –55°C to +150°C. Semiconductor temperature sensors are often categorized by their output signal type, which can be analog (voltage and current), logic, or digital (Gyorki, 2009). The key advantages of this sensor type are ease of integration into a circuit, general ruggedness, and low cost. Their primary disadvantages are limitations of accuracy and stability, often poor thermal chip design, and slow response time (CAPGO, 2010)(Fraden, 2010).

Magnetic Sensors

Semiconductor magnetic sensors detect changes or disturbances in magnetic fields and convert these changes into a measureable electrical signal. They can produce information on properties, such as directional movement, position, rotation, angle, or electrical currents in machines or devices. They are used in medical devices such as ventilators to control the extent of movement; in enclosures for consumer electronic devices to detect opening and shutting of a device; and in renewable-energy scenarios, such as solar installations. For example, in domestic solar installations, magnetic sensors are used in power invertors that convert the electricity generated by the solar panels into usable electrical current for the home. They can also be used to monitor the charge level of batteries used in conjunction with solar panels for energy storage (Racz, 2011). The most common semiconductor magnetic integrated circuits apply the Hall effect (discovered by Edwin Hall in 1879) or magnetoresistive principles (ansiotropic, giant, or tunnel magnetoresistivity).

Hall-effect sensors comprise a thin layer of p-type (or n-type) semiconductor material that carries a continuous current. When the device is placed within a magnetic field, the measured voltage difference across the semiconductor depends on the intensity of the magnetic field applied perpendicular to the direction of the current flow. Charge carriers (electrons) moving through the magnetic field are subjected to Lorentz force (the force experienced by a charged particle as it moves through an electromagnetic field) at right angles to the direction of motion and the direction of the field. A voltage called the Hall voltage is generated in response to Lorentz force on the electrons. This voltage is directly proportional to the strength of the magnetic field passing through the semiconductor material. Semiconductor materials that have high electron mobility, such as indium (In), indium antimonide (InSb), indium arsenide (InAs), or gallium arsenide (GaAs) are commonly used in Hall-effect sensors (Eren, 2001). The output voltage is often relatively small—no more than a couple of microvolts—which requires amplification and signal conditioning to improve sensitivity and compensate for hysteresis (the difference in output between the rising and falling output values for a given input). In commercial sensors, sensing, signal amplification, voltage regulation, and signal conditioning are contained in a single package.

Hall-effect sensors demonstrate good environmental immunity to problems such as dust, vibration, and moisture. However, they can be affected by other sources of magnetic flux that are in close proximity, such as those generated by electrical wires. They are robust, having no mechanical contacts for sensing. They are, however, effective only over a limited distance and do not work at distances great than 10cm unless the magnetic field strength is very high.

Optical Sensors

There are a variety of optical semiconductor sensors, the most common of which is the photodiode, a type of photodetector that converts light into either current or voltage. Photodiodes normally have a window or optical fiber connection to allow light to reach a p-n or a PIN junction (an intrinsic semiconductor region between p-type and n-type semiconductor regions). Photodiodes often use a PIN junction rather than a p-n junction to increase the speed of response. When a photon of sufficient energy strikes the depletion region of the diode, it may hit an atom with sufficient energy to release an electron, thereby creating a free electron (and a positively charged electron hole). Free electrons and holes in the depletion region, or one diffusion length away, are pulled away in an applied electrical field. The holes move toward the anode, and electrons move toward the cathode, resulting in a photocurrent. This photocurrent is the sum of both the dark current (without light) and the light current, so the dark current must be minimized to enhance the sensitivity of the device. Photodiodes are used in a variety of applications, including pulse oximeters, blood particle analyzers, nuclear radiation detectors, and smoke detectors.

Another form of photodetector is the phototransistor, which is essentially a bipolar transistor with a transparent window, like the photodiode, that allows light to hit the base-collector junction. The intensity of the light shining on the phototransistor's base terminal determines how much current can pass into its collector terminal and out through its emitter terminal. Higher light intensity results in more current and, inversely, less light results in less current. Phototransistors have the advantage of being more sensitive than photodiodes. However, they have a slower response time. Applications for phototransistors include detecting ambient light, monitoring intravenous (IV) infusion rates, and atmospheric monitoring. For IV applications, the phototransistor is used as a drip sensor that attaches to the IV bag drip chamber. It counts the number of drips per unit time, which is feedback to an infusion pump controller to ensure that the set point flow rate is maintained (Times, 2004). In atmospheric monitoring applications, phototransistors with sensitivity in the IR spectral region are used for Lidar sensing, a laser-based technique that can be used for monitoring and profiling atmospheric species and constituents such as water vapor, carbon dioxide (CO_2), CO, methane (CH_4) and ethane (C_2H_6). Phototransistors are used in detectors that convert the collected returned optical signal into an electrical signal. Differences in the return optical signal are due to absorption by the gas of interest (Refaat, et al., 2007).

A third type of photodetector is the light-dependent resistor (LDR), the conductivity of which changes in proportion to the intensity of light. When light strikes the LDR, photons are absorbed, resulting in excitation of electrons from the valence band into the conduction band of the semiconductor material. As a consequence, the electrical resistance of the device decreases. The cells exhibit very high resistance (1–10 MΩ) when in the dark, decreasing to a few hundred ohms when fully illuminated. LDRs can be constructed from various materials, including lead sulfide (PbS), lead selenide (PbSe), indium antimonide (InSb), cadmium sulfide (CdS), and cadmium selenide (CdSe). The semiconductor material utilized determines the wavelengths of greatest sensitivity, ranging from the visible (390–700 nm) to the infrared region (>700 nm). Applications for LDRs include lighting control, camera shutter control, and commercial light meters.

Ion-Sensitive Field-Effect Transistors (ISFETs)

ISFETs are used for measuring ion concentrations in solution, such as H^+ in pH measurements. In devices with ISFETs, the sample solution is in direct contact with the FET gate-electrode material, and this determines the gate voltage, which in turn controls the source-to-drain current through the transistor. Hence, changes in the source-to-drain current occur as the sample ion concentration varies. To convey a degree of selectivity to this effect, the transistor gate surface in the ISFET is typically covered by an ion-sensitive membrane, for example, one sensitive to hydrogen ions for pH measurements. SiO_2 films can be used for pH measurements, but materials such as silicon nitride (Si_3N_4), alumina (Al_2O_3), zirconium oxide (ZrO_2), and tantalum oxide (Ta_2O_5) are normally employed as they have better properties in relation to pH response, hysteresis, and drift. The key advantages of ISFETs are their small size, which allows them to be used with small volumes; low cost; good stability; and ability to work in wide temperature ranges. Their key disadvantages are long-term drift, hysteresis, and relatively short life span. Additionally, the availability of miniature reference electrodes remains an issue. While conventional silver chloride (AgCl) or mercury(II) chloride ($HgCl_2$) reference electrodes can be used, they are unsuitable for many biological and in vivo analyses that require miniaturization. The development of suitable reference electrodes, such as solid state electrodes for ISFETs, remains an area of active research (Adami, et al., 2014)(Guth, et al., 2009). ISFET sensing approaches that do not require a reference electrode have also been reported in the literature (Kokot, 2011).

Electrochemical Sensors

An electrochemical sensor is composed of a sensing or working electrode, a reference electrode, and, in many cases, a counter electrode. These electrodes are typically placed in contact with either a liquid or a solid electrolyte. In the low-temperature range (<140° C), electrochemical sensors are used to monitor pH, conductivity, dissolved ions, and dissolved gases. For measurements at high temperatures (>500° C), such as the measurement of exhaust gases and molten metals, solid electrolyte sensors are used (Guth, et al., 2009). Electrochemical sensors work on the principle of measuring an electrical parameter of the sample of interest. They can be categorized based on the measurement approach employed.

Electrochemical sensors present a number of advantages, including low power consumption, high sensitivity, good accuracy, and resistance to surface-poisoning effects. However, their sensitivity, selectivity, and stability are highly influenced by environmental conditions, particularly temperature. Environmental conditions also have a strong influence on operational lifespan; for example, a sensor's useful life will be significantly reduced in hot and dry environments. Cross-sensitivity to other gases can be problem for gas sensors. Oversaturation of the sensor to the species of interest can also reduce the sensor's lifespan. The key electrochemical sensor types follow.

Potentiometric Sensors

This type of sensor measures differences in potential (voltage) between the working electrode and a reference electrode. The working electrode's potential depends on the concentration (more exactly, the ion activity) of the species of interest (Banica, 2012). For example, in a pH sensor, the electric potential, created between the working electrode and the reference electrode, is a function of the pH value of the solution being measured. Other applications of potentiometric sensors include ion-selective electrodes for both inorganic (for example, monitoring of metal ion contamination in environmental samples or profiling of blood electrolytes) and organic ions (for example, aromatic aldehyde or ibuprofen in human serum samples).

Amperometric Sensors

This form of electrochemical sensor measures changes in current. The potential of the working electrode is maintained at a fixed value (relative to a reference electrode) and the current is measured on a time basis. Electron transfer (current) is determined by redox (reduction-oxidation) reactions at the electrode surface that are driven by the applied potential (Wang, et al., 1995). The working electrode is designed so the measured current is directly proportional to the concentration of a redox active species of interest in the sample solution. Typical applications include oxygen-sensing ($_pO_2$ and $_pCO_2$ patient monitoring), fire detection (for example, CO from smoldering fires), and toxic gas detection (such as chlorine (Cl)).

Coulometric

Coulometric sensors measure the quantity of electricity in coulombs as a result of an electrochemical reaction. This is achieved by holding a working electrode at a constant potential and measuring the current that flows through an attached circuit. The analyte of interest is fully oxidized or reduced at the electrode. As the analyte is consumed, the current being measured decreases towards zero. The rate of reaction is dependent on the rate that the analyte is transferred to the working electrode. Some oxygen sensors utilize a variation of this configuration where both a cathode and an anode are used with a DC voltage maintained between them. Oxygen atoms from the sample diffuse to the cathode through a porous membrane where they are reduced. The oxygen ions, O^{2-}, are attracted though a solid electrolyte that is heated to 400°C. The oxygen ions are then converted back to molecular oxygen at the anode electrode.

Coulometric sensors also find application in detecting glucose. The enzyme used in the sensor, glucose oxidase, is specific for glucose, so all of the charge measured by the sensor corresponds to the complete concentration of glucose in the sample—provided the enzymatic reaction completes. A great advantage of this under-utilized method is that in principle, no calibration is required; you just count the electrons and convert this into the number of glucose molecules. Removing the need for calibration greatly simplifies the complexity of the device for on-body sensing, or for implantable sensors (Andoralov, et al., 2013).

Coulometric sensors have a number of advantages over amperometric sensors, including higher sensitivity, greater selectivity, and better stability. Another key advantage of this sensor is that, if used correctly, it can offer absolute quantitation. If the cell volume of the sensor is known and the species of interest is fully electrolyzed, the corresponding charge is an absolute measure of quantity and concentration (Carroll, et al., 2011).

Conductometric Sensors

This form of sensor operates on the principle that electrical conductivity can change in the presence or absence of some chemical species. Two configurations are commonly used. The first arrangement consists of two elements—a sensitive conducting layer and contact electrodes. DC voltage is applied to the sensor and the resistance is measured. This configuration is typically used for chemiresistors in gas-sensing applications. The conducting layer can either be a porous thick film (2–300 μm), which allows the gas to diffuse through it, resulting in good sensitivity, or a thin film (5–500 nm), on which the source material is sputtered (a process where atoms are ejected from a target or source material and deposited onto a substrate) or deposited using chemical vapor deposition onto a substrate layer, mainly oxide semiconductors (Janta, 2009). In the second configuration, an electrode (often glass) with a chemically interactive layer on the top is placed in an electrolytic solution to which the analyte of interest is added. A counter electrode is used to complete the circuit. This form of configuration is often used for biosensors. Conductometric sensors are generally inexpensive, making them popular.

Biosensors

Biosensors use biochemical mechanisms to identify an analyte of interest in chemical, environmental (air, soil, and water), and biological samples (blood, saliva, and urine). The sensor uses an immobilized biological material, which could be an enzyme, antibody, nucleic acid, or hormone, in a self-contained device (see Figure 2-5). The biological material being used in the biosensor device is immobilized in a manner that maintains its bioactivity. Methods utilized include membrane (for example, electroactive polymers) entrapment, physical bonding, and noncovalent or covalent binding. The immobilization process results in contact being made between the immobilized biological material and the transducer. When an analyte comes into contact with the immobilized biological material, the transducer produces a measurable output, such as a current, change in mass, or a change in color. Indirect methods can also be utilized, in which a biochemical reaction occurs between the analyte and sensor material, resulting in a product. During the reaction, measurable quantities such as heat, gas (for example, oxygen), electrons, or hydrogen ions are produced, and can be measured.

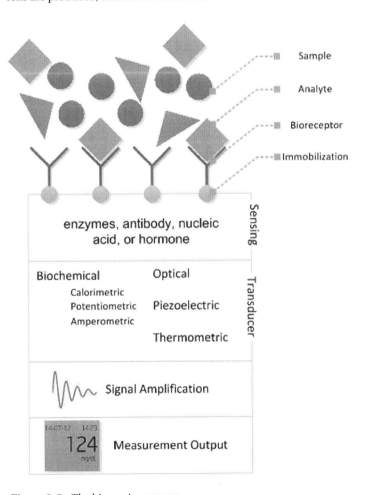

Figure 2-5. *The biosensing process*

The use of biosensors has increased steadily since Yellow Springs Instruments produced the first commercially successful glucose biosensor in 1975 (Setford, et al., 2005). Biosensors are now available over the counter for a large variety of consumer applications, including cholesterol measurement, fertility monitoring, ovulation status, bacterial infection or exposure (such as Heliobacter pylori), allergies, and STD detection. A report by Global Industry Analysts (GIA) estimates that the biosensors market will be worth approximately USD 16.5 billion by 2017 (PRWeb, 2012). Biosensors have also found niches in domains outside of healthcare. The key biosensor application domains are summarized in Table 2-3.

Table 2-3. *Key Biosensor Application Domains*

Domain	Application
Healthcare	Chronic disease management, such as glucose monitoring in diabetes Diagnosis and screening for home pregnancy testing; stomach ulcers: Helicobacter pylori Biochemistry, for example, cholesterol testing Bacterial infection testing Acute disease evaluation, as for cancers, such as prostate
Biotechnology/fermentation	Wine fermentation Citric acid Brewing Enzyme production Biopharmaceutical production
Food quality	Chemical contaminant detection, such as contamination with antibiotics Toxin detection Pathogen detection Hormone detection, as in milk
Personal safety/law enforcement/ employment	Alcohol testing Drug testing
Environmental monitoring	Pollution, such as testing for fecal coliforms in water Agriculture Pesticides in water such as organophosphates Heavy metals Hormones
Security	Chemical and warfare agent detection

Transducers for Biosensors

The transduction process in a biosensor involves converting the biological activity that the sensor has measured via a bioreceptor into a quantifiable signal, such as current, an optical signal, or a change in measurable mass. The most commonly utilized transducer mechanisms are electrochemical, optical, piezoelectric, and thermometric.

- There are three common electrochemical sensing approaches used in biosensors (Pohanka and Skládal, 2008).

  - Conductometric and impedimetric biosensors measure changes in conductivity (the inverse of resistivity) during enzymatic redox reactions (Yoon, 2013).

  - Potentiometric biosensors measure potential changes due to biochemical reactions using ISE and ISFETs (Lee, et al., 2009).

- Amperometric biosensors function by measuring the current produced by a biochemical redox reaction, such as glucose oxidization by glucose dehydrogenase (Corcuera, et al., 2003)

- Coulometric biosensors measure the current generated during an enzymatic reaction in coulombs. Biomedical applications include glucose measurements in blood samples (Wang, 2008)(Peng, et al., 2013).

- In optical biosensors, an immobilized biological component on an optical fiber interacts with its target analyte, forming a complex that has distinct and measurable optical properties. Alternatively, in immunoassays, the biological component (such as an antibody) is immobilized in an assay tray. When the sample is added, a measureable, visible change in color or luminescence occurs. Measurement approaches include photometric and colorimetric detection.

  - Piezoelectric biosensors are based on a change in mass or elastic properties that results in a change to the resonant frequency of a piezoelectric crystalline structure (for example, in quartz, cadmium sulfide, lithium niobate ($LiNbO_3$), or gallium nitride (GaN)). There are two common implementations of piezoelectric biosensors: bulk acoustic wave (BAW) and surface acoustic wave (SAW) devices. An acoustic wave is applied to an oscillating electric field to create a mechanical wave, which propagates either through the surface (SAW) or substrate (BAW), before conversion back to an electric field for measurement. In a biosensor configuration, the resonant frequency is a function of the biosensing membranes attached to a crystal resonator, such as immobilized monoclonal antibodies. As the analyte of interest binds with the antibodies, a change in mass occurs that changes the resonant frequency. BAW implementations are generally favored over SAW for biosensor applications since the shear horizontal wave generated during the detection process radiates limited energy in liquid samples, impacting the signal-to-noise ratio (Durmus, et al., 2008).

  - Thermometric and calorimetric biosensors are based on the measurement of heat effects. Many enzyme-catalyzed reactions are exothermic in nature, resulting in heat generation that can be used for measuring the rate of reaction and hence the analyte concentration. The heat generated can be measured by a transducer such as a thermistor.

Key Characteristics of Biosensors

Biosensors have a unique set of characteristics, due to the use of bioreceptors that differentiate them from other sensing approaches. Biosensors can offer superior sensitivity and specificity over other sensor types. However, they can lack robustness due to sensitivity to the operating environment. The key characteristics that affect biosensors in most applications are:

- Because biosensors rely on biological components, they can have stability or time-dependent degradation of performance; that is, the enzymes or antibodies can lose activity over time. Storage conditions and the method of manufacture can significantly influence operational lifespan.

- Biosensors are normally for single use only. They are generally suitable for point-of-care applications, but they are currently not suitable for long-term monitoring where continuous measurements are required, such as the monitoring of bacteria in water.

- Biosensors often have a limited operational range, in terms of factors such as temperature, pH, or humidity, in which they will operate reliably.

- Sample preparation, such as the preparation of biological samples before presentation to the sensor, is often necessary and this can increase the complexity of the sensor system as well as the sample turnaround time.

- Sensor fouling can be a significant issue, particularly with biological samples, as in the case of protein deposits. These issues can be addressed in part through the use micro- and nanofluidic systems, such as micro-dialysis, to prepare the sample before presentation to the sensor.

- Some compounds can interfere with the sensor readings, particularly biochemical transducers, as in the case of paracetamol interference in glucose measurements.

- Generally, biosensors exhibit very high sensitivity and specificity.

Application Domains

As outlined in the previous section, researchers and commercial solution providers have at their disposal many different sensing options. As a result, more than one sensor type is usually available to measure a quantity of interest. Each sensing option presents its own unique set of advantages and disadvantages. These must be weighed in the context of the use case or application being implemented to determine which sensing technology should be selected. Depending on the specific application, this can involve a complex mixture of competing variables that need to be thought through. Factors such as the sensor type, hardware options, form of enclosure, and the application protocol should be carefully considered. Let us now look briefly at the key challenges and requirements for our application domains.

Environmental Monitoring

Increased urbanization, intensive agricultural methods, industrialization, demands for power, and climate change have significantly impacted our ability to maintain a clean environment. Contaminants and pollutants from a large variety of sources can affect our air, water, soil, and ambient environment. These range from chemical pollutants, biological blooms, heavy metals, gases, and bacterial pathogens, to ambient noise sources (Ho, et al., 2005).

Protection of human health and ecosystems is of the highest priority, requiring rapid, sensitive, robust, and scalable sensor solutions that are capable of detecting pollutants, often at very low concentrations and on a widespread basis. While many solutions are already available for environmental monitoring, there are on-going pressures to develop new sensor technologies that are even more accurate and more sensitive, in order to drive effective, scalable solutions. This will enable improvements in real-time decision-making, sensing-granularity, and compliance-monitoring.

Many analyses especially for bacterial contamination still require in-situ sampling with laboratory-based analysis of samples. Strict protocols must be adhered to in the sampling process, particularly for regulated monitoring; otherwise the integrity of the samples and results can be compromised. Sensors, which operate in situ, can address these issues but bring their own set of challenges; particularly relating to sensor fouling, sensitivity stability, accuracy, and environmental influences. Growth in the use of sensors for these applications is currently inhibited by significant technological barriers that must be overcome. Progress towards sustainable performance, comparable to a laboratory, must also be demonstrated and maintained in sensor networks distributed over a wide geographical area.

Air

Air pollutants come in many forms, including: sulfur dioxide (SO_2), CO, NO_2, and volatile organic compounds, such as benzene (C_6H_6). The sources of these pollutants include vehicle emissions, electric power plants, farming, and industrial manufacturing. Air pollution remains an issue both in the developed and developing world. Fossil fuel power generation facilities are a major source of air pollution and demand for solutions is likely to grow, given the public outcry and government policy changes with respect to nuclear power plants in countries such as Germany and Japan following the Fukushima nuclear power plant explosions in 2011 (Inajima, et al., 2012). The burning of fossil fuels generates particulate matter, sulfur dioxides, nitrogen oxides, and mercury (Hg), which can impact human health. In parallel, increased urbanization and personal car ownership, resulting in concentrated vehicular emissions in large cities, such as Mexico City and Rio de Janeiro, can also have a negative impact on human health (Schwela, 2000). In China, more than 13 million cars were sold in 2012 alone. This rapid proliferation of cars has resulted in serious air pollution problems, like $PM_{2.5}$ (fine particulate matter with a diameter of 2.5 micrometers or less), in cities such as Beijing (Watt, 2013). For the first time, the Chinese government has publically admitted the link between extensive environmental pollution and cancer in China (Wee, et al., 2013).

In many parts of the world, air quality specifications and monitoring regimes are now controlled on a regulatory basis (for example, with the Clean Air Act in the US) by national bodies such as the Environmental Protection Agency (EPA) in the United States. Limits are in place for various gases, hydrocarbons, metals and particulate matter in air to safeguard public health. Concentrations of the various pollutants and contaminants are monitored on a continuous basis to ensure compliance with the regulations. These regulations are discussed in more detail in Chapter 6.

Many different combinations of sensors may come with an air-monitoring station. Air sensing can range from monitoring a single gas species, using a single sensor, to monitoring multiple gases, particulate matter, hydrocarbons, and metals sensing, as defined by regulatory requirements for air quality. Regulatory monitoring utilizes expensive analytical instrumentation, including spectroscopy analysis, as in the case of sulfur dioxide monitoring by UV fluorescence, and O_3 absorption of UV light at 254nm (EPA, 2012). As a result, only a small number of high functionality, high cost monitoring stations are deployed in any given geographical area. This low-density deployment results in less than satisfactory resolution of the data; particularly in highly urbanized areas where local effects due to specific emission sources, traffic patterns, or the types of buildings can affect local air quality. With the availability of low-cost sensors, there is growing interest, particularly in the research community, in using high-density sensor deployments to provide high-granularity air quality sensing. A detailed description of such applications is presented in Chapter 11. A variety of sensor technologies are being utilized for air quality and ambient environmental applications, including:

- Semiconductor sensors are used to monitor atmospheric gases (CO, CO_2, O_3, ammonia (NH_3), CH_4, NO_2), as well as ambient temperature, humidity and atmospheric pressure (Fine, et al., 2010, Kumar, et al., 2013).

- Optical and optical fiber sensors are used for ambient monitoring of humidity and temperature, as well as for monitoring atmospheric gases (SO_2, NO_2, O_2 H_2, CH_4, NH_3) (Diamond, et al., 2013, Zhang, et al., 2010, Borisov, et al., 2011)

- Electrochemical sensors are used for atmospheric gases monitoring (O_3, CO, H_2S, H_2, NO, NO_2, SO_2) (Mead, et al., 2013, Bales, et al., 2012, Kumar, et al., 2011, Korotcenkov, et al., 2009)

Water

The increasing need for clean water, driven by global demand for drinking water and industrial water requirements, has created a critical requirement for monitoring water quality. Similar to air quality, strict regulations are set out by national bodies (such as the EPA) and geopolitical bodies (such as the EU) that apply to public water systems. These are legally enforceable and drive the need for reliable sensor technologies that can monitor different water quality parameters with the required sensitivity. Sensor technologies need to provide real-time or near real-time readings in order to ensure that any anomalous changes in water quality will have the minimum impact on human health or manufacturing operations. The absence of such monitoring can led to incidents like the one experienced by Perrier. Benzene, a known carcinogen, was found in the company's bottled water, resulting in a recall of their entire inventory from store shelves throughout the United States (James, 1990). Numerous parameters can be monitored in a water-quality regime. The specific mix of parameters depends on the application area, whether it be drinking water, an industrial application (such as beverage manufacturing), or monitoring industrial discharges or storm drains. There are normally three major categories of interest: physical (turbidity, temperature, conductivity,) chemical (pH, dissolved oxygen, metals concentration, nitrates, organics), and biological (biological oxygen demand, bacterial content).

A number of sensor technologies are being used commercially or are currently being evaluated to measure water quality parameters, including:

- Electrochemical (pH (ISFET), ammonium, conductivity)

  - Amperometric (chlorine, biochemical oxygen demand (BOD), dissolved oxygen, nitrates)

  - Colorimetric (organics, pesticides such as methyl parathion, Cl)

- MEMS (dissolved oxygen, NH_3)

- Optical (dissolved oxygen, turbidity, calcium (Ca), metal ions)

- Natural biosensors (bacteria, toxins)

The use of species-specific reagents is also popular for many water-analysis applications. While reagent-based approaches are not conventional sensors, they are used to sense or monitor many key water-quality parameters, such as the presence of nitrates. The reagent reacts with the analyte of interest in the water sample, resulting in a measurable color change using optical detection methods (Czugala, et al., 2013, Cogan, et al., 2013). In addition to water-quality monitoring, sensors (such as MEMS pressure sensors) are also being used to monitor the water distribution infrastructure, in order to improve the control and manageability of the system. Concepts such as smart water grids and predictive models are starting to emerge in the applied research domain. Sensors deployed in the water distribution infrastructure will assist in the identification of leaks through pressure drops, thus enabling rerouting of flow and minimizing water loss. Another area of interest in the research domain is predictive model-based water quality monitoring. This approach is based on fusing data from water quality, environmental sensors, and metrological sensors to predict potential changes in future water quality.

Sound (Noise Pollution)

As our society becomes more urbanized and we live in closer proximity to each other, noise and noise pollution becomes more problematic. Noise can have significant implications for the quality of life, ranging from being a nuisance to having a substantial physiological or psychological impact. Noise pollution can be described as unwanted sound that affects our daily lives and activities. Noise pollution can be transient or continuous. Common sources include cars, rail, and air transport, industry, neighbors, and recreational noise. Noise pollution monitoring is becoming increasingly regulated. The European Directive 2002/49/EC now requires member states to provide accurate mappings of noise levels in urban areas of more than 250,000 inhabitants on a regular basis, and to make this data easily available to the public (Santini, et al., 2008).

Spanish company Libelium, for example, offers noise-pollution sensing as part of its Smart Cities wireless sensor platform. More recently, with the rapid adoption of smartphones, citizen-led monitoring of noise levels in urban environments has gained popularity. Smartphone apps use the phone's built-in microphone (MEMS) to collect noise-level data points, which are tagged with location information from the phone's GPS coordinates and uploaded to the Web over 3G or Wi-Fi. Citizens can then use the data to create noise maps to influence city planners to make changes that improves quality of life within the city (Maisonneuve, et al., 2009).

Soil

A number of handheld instruments to measure the characteristics and quality of soil are in commonly use. Among the most popular are field-portable X-ray fluorescence (FP-XRF) instruments to measure metal contamination. A key advantage of the technique is that it requires almost no sample preparation, such as acid digestion. However, the technique is limited to bulk concentration analysis in which high concentrations of an element are likely to be present in a sample (Radu, et al., 2013). Other commonly used instruments include temperature and moisture meters and penetrometer for the measurement of soil strength. While the performance of these instruments is normally very accurate, they suffer from the limitation of being able to provide only a single measurement in time. For applications such as horticulture that require more frequent data points, sensors are now available to address that need.

When using sensors to monitor or analyze soil, we are normally interested in the soil's physical, chemical, and biological content. This type of data has a broad range of application, including agricultural, contamination, and geophysical monitoring. Key measurements include water content (capacitance, neutron moisture gauge, time-domain transmission (TDT), and time-domain reflectometry (TDR), temperature, pH, organic matter content (optical reflectance), and nitrogen levels.

Soil contaminants can be classified as microbiological (such as fecal coliforms), radioactive (such as tritium), inorganic (such as chromium (Cr)), synthetic organic (such as organophosphate pesticides), and volatile organic compounds (such as benzene). Sensors can serve two roles in soil contamination applications: the detection of the contaminants using species-specific sensors, and monitoring the physical characteristics of the soil during clean-up operations, including moisture content (ground water contamination) and soil temperature (soil temperatures play an important role when using fungal treatment of soil to remove contamination).

Geophysical monitoring of soil employs many of the same physical sensor readings that are used in agricultural applications. This type of monitoring is applied to dikes and dams to determine structural integrity. Motion sensors (MEMS accelerometers) and GPS sensors are also commonly used. Other typical applications include monitoring areas subject to landside threats, monitoring buildings that may have subsidence issues, landfill leachate monitoring, and biogas monitoring.

Healthcare

Sensor applications in the healthcare domain range from physiological monitoring, such as heart rate, to screening applications, such as blood biochemistry, to falls risk estimation. Sensors and applications utilized in the healthcare domain are typically developed by companies implementing a specific medical use case requiring approval and registration with an appropriate regulatory body, such as the US FDA. In the home and community, telehealth, telemonitoring, and mHealth (or mobile health) sensor applications enable remote monitoring and management of patients with chronic diseases, including diabetes, chronic obstructive pulmonary disease (COPD), and congestive heart failure (CHF). Sensor use in hospitals and primary healthcare facilities focuses more on medical screening and diagnostics applications, such as point-of-care blood chemistry testing, electrolyte-level measurement, and analyzing blood gas concentrations. There is also a growing market for over-the-counter diagnostic sensors that perform cholesterol monitoring, pregnancy testing, food allergy testing, and DNA testing. While often not strictly diagnostic in terms of accuracy, in many cases these over-the-counter sensors can deliver indicative results, which can assist decision-making prior to seeking formal clinical intervention and care.

Key to the proliferation of sensors in healthcare has been the development of low-cost microsystem sensor technologies coupled, in some cases, with low-cost, low-power microcontrollers (MCUs) and radios. These devices have enabled the development of small form-factor, reliable, robust, accurate, low-power sensor solutions. Some key application areas of sensors in clinical healthcare are:

- *Screening and Diagnostics:* Biochemical and optical sensors are used for point-of-care monitoring and diagnostics applications, including blood and tissue analysis (Yang, et al., 2013, Girardin, et al., 2009). Biosensors can be used to identify bacterial infection, drugs, hormones, and proteins levels in biological samples (Swensen, et al., 2009)(McLachlan, et al., 2011, Wang, et al., 2011).

- *Motion and Kinematics:* Body-worn wireless sensors, such as accelerometer and gyroscopes, can be used to identify balance and falls risk issues and to monitor the impact of clinical interventions. Kinematic sensors can be used in the assessment of prosthetic limb replacements (Arami, et al., 2013). They are also used in stroke rehabilitation to monitor the performance of targeted physical exercises (Uzor, et al., 2013) (Shyamal, et al., 2012). Sensors have also be been printed onto fabrics for motion-detection applications (Wei, et al., 2013) (Metcalf, et al., 2009).

- *Physiological:* Sensors in this category are used to measure key physiological indicators of health, such as ECG/EKG and blood pressure (Mass, et al., 2010) (Brown, et al., 2010). IR sensors can be found in noncontact thermometers (Buono, et al., 2007).

- *Musculoskeletal:* Body-worn sensors, such as an EMG, are used to assess muscular issues and tissue damage (Spulber, et al., 2012); (Reaston, et al., 2011) Sensors integrated directly into fabrics for rehabilitation applications have also been reported in the literature (Shyamal, et al., 2012)

- *Imaging:* Low cost CCD and ultrasound sensors are used for medical imaging (Jing, et al., 2012, Ng, et al., 2011). Smart pills can be used for intestinal imaging (McCaffrey, et al., 2008).

Wellness

Wellness is generally described as maintaining a healthy balance between the mind, body, and soul in order to create an overall feeling of well-being in an individual. The National Wellness Institute definition is (Institute, 2013):

> *Wellness is multi-dimensional and holistic, encompassing lifestyle, mental and spiritual well-being, and the environment.*

The use of sensors in the wellness domain encompasses a broad range of applications, from monitoring activity levels during recreational sporting activities, to sleep quality, to personal safety in the home.

Monitoring Recreational Activity

As people have become more aware of their health, there is a growing market for off-the-shelf sensors that had been found previously only in clinical applications. Such sensors are now used by consumers to track progress in wellness programs, such as those for obesity prevention, that encompass fitness and increased activity levels. Devices such as body-worn heart-rate and blood-pressure monitors, integrated activity monitors, and pulse oximeters are increasingly being used in this emerging domain. These sensors are supplemented by standard activity monitoring sensors, such as body-worn pedometers, which are coupled with software applications to provide analysis of activities and to encourage goal-directed behavior. There are a variety of commercial solutions that provide hybrid software/hardware solutions, including the Nike+ Fuelband, which features three accelerometers, user-defined goal setting, and visualization of daily activities.

Companies such as Freescale are already offering silicon building blocks for multisensor activity and wellness monitoring solutions (Freescale, 2012). Their use will increase as the cost of these sensors falls and as they are integrated into lifestyle elements of consumer electronic devices, particularly smartphones. The Nike+ iPhone application is a good example of a sensor/CE application (Apple, 2012). The ease of building new consumer applications will also increase as new standards emerge, driven by bodies such as the Continua Health Alliance (Alliance, 2010) and the ever-growing electronics hobbyist community.

Personal Safety

Another key element of wellness is personal safety, particularly in the home. The use of smoke detectors and CO sensors is long established. Semiconductor or electrochemical sensors are commonly used in residential CO sensors. Electrochemical instant detection and response (IDR) sensors are frequently used by emergency personnel, such as fire fighters, to determine almost immediately if a building contains dangerous levels of CO. Smoke detectors are generally based on one of two sensor types: ionization detectors or photoelectric detectors. Both types are effective, but differ in their response characteristics. Ionization detectors demonstrate a faster response to fires with flames, while photoelectric detectors respond faster to fires that generate more smoke (such as a smoldering fire from an electrical fault or initial furniture fire). Ionization detectors have the disadvantage of giving false alarms due to their sensitivity to small smoke particles, which result from normal cooking. In modern homes, smoke detectors (ionization and photoelectric) are normally AC powered with batteries as a backup power source (Helmenstine, 2013), thus eliminating issues with batteries dying.

Activity and Location Detection

As the average lifespan of the global population increases due to better healthcare, nutrition, and lifestyles, there is an increasing focus on allowing older adults to remain in their homes as long as possible. Sensor-based applications can enable this by providing in-home location and presence monitoring. Location data, usually measured using PIR sensors, can be combined with machine-learning algorithms and data from other sources, such as temperature and humidity, to determine the wellness of an individual and to trigger intervention if required. In situations where a resident has mild cognitive impairment, the perimeter of the house could be monitored using sensors (for example, magnetic contact sensors) on exit doors to determine if the individual leaves the home—and alert family members if required. Ambient sensing can be further augmented with body-worn sensors (MEMS accelerometers and gyroscopes) to detect problems such as falls.

The availability of GPS trackers and other sensors, such as accelerometers in smartphones, has enabled new personal location-tracking capabilities. This category of sensing can be used for recreational purposes, to provide real-time pace, location, elevation, and direction information to a jogger; as well as for personal safety applications, where the GPS trackers can be used by parents to determine the location of a child or a cognitively impaired older adult. There are limitations, however, particularly in determining the type or intensity of the monitored activity, such as walking on flat ground versus walking up steps.

Sensor Characteristics

Sensors provide an output signal in response to a physical, chemical, or biological measurand and typically require an electrical input to operate; therefore, they tend to be characterized in sensor specifications (commonly called "specs") or datasheets in much the same way as electronic devices. To truly understand sensors, and how sensors that measure the same measurand can differ, it is necessary to understand sensor performance characteristics. Unfortunately, there is no standard definition for many of these characteristics and different parts of the sensor community have different names for these characteristics, depending on the sensing domain. This confusion is compounded by manufacturers publishing an abundance of performance characteristics, that make it even more difficult for potential users to identify the ones relevant to their applications, and how they should be applied. The following section will describe these characteristics, using their most common names, and will reference alternative names where relevant.

Sensor characteristics can be categorized as systematic, statistical, or dynamic. Bently defines systematic characteristics as "those which can be exactly quantified by mathematical or graphical means;" statistical characteristics as "those which cannot be exactly quantified;" and dynamic characteristics as "the ways in which an element responds to sudden input changes" (Bently, 1995).

Range

Range is a static characteristic and, as the name implies, it describes both the minimum and maximum values of the input or output. The term range is commonly used in the following ways in datasheets:

- Full-scale range describes the maximum and minimum values of a measured property. Full-scale input is often called *span*. Full-scale output (FSO) is the algebraic difference between the output signals measured at maximum input stimulus and the minimum input stimulus. Span (or dynamic range) describes the maximum and minimum input values that can be applied to a sensor without causing an unacceptable level of inaccuracy.

- Operating voltage range describes the minimum and maximum input voltages that can be used to operate a sensor. Applying an input voltage outside of this range may permanently damage the sensor.

Transfer Function

Sensor characteristics describe the relationship between the measurand and the electrical output signal. This relationship can be represented as a table of values, a graph, or a mathematical formula. Expensive sensors that are individually calibrated may even provide a certified calibration curve. If this relationship is time-invariant, it is called the sensor transfer function. A mathematical formula describing the transfer function is typically expressed as follows:

$$S = F(x)$$

Where x is the measurand and S is the electrical signal produced by the sensor. It is rare to find a transfer function that can be completely described by a single formula, so functional approximations of the actual transfer function are used.

Linear Transfer Functions

The simplest transfer function is a linear transfer function, with the following form:

$$S = A + Bx$$

where A is the sensor offset and B is the sensor slope. The sensor offset is the output value of the sensor when no measurand is applied. The slope of a linear transfer function is equal to the sensor's sensitivity, which is described later. In practice, very few sensors are truly linear, but they are considered to have linear characteristics if the plot of measurand versus the output values is approximately a straight line across the specified operating range. An ideal straight line, that is a linear approximation of the transfer function, is most commonly drawn using one of the following methods (see Figure 2-6):

- *End-point method:* The ideal straight line is drawn between the upper- and lower-range values of the sensor. This method is generally less accurate than the best-fit method.

- *Best-fit method:* Also called independent linearity, the ideal straight line can be positioned in any manner that minimizes the deviations between it and the device's actual transfer function. This method is most commonly used by sensor manufacturers to describe their sensor performance as it provides the best fit or smallest deviation from the actual data. The least-squares method is the most common method to determine best fit. This statistical method samples a number of different points to calculate the best fit.

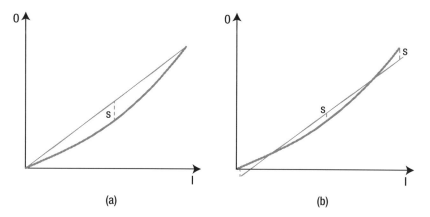

Figure 2-6. *An ideal straight line drawn using the (a) end-point and (b) best-fit methods. Nonlinearity is indicated by the dotted line(s) between the actual data and the ideal straight line*

Linearization

There are a number of advantages to linear transfer functions. First, it is simple to calculate the measurand value from the electrical output of a sensor and to predict the electrical output based on the measurand value. Second, the sensor offset and sensor slope characteristics are easily read from the transfer function. Third, non-ideal characteristics, such as nonlinearity and hysteresis, can be defined relative to a linear transfer function. A non-linear sensor output can be "linearized" using hardware or software to leverage the advantages of linear sensors (van der Horn, et al., 1998). The traditional hardware-based linearization method often requires manual calibration and precision resistors to achieve the desired accuracy. Modern smart sensors employ less complex and less costly digital techniques to create a linear output. These techniques perform digital linearization and calibration by leveraging the smart sensor's integrated microcontroller and memory to store the factory calibration results for each individual sensor. The microcontroller can correct the sensor output by searching for the compensation value or the actual linearized output in a look-up table. If memory is limited, calibration coefficients, rather than a full-look up table, are used to construct a linearized output.

Non-Linear Transfer Functions

Some transfer functions do not approximate well to linear transfer functions. However, they can be approximated using other mathematical functions (Fraden, 2010), including:

Logarithmic functions: $S = A + B.\ln(x)$

Exponential functions: $S = A.e^{k.x}$

Power functions: $S = A + B.x^k$

where x is the measurand, S is the electrical signal produced by the sensor, A and B are parameters, and k is the power factor. A polynomial function can be used when none of the functions previously described can be applied to describe the sensor transfer function. Second- and third-order polynomials can be described using the following transfer functions:

Second-Order Polynomial functions: $S = A.x^2 + B.x + C$

Third-Order Polynomial functions: $S = A.x^3 + B.x^2 + C.x + D$

A third-order polynomial will provide a better fit to the sensor transfer function than a second-order polynomial. However, a second-order polynomial may provide a sufficiently accurate fit when applied to a relatively narrow range of input stimuli.

Linearity and Nonlinearity

Nonlinearity, which is often called linearity in datasheets, is the difference between the actual line and ideal straight line. As nonlinearity may vary along the input-output plot, a single value, called maximum nonlinearity, is used to describe this characteristic in datasheets. Maximum nonlinearity is typically expressed as a percentage of span. Nonlinearity can often be affected by environmental changes, such as temperature, vibration, acoustic noise level, and humidity. It is important to be aware of the environmental conditions under which nonlinearity is defined in the datasheet, particularly if they differ from the application operating environment.

Sensitivity

Sensitivity is the change in input required to generate a unit change in output. If the sensor response is linear, sensitivity will be constant over the range of the sensor and is equal to the slope of the straight-line plot (as shown in Figure 2-7). An ideal sensor will have significant and constant sensitivity. If the sensor response is non-linear, sensitivity will vary over the sensor range and can be found by calculating the derivative of S with respect to x (dS/Dx).

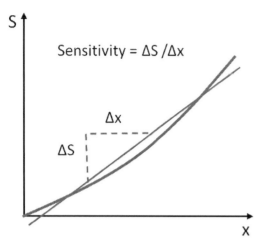

Figure 2-7. *Sensor sensitivity*

Common sensitivity-related issues include dead-bands and saturation. The dead-band is a specific range of input signals in which the sensor is unresponsive or insensitive. In that range, the output may remain near a certain value (generally zero) over the entire dead-band zone. Dead-band is usually expressed as a percentage of span. The saturation point is the input value at which no more changes in output can occur.

Environmental Effects

Sensor outputs can be affected by external environmental inputs as well as the measurand itself. These inputs can change the behavior of the sensor, thus affecting the range, sensitivity, resolution, and offset of the sensor. Datasheets specify these characteristics under controlled conditions (such as fixed temperature and humidity, fixed input voltage, and so on). If a sensor is to be operated outside these conditions, it is highly recommended to recalibrate the sensor under the conditions in which it will be used.

Modifying Inputs

Modifying inputs changes the linear sensitivity of a sensor. The voltage supplied to the sensor, V_s, is a common example of a modifying input as it can modify the output range of the sensor, which in turn modifies the resolution and sensitivity.

Interfering Inputs

Interfering inputs change the straight-line intercept of a sensor. Temperature is a common example of an interfering input, as it changes the zero-bias of the sensor. An example of a temperature effect on sensor output is shown in Figure 2-8.

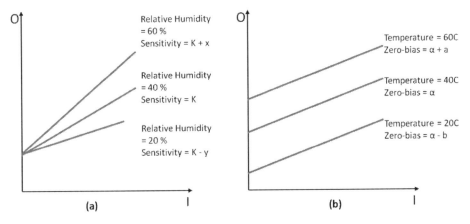

Figure 2-8. *(a) Effect of a modifying input (relative humidity) on the sensor's sensitivity, K; (b) Effect of an interfering input (temperature) on the sensor*

Hysteresis

The output of a sensor may be different for a given input, depending on whether the input is increasing or decreasing. This phenomenon is known as *hysteresis* and can be described as the difference in output between the rising and falling output values for a given input as illustrated in Figure 2-9. Like nonlinearity, hysteresis varies along the input-output plot; thus maximum hysteresis is used to describe the characteristic. This value is usually expressed as a percentage of the sensor span. Hysteresis commonly occurs when a sensing technique relies on the stressing of a particular material (as with strain gauges). Elastic and magnetic circuits may never return to their original start position after repeated use. This can lead to an unknown offset over time and can therefore affect the transfer function for that device.

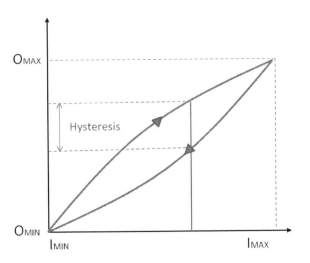

Figure 2-9. *Hysteresis curve, illustrating the different responses of a sensor to an increasing input and a decreasing input*

Resolution

Resolution, also called discrimination, is the smallest increment of the measurand that causes a detectable change in output. The resolution of modern sensors varies considerably, so is important to understand the resolution required for an application before selecting a sensor. If the sensor resolution is too low for the application, subtle changes in the measurand may not be detected. However, a sensor whose resolution is too high for the application is needlessly expensive. Threshold is the name used to describe resolution if the increment is measured from zero, although it is more commonly described as the minimum measurand required to trigger a measurable change in output from zero.

Accuracy

Accuracy refers to a sensor's ability to provide an output close to the true value of the measurand. Specifically, it describes the maximum expected error between the actual and ideal output signals. Accuracy is often described relative to the sensor span. For example, a thermometer might be guaranteed to be accurate to within five percent of the span. As accuracy is relative to the true value of the measurand, it can be quantified as a percentage relative error using the following equation:

$$Percentage\ Relative\ Error = \frac{(Measured\ Value - True\ Value)}{(True\ Value)} \times 100$$

Precision

Precision is sometimes confused with accuracy. Figure 2-10 illustrates the key differences between the two. Precision describes the ability of an output to be constantly reproduced. It is therefore possible to have a very accurate sensor that is imprecise (a thermometer that reports temperatures between 62–64° F for an input of 63° F), or a very precise sensor that is inaccurate (a thermometer that always reports a temperature of 70° F for an input of 63° F). As precision relates to the reproducibility of a measure, it can be quantified as percentage standard deviation using the following equation:

$$Percentage\ Standard\ Deviation = \frac{(Standard\ Deviation)}{(Mean)} \times 100$$

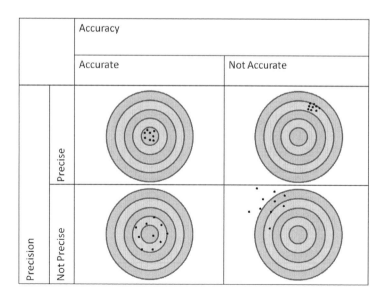

Figure 2-10. *The difference between accuracy and precision, illustrated using a dartboard analogy*

Error

Error is the difference between the measured value and true value, where true value is a reference to an absolute or agreed standard. There are two forms of error: systematic error and random error.

Systematic Errors

Systematic errors are reproducible inaccuracies that can be corrected with compensation methods, such as feedback, filtering, and calibration (Wilson, 2004). These errors result from a variety of factors including:

- Interfering inputs, which introduce error by changing the zero-bias of the sensor.

- Modifying inputs (such as humidity) introduce error by modifying the relationship between the input and the output signal.

- Changes in chemical structure or mechanical stresses, due to aging or long-term exposure to elements (such as UV light), can result in the gain and the zero-bias of the sensor to drift. This gradual deterioration of the sensor and associated components can result in outputs changing from their original calibrated state. This source of error can be compensated for through frequent recalibration.

- Interference, also called loading error, can occur when the sensor itself changes the measurand it is measuring. A simple example of this is a flow-rate sensor that may disrupt the flow, resulting in an erroneous reading. In chemical sensors, interference relates to a process by which other species in the sample compete with the target (primary) species of interest.

- Signal attenuation, and sometimes signal loss, can occur when the signal moves through a medium.

- Humans can inadvertently introduce a number of errors into a system, including parallax errors, due to incorrect positioning; zero error, due to incorrectly calibrated instruments; and resolution error, where the resolution of the reference device is too broad. Human errors are commonly called "operator errors".

Random Errors (Noise)

Random error (also called noise) is a signal component that carries no information. The quality of a signal is expressed quantitatively as the signal-to-noise ratio (SNR), which is the ratio of the true signal amplitude to the standard deviation of the noise. A high SNR represents high signal quality. Noise can be measured by recording the signal in the absence of the measurand, or by recording a known measurand several times, then subtracting the known true signal from the measured signal. SNR is inversely proportional to the relative standard deviation of the signal amplitude used to measure precision. Therefore, a noisy signal is also an imprecise signal.

In analytical chemistry, the limit of detection (LOD) and limit of quantification (LOQ) have a particular relevance to noise. The LOD is the lowest quantity of a substance that can be distinguished from the absence of that substance (noise). The LOQ is the limit at which the difference between the substance and absence of that substance can be quantified. LOD is quantified as three times the standard deviation of noise and LOQ is defined as 10 times the standard deviation of noise. True random errors (white noise) follow a Gaussian distribution. Sources of randomness include:

- Noise in the measurand itself (such as the height of a rough surface)

- Environmental noise (such as background noise picked up by a microphone)

- Transmission noise

Error Bands

Error bands combine several sensor characteristics (including nonlinearity, hysteresis, and resolution) into a single measure and guarantee that the output will be within a ±h of the ideal straight line. The value "h" is typically a percentage, such as ±5 percent; or a value, such as ± 0.5°C. Figure 2-11 illustrates the concept of error bands around an ideal straight line sensor output. They are advantageous to users as they reduce the number of characteristics that need to be considered when designing an application and are advantageous to manufacturers as they eliminate individual testing and calibrating of each separate characteristic of a sensor.

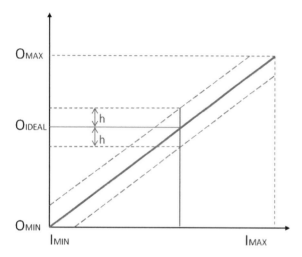

Figure 2-11. *Error bands around an ideal straight line*

Statistical Characteristics

Statistical characteristics are characteristics that can't be exactly described by formulas or graphical means. These characteristics describe a summary of numerous measurements taken with a single or multiple sensors. The most commonly used statistical characteristics in sensor datasheets are repeatability and tolerance.

Repeatability

Repeatability is the ability of a sensor to produce the same output when the same input is applied to it. Lack of repeatability generally occurs due to random fluctuations in environmental inputs or operator error.

Tolerance

Tolerance describes the variations in the reported output among a batch of similar elements due to small random manufacturing variations. If a manufacturer reports a tolerance of ±5 percent, it can't sell any sensors that fall outside of this range.

Dynamic Characteristics

Dynamic characteristics are time-dependent characteristics of a sensor. Sensor dynamics are less important in applications that have sensor inputs that are constant over long periods of time. Dynamic characteristics can be classified as zero-order, first-order, and second-order systems. The most common dynamic characteristics found in datasheets are response time and dynamic linearity.

Response Time

Sensors do not change their output immediately following a change in the input. The period of time taken for the sensor to change its output from its previous state to a value within a tolerance band of the new correct value is called response time (see Figure 2-12). The tolerance band is defined based on the sensor type, sensor application, or the preferences of the sensor designer. It can be defined as a value, such as 90 percent of the new correct value. Response time is commonly defined using time constants in first-order systems (Fraden, 2010). A time constant is the time required by a sensor to reach 63.2 percent of a step change in output under a specified set of conditions. A time constant can be easily estimated by fitting a single exponential curve to the response curve.

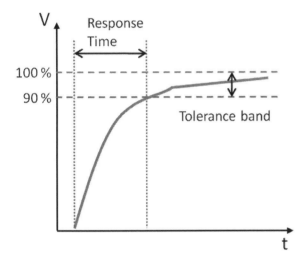

Figure 2-12. *Response time for a sensor based on a tolerance band set to 90–100 percent*

Dynamic Linearity

The dynamic linearity of a sensor is a measure of its ability to follow rapid changes in the input parameter. Amplitude distortion characteristics, phase distortion characteristics, and response time are important in determining dynamic linearity.

Summary

The terms sensor and transducer are commonly used interchangeably, and both devices are encapsulated in sensor systems for a given application. As described in this chapter, a great variety of sensing techniques are available for measuring physical, chemical, and biological quantities of interest. We have briefly outlined the various techniques—mechanical, optical, semiconductor, and biosensing—and have highlighted their respective advantages and disadvantages. We introduced our key sensing domains and described how the various sensor technologies can be utilized within these domains to address problems associated with increased urbanization, global ageing, pollution, and climate change. The role of regulation in driving sensor applications for monitoring air and environmental compliance was also outlined. Finally, sensor characteristics were defined to simplify the process of reading datasheets and comparing performance characteristics of different sensors.

References

Fraden, Jacob, *Handbook of Modern Sensors*, 4th ed. New York: Springer, 2010.

Jones, Deric P., *Biomedical Sensors*, 1st ed. New York: Momentum Press, 2010.

Chen, K. Y., K. F. Janz, W. Zhu, and R. J. Brychta, "Redefining the roles of sensors in objective physical activity monitoring," *Medicine and Science in Sports and Exercise,* vol. 44, pp. 13–12, 2012.

Sutherland, John W., *An Introduction to Sensors and Transducers*, Last Update: 2004, `http://www.mfg.mtu.edu/cyberman/machtool/machtool/sensors/intro.html`

ANSI, Americian National Standards Institute, "ISA S37.1–1975 (R1982)," ed, 1975.

NRC, (National Research Council) - Committee on New Sensor Technologies: Materials Applications Commission on Engineering Technical Systems, *Expanding the Vision of Sensor Materials*: The National Academies Press, 1995.

AALIANCE. (2010). *Ambient Assisted Living Roadmap*, Broek, Ger Van Den, Filippo Cavallo, and Christian Wehrman, Eds., vol. 6, IOS Press, `http://ebooks.iospress.nl/volume/aaliance-ambient-assisted-living-roadmap`

Khanna, Vinod Kumar, *Nanosensors: Physical, Chemical, and Biological*. Boca Raton: CRC Press, 2012.

Wang, Ping and Qingjun Liu, *Biomedical Sensors and Measurement*, Berlin Heidelberg: Springer-Verlag, 2011.

Fink, Johannes Karl, "Mechanical Sensors," in *Polymeric Sensors and Actuators*, Hoboken, Massachusetts, Wiley-Scrivener, 2012, pp. 131–138.

Patranabis, D, *Sensors and Transducers*, 2nd ed. New Delhi: PHI Learning Pvt Ltd, 2004.

Kyowa, "What's a Strain Guage", `http://www.kyowa-ei.co.jp/eng/`, 2013.

Kasukawa, Yuji, *et al.*, "Relationships between falls, spinal curvature, spinal mobility and back extensor strength in elderly people," *Journal of Bone and Mineral Metabolism,* vol. 28, (1), pp. 82–87, 2010.

Bohannon, Richard W., "Literature reporting normative data for muscle strength measured by hand-held dynamometry: A systematic review," *Isokinetics and Exercise Science,* vol. 19, (3), pp. 143–147, 2011.

PCB Piezotronics[1]. "MEMS Accelerometers", `http://www.pcb.com/Accelerometers/MEMS.asp`, 2013.

PCB Piezotronics[2]. "Sensing Technologies used for Accelerometers", 2013. `http://www.pcb.com/Accelerometers/Sensing_Technologies.asp`, 2013.

Nanogloss. "What is a MEMS Accelerometer?", `http://nanogloss.com/mems/what-is-a-mems-accelerometer/#more-190`, 2009.

Nasiri, Steven, "A Critical Review of MEMS Gyroscopes Technology and Commericalisation Status", InvenSense, Santa Clara, `http://invensense.com/mems/gyro/documents/whitepapers/MEMSGyroComp.pdf`, 2013.

Cadena, Richard, "Electromechanical Systems," in *Automated Lighting: The Art and Science of Moving Light in Theatre, Live Performance, Broadcast and Entertainment*, Burlington, MA, Elsevier, 2013.

Fried, Limor. *PIR Motion Sensors*, Last Update: April 27th 2012, `http://www.ladyada.net/learn/sensors/pir.html`

EngineersGarage. "Infrared Sensors or IR Sensors", `http://www.engineersgarage.com/articles/infrared-sensors?page=3`, 2012.

Udd, Eric, "Fiber Optic Sensors - An Introduction for Engineers and Scientists," in *Pure and Applied Optics* vol. 2013, Udd, Eric and William B. Spillman, Eds., 2nd ed. Hoboken, New Jersey: John Wiley & Sons, 2011.

Lee, Byeong Ha, *et al.*, "Interferometric Fiber Optic Sensors," *Sensors* vol. 12, pp. 2467–2486, 2012.

Morendo-Bondi, Maria C., Guillermo Orellana, and Maximino Bedoya, "Optical Sensor-- Industrial, Environmental and Diagnostic Applications," in *Chemical Sensors and Biosensors* Wolfbeis, O. S., Ed., Berlin Heidelberg, Springer-Verlag, 2004, pp. 251–278.

Baldini, Francesco and Anna Grazia Mignani, "Biomedical Fibre Optic Sensors," in *Handbook of Optical Fibre Sensing Technology*, López-Higuera, José Miguel, Ed., Chichester, John Wiley & Sons Ltd, 2002, pp. 705–722.

Nihal, Kularatna and B. H. Sudantha, "An Environmental Air Pollution Monitoring System Based on the IEEE 1451 Standard for Low Cost Requirements," *Sensors Journal, IEEE,* vol. 8, (4), pp. 415–422, 2008.

Wetchakun, K., *et al.*, "Semiconducting metal oxides as sensors for environmentally hazardous gases," *Sensors and Actuators B: Chemical,* vol. 160, (1), pp. 580–591, 2011.

Knott, Barry. *Semiconductor Technology - Personal Breathalyzer*, Last Update: January 10th 2010, `http://ezinearticles.com/?Semiconductor-Technology---Personal-Breathalyzers&id=3511961`

Gómez-Pozos, Heberto, *et al.*, "Chromium and Ruthenium-Doped Zinc Oxide Thin Films for Propane Sensing Applications," *Sensors,* vol. 13, (3), pp. 3432–3444, 2013.

Fraden, Jacob, "Temperature Sensors," in *Handbook of Modern Sensors*, Springer New York, 2010, pp. 519–567.

Coey, J. M. D., "Magnetic Sensors," in *Magnetism and Magnetic Materials*, Cambridge University Press, 2010, pp. 516–521.

Sze, Simon M. and Kwok K. Ng, "Magnetic Sensors," in *Physics of Semiconductor Devices*, Hoboken, New Jersey, Wiley, 2007, pp. 758–764.

CHEM EUROPE.COM. "Charge-coupled device", `http://www.chemeurope.com/en/encyclopedia/Charge-coupled_device.html`, 2013.

AppliedSensor, "Metal Oxide Semiconductor (MOS) Sensors", `http://www.electronics-base.com/images/stories/General_descriptions/Gas%20sensors/Metal_Oxide_Semiconductor_(MOS).pdf`, 2008.

Gyorki, John R., *Designing with Semiconductor Temperature Sensors*, Last Update: 2009, `http://www.sensortips.com/temperature/designing-with-semiconductor-temperature-sensors/`

CAPGO. "Introduction to Semiconductor Temperature Sensors", `http://www.capgo.com/Resources/Temperature/Semiconductor/Semi.html`, 2010.

Racz, Robert. *A Novel Contactless Current Sensor HEV/EV and Renewable Energy Applications*, Last Update: 28th March, 2011, `http://www.digikey.com/us/es/techzone/sensors/resources/articles/a-novel-contactless-current-sensor-hev-ev.html`

Eren, Halit, "Magnetic Sensors," in *Wiley Survey of Instrumentation and Measurement*, Dyer, Stephen A., Ed., New York, Wiley, 2001, pp. 40–60.

EE TImes. "Non-Contact Fluid Sensor - detects liquid through transparent tubing", `http://www.eetimes.com/document.asp?doc_id=1294625`, 2004.

Refaat, Tamer F., *et al.*, "Infrared phototransistor validation for atmospheric remote sensing application using the Raman-shifted eye-safe aerosol lidar," *Optical Engineering,* vol. 46, (8), pp. 086001-086001-8, 2007.

Adami, Andrea, Severino Pedrotti, Cristian Collini, and Leandro Lorenzelli, "Development of a pH Sensor with Integrated Reference Electrode for Cell Culture Monitoring," in *Sensors.* vol. 162, Baldini, Francesco, Arnaldo D'Amico, Corrado Di Natale, Pietro Siciliano, Renato Seeber, Luca De Stefano, Ranieri Bizzarri, and Bruno Andò, Eds., Springer New York, 2014, pp. 481–485.

Guth, U., F. Gerlach, M. Decker, W. Oelßner, and W. Vonau, "Solid-state reference electrodes for potentiometric sensors," *Journal of Solid State Electrochemistry,* vol. 13, (1), pp. 27–39, 2009.

Kokot, Maciej, "Measurement of sub-nanometer molecular layers with ISFET without a reference electrode dependency," *Sensors and Actuators B: Chemical,* vol. 157, (2), pp. 424–429, 2011.

Guth, Ulrich, Winfried Vonau, and Jens Zosel, "Recent developments in electrochemical sensor application and technology — a review," *Measurement Science and Technology,* vol. 20, (4), 2009.

Banica, Florinel-Gabriel, "Potentiometric Sensors," in *Chemical Sensors and Biosensors: Fundamentals and Applications*, Chichester, UK, John Wiley & Sons, 2012, pp. 165–216.

Wang, Joseph and Kim Rogers, "Electrochemical Sensors for Environmental Monitroing: A Review of Recent Technology", U.S. Environmental Protection Agency, Office of Research and Development, Environmental Monitoring and Support Laborator, `http://www.clu-in.org/download/char/sensr_ec.pdf`, 1995.

Andoralov, Viktor, Sergey Shleev, Thomas Arnebrant, and Tautgirdas Ruzgas, "Flexible micro(bio)sensors for quantitative analysis of bioanalytes in a nanovolume of human lachrymal liquid," *Analytical and Bioanalytical Chemistry,* vol. 405, (11), pp. 3871–3879, 2013.

Carroll, S., M. M. Marei, T. J. Roussel, R. S. Keynton, and R. P. Baldwin, "Microfabricated electrochemical sensors for exhaustive coulometry applications," *Sensors and Actuators B: Chemical,* vol. 160, (1), pp. 318–326, 2011.

Janta, Jiří, *Principles of Chemical Sensors*, 2nd ed. Heidelberg: Springer, 2009.

Setford, Steven J. and Jeffrey D. Newman, "Enzyme Biosensors," in *Microbial Enzymes and Biotransformations*. vol. 17, Barredo, Jose Luis, Ed., Totowa, New Jersey, Humana Press, 2005, p. 30.

"Global Market for Biosensor in Medical Diagnostics to Reach US$16.5 Billion by 2017, Accoring to New Report by Global Industry Analysts, Inc", http://www.prweb.com/releases/medical_biosensors/environmental_biosensors/prweb9242715.htm, 2012.

Yoon, Jeong-Yeol, *Introduction to Biosensors - From Circuits to Immunosensors*. New York: Springer, 2013.

Lee, Chang-Soo, Sang Kyu Kim, and Moonil Kim, "Ion-Sensitive Field-Effect Transistor for Biological Sensing," *Sensors,* vol. 9, (9), pp. 7111–7131, 2009.

Corcuera, José I. Reyes De and Ralph P. Cavalier, "Biosensors," in *Encyclopedia of Agricultural, Food, and Biological Engineering*, Heldman, Dennis R., Ed., New York, Marcel Dekker Inc., 2003, p. 121.

Wang, Joseph, "Electrochemical Glucose Biosensors," *Chemical Reviews,* vol. 108, (2), pp. 814–825, 2008.

Peng, Bo, *et al.*, "Evaluation of enzyme-based tear glucose electrochemical sensors over a wide range of blood glucose concentrations," *Biosensors and Bioelectronics,* vol. 49, (0), pp. 204–209, 2013.

Durmus, N. Gozde, *et al.*, "Acoustics Based Biosensors," in *Encyclopedia of Microfluidics and Nanofluidics*, Li, Dongqing, Ed., Heidelberg, Springer, 2008, pp. 15–24.

Ho, Clifford K., Alex Robinson, David R. Miller, and Mary J. Davis, "Overview of Sensors and Needs for Environmental Monitoring," *Sensors,* vol. 5, pp. 4–37, 2005.

Inajima, Tsuyoshi, Takashi Hirokawa, and Yuji Okada. *Japan Draws Curtain on Nuclear Energy Following Germany*, Last Update: 2012, http://www.bloomberg.com/news/2012-09-14/japan-draws-curtain-on-nuclear-energy-following-germany.html

Schwela, Dietrich, "Air Pollution and Health in Urban Areas," *Reviews on Environmental Health,* vol. 15, (1–2), pp. 13–42, 2000.

Watt, Louise. *China Pollution: Cars Cause Major Air Problems in Chinese Cities*, Huffington Post, http://www.huffingtonpost.com/2013/01/31/china-pollution-cars-air-problems-cities_n_2589294.html, 2013.

Wee, Sui-Lee and Adam Jouran. *In China, public anger over secrecy on environment*, Last Update: March 10th 2013, http://www.reuters.com/article/2013/03/10/us-china-parliament-pollution-idUSBRE92900R20130310

EPA, "List of Designated Reference and Equivalent Methods," vol. MD-D205-03, ed. Research Triangle Park, North Carolina: National Exposure Reseach Laboratory, 2012, p. 60.

Fine, George F., Leon M. Cavanagh, Ayo Afonja, and Russell Binions, "Metal Oxide Semi-Conductor Gas Sensors in Environmental Monitoring," *Sensors,* vol. 10, (6), pp. 5469–5502, 2010.

Kumar, A., H. Kim, and G. P. Hancke, "Environmental Monitoring Systems: A Review," *Sensors Journal, IEEE,* vol. 13, (4), pp. 1329–1339, 2013.

Diamond, Dermot, Fiachra Collins, John Cleary, Claudio Zuliani, and Cormac Fay, "Distributed Environmental Monitoring," in *Autonomous Sensor Networks*. vol. 13, Filippini, Daniel, Ed., Springer Berlin Heidelberg, 2013, pp. 321–363.

Zhang, C., W. Zhang, D. J. Webb, and G. D. Peng, "Optical fibre temperature and humidity sensor," *Electronics Letters,* vol. 46, (9), pp. 643–644, 2010.

Borisov, Sergey M., Roman Seifner, and Ingo Klimant, "A novel planar optical sensor for simultaneous monitoring of oxygen, carbon dioxide, pH and temperature," *Analytical and Bioanalytical Chemistry,* vol. 400, (8), pp. 2463–2474, 2011.

Mead, M. I., *et al.*, "The use of electrochemical sensors for monitoring urban air quality in low-cost, high-density networks," *Atmospheric Environment,* vol. 70, pp. 186–203, 2013.

Bales, E., *et al.*, "Citisense: Mobile air quality sensing for individuals and communities Design and deployment of the Citisense mobile air-quality system," in *Pervasive Computing Technologies for Healthcare (PervasiveHealth), 2012 6th International Conference on*, 2012, pp. 155–158.

Kumar, A., I. P. Singh, and S. K. Sud, "Energy efficient air quality monitoring system," in *Sensors, 2011 IEEE*, 2011, pp. 1562–1566.

Korotcenkov, Ghenadii, Sang Do Han, and Joseph R.Stetter, "ChemInform Abstract: Review of Electrochemical Hydrogen Sensors," *ChemInform,* vol. 40, (22), 2009.

James, George. *Perrier Recalls Its Water in U.S. After Benzene Is Found in Bottles*, The New York Times, New York, http://www.nytimes.com/1990/02/10/us/perrier-recalls-its-water-in-us-after-benzene-is-found-in-bottles.html, 1990.

Czugala, Monika, *et al.*, "CMAS: fully integrated portable centrifugal microfluidic analysis system for on-site colorimetric analysis," *RSC Advances,* vol. 3, (36), pp. 15928–15938, 2013.

Cogan, Deirdre, *et al.*, "Integrated flow analysis platform for the direct detection of nitrate in water using a simplified chromotropic acid method," *Analytical Methods,* vol. 5, (18), pp. 4798–4804, 2013.

Santini, Silvia, Benedikt Ostermaier, and Andrea Vitaletti, "First experiences using wireless sensor networks for noise pollution monitoring," presented at the Proceedings of the workshop on Real-world wireless sensor networks, Glasgow, Scotland, 2008.

Maisonneuve, Nicolas, Matthias Stevens, Maria E. Niessen, Peter Hanappe, and Luc Steels, "Citizen Noise Pollution Monitoring," presented at the 10th International Digital Government Research Conference, Puebla, Mexico 2009.

Radu, Tanja, *et al.*, "Portable X-Ray Fluorescence as a Rapid Technique for Surveying Elemental Distributions in Soil," *Spectroscopy Letters,* vol. 46, (7), pp. 516–526, 2013.

Yang, Chin-Lung, *et al.*, "Design and evaluation of a portable optical-based biosensor for testing whole blood prothrombin time," *Talanta,* vol. 116, (0), pp. 704–711, 2013.

Girardin, Céline M., Céline Huot, Monique Gonthier, and Edgard Delvin, "Continuous glucose monitoring: A review of biochemical perspectives and clinical use in type 1 diabetes," *Clinical Biochemistry,* vol. 42, (3), pp. 136–142, 2009.

Swensen, James S., *et al.*, "Continuous, Real-Time Monitoring of Cocaine in Undiluted Blood Serum via a Microfluidic, Electrochemical Aptamer-Based Sensor," *Journal of the American Chemical Society,* vol. 131, (12), pp. 4262–4266, 2009.

McLachlan, Michael J., John A. Katzenellenbogen, and Huimin Zhao, "A new fluorescence complementation biosensor for detection of estrogenic compounds," *Biotechnology and Bioengineering,* vol. 108, (12), pp. 2794–2803, 2011.

Wang, Xuefeng, Ming Zhao, David D. Nolte, and Timothy L. Ratliff, "Prostate specific antigen detection in patient sera by fluorescence-free BioCD protein array," *Biosensors and Bioelectronics,* vol. 26, (5), pp. 1871–1875, 2011.

Arami, A., A. Vallet, and K. Aminian, "Accurate Measurement of Concurrent Flexion-Extension and Internal-External Rotations in Smart Knee Prostheses," *IEEE Transactions on Biomedical Engineering,* vol. 60, (9), pp. 2504–2510, 2013.

Uzor, Stephen and Lynne Baillie, "Exploring & designing tools to enhance falls rehabilitation in the home," presented at the Proceedings of the SIGCHI Conference on Human Factors in Computing Systems, Paris, France, 2013.

Shyamal, Patel, Park Hyung, Bonato Paolo, Chan Leighton, and Rodgers Mary, "A review of wearable sensors and systems with application in rehabilitation," *Journal of NeuroEngineering and Rehabilitation,* vol. 9, (1), pp. 21–21, 2012.

Wei, Yang, Russel Torah, Kai Yang, Steve Beeby, and John Tudor, "Design optimized membrane-based flexible paper accelerometer with silver nano ink," *Applied Physics Letters,* vol. 103, (7), 2013.

Metcalf, Cheryl D., *et al.*, "Fabric-based strain sensors for measuring movement in wearable telemonitoring applications," presented at the IET Conference on Assisted Living, London, UK, 2009.

Mass, Fabien, Julien Penders, Aline Serteyn, Martien van Bussel, and Johan Arends, "Miniaturized wireless ECG-monitor for real-time detection of epileptic seizures," presented at the Wireless Health 2010, San Diego, California, 2010.

Brown, L., *et al.*, "A low-power, wireless, 8-channel EEG monitoring headset," in *Engineering in Medicine and Biology Society (EMBC), 2010 Annual International Conference of the IEEE*, 2010, pp. 4197–4200.

Buono, Michael J, Amy Jechort, Raquel Marques, Carrie Smith, and Jessica Welch, "Comparison of infrared versus contact thermometry for measuring skin temperature during exercise in the heat," *Physiological Measurement,* vol. 28, (8), pp. 855–859, 2007.

Spulber, I., *et al.*, "Frequency analysis of wireless accelerometer and EMG sensors data: Towards discrimination of normal and asymmetric walking pattern," in *Circuits and Systems (ISCAS), 2012 IEEE International Symposium on*, 2012, pp. 2645–2648.

Reaston, P., M. Reaston, and B. Kuris, "Wireless Diagnostics," *Pulse, IEEE,* vol. 2, (2), pp. 20–26, 2011.

Jing, Meng, Liang Dong, and Song Liang, "Compressed sensing photoacoustic tomography in vivo in time and frequency domains," in *Biomedical and Health Informatics (BHI), 2012 IEEE-EMBS International Conference on*, 2012, pp. 717–720.

Ng, J. H. G., *et al.*, "Design, manufacturing and packaging of high frequency micro ultrasonic transducers for medical applications," in *Electronics Packaging Technology Conference (EPTC), 2011 IEEE 13th*, 2011, pp. 93–98.

McCaffrey, C., O. Chevalerias, C. O'Mathuna, and K. Twomey, "Swallowable-Capsule Technology," *Pervasive Computing, IEEE,* vol. 7, (1), pp. 23–29, 2008.

National Wellness Institute. "The Six Dimensions of Wellness", http://www.nationalwellness.org/?page=Six_Dimensions, 2013.

Freescale, "Medical Applications - User Guide", http://www.freescale.com/files/microcontrollers/doc/user_guide/MDAPPUSGDRM118.pdf#page=44, 2012.

Apple. "Nike + iPod - Meet Your New Personnal Trainer", http://www.apple.com/ipod/nike/, 2012.

Continua Health Alliance. "Health & Wellness - Fitness goals will be more easily attainable", http://www.continu-aalliance.org/connected-health-vision/health-and-wellness.html, 2010.

Helmenstine, Anne Marie. *How Do Smoke Detectors Work? - Photoelectric & Ionization Smoke Detectors*, Last Update: 2013, http://chemistry.about.com/cs/howthingswork/a/aa071401a.htm

Bently, John P., *Principles of Measurements Systems*, 3rd ed. Singapore: Longman, 1995.

van der Horn, Gert and Johan Huijsing, "Calibration and Linearization Techniques," in *Integrated Smart Sensors: Design and Calibration*, Springer, 1998.

Wilson, Jon S., *Sensor Technology Handbook*. Burlington, MA: Newnes, 2004.

■ ■ ■

CHAPTER 3

Key Sensor Technology Components: Hardware and Software Overview

Sensors measure a variety of chemical, biological, and physical quantities using a wide range of sensing techniques as outlined in the previous chapter. The action of sensing creates an output signal, via a transduction process, that must be processed and transmitted in some manner in order for a person or another device to do something useful with it. Sensors that have the capability to acquire, process, and output measurements over a data bus in a single package are referred to as smart sensors. The capabilities of these smart sensors can be further augmented with features, such as radio communications, sampling, remote manageability, and enclosures, to deliver smart sensor systems. The combination of hardware and software enables signal conditioning, data processing, transmission, storage, and display of the sensor measurement. In this chapter, we will examine the key hardware and software features that are important in the design of sensors and sensor systems.

Smart Sensors

The difference between a smart sensor and a sensor system isn't always clear. Smart sensors are generally expected to incorporate sensing and transduction functions with an analog interface circuit, a microcontroller with an integrated analog-to-digital converter (ADC), and an input/output (I/O) bus interface in a single integrated package (Huijsing, 2008). Apart from the system requirements, smart sensors are also functionally expected to have features such as auto-calibration, compensated measurements (baseline drift adjustment, environmental variation correction—for example, temperature) and self-health evaluation. In addition, smart sensors may have firmware-based signal processing capabilities, processed data validation, and multisensing capabilities (Mathas, 2011). Many smart sensor features are driven primarily by the use of a modern microcontroller (MCU). The inclusion of an MCU in a smart sensor enables digital signal processing (DSP), ADC, baseline correction, data processing, data storage support, power management, and interfacing functions such as external communications.

Smart sensors normally have their components integrated onto the same printed circuit board (PCB). This level of integration improves both reliability and performance, while reducing production testing costs. The small form factor also enables flexibility in terms of platform design, which can be important for applications such as on-body vital signs monitoring. However, upfront development costs can be significant, and high volumes are often required to make smart sensors economical. Due to the small footprint of PCBs, designers must carefully consider board layout effects on the sensor's operational performance. Issues such as local heating effects and radio frequency (RF) interference need to be considered to avoid any influence on sensor performance.

The market for smart sensors is likely to increase to USD 6.7 billion by 2017, as advances in microelectromechanical systems (MEMS) fabrication techniques drive down sensor manufacturing costs (PRWeb, 2012). As the dimensions of smart sensors continue to decrease, new applications are sure to emerge, such as implantable biosensors (Córcoles et al., 2013).

Sensor Systems

Sensor systems extend the capabilities of smart sensors by adding more capabilities, such as communications (wired and wireless), display, sample acquisition and preparation, enclosures and mounts, remote manageability, and security. The specific mix of system capabilities is generally dictated by application requirements. The high-level architecture of a sensor system is illustrated in Figure 3-1. Meijer describes a sensor system as the combination of the sensing function with various interfaces, a microcontroller, storage, digital and analog I/O, enclosures, and mountings into an integrated system (Meijer, 2008).

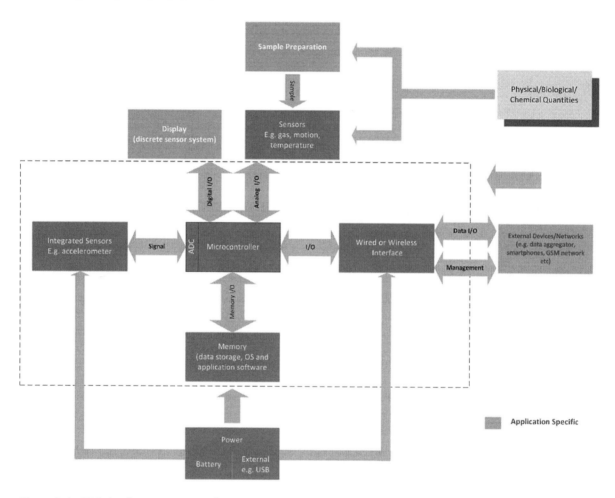

Figure 3-1. *High-level sensor system architecture*

Sensor systems comprise several hierarchical functional layers, including sensing and transduction, signal processing (filtering, conditioning, ADC conversion), data-integrity checking, data processing, signal transmission and display, and, in some cases, remote device manageability. In multisensor systems, it is possible to optimize the performance of individual sensors by using the data from a sensor to improve the accuracy of the reading from another sensor (for example, temperature drift compensation). This capability enables the system to adapt and compensate for environmental variations in order to maintain robust system health (Hunter et al., 2010).

For some application domains, such as healthcare, the physical attributes of a sensor system are important selection criteria, particularly for body-worn configurations. These attributes include weight, physical dimensions, enclosure type, sensor-mounting system, ability to wipe down, and waterproofing (that is, preventing biological fluid ingress). The weight of the sensor system is also important for mobile applications, such as those for smartphones, or in vibration applications, where the weight of the sensor could directly impact the accuracy of the measurement (Pecht, 2008).

Sensor Platforms

Sensor platforms are a subset of smart sensors. Like smart sensors, they feature a microcontroller, a wired/wireless interface, and memory. However, sensor platforms are designed for non-specific applications. They have the functionality to integrate with unspecified external sensors, and an interface for programming the microcontroller to perform a specific function. These platforms are very useful for rapid prototyping—sensor hardware and actuators can be physically or wirelessly connected to the platform's sensor interface (digital or analog). Most sensor platforms are accompanied by an integrated development environment (IDE) and sample application code that can be combined to program the sensors or actuators. If the prototype is successful, it can form the basis of a specific smart sensor design. If not, the sensors can be quickly reconfigured and retested, or they can be discarded and the platform reused for a different application. However, this flexibility has some drawbacks: sensor platforms are physically larger and more expensive than smart sensors, and the user may not require all of the features available on the sensor platform.

Sensor platforms are very popular among hobbyists, designers, researchers, and educators. Many sensor platforms exist, including Parallax Basic Stamp, Netmedia's BX-24, Phidgets, and MIT's Handyboard. The most common sensor platforms in the health, wellness, and environmental domains are Arduino, Shimmer, and smartphones.

The Arduino I/O Board

The Arduino (`www.arduino.cc`) was developed in Italy in 2005 to allow non-experts, including artists, designers, and hobbyists, to rapidly create interactive prototypes. The Arduino I/O board is commonly referred to as "an Arduino." However, the term "Arduino" describes not only the open source hardware sensor platform, but also open source software and the active user community.

Traditionally, Arduino I/O boards are developed around a member of the Atmega MegaAVR MCU family (Atmel, 2013), although there is nothing to prevent someone from creating an Arduino-compatible I/O board using a different MCU. For example, the Arduino UNO R3 board (shown in Figure 3-2) is based on an Atmel ATmega328 (`www.atmel.com`), which is a 8-bit Atmega core microcontroller. The functionality of Arduino I/O boards can be extended by plugging an Arduino shield into the four expansion connectors found on most official Arduino I/O boards. There are currently hundreds of Arduino shields (many of them are listed on `http://shieldlist.org/`), providing radio and sensor functionality or prototyping functionality to the Arduino board. A key feature of Arduino is its open source ethos. Arduino releases all of its hardware CAD-design files under an open source license, and these designs can be used or adapted for personal and commercial use, provided Arduino is credited. As a result, several commercial vendors sell official Arduino and Arduino-compatible sensor platforms and shields. The newly introduced Galileo board from Intel is part of the Arduino Certified product line. The functionality of this board is described in Chapter 4.

Figure 3-2. Arduino UNO R3 board

The Arduino I/O board MCU is programmed using the open source Arduino programming language (an implementation of the Wiring programming language) and the open source Arduino IDE (based on the Processing IDE). It can also be programmed using Atmel's AVR-studio or other software environments.

Shimmer

Shimmer is a wireless sensor platform that can capture and transmit sensor data in real time or log the data to a microSD card. Shimmer is a mature sensor platform, targeted at researchers, clinicians, and scientists who want to capture data from sensors without worrying about the underlying sensor electronics, power, or casing. Its small size makes it ideal for body-worn applications, although it has also been used for ambient sensing applications (Burns et al., 2010).

Shimmer is the name given to the main board, as shown in Figure 3-3, which features an MSP430 MCU, two radios (802.15.4 and Bluetooth), a microSD connector, a 3-axis accelerometer, and a 20-pin Hirose connection. The Shimmer main board is a smart sensor itself, having the capability to perform basic motion sensing, data capture, processing, and wireless transmission of sensed data. The sensing capability of Shimmer can be extended by connecting a Shimmer daughterboard with the required sensing functionality, or the Shimmer prototyping board, to support the connection of other sensors. Shimmer has daughterboards for complex motion sensing, vital signs and biophysical sensing, and environmental and ambient sensing applications.

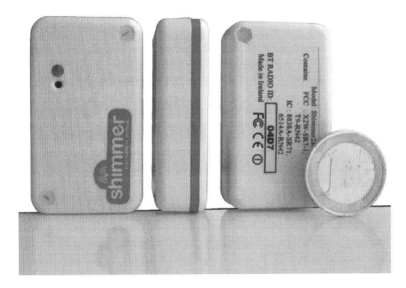

Figure 3-3. *Shimmer Kinematic Sensors (main board, kinematic daughter board,and battery enclosed in a custom sensor casing) (image used with permission from Shimmer Research)*

Shimmer can be programmed in two ways. First, Shimmer provides a number of precompiled firmware images for its various sensor modules that can be downloaded to the Shimmer using the Shimmer Bootstrap Loader and a universal serial bus (USB) docking station. Second, firmware developers can write their own firmware code using open source TinyOS modules, which are freely available from the TinyOS repository on code.google.com. On the application side, Shimmer can interface with a PC or smartphone using a Matlab, Labview, C#, or Android module, which are available on the Shimmer web site (`www.shimmersensing.com`); or with the PAMSys physical activity monitoring platform.

Smartphones and Tablets

Smartphones and tablets contain many integrated sensors, which the operating system employs to improve the user experience. These may include motion and location sensors (accelerometers, gyroscopes, magnetometers, and pressure sensors), optical sensors (ambient light sensors, proximity sensors, image sensors, and display sensors), silicon microphones, and many environment sensors. The major mobile operating systems (iOS, Android, and Windows 8) provide sensor frameworks that allow application developers to easily access these real time data streams within their applications. "Run Keeper" is an example of a popular mobile application that uses a smartphone's embedded sensors for an alternative use (`http://runkeeper.com`).

These mobile devices compare very favorably to other sensor platforms in many aspects. The sensors are integrated into an existing, frequently used technology, ensuring that user compliance will be high. The combination of a high-performance microcontroller and substantial memory storage can support complex data analysis over long periods of time. And the integration of a sensor framework into the software development environment greatly simplifies the development process.

However, there are also disadvantages to sensing using mobile devices. The sensor framework abstracts the sensor details and control, making it difficult to achieve the granularity you can realize with a discrete sensor. Moreover, sensing is a secondary function of the device and can be paused or killed by the operating system when a higher priority task occurs. Finally, Android and Windows 8 run on various hardware configurations, which means the programmer has no control over the sensor specification or how its data is translated by the sensor framework. In fact, the only way to ensure that sensor data is accurate is to use a discrete sensor that is wirelessly connected to the phone. Mobile devices can also be used as aggregators for internal and external sensors (discussed in Chapter 4).

Microcontrollers for Smart Sensors

We have already defined a smart sensor as sensing capabilities combined with computing, I/O, and communications in a single, integrated package. Many smart-sensor features are driven primarily by an MCU, which includes ADC, data storage support, power management, and interfacing functions such as external communications. We now look in detail at the key architectural components of a modern MCU, and at how they enable smart sensors.

The terms "microprocessor," "microcomputer," and "microcontroller" are often confused, but they have very different and distinct meanings. A microprocessor is a central processing unit (CPU), implemented on a single chip. In fact, the "micro" in "microprocessor" refers to this single-chip implementation. Prior to 1970, CPUs were not integrated on a single chip and consisted of many chips or many discrete devices connected together.

Microcomputers are computing devices containing microprocessors and peripherals, including I/O interfaces, data memory, program memory, interrupt handling, and timers, as shown in Figure 3-4. Microcomputers are not necessarily small computers; they are simply computing devices containing a microprocessor. For example, a PC containing an Intel Core i5 microprocessor can be described as a microcomputer.

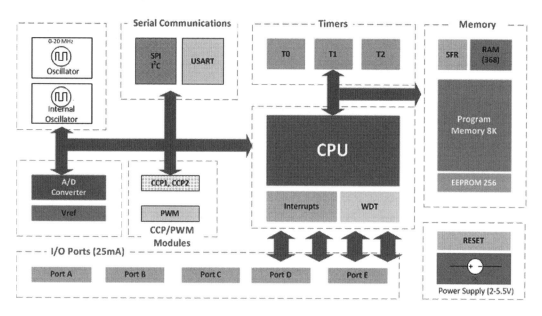

Figure 3-4. *Block diagram of a microcontroller*

Microcontrollers are designed to perform specific tasks, where the relationship between the input and output is defined. They can be found in microwaves, telephones, and washing machines, as well as in the sensing applications described in this book. Since these applications are very specific, the resources required (for example, random access memory (RAM), read only memory (ROM), and I/O ports) can be defined in advance, and a low-cost microcontroller can be identified to meet these requirements. Microcontrollers generally exist in families, such as the Atmel MegaAVR family, that have a common CPU but different input/output configurations. When selecting a microcontroller, you generally select the microprocessor family first and then choose a member of that family that best meets your input, output, and memory requirements.

CPUs

CPU design is a broad and complex topic that is beyond the scope of this text. However, this section provides a brief overview of CPUs and the terms used to describe them in the context of microcontrollers.

A CPU, at its most basic level, consists of five parts:

- *Arithmetic and logic unit (ALU)*: The ALU is responsible for performing calculations on data. A basic CPU might contain just one ALU that can perform only addition, subtraction, and basic logic. More sophisticated CPUs may contain several ALUs that are capable of advanced floating point operations. When the internal bus in an MCU is a 16-bit bus and the ALU performs operations on 16 bits at an instruction level, the MCU is described as a 16-bit microcontroller. A 16-bit MCU provides greater precision and performance than an 8-bit MCU, but less than a 32-bit MCU.

- *Control unit (CU)*: The CU controls the movement of instructions in and out of the processor, as well as the operation of the ALU.

- *Register array*: A register array consists of small units of internal memory used for quick storage and retrieval of data and instructions. All processors contain at least one program counter, an instruction register, an accumulator, a memory address register, and a stack pointer register, as shown in Figure 3-5.

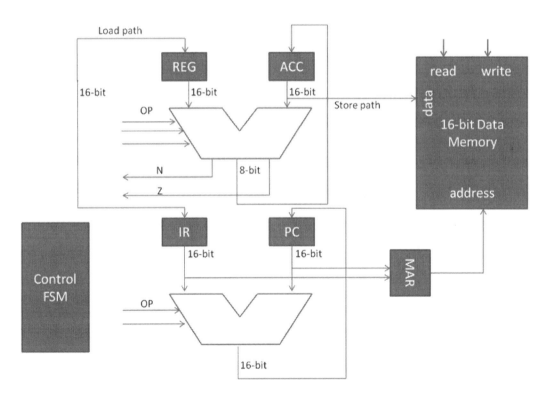

Figure 3-5. *A register view of the Princeton architecture CPU*

- *System bus*: The system bus comprises a data bus, an address bus, and a control bus and is used to transfer data between the processor, memory, and peripherals. The address bus carries the address of a specified location. If an address bus has n address lines, it can access 2^n locations. For example, a 16-bit address bus can access $2^{16} = 65,536$ locations (or 64K memory). The data bus carries information between the CPU and memory, or between the CPU and I/O devices. The control bus carries commands from the CPU and returns status signals from the devices.

- *Memory*: Although not actually part of the CPU, memory is an essential part of CPU operation as it stores data and the program being executed.

The instruction set architecture (ISA) describes a list of instructions that a processor understands. Different processors have different instruction sets, which are optimized for the features of that processor. Each instruction consists of a short code, called an opcode, describing the operation the CPU is expected to perform; and an operand, describing where the data required for the operation can be found. Programmers almost never write their programs using this instruction set, but their code is translated into this form at some point before execution so the CPU can manipulate it.

Processors are generally described as having either a reduced instruction set computer (RISC) or a complex instruction set computer (CISC) architecture. RISC describes a simple instruction set in which instructions have fixed length and are implemented in a single cycle using distinct hardwired control. RISC architecture includes many registers, reducing the need for external fetches from memory. RISC processors have a simpler design than CISC, with smaller chips, smaller pin counts, and very low power consumption. RISC is a cheaper architecture to produce.

CISC has a larger instruction set, featuring varying code lengths, varying execution times, and a complex architecture. CISC allows memory access during ALU and data transfer instructions. Many CISC architecture instructions are macro-like, allowing a programmer to use one instruction in place of several simpler instructions. The differences between RISC and CISC have become less dramatic as both architectures have borrowed features from each other. Modern microcontrollers typically have a RISC core but are capable of running some CISC features by using on-chip compilers.

Registers

Registers are small RAM memory elements, 1–2 bytes in size. There are two types of registers: general purpose and special function. General purpose registers are used by the ALU to store interim calculation results because they can be accessed faster than external memory. Special function registers (SFRs) are registers whose function is defined by the manufacturer. The bits of these registers are connected directly to internal circuits, including the ADC and universal synchronous/asynchronous receiver/transmitter (USART), giving them direct control of these circuits. SFR registers and their bits can be called by name in software.

Memory

A microcontroller contains three types of memory: RAM, ROM, and electrically erasable programmable read-only memory (EEPROM), all of which are connected to the CPU via the address bus.

- RAM stores data that can be changed during program execution. The data contained in RAM is usually lost when the microcontroller is switched off; therefore, RAM should not be used to store programs or settings that must be saved between power cycles.

- ROM is non-volatile data memory, meaning it does not lose its data when powered off. For this reason, it is used to store program and permanent data and is often called "program memory." Several different technologies are used to implement ROM in an MCU, including EEPROM and flash memory.

- EEPROM can be electrically erased and rewritten, negating the need for physical removal. EEPROM memory uses NOR gates to support fast access time and byte-level erasure. But it is more expensive than other erasable forms of memory, such as flash.

If an MCU has different address spaces for program and data memory, it is said to have a Harvard memory architecture (Figure 3-6a). In this model, program memory is read-only, and data memory is read-write. Modern microprocessors and MCUs implement a modified Harvard architecture that allows concurrent data and instruction access to speed processing, as well as different bit-widths (`www.microchip.com/pic`). An MCU has a von Neumann (Princeton) architecture if it contains a common memory space that can be used for both program and data (Figure 3-6b).

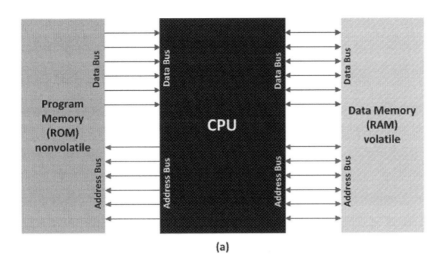

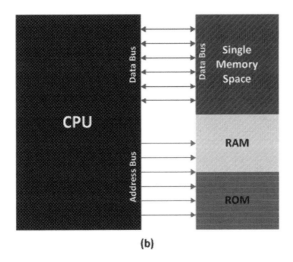

Figure 3-6. *Block diagrams representing (a) Harvard and (b) von Neumann memory architectures*

Timers and Counters

Most microcontrollers have one or more built-in timers that can be used to generate precise time delays by counting fixed intervals of time or occurrences of an event. A timer can also act as a real-time clock by generating repeated interrupts at regular intervals that can be used to initiate events:

- *Oscillators*: Microcontrollers use quartz crystal oscillators to generate precise, stable time pulses. A timer counts the number of pulses generated by the oscillator to generate a time signal.

- *Timers*: Functionally, a timer is an 8- or 16-bit SFR that is automatically incremented by each incoming pulse. A timer that counts the pulses of the internal quartz oscillator to measure time between two events is called a timer; a timer that counts pulses from an external source is called a counter. An 8-bit timer can only count to 255; a 16-bit timer can count to 65,535. The timer is automatically reset and counting restarts when the limit is exceeded; this is known as overflow. An interrupt can be generated to notify the user each time the timer overflows. The timer prescaler reduces the number of pulses supplied to the timer to slow the speed of the timer. The timer postscaler adjusts how often the timer interrupt is called but doesn't affect the timer itself. Both the timer prescaler and postscaler can be modified using the relevant SFRs.

- *Interrupts*: An interrupt is a call sent to the MCU to stop the normal execution of a program so the MCU can do something else. An interrupt service routine (ISR) is a piece of code that the MCU starts on receipt of a specific interrupt. When the ISR has completed, the MCU returns to whatever it was doing before the interrupt was received. There are several sources for interrupts, both hardware and software. Common hardware interrupts are raised when the timer counter overflows, data is received on the serial port, or an external interrupt pin is brought high. The processor can also interrupt itself if a procedure is called during normal execution of a program. Non-critical interrupts can be disabled, using the Interrupt Enable SFR, but interrupts indicating critical issues, such as a drop in source voltage, can't be disabled.

- *Watchdog timer*: The watchdog timer (WDT) is a resistor-capacitor (RC) oscillator-based timer that operates independently of other timers in the MCU. Its function is to ensure that the program does not get trapped in an inconsistent state. If the WDT is enabled, it begins to count. If the WDT counter overflows, the microcontroller program is reset and program execution starts from the first instruction. To avoid WDT resetting your program and affecting program execution, the WDT should be reset at regular intervals within the program code.

Debugging Interfaces

Microcontroller-based embedded systems lack user interfaces, including the keyboards, monitors, and disk drives that are present on computers. Therefore, different methods must be applied to debug hardware and firmware issues. These methods range from illuminating a light-emitting diode (LED) to indicate success or failure to using logic analyzers for monitoring traces on a system bus. Microcontrollers usually provide a hardware interface that can be used to debug microcontroller hardware and software. We'll briefly describe the hardware interfaces here (Hector, 2002), and debugging methods and software-based debugging later in the chapter.

- In-circuit emulators (ICE) are hardware devices that emulate the CPU of the embedded processor. These devices are connected between the embedded system and a PC and provide a user interface that lets the software developer monitor and control the embedded system. The device normally replaces the system's MCU with a "pod" and box that emulates the processor being replaced. ICE devices provide complete control of the MCU, and can trace data on the system bus. They are expensive tools, however, and are typically used only by hardware developers.

- In-circuit debuggers (ICD), also called background mode emulators (BME, and are often mistakenly referred to as ICE), are fundamentally different from ICE devices. ICE devices enable debugging by replacing the device under test with a device that emulates that device, whereas ICD devices use the Joint Test Action Group (JTAG) debug interface on the MCU to debug using the actual device under test. The debugging capabilities of the ICD are dependent on the debug features enabled by the manufacturer for a particular MCU or MCU family. Typically, an ICD allows the developer to step through code actually running in the target MCU, start and stop it, and read the register and processor state. It does not provide trace functionality or the ability to overlay memory that can be found in ICE devices. Because all processors that support ICD have the ICD hardware built in, the only extra cost is the ICD communication hardware (between the PC and the processor/microcontroller). ICDs are typically 3–10 times cheaper than ICEs and are suitable for software developers who use ready-built boards. Processor manufacturers and emulator manufacturers are creating hybrid technologies that provide ICE-like functionality over ICD interfaces.

- ROM monitors are the cheapest of the emulator types. They provide debug information to the development environment on the PC via the universal asynchronous receiver/transmitter (UART) interface. The ROM monitor allows both line-by-line execution and code breakpoints, but it does not offer real-time control. It is not suitable for debugging embedded applications that use a UART because the ROM monitor needs the UART to communicate with the PC.

Common Microcontrollers

When selecting an MCU for an application, it is important to perform a detailed requirements analysis: How many I/O lines and timers will be required? How much RAM? Are serial communications necessary? What is the sensor interface? What is the speed of operation? How much will one or several devices cost? What is the software development environment? Once all the questions have been answered, you should select a manufacturer and identify a device family with a CPU that will meet your processing needs. Then, study that family and identify the device that best meets your interfacing requirements. A key advantage of selecting an MCU from a large family is the ease of switching to another device in that family if it turns out you must upgrade or downgrade the MCU. Table 3-1 shows details of three popular microcontroller families.

Table 3-1. *Key Features of Popular Microcontroller Families*

	PIC16C5X family	MSP430 family	MegaAVR family
Manufacturer	Microchip Technology	Texas Instruments	Atmel
Processor	8-bit	16-bit	8-bit AVR
Instruction set	RISC	RISC	RISC
Memory Architecture	Modified Harvard	Von-Neumann	Modified Harvard
Processor Speed	40MHz	16MHz	16–20MHz
Flash	Up to 2K EEPROM	Up to 512KB	4–256KB
Software Development Tools	PBASIC MPLAB PIC Start Plus	Code Composer Studio IAR Embedded Workbench MSPGCC, TinyOS	AVR Studio Arduino IDE

Interfaces and Embedded Communications

Various methods are employed to communicate between subsystems in a sensor system, and from a sensor system to external interfaces. Digital interfaces with lightweight protocols are normally used for subsystem-to-subsystem communications (for example, digital sensor to MCU communication). They are also used to provide bidirectional input and output between the sensor system and larger systems. General purpose input/output (GPIO) pins are commonly found in embedded systems or on chips that have limited pins. As the name suggests, GPIO pins have no specific purpose but can be programmed to act as an input for sensor data or as an output that controls external components, such as LED indicators. Analog interfaces are used to transfer signals between analog sensors, signal conditioning circuitry, and the MCU's analog interfaces.

In an effort to standardize how smart sensors should be integrated into larger systems, the IEEE developed the 1451 standard, which "describes a set of open, common, network-independent communication interfaces for connecting transducers (sensors or actuators) to microprocessors, instrumentation systems, and control/field networks." The 1451.4 standard defines the format of the transducer electronic data sheet (TEDS), which holds key information that is unique to a sensor type for a specific manufacturer. A TEDS is typically stored in the sensor's EEPROM and contains information such as serial numbers, calibration dates, output scaling factors, and baseline offsets. The TEDS smart transducer interface makes it easier for transducer manufacturers to develop smart devices that can interface to networks, systems, and instruments using existing and emerging sensor and networking technologies. The standard does not specify interfaces or define physical connections. However, standard wired interfaces such as USB and Ethernet, and wireless such as 802.15.4, 802.11, and 6LoWPAN are suitable (Lee, 2005).

Embedded Digital Interfaces and Protocols

Digital interfaces for sensor systems are generally serial in nature. However, some sensors that require very high data throughput, such as digital imaging sensors, can feature parallel interfaces. Serial interfaces can be categorized as asynchronous (for example, RS232/RS485) or synchronous (such as I²C and SPI). Many modern MCUs feature integrated USART interfaces that can be programmatically defined to implement synchronous or asynchronous standard communication protocols, as shown in Figure 3-7. Serial interfaces have certain advantages over parallel interfaces. The most significant advantage is simpler wiring. In addition, serial interface cables can be longer than parallel interface cables because there is much less interaction (crosstalk) among the conductors in the cable (Rouse, 2011). Let us look briefly at some of the most common digital interfaces and protocols in sensors and sensor systems.

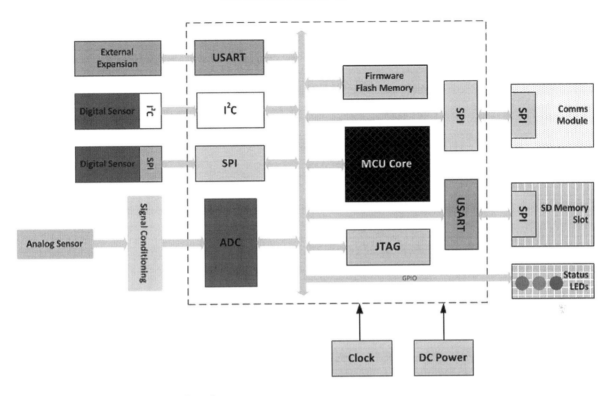

Figure 3-7. *Common digital interfaces for a smart sensor system*

Serial Peripheral Interface (SPI)

The SPI bus is a synchronous serial data link communications protocol that operates in full-duplex mode (meaning data can be sent and received simultaneously). It was originally developed by Motorola and has been widely adopted in the industry. SPI can be used to communicate with serial peripheral devices, such as digital sensors. It can also allow a microcontroller to communicate with a subsystem, such as a wireless communications module. SPI interfaces are available on many popular MCUs, such as the MSP430 (www.ti.com/msp430). However, the SPI standard is somewhat loosely defined, leading to differences among manufacturer implementations. Therefore, some sensors with SPI interfaces may require firmware tweaks to enable successful communications with an MCU.

The SPI bus is usually a four-wire serial communications interface with one master device (normally the MCU in a sensor system) that initiates and controls the communication, and one or more slaves that receive and transmit to the master. The use of an SPI bus is normally confined to a PCB. The bus is designed to transfer data between various subsystems on the same PCB at speeds up to 100Mbps. However, reactance ((X) - opposition of a circuit element to a change of current or voltage, due to that element's inductance or capacitance) increases with line length, making the bus unusable over longer lengths. National Semiconductor has an equivalent interface called Microwire, which is based on a three-wire synchronous interface with a similar master/slave bus, serial data in and out to the master, and a signal clock configuration. Microwire can support speeds up to 625Kbps with the same short-range communication restrictions as SPI (EE Herald, 2006).

SPI is suited to applications where devices have to transfer data streams. SPI is extremely simple and efficient for single-master to single-slave applications, due to its full-duplex communication capability and data rates (ranging up to several megabits per second).

The I²C Bus

The I²C bus was developed by Philips in the 1980s to facilitate low-bandwidth serial communications between components residing on the same PCB. It operates in a multi-master mode over short distances, and has been widely adopted as a means to attach low-speed peripheral devices and components to a motherboard or to a smart sensor, as shown in Figure 3-8. The I²C bus is a two-wire bidirectional bus; one wire carries a clock signal and the other carries the data. Speeds of 100 kbps are possible in standard mode, 400Kbps in enhanced or fast mode, and up to 3.4Mbps in high-speed mode.

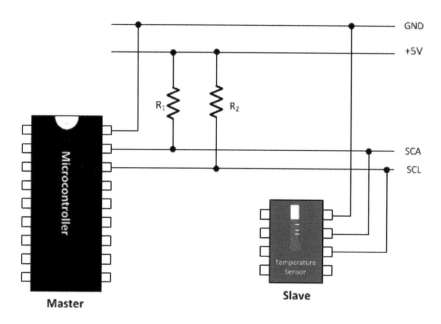

Figure 3-8. *Interfacing a temperature sensor with a microcontroller using the I²C bus*

Simplicity and flexibility are key characteristics that make this bus attractive for many applications, including sensor interfacing. Simple master/slave relationships exist between all components. The I²C protocol supports multiple masters, though most system designs include only one, and there may be one or more slaves on the bus. Both masters and slaves can receive and transmit data, but only the master initiates communications—it can send commands to the slaves and query them for data. The slaves only respond; they can't initiate communications with the master. Slaves have 7-bit addresses; therefore a maximum of 128 slave devices can be supported on the bus. When addressing slave devices, 8 bits are sent; the first 7 bits identify the slave, and the eighth bit is used to tell the slave whether the master is writing to it or reading from it.

Analog Interfacing

Analog sensor outputs (voltage, resistance, current) are typically converted to digital form to enable easier processing, transmission, or storage of the data. If the voltage output of the analog sensor is compatible with an ADC input voltage range, it can be connected directly to a discrete ADC, or to an MCU's built-in ADC. However, most sensor signals require some form of conditioning, such as voltage conversion, filtering, or signal isolation, to ensure they are in the correct voltage range for analog-to-digital conversion.

There are three types of voltage conversions: division, amplification, and shifting. Voltage division is needed when the voltage range exceeds the ADC's input voltage range. It is easily achieved using a resistor-based voltage divider circuit. Voltage amplification is required for sensors that create small voltages, such as accelerometers. The output voltage is multiplied using an op-amp-based circuit to increase the range and sensitivity of the circuit. The ratio of signal output to signal input following linear amplification is commonly known as gain. Care must be taken in selecting the correct gain to ensure that the amplified output does not exceed the input range of the ADC, which would cause signal saturation. If the amplified sensor output voltage falls beneath the minimum input voltage to the ADC, the sensor output must be shifted to the ADC's minimum input. A summing circuit, based on op-amps, is typically used to achieve voltage shifting. A common example of analog signal conditioning is using a Wheatstone bridge to convert impedance measurements from a sensor, such as a strain gauge, into voltages (see mechanical sensors, Chapter 2) that can be further amplified to increase the sensitivity of the sensor reading.

The frequency response of the amplifier can be stabilized at low frequencies through the addition of a capacitive element. However, the signal characteristics should be fully understood beforehand to ensure that appropriate sensor response times are used (Bates, 2006). Filtering the sensor signal limits the frequency range and removes noise from the signal, allowing the signal of interest to be measured more accurately. The frequency range removed is determined by the type of filter—low-pass, high-pass, or band-pass. If a sensor has a slow response time, a low-pass filter can be used to remove high-frequency signals. Inversely, if the response is high frequency, then low-frequency signals can be removed. Noise at an AC electrical frequency is typically removed using a notch filter to eliminate signals in the 50–60 Hz range. Keep in mind that filters should be carefully selected to ensure that no useful information is removed. For example, valuable information that may exist in higher frequency harmonics of the fundamental frequency will be lost if a low-pass filter is used at the fundamental frequency. It is therefore of critical importance to fully characterize the sensor signal before designing the filtering regime.

In healthcare applications, where there may be direct contact between a patient's body and the sensor, signal isolation between the source and the measurement and conversion circuits is an important safety consideration. Isolation amplifiers should be used to ensure there is no direct electrical connection with the measurement. This provides a safeguard against the possibility of dangerous voltages or currents passing into the sensor, preventing damage or potential injury to the patient. The inverse case is also applicable to ensure that damaging signals are not passed from the sensing environment into the measurement circuits (Kester, 2005).

Sensor Communications

A sensor's ability to communicate its results to a person or another device is fundamental to its usefulness. There are three main ways in which a sensor communicates: it can display data directly to the user, transfer data over a wired interface, or transfer data wirelessly.

Sensors can communicate binary status information, such as power on or off, using a light-emitting diode (LED). Single-use discrete sensors, such as pregnancy-testing kits, can communicate using a color-changing indicator or a simple, inexpensive liquid-crystal display (LCD). As the complexity of the data from the sensor increases, larger and more complex LCD screens may be required. LCD screens can display characters, symbols, or graphics. They range in size, price, and configuration, from showing just a couple of lines to large displays. Single-application LCDs display only predefined graphics, whereas large displays, such as those for weather stations and home heating control panels, can display multiple values or symbols from their sensor inputs.

Simple LCD screens and the underlying sensors are typically controlled by a simple microcontroller. When sensor data is an input to a graphical display, such as for a smartphone game, a more complex display and a graphical processing unit capable of displaying complex graphics may be required.

Standard Wired Interfaces

A serial port is a communication interface through which data is transferred one bit at a time between data terminal equipment (DTE) and data circuit-terminating equipment (DCE). Although Ethernet, FireWire, and USB all transfer their data serially, the term serial port is generally associated with the RS232 standard.

To achieve successful data communication, the DTE and DCE must agree on a communication standard, the transmission speed, number of bits per character, and whether stop and parity framing bits are used. Speed, also called the baud rate, is the number of bits transferred per second. Baud rate includes the data and the framing bits, meaning that if 2 framing bits are transmitted with 8 data bits, only 80% of the bits transferred are data. Parity bits are a simple method of detecting errors in a transmitted packet. A parity bit indicates whether the number of logical 1 bits in each packet is odd or even. If a received packet has a different number of 1s, then a bit in the packet has been corrupted. However, this simple method of error checking can't tell if an even number of bits have been corrupted. Stop bits are sent at the end of every character to notify the receiver that the end has been reached.

The most common communication configuration is 8-N-1, which indicates 8 data bits, no parity bit, and 1 stop bit. Clearly, the sender and receiver circuit must use the same parameters or the data will be incorrectly translated by the receiver and will appear as nonsense on the screen or to the processor. These parameters can be modified by software on a UART integrated circuit. Some serial standards, including Ethernet, FireWire, and USB, fix or automatically negotiate these parameters so users don't need to change the configuration.

Flow control is required between the DTE and DCE to indicate when both parties are ready to send and receive data. The RS232 standard uses the request to send (RTS) and clear to send (CTS) signals to indicate readiness for transmission/receipt of data. This is known as hardware flow control. In software flow control, special characters (XON and XOFF) are sent by the receiver to the sender (in the opposite direction to which the data will flow) to control when the sender will send the data. XON tells the sender to send data, while XOFF says to stop sending data.

RS-232

The RS-232 standard was once the accepted interface for personal computers to communicate with peripheral devices (modems, mice, printers). Although USB now performs this function in PCs, RS-232 interfaces can still be found in medical, retail, and military instruments. The RS-232 port transforms signals from UART logic levels to higher voltages (between –3 and –15V for logical 1s, and between +3V and +15V for logical 0s) for transmission, and transforms the signals back to UART levels at the receiver. These large voltage swings give the cable more immunity against electromagnetic interference and protect against voltage loss over long cable lengths. RS-232 can transfer data for up to 50 feet on a standard cable and up to 1,000 feet on low-capacitance cables. This compares favorably to USB cables, which have a maximum length of about 16 feet. However, the large voltage swings required to achieve this noise immunity increase the power consumption of the interface. The connectors for 9-way and 5-way RS-232 devices are larger than USB, and the standard does not provide a method to power other devices. Because the voltages defined by RS-232 are much larger than logic-level voltages on a sensor board, connecting an RS-232 device directly to a sensor board without using logic-level converters is not recommended.

Virtual Serial Ports

A virtual serial port, as the name suggests, is a software emulation of a standard serial port, which provides all the functionality (baud rate, data bits, and framing bits) of a physical serial port and can use serial port APIs and libraries. Bluetooth and USB devices are commonly implemented as virtual serial ports. In microcontrollers, virtual COM ports are usually implemented using a dedicated chip, such as an FTDI (Future Technology Devices International Ltd) FT232R-USB UART. The chip handles all USB-specific communications in hardware and interfaces to the microcontroller using an asynchronous serial port. FTDI provides drivers for Windows and other operating systems to interface to the chip. A virtual serial port can also be implemented in software using the USB communication devices class (CDC) drivers on the PC's operating system. Early Arduino boards, such as the Arduino Uno and Mega 2560, used USB CDC drivers, but newer boards implement this function using the FTDI chip.

RS-485

The RS-485 standard is used to configure inexpensive local networks and multidrop communications links. It can span large distances at low data rates (4000 feet at 100Kbps) or short distances at high data rates (50 feet at 35Mbps). Devices can be daisy-chained together on a shared circuit, and terminating resistors at each end of the shared cable promote noise immunity. RS-485 driver chips perform voltage-level shifting at the receiving end. As serial transmission runs over a shared pathway, the RS-485 data will be lost if two devices try to talk at the same time. Therefore, the serial port software must implement methods to ensure accurate data delivery, including resending and an acknowledgements scheme for received data. RS-485 is gradually being replaced by Controller Area Networks (CAN), but is still commonly found in automated factories and warehouses, and in television studios.

Universal Serial Bus (USB)

The USB standard was developed to simplify the connection, communication, and power supply between computers and computer peripherals and has effectively replaced serial ports, parallel ports, and portable device charger interfaces. The USB standard defines the cable connectors, and communications protocols required to support them. Three versions of the USB standard have been released to date: USB 1.x (full speed, up to 12Mbps), USB 2.0 (high speed, up to 480Mbps), and USB 3.0 (super speed, up to 5Gbps). Each subsequent version adds higher speed, new interfaces, and more functionality.

USB hubs can be added to increase the number of USB interfaces usable from a single USB host. A single USB host can control up to 127 devices. A physical USB device can have several sub-functions; for example, a webcam may have both video and audio functions. If a single address is associated to many functions in the device, the device is known as a composite device. If each function is assigned a unique address, it is known as a compound device. When a USB device is first connected to a USB host, the host reads the USB data rate and device information. If the device functionality is supported by the host, as defined by the USB device class, the USB device drivers are loaded. USB devices can draw 5V and a maximum of 500mA from a USB host. High-power devices requiring more current than this may use a Y-shaped cable that has 2 USB connectors (one for power and data, and the other for power only) or an external power supply. USB is commonly used to interface sensors to a PC or data aggregator for data acquisition, programming, and powering the device.

Short- and Medium-Range Standards for Wireless Communications

Wireless communications have been a key research focus over the last fifteen years. The use of wireless communications provides a number of significant advantages: reduced infrastructure requirements (no cabling), lower deployment costs, the ability to accommodate new devices at any time, and protocol flexibility. The initial focus was on the physical, media access control (MAC), and network layers to improve power efficiency and the reliability and robustness of communications. This led to the development at the physical layer of low-power radios, such as 802.15.4 and ultra-wideband (UWB), and the adoption of frequency-hopping spread spectrum (FHSS) techniques to improve transmission interference immunity. At the MAC layer, the focus has been on power-efficient protocols (for example, variants of time division multiple access (TDMA) and low-power duty cycles). Finally, at the network layer, the focus has been on the network structure, such as multi-hop routing to support sensor deployment over geographically dispersed areas.

Four key short-range, low-power, wireless communication standards predominate in the sensor application domain. These are: Bluetooth (IEEE 802.15.1) (Eliasson et al., 2008), UWB (IEEE 802.15.3), ZigBee (IEEE 802.15.4), and Wi-Fi (IEEE 802.11). Each of these standards has different data throughputs and ranges (Lee et al., 2007), as shown in Figure 3-9. Bluetooth has been heavily adopted for body-worn applications; Zigbee or 802.15.4 is used for indoor and outdoor multinode network applications; and UWB supports a variety of applications, ranging from implantable sensors (Yuan et al., 2011) to high-precision geolocation determination (Win et al., 2009). Wi-Fi is usually applied in ambient applications where longer ranges, higher data rates, and immunity to signal attenuation in high blockage environments are required. The advantages and disadvantages of each protocol as outlined in Table 3-2 should be considered when selecting the communications method for an application.

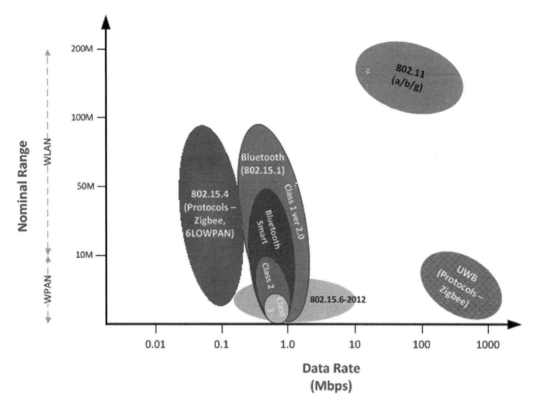

Figure 3-9. *Common protocols used for wireless sensor applications*

Table 3-2. *Advantages and Disadvantage of Common Wireless Protocols*

Standard/Protocol	Advantages	Disadvantages
Bluetooth	Low power < 15mA (Bluetooth Smart) Data throughput up to 24Mbps (ver 3) Good interference immunity; multi-hop protocol Low cost Mature technology with large installed base Flexible data packet sizes Supported by smartphones and tablets Does not require a clear line of sight between devices Bluetooth Smart (4.0);-theoretically unlimited number of slaves	Classic Bluetooth (BR/EDR) Limited number of nodes (7 slaves, 1 master) Not suitable for high-speed data applications Device discovery is slow, power-consuming High power overhead for active connections Difficult to implement high granularity time synchronization in Bluetooth stack.

(*continued*)

Table 3-2. (*continued*)

Standard/Protocol	Advantages	Disadvantages
802.15.4/Zigbee	Good power management Simple protocol Meshed networking support with support for a large number of nodes Significant commercial support and large installed base Good data security; authentication, encryption, and integrity services support (802.15.4)	Communications interference issues due to lack of multihop protocol Operation difficulties in high blockage environments Limited data throughput (>250kbps) Small data packet transmissions No native smartphone support
UWB	Good noise immunity Low power High immunity to multipath fading Signals can penetrate a variety of materials Potentially very high data rates	High cost Slow adoption rate Long signal acquisition times FCC emission restrictions—less than 0.5 mW max power over 7.5 GHz band Ongoing issues of coexistence and interference with other radios
802.11	Good coverage in high-blockage environments High data rates Supported by smartphones and tablets Scalable and adaptable Good security possible	High power requirements Significant overhead of listening without receiving messages Single hop networks Expensive relative to Bluetooth and 802.15.4

The demand for wireless devices that integrate seamlessly into our daily lives, coupled with ever-increasing smartphone adoption rates, is accelerating innovation in the performance and capability of radios and supporting protocols. One key development is Bluetooth Smart, which addresses the need for connectivity and interoperability among sports and healthcare devices (see Chapter 10). Bluetooth Smart significantly reduces power consumption and is capable of delivering operational lifespans of years with standard lithium-ion batteries, depending, of course, on the specific use case. The protocol is found in a variety of smartphones, including the iPhone 4S/5 and Motorola Droid Razr (`www.bluetooth.com/pages/Bluetooth-Smart-Devices`). Bluetooth is already pervasive in smartphones and tablets, so most manufactures can simply upgrade their hardware to Bluetooth Smart.

Smartphones give users access to hundreds of apps that communicate with, process, and visualize sensor data. The low power performance of Bluetooth Smart and smartphone support is helping it to make a quick impact in the personal fitness market, where it is found in devices such as the Nike Fuelband, Fitbit, and Motorola MOTACTV (Bennett, 2012). Because the Bluetooth Smart profile definition is still somewhat in its infancy, some interoperability issues are still being resolved. As an interim step, some manufacturers are providing support for both Bluetooth Smart and the proprietary ANT+ protocol that is widely used in the health and fitness device market (Marker, 2012).

Another protocol, 6LOWPAN, specifies IP networking capabilities for IEEE 802.15.4 networks. 6LOWPAN is driven by the concept that low-power devices, such as sensors, should be able to join the Internet of Things using connectivity at low data rates and low duty cycles. The standard specifies an adaptation layer between a simplified IPv6 layer and the IEEE 802.15.4 MAC layer that can adapt packet sizes, provide address resolution, and support mesh topologies as well as device and service discovery (Higuera et al., 2011). The protocol is finding initial adoption in the smart meter space; however this is likely to grow into other areas, such as healthcare applications (Jin Ho et al., 2010)

In 2012, the IEEE announced the 802.15.6-2012 protocol for short-range, wireless communications in proximity to or inside a human body with data rates up to 10Mbps. It is designed specifically to compensate for issues associated with on-body sensor communications. Compliant devices utilize very low transmission power to minimize the specific absorption rate into the body and to increase the battery life. The standard supports quality of service (QoS) and strong security, essential given the nature of its intended applications, which include EEG, EKG/ECG, and monitoring vital signs such as temperature, heart rate, oxygen, and blood pressure. Beyond healthcare, 802.15.6-2012 may find application in areas such as body-worn game controllers (WPAN-Working-Group, 2012) (Wang et al., 2012).

Another recent wireless standard is ISO/IEC 1453-3-10, which is based on a protocol developed by EnOcean and is optimized for energy harvesting. Sensors based on this standard are mainly focused on monitoring and industrial automation applications (EnOcean, 2012).

Proprietary Wireless Protocols

A number of propriety wireless protocols can be found in commercial sensors. These protocols can operate in either the industrial, scientific, and medical (ISM) band or on propriety radio frequencies. They are normally focused on optimizations for specific applications, such as ultra-low power to deliver battery lifespans of years (Smith, 2012). Because of the specific application focus, these protocols are lighter weight, have less overhead, and generally provide more predictable performance than standards-based protocols. It is up to application developers to decide whether the advantages of specific optimizations afforded by proprietary solutions outweigh the flexibility and openness of standard protocols.

ANT is a proprietary ISM band wireless sensor network protocol designed and marketed by Dynastream Innovations Inc. (a subsidiary of the GPS manufacturer, Garmin). It has been incorporated into a number of low-power RF transceivers from companies such as Nordic Semiconductor and Texas Instruments (TI). ANT focuses primarily on applications with low frequency parameters and has been widely adopted in the health and fitness domain, with over 300 companies offering products based on this protocol. A key limitation of ANT, however, is the lack of smartphone and tablet support; only the HTC Rhyme and Sony Ericsson Xperia phones offer native ANT support.

Sensium, a system on a chip (SoC) developed by Toumaz Technology Ltd, is used in ultra-low power body-worn applications to continuously monitor vital signs, such as temperature, heart rate, pulse, and respiration at date rates up to 50Kbps. Data is streamed over 868/915MHz radio to a base station for storage. Sensium is based on a mixed signaling approach, where digital elements are used to dynamically control analog processing blocks to achieve low power utilization. The sensor is designed to operate for a year on a single 30mAhr battery (Bindra, 2008) (Toumaz, 2013).

The BodyLAN wireless protocol from FitLinxx is another proprietary solution for body-worn applications, reportedly used in over 4 million activity, wellness, fitness, and medical devices (FitLinxx, 2013). SimpliciTI from TI is a low-power protocol that runs on the RF SoC series or MSP430 MCU, both from TI, for simple ambient applications such as occupancy detection, carbon monoxide sensing, smoke detection, and automatic meter reading (Texas Instruments, 2008). Other solutions include MicrelNet from Micrel (Micrel, 2012) and MiWi/MiWi P2P from Microchip Technology, based on the IEEE 802.15.4 for wireless personal area network (WPAN) implementations (Microchip, 2013).

Power Management and Energy Harvesting

Many sensors, particularly wireless sensors, rely on batteries as their power source. Energy becomes a significant constraint in applications where the sensor must operate unattended for long durations. Replacing batteries can be a costly overhead, particularly if deployments are geographically dispersed or if there are logistical issues in accessing the sensors—for example, sensors attached to a street light post. As a result, much effort has been invested in the efficient use of battery energy and in the harvesting of energy from the environment. Power management has focused primarily in the wireless sensor domain; however, it is relevant to any sensor with a battery power source. Power management employs a variety of mechanisms to minimize power consumption, including turning off sensor subsystems, such as radio communications; using more power-efficient protocols; and optimizing message structures. The choice of power-management technique is determined by the application's environmental characteristics and performance requirements, such as reliability, and protocol needs. We will briefly look at the most important elements of power management and energy harvesting that application developers should be cognizant of.

Power Management

Although an in-depth analysis of power control algorithms and protocols is beyond our current scope, we will briefly look at the key elements of power management. Communications—particularly the physical, data link, and network protocol layers of wireless communications—consume a significant proportion of the overall sensor energy (Lin et al., 2009). One area of focus has been the development of energy-efficient MAC protocols. Overhead— associated with managing network functions, such as collision management, control packets, and listening to send/ resend—is a constant power drain. Contention-based MAC protocols, such as CSMA/CA (carrier sense multiple access/collision avoidance), require nodes to contend for access to the transmission medium and are therefore are less power-efficient due to that overhead. Scheduled-based protocols, such as TDMA, offer more predictable network behavior as each node has a transmission slot to transmit in. This results in lower overhead, lower power requirements, and the ability to switch sensors off between communications cycles. This off-on cycle is not without overhead, however, and needs to be balanced against the potential energy savings (Chin et al., 2012).

A variety of energy-efficient MAC protocols based on TDMA have been reported in the literature, such as using the frequency of the heartbeat to perform TDMA synchronization, avoiding the energy consumption associated with transmitting time synchronization beacons. In environments where the radio link quality is marginal or there is intermittent inference, the reliability of the packet transmission is related to packet size. Reducing the packet size can improve transmission reliability in fading environments. However, if the packet size is too small, excessive transmissions are required, resulting in energy inefficiency.

Other approaches to power management include policy-based methods such as *timeouts,* which are implemented in firmware. The sensor is automatically switched into low-power sleep mode if it is idle for a defined period of time. It "wakes up" from its sleep state to make measurements or send and receive transmissions before returning to its sleep state. This approach can be augmented with the addition of a tilt or vibration sensor for detecting movement or motion, which can be used to wake other subsystems that are maintained in a sleep state until required. Alternatively, acoustic or optical sensors (for example, near-infra red) can also be used as the triggering mechanism. The rendezvous approach, where sensor nodes are synchronized to periodically wake and communicate with each other, is also used in the sensor world. Similarly, asynchronous wakeup can be used to wake sensor nodes individually on a scheduled basis. The waking time for each sensor is designed to overlap sufficiently with neighboring nodes to enable the exchange of messages. Another method is topology control, where the power output of the radio is adjusted based on the known position of each node in the network. This can be used effectively in static networks, where the distance between the nodes does not change (Zheng et al., 2006).

Energy Harvesting

The operational lifespan of many sensors is based the availability of power. A variety of battery types are commonly used in sensors, ranging from standard alkaline to Li-ion/NiMH/Li-polymer. However, batteries have a finite energy capacity, and this limitation has generated significant interest in the use of energy-harvesting or energy-scavenging techniques to increase battery life by either recharging them on an on-going basis or at regular intervals, coupled with effective power management to maximize operational lifetime.

Alternatively, an energy-harvesting mechanism can replace a battery altogether, allowing the sensor to operate perennially. This can be thought of as an energy-neutral operation, as the harvesting node consumes only as much energy as the energy-harvesting source is generating (Kansal et al., 2006). The use of energy harvesting with wireless sensors is challenging, as sensors normally require power in the range of 1 to 100 milliwatts (depending on configuration and sensor types) when fully powered up. Current energy-harvesting technologies generally can't supply this level of power continuously.

To address this limitation, wireless sensor nodes often adopt an intermittent mode where the sensor remains in a deep sleep or standby mode between measurement cycles. An energy-harvesting mechanism, such as solar, charges a high-capacity energy storage device that can supply the short term high-energy output required during the wake cycle (Boisseau et al., 2012). A variety of methods have been utilized for energy harvesting. A summary of these methods with their respective advantages and disadvantages is presented in Table 3-3 (Gilbert et al., 2008)

(Chalasani et al., 2008). IDTechEx has estimated the market for energy-harvesting devices will exceed USD 4 billion in 2021, with healthcare and wellness providing substantial growth (Harrop et al., 2011).

Table 3-3. *Common Energy Harvesting Mechanisms for Sensors*

Source	Conversion Mechanism	Advantages	Disadvantages
Solar	Photo voltaic cell	Efficiency (up to 15mW/cm^2) Simple Cheap	Unpredictable source Can't power sensor directly Requires overcharge protection
Mechanical	Vibration Electrostatic Electromagnetic Piezoelectric Wind Fluid Flow Strain Piezoelectric Human body Breathing Blood pressure Kinetic, for example, walking	Predictable energy output Potentially high energy output Reliable Many devices enclosed – environmentally protected	Wear on parts may limit lifespan Piezoelectric materials used in some devices degrade over time; may, for example, become brittle Size can be an issue, particularly with electromagnetic devices Human body Biocompatibility Limited power output Limited practical operational duration
Thermal (Pyroelectric)	Thermogenerators Peltier element	No moving parts—longer lifespan Potential for human body-worn applications	Low energy—power output depends on thermal gradient Conversion efficiency High cost Low power output (40μW/cm^3) Limited usage due to high temperature gradient requirements
Biochemical	BioFuel cells redox reactions such as glucose/O$_2$	Implantable human applications Constant fuel source—implantable applications	Lifetime and reliability of biological components limitations Specialized applications only Not commercially available Sensitive to external environment

Energy sources can be characterized as either controllable or uncontrollable. A controllable source, such as the human body, can provide energy as required; while an uncontrollable source, such as wind, can be harvested only when it is available. Energy sources can also be characterized based on the source of power—for example, ambient (wind, solar, thermal) or human power (human motion) (Sudevalayam et al., 2011).

Microcontroller Software and Debugging

Reduced time to market and low development costs are key requirements in selecting a microcontroller. As discussed earlier, sensor platforms and prototyping kits enable rapid hardware development. An intuitive integrated development environment, familiar programming language, and availability of sample code and tutorials all facilitate rapid software development. Reductions in development cost can be achieved using free IDEs, such as the Arduino IDE, the MPLAB IDE (for PIC microcontrollers) and Eclipse (plus the Android SDK for Android devices). For complex applications, however, commercial IDEs that include optimized machine code generators and debug tools, such as Keil μVision (www.keil.com/uvision/), may provide time savings and prove less costly overall.

Programming a microcontroller requires two computers: a target computer (the microcontroller to be programmed) and a host computer (the PC used to develop the microcontroller software and send it to the target). Several types of software are required at various stages of the development process: editors, to create and edit code; compilers, to convert code to a machine-readable format; device-programming software, to download the machine code to the target; and a bootloader, to invoke the machine code on the target device. Of course, the compiled code, which is used to control the microcontroller, is also software.

This section covers the different types of software and their use during the software development lifecycle. It also describes the software and hardware debugging methods employed to test embedded applications.

IDEs

An IDE (as shown in Figure 3-10) is a desktop computer application that integrates the various software tools required to create, test, and deploy firmware onto the microcontroller. These tools include some or all of the following: editors, build tools (compilers or assemblers, and linkers), and debug tools (simulators and emulators).

Figure 3-10. *The Arduino IDE*

- A source code editor is a text editor designed specifically for editing source code. Although any text editor can be used to write and edit source code, source code editors are easier for programmers to use because they include features such as syntax highlighting, autocomplete, and bracket matching.

- A compiler is a computer program that evaluates and optimizes high-level source code, such as C, against the programming language's syntax. If the source code correctly follows the rules of the syntax, the compiler translates the source code into machine code and places it in an object file. The compilers in microcontroller IDEs are more accurately described as "cross compilers," because the code is compiled on one type of computer and deployed on another.

- An assembler translates low-level assembly code into machine code.

- A linker links the object file from the compiler to object files from other sources, including other compiled files, real-time operating system (RTOS) modules, and system libraries. The result is an executable file, called a hex file. In microcontroller IDEs, the linker is often part of the compiler rather than a standalone piece of software.

- Most modern MCUs support in-system programming (ISP), which allows the user to program the device in the circuit by connecting an adapter between the circuit board and the PC. The device-programming software is usually integrated into the IDE, but it can also be used as standalone software.

- The bootloader is a piece of software that resides in the ROM of the MCU and executes when it is started or reset. It is a key component in supporting the ISP features of an MCU.

The most common IDEs are the Arduino IDE, MPLAB for the PIC microcontroller (`www.microchip.com/pic`) and Keil μVision. Each of these IDEs offers a code editor, an integrated compiler and linker, and a device programmer. The Keil IDE also features debug and emulation tools and can be used to program 8051-based and ARM devices from various manufacturers.

Development Languages

The CPU can only understand and execute machine code, which consists of very simple instructions (opcodes) and data (operands) that must be processed. Machine code instructions are difficult to read and vary greatly among individual processors. Almost all MCU programs are written in assembly language or C, which are closer to natural language than obscure machine code. However, they still support key system functionality, such as access to registers. Java can also be used to program embedded devices, but this is less common.

- Assembly is a low-level language, in which each instruction corresponds to a single machine code instruction. Opcodes are described using an English word, such as *jump*, rather than a number. As with machine code, it is very closely coupled to an individual processor and produces very efficient code. However, it is slow and difficult to program.

- C (or variants of C including the Arduino programming language and nesC) is the most common programming language for microcontrollers. It provides all the features of a higher-level language while allowing the programmer to insert assembly statements if granular control is required. Modern C compilers generate efficient machine code for the MCU, without the programmer having to understand machine code. In many cases, this layer of abstraction from the MCU ensures that code can be recompiled and used for similar MCUs with minimal effort.

- nesC (network embedded systems C) is a C-variant language used to create real-time TinyOS applications. It consists of components that are wired together via their interfaces to create an application. Shimmer and TelosB motes are programmed using this language.

- Java is an interpreted object-orientated language and therefore requires a more powerful processor than 8-bit and 16-bit MCUs. However, it is becoming more widely used: Java is the main programming language for Android applications, and a Java runtime (Java ME Embedded) has been developed especially for ARM-based MCUs.

Testing Code

Debugging embedded systems requires different methods than debugging PC-based applications, because of the different peripherals available to each computer type. Embedded systems lack a mouse, keyboard, and monitor; however, they have easy access to LEDs, LCDs, and breakout pins, which can be used to provide debug information to the user. In-circuit emulation, background debug mode (BDM), and simulators are the most common methods for performing step-by-step debugging of the source code.

- *Line-by-line debugging*: ICE and BDM were described earlier: ICE physically replaces the target processor with a processor that emulates the target's functionality, while BDM uses the target processor to step through and test the code. Simulators model the behavior of the target microcontroller in software (and some simulators allow the programmer to model basic external events). However, simulators are not fast enough to replicate a microcontroller's real-time behavior, nor can they accurately model the behavior of external components. Simulators are most useful for evaluation of software, which does not use external peripherals, or for initial evaluation of software before debugging the hardware.

- *Verbose error messages*: The RS232 interface can be used to print error and debug messages from the microcontroller to the serial port. Data from the serial port can be entered and viewed on a terminal emulator on the PC. Verbose messages can also be printed to the microcontroller's LCD display, if one exists.

- *Pin debugging*: Setting or clearing a port pin is a quick and crude method for indicating that a certain point in code has been activated, and controlling the timing between events. Similarly, an LED can be set and cleared to provide a visual indication of the software status.

Summary

In this chapter we have described features and differences among smart sensors, sensor systems, and sensor platforms. We've also outlined the hardware and software components required to interface with sensors, build sensor systems, and integrate sensors into high-level systems or to display data to end users. Microcontrollers, the building blocks of low-cost sensor-based systems, have been described in detail, as were the internal and external communication protocols used to transfer data. Finally, we reviewed the software languages and development environments required to control a smart sensor and discussed various debug methods that are commonly used.

References

Huijsing, Johan H, "Smart Sensor Systems: Why? Where? How?," in *Smart Sensor Systems*, Meijer, Gerard C. M., Ed., New York, Wiley, 2008.

Mathas, Carolyn. "*Smart Sensors - Not Only Intelligent, but Adaptable*", Last Update: 2011, `http://www.digikey.com/us/en/techzone/sensors/resources/articles/intelligent-adaptable-smart-sensors.html`

PRWeb. "*Global Smart Sensors Market to Reach US$6.7 Billion by 2017, According to New Report by Global Industry Analysts, Inc.*", Last Update: 2012, `http://www.prweb.com/releases/smart_sensors/flow_pressure_sensors/prweb9251955.htm`

Córcoles, Emma P. and Martyn G. Boutelle, "Implantable Biosensors," in *Biosensors and Invasive Monitoring in Clinical Applications*, Springer International Publishing, 2013, pp. 21–41.

Meijer, Gerard, "Interface Electronics and Measurement Techniques for Smart Sensor Systems," in *Smart Sensor Systems*, Meijer, Gerard, Ed., Chichester, John Wiley & Sons, 2008, pp. 23–24.

Hunter, Gary W., Joseph R. Stetter, Peter J. Hesketh, and Chung-Chiun Liu, "Smart Sensor Systems", *Interface*, vol. 19 (4), 29–34, 2010.

Pecht, Michael G., *Prognostics and Health Management of Electronics*. Hoboken, New Jersey: Wiley, 2008.

Burns, Adrian, *et al.*, "SHIMMER™ – A Wireless Sensor Platform for Noninvasive Biomedical Research," *IEEE Sensors*, vol. 10 (9), pp. 1527–1534, 2010.

Hector, Jonathan. "*How to choose an in-circuit emulator*", Last Update: 2002, `http://eetimes.com/electronics-news/4134723/How-to-choose-an-in-circuit-emulator`

Lee, Kang, "A Smart Transducer Interface Standard for Sensors and Actuators," in *The Industrial Information Technology Handbook*, Zurawski, R., Ed., Boca Raton, FL, CRC Press, 2005, pp. 1–16.

Rouse, Margaret. "*Serial Peripheral Interface (SPI)*", Last Update: March 2011, `http://whatis.techtarget.com/definition/serial-peripheral-interface-SPI`

EE Hearld, "SPI Bus interface", `http://www.eeherald.com/section/design-guide/esmod12.html`, 2006.

Bates, Martin, "Sensor Interfacing," in *Interfacing PIC Controllers*, Oxford, Newnes, 2006, pp. 236–238.

Kester, Walt, "Sensor Signal Conditioning," in *Sensor Technology Handbook*, Wilson, Jon S., Ed., Burlington, MA, Elsevier, 2005, pp. 87–89.

Eliasson, Jens, Per Lindgren, and Jerker Delsing, "A Bluetooth-based Sensor Node for Low-Power Ad Hoc Networks," *Journal of Computers*, vol. 3 (5), pp. 1–10, 2008.

Lee, Jin-Shyan, Yu-Wei Su, and Chung-Chou Shen, "A Comparative Study of Wireless Protocols: Bluetooth, UWB, ZigBee, and Wi-Fi," presented at the 33rd Annual Conference of the IEEE Industrial Electronics Society (IECON), Taipei, Taiwan, 2007.

Yuan, Gao, *et al.*, "Low-Power Ultrawideband Wireless Telemetry Transceiver for Medical Sensor Applications," *Biomedical Engineering, IEEE Transactions on*, vol. 58 (3), pp. 768–772, 2011.

Win, Moe Z., Davide Dardari, Andreas F. Molisch, and Jinyun Zhange, "History and Applications of UWB," *Proceedings of the IEEE*, vol. 97 (2), pp. 198–204, 2009.

Bennett, Brian. "*The Power of Bluetooth 4.0: It'll change your life*", Last Update: March 2nd 2012, `http://news.cnet.com/8301-1035_3-57389687-94/the-power-of-bluetooth-4.0-itll-change-your-life/`

Marker, Ray. "*The current state of Bluetooth Smart/Low Energy in Sports Technology (and why it matters to you)*", Last Update: July 31st 2012, `http://www.dcrainmaker.com/2012/07/the-current-state-of-bluetooth-smartlow.html`

Higuera, Jorge E. and Jose Polo, "IEEE 1451 Standard in 6LoWPAN Sensor Networks Using a Compact Physical-Layer Transducer Electronic Datasheet," *Instrumentation and Measurement, IEEE Transactions on*, vol. 60 (8), pp. 2751–2758, 2011.

Jin Ho, Kim, Haw Rim, and Hong Choong Seon, "Development of a Framework to Support Network-based Mobility of 6LoWPAN Sensor Device for Mobile Healthcare System," in *Consumer Electronics (ICCE), 2010 Digest of Technical Papers International Conference on*, 2010, pp. 359–360.

Wireless Personal Area Network WPAN Working Group, "802.15.6-2012 - IEEE Standard for Local and Metropolitan Area Networks - Part 15.6: Wireless Body Area Networks", `http://standards.ieee.org/findstds/standard/802.15.6-2012.html`, 2012.

Wang, Jianqing and Qiong Wang, "Introduction to Body Area Communications," in *Body Area Communications: Channel Modeling, Communication Systems, and EMC*, Singapore, Malaysia Wiley-IEEE Press, 2012.

EnOcean. "*EnOcean Wireless Standard - First ISO/IEC wireless standard optimized for solutions with ultra-low power consumption and energy harvesting*", Last Update: 2012, `http://www.enocean.com/en/enocean-wireless-standard/`

Smith, Phil. "*Comparing Low-Power Wireless Technologies*", Last Update: 2012, `http://www.digikey.com/us/en/techzone/wireless/resources/articles/comparing-low-power-wireless.html`

Bindra, Ashok, "Medical Info-communications Signals an Era of Body Area Networking", *Microwaves and RF*, vol. 47, 10–14, 2008, `http://rfdesign.com/next_generation_wireless/short_range_wireless/0208RFDFeature1.pdf`

Toumaz. "*SensiumVitals*"', Last Update: 2013, `http://www.toumaz.com/toumaz-healthcare#.UoNbQ_nQCSp`

FitLinxx. "*BodyLAN Wireless Protocol*", Last Update: 2013, `http://www.fitlinxx.net/bodylan-wireless-protocol.htm`

Texas Instruments, "SimpliciTI™ - RF Made Easy", `http://www.ti.com/corp/docs/landing/simpliciTI/index.htm?DCMP=hpa_rf_general&HQS=NotApplicable+OT+simpliciti`, 2008.

Micrel. "*Introducing the RadioWire° MicrelNet™*", Last Update: 2012, `http://qwikradio.com/page.do?page=product-info/Micrelnet/Micrelnet.shtml`

Microchip. "*MiWi™ Protocol*", Last Update: 2013, `http://www.microchip.com/pagehandler/en-us/technology/personalareanetworks/technology/home.html`

Lin, Xiao-Hui, Yu-Kwong Kwok, and Hui Wang, "Energy-Efficient Resource Management Techniques in Wireless Sensor Networks," in *Guide to Wireless Sensor Networks*, Misra, Sudip, Subhas Chandra Misr, and Isaac Woungang, Eds., London, Springer-Verlag, 2009, pp. 439–468.

Chin, Craig A., Garth V. Crosby, Tirthankar Ghosh, and Renita Murimi, "Advances and Challenges of Wireless Body Area Networks for Healthcare Applications," in *Computing, Networking and Communications (ICNC), 2012 International Conference on*, 2012, pp. 99–103.

Zheng, Rong, Jennifer C. Hou, and Ning Li, "Power Management and Power Control in Wireless Networks," in *Ad Hoc and Sensor Networks*, Pang, Yi and Yang Xiao, Eds., New York, Nova Science, 2006, pp. 1–30.

Kansal, Aman, Jason Hsu, Mani Srivastava, and Vijay Raghunathan, "Harvesting Aware Power Management for Sensor Networks," in *43rd Annual Design Automation Confernce* San Francisco, California, 2006, pp. 651–656.

Boisseau, Sebastien and Ghislain Despesse. "*Energy Harvesting, Wireless Sensor Networks & Opportunities for Industrial Applications*", Last Update: 27th Febuary, 2012, `http://www.eetimes.com/design/smart-energy-design/4237022/Energy-harvesting--wireless-sensor-networks---opportunities-for-industrial-applications?pageNumber=1`

Gilbert, James M. and Farooq Balouchi, "Comparison of Energy Harvesting Systems for Wireless Sensor Networks," *International Journal of Automation and Computing*, vol. 5 (4), pp. 334–347, 2008.

Chalasani, Sravanthi and James M. Conrad, "A Survey of Energy Harvesting Sources for Embedded Systems," in *IEEE Southeastcon 2008*, pp. 442–447.

Harrop, Peter and Raghu Das, "Energy Harvesting and Storage for Electronic Devices 2011–2021", IDTechEx, Cambridge, UK, 2011.

Sudevalayam, Sujesha and Purusgottam Kulkarni, "Energy Harvesting Sensor Nodes: Survey and Implications," *IEEE Communications Surveys & Tutorials,* vol. 13 (3), pp. 443–461, 2011.

■ ■ ■

CHAPTER 4

Sensor Network Topologies and Design Considerations

Connecting the devices in our lives, from toasters to fitness devices, to each other and to the Internet is the fundamental principle of the Internet of Things (IoT). Enabling this connectivity requires at the very least a direct connection to the Internet, but often data is routed and processed at a local network stage before being passed to the Internet. Some sensor networks are not connected to the Internet at all, and their data is simply aggregated and displayed at a local aggregation point, such as a smartphone or PC. The topology of the sensor network depends largely on the overall system application: a personal area network may simply stream data from all sensors to a single central aggregator (star topology), whereas a home monitoring network may use a self-healing mesh topology. The different sensor topologies and the applications to which they are most suited are discussed in this chapter.

As more and more devices are connected to the Internet, big data challenges emerge: volume, velocity, variety, and veracity. Sensor data is cheap to generate, but expensive to move, store, and manage. Not all data is useful. The sensor network, or more specifically the aggregator on the sensor network, has a key role in aggregating data: identifying which data should be presented to the user or a remote network and which data should be discarded. The earlier data is processed in the sensor lifecycle, the cheaper the overall system will be. Increasingly capable, low-power, low-cost devices are being developed for this edge-processing role. We discuss these aggregation devices in detail in this chapter.

Managing large numbers of different sensors across a sensor network is a challenging task, particularly if the sensors are deployed in remote locations. Cloud-based sensor-network management tools are becoming increasingly popular. These tools provide real-time network status information, the ability to remotely change a sensor's configuration, and basic data storage and visualization. Many popular cloud-based services can be quickly integrated with popular sensor platforms, such as Arduino. Therefore, they are becoming a popular tool for the maker community and IoT enthusiasts. The most popular sensor-network management tools and their sensor interfaces are discussed and compared at the end of this chapter.

Sensor Network Components

A sensor network consists of a group of smart sensors that are wired or wirelessly connected to another smart sensor or to a common aggregator. In networking terminology, each component in the network that has a communications module is called a *node*. A node that generates data is called a *source node*, while a node that requests data is called a *sink* or *sink node*. A sink can be another sensor node on the network, a gateway to another larger network, or a local aggregator. A source node can report routine data, an alert, or maintenance data. The sensor network performs two key tasks: data gathering and data dissemination. *Data gathering* is term used to describe the capture and transfer of data from each sensor node to a sink. The source sends data to the sink periodically or on demand, and the sink processes the data. *Data dissemination* is the term used to describe the process for routing queries or data around the sensor network. Data dissemination is a two-step process. In the first step, the sink node describes the data it is interested in and broadcasts this descriptor, which is called "interest," across the network. Each node maintains an interest cache of all data to be reported. In the second step, the nodes that have data of interest send this data to the sink.

Sensor networks can consist of a number of the same types of sensors distributed over a region, providing the same sensor data (a homogenous sensor network); or they may involve a number of different sensors (a heterogeneous sensor network), which provide different sensor data to the system. Homogenous sensor networks can be applied to extend the sensing region of a sensor. For example, a network of weather sensors distributed across a city can provide richer information than a single weather sensor placed in a solitary location, and could even be applied to study microclimates across the city. In this scenario, a homogenous network, sensing the same range of target parameters over a different region can also offer a degree of fault tolerance, as spurious data from a single sensor in the network could be identified by comparing it to data from neighboring sensors. This spatial sensor redundancy can also be applied, along with prediction-monitoring techniques, to reduce unnecessary transmission of events, thus making the sensor network more energy-efficient (Hongbo, 2011). Another application of homogenous networks could be using the same sensor type to measure different aspects of a system. For example, a personal area network, in which an inertial sensor is connected to each limb, would produce different data from each limb. In this scenario, the sensor network can capture and synchronize data from each sensor, allowing the end user to examine the motion of each limb in comparison with the others for a given period of time.

Heterogeneous sensor networks integrate data from different sensor types into the system. The different data sources are typically used for a common purpose. A home alarm system is a typical example of a heterogeneous network. These systems feature magnetic switches to detect the opening and closing of windows and doors and passive infrared sensors to detect motion. The network may also contain an actuator, such as a siren, to raise an alert if a home intrusion is detected. Although the sensing modality differs in all these devices, the purpose of each device is the same—to detect an intrusion.

Wireless sensor networks (WSNs) are a subset of sensor networks, and consist of a sink node, which is usually called a "base station," and a number of wireless, battery-powered sensor nodes. The base station typically has significantly higher processing and data storage capabilities than the other nodes on the network. A base station is often AC-powered, but this is not always the case. A smartphone can act as a base station in a wireless personal area network (WPAN) despite being battery-powered; the smartphone will have significantly more battery power than the sensor nodes in the network and will be regularly charged. The lifetime of the sensor network depends on how well the energy consumption of the sensing and processing of the communications components of the WSN node are balanced against the battery life. Selection of low-power radios and efficient network protocols and messaging are key factors in extending the lifetime of the WSN.

Sensor Nodes

A sensor node is a smart sensor that is capable of gathering sensory information, performing some processing, and communicating with other connected nodes on the network. Smart sensors are discussed in detail in Chapter 3. Sensor platforms such as Arduino allow users to connect sensor and communications modules to a base platform. The ability to seamlessly interchange hardware radio modules means users can change not only their communication protocol but also the network topology employed. For example, replacing a Wi-Fi module with an XBee 868 module allows the user to replace a star-based network with a self-healing mesh network that has a wider sensing range.

Aggregators, Base Stations, and Gateways

Sensor nodes require a collection point where the data can be processed, stored, or forwarded onward to other networks via longer-range and higher-throughput wired or wireless communications mechanisms. A variety of terms are used to describe various data collection and translation points in sensor networks. Computing devices, such as M2M devices or PCs, can be configured to act as aggregators, gateways, bridges, base stations, or coordinators, which can lead to confusion in the meanings of these terms. The complexity of the network architecture or the domain in which they're applied can also influence the term used to describe a particular function. In an attempt to clarify, we offer the following definitions:

> *Routers* forward data packets between two or more computer networks.

> *Gateways* perform protocol translation between different networks. A gateway can operate at any network layer, and, unlike a router or a switch, a gateway can communicate using more than one protocol. PCs, servers, and M2M devices can function as gateways, although they are most commonly found in routers. In a sensor network, a gateway is responsible for interfacing the data from the sensor nodes to another network that uses a different protocol, and delivering commands back from that network to the nodes. Gateways work on OSI layers 4-7.

> *Bridges* connect two or more network segments along the data link layer (OSI layer 2) to create an aggregate network.

> *Aggregators* are sink nodes, which capture raw data from the nodes in the sensor network and reduce the overall size of the data by aggregating redundant or correlated data. This decreases the volume of network traffic and the energy consumption of the system, thus reducing cost.

> In WSNs, a *base station* is a node that has far more computational, energy, and communication resources than the other sensor nodes. A base station typically acts as a gateway between sensor nodes and the end user as its role is to forward data from the WSN to a server.

> In a Zigbee network, a ***coordinator node*** is responsible for managing the sensor network. Specifically, the coordinator acts at the network layer to select the frequency channel to be used by the network, starts the network, and allows other devices to join the network. The coordinator can also provide message routing, security management, and other services.

Machine-to-Machine Devices

Machine-to-machine (M2M) devices are networked devices that can exchange information and perform actions without the manual assistance of humans. An M2M system includes sensors, a back-haul communications link, such as cellular or Wi-Fi, and application software, which can automatically interpret data and make decisions. M2M systems are often used for remote monitoring or automation tasks in which sensor inputs and the decision tree are clearly defined. A common example of an M2M system is a vending machine, which can alert a distributor when a particular item is running low. Initially used only in scientific, engineering, and manufacturing domains, M2M technology is becoming increasingly relevant to end users as more and more home devices have network connectivity and open data interfaces. M2M technology is now found in heating units, water meters, and even in coffee makers (www.nespresso.com/pro/aguila/#/aguila). Devices with M2M communications capabilities are often marketed to end users as "smart" devices.

There is currently no standard M2M radio or messaging protocol, although many de facto standards, such as MQ Telemetry Transport (MQTT) messaging, are beginning to emerge. As the IoT concept continues to grow and M2M becomes more pervasive, it is widely expected that vendors will have to agree on standards for device-to-device communications.

In recent years, the number of M2M devices has dramatically increased. They can be sold as components in an end-to-end solution or as standalone devices that must be configured by the user. An M2M device is simply a piece of hardware that can be configured by software to operate as part of an M2M solution. The software components of an end-to-end solution are discussed in more detail later in this chapter.

Proprietary M2M solutions

Proprietary solutions, such as the Libelium Meshlium M2M device (`www.libelium.com/products/meshlium`), provide out-of-the-box connectivity between a manufacturer's sensor solution and its cloud solution. Proprietary solutions provide a quick and easy method to transfer data from predefined sensors to a predefined cloud. The software in a proprietary solution is typically optimized to interface with the manufacturer's own sensors using a predefined messaging protocol over a predefined radio. It is usually difficult to interface sensors from another manufacturer with the system. The key advantage of a proprietary solution is ease of use for the end user, who can typically configure a sensor network using a web interface on the M2M device or a cloud solution. Preexisting knowledge of a sensor type and messaging protocol allows the manufacturer to add advanced features, such as over-the-air programming, to the system's management suite without the complexity of supporting numerous device types.

Smartphones

Smartphones are discussed in Chapter 2 as sensor platforms, due to their integrated sensors and processing and communication abilities. However, smartphones can also act as M2M devices that can aggregate data from external sensors and other data sources, store and analyze data, and interface with cloud-based services. The key advantage of smartphones as M2M devices is the number of sensor devices available to connect to them. Smartphone "app-enabled accessories," such as smart watches or blood-pressure monitors, can interface with a smartphone over a physical or wireless connection using a messaging protocol defined by the operating system. The Apple App Store and Google Play provide intuitive access to a repository of software apps that can interface with these sensors and actuators. These apps are proprietary software written by the sensor manufacturer or a third party and are designed to interpret and process data from a proprietary sensor. Apps may also upload data to proprietary cloud-based storage for long-term tracking. Although the processing and communications specifications of smartphones and traditional M2M devices are fundamentally very similar, they differ greatly in their application software. A traditional M2M device is typically a headless device that can operate with little or no user interaction for years at a time. It has a single purpose: to aggregate data from numerous sources into a single database for analysis and decision-making and trigger the appropriate response when an event is detected. Although a smartphone can perform the same data capture, processing, and decision-making tasks as an M2M device, it is primarily a phone and an entertainment device. The processing, data storage, and display features of each app are independent of the processing, data storage, and display features of other apps on the device. This siloing of data, though important for security purposes, is inefficient and makes it difficult for the user to make interesting correlations between data captured from different apps.

Traditional M2M Platforms

There has been a rapid increase in the number of low-power M2M-capable devices in recent years. ARM-based devices, such as the Raspberry Pi (`aspberrypi.org`) and BeagleBoard (`beagleboard.org`), have been widely used by the maker community as M2M devices for monitoring and actuation projects. These boards can be interfaced with sensors and actuators using the onboard general-purpose input/output (GPIO) headers, and a hardware ecosystem has developed to create sensor shields for these devices. The USB interface on the board can be used to add radio dongles that interface with wireless sensors or provide wireless Internet connectivity over Wi-Fi or general packet radio service (GPRS). The Intel Galileo (`arduino.cc/en/ArduinoCertified/IntelGalileo`), shown in Figure 4-1, is a 32-bit microcontroller that is hardware and software pin-compatible with the Arduino 1.0 pinout. It is therefore compatible with the hundreds of existing Arduino shields and can be programmed using the Arduino IDE. The Galileo board also features two USB ports and a full-sized mini-PCI Express slot, which can be used to add Wi-Fi, Bluetooth, GSM cards, or a solid-state drive. Both the ARM and Intel-based devices run embedded Linux (eLinux) distributions. An eLinux distribution, such as Raspbian or Yocto, is becoming the de facto standard for M2M operating systems. It provides a familiar interface to users who are already familiar with Linux on PCs and servers and allows users to leverage thousands of existing free and open source packages for networking, multimedia, and data processing.

Figure 4-1. *The Intel Galileo board (photo courtesy of Intel)*

The RaspberryPi, BeagleBoard, and Intel Galileo are currently used only by hobbyists and are not part of any integrated device-to-cloud solution, although platform-as-service providers such as Xively (`xively.com`) and Device Cloud (`etherios.com/products/devicecloud`) supply APIs to interface these devices to their cloud storage platforms. The Kontron M2M Smart Services Developer Kit is a commercial solution that includes an Intel Atom-based M2M device, a Wind River IDP operating system, and Cumulocity Device Cloud. The Kontron M2M device has integrated Wi-Fi, 802.15.4, and USB interfaces to connect to sensors and Wi-Fi, Ethernet, and GPRS to communicate with the device cloud.

Sensor Network Topologies

In chapter 3 we looked at the architectures of sensors, smart sensors, and sensor systems. They typically combine sensing, processing, communication, and power subsystems in a single integrated system. While sensors can be used in isolation for specific applications, multiple sensors are commonly integrated into higher-level topologies to deliver real world applications. These topologies can vary in complexity from a single node connected to an aggregator to fully meshed networks distributed over a large geographical area. Sensor topologies can also be described as having either a flat or hierarchical architecture. In a flat (peer-to-peer) architecture, every node in the network (sink node and sensor node) has the same computational and communication capabilities. In a hierarchical architecture, the nodes operate in close proximity to their respective cluster heads. Hence, nodes with lower energy levels simply capture the required raw data and forward it to their respective cluster heads. Usually the cluster heads possess more processing and storage capacity than any ordinary sensor node. The most common forms of network topologies are shown in Figure 4-2. Sensor networks that are physically wired together commonly use star, line, or bus topologies. Wireless sensors networks are often built using star, tree, or mesh topology configurations:

> ***Point-to-point topology*** links two endpoints, as shown in Figure 4-2 (a). This topology can be permanent or switched. A permanent point-to-point topology is a hardwired connection between two points. A switched connection is a point-to-point connection that can be moved between different end nodes. This topology is commonly used in many of the applications described in Chapters 9–11, where a single sensor is used with a smartphone or tablet acting as a data aggregator

> ***Bus topology*** is a configuration in which each node is connected to a shared communication bus, as shown in Figure 4-2 (b). A signal is transmitted in both directions along the bus until it reaches its intended destination. Bus networks must include a collision avoidance system to resolve issues when two nodes simultaneously send out data on the bus. Bus networks are simple and easy to install. However, there is a single point of failure: if the bus fails, the entire network fails.

Linear topology is a two-way link between one node and the next node, as shown in Figure 4-2 (c). There are two terminating nodes at the end of the network that have a single connection to a nearby node, and all other nodes are connected to two other nodes. In this topology, the nodes depend on each other to propagate a message to the next node. If a node fails, any nodes connected to that node are disconnected from the network.

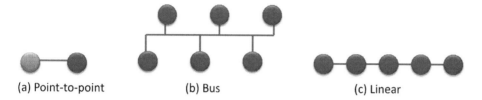

(a) Point-to-point   (b) Bus   (c) Linear

Figure 4-2. *Graphical representation of (a) point-to-point, (b) bus, and (c) linear network topologies*

Ring topology is a network set up in a circular fashion, as shown in Figure 4-3 (a). It is similar to a linear topology, in which the end nodes are connected to each other. In this configuration, each node connects to exactly two other nodes and data flows in one direction from the source to each node until it finds the intended recipient. This topology is easy to install and reconfigure. However, it is costly to manage as a ring network can be disturbed by the failure of a single node. Many networks add a second communication ring that can transmit data in the opposite direction to overcome this issue. This topology was a common way to link small offices and schools, but is rarely used anymore.

Star topology consists of a single "central node," such as a hub or a switch that every node in the network connects to, as shown in Figure 4-3 (b). This topology is easy to design, implement, and extend. All data traffic flows through the central node; therefore, an intelligent central node is required. Failure of this node will result in failure of the entire network. The star network topology is one of the most common sensor network topologies. A wireless personal area network (WPAN), consisting of a smartphone connected to several wireless sensors, is a common example of this topology.

Tree topology is a hierarchy of nodes in which the highest level of the hierarchy is a single "root node," and this node is connected to one or many nodes in the level below, as shown in Figure 4-3 (c). A tree topology can contain many levels of nodes. The processing and power in nodes increase as the data moves from the branches of the tree toward the root node, allowing data to be processed close to where it is generated. This topology is scalable and the simple structure makes it easy to identify and isolate faults. Tree networks become increasingly difficult to manage as they get larger.

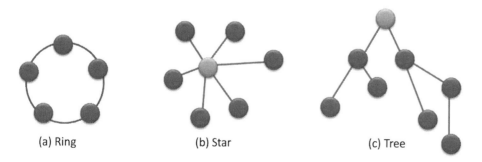

(a) Ring   (b) Star   (c) Tree

Figure 4-3. *Graphical representation of (a) ring, (b) star, and (c) tree network topologies*

Mesh topology nodes disseminate their own data and also act as relays to propagate the data from other nodes. There are two forms of mesh topology: a ***partially connected mesh***, in which some nodes are connected to more than one other node, shown in Figure 4-4 (a); and a ***fully connected mesh***, in which every node is connected to every other node in the mesh, shown in Figure 4-4 (b). Mesh networks are self-healing, as data can be routed along a different path if a node fails. Fully connected mesh networks are not suitable for large sensor networks as the number of connections required become unmanageable. Partially connected mesh networks provide the self-healing capability of a fully connected network without the connection overhead. Mesh topologies are most commonly found in wireless networking.

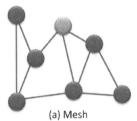
(a) Mesh

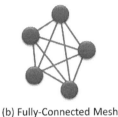
(b) Fully-Connected Mesh

Figure 4-4. *Graphical representation of (a) partially connected and (b) fully connected mesh network topologies*

Sensor networks can also be described by their logical topology—the method they use to move data around the network. There are two types of logical topology: shared media and token-based. In the shared media topology, all nodes can access the transport media when they want. This can lead to collisions, which must be managed by a collision-avoidance protocol. This logical topology is used in bus, star, or hybrid physical topology networks, due to their shared data bus or shared node. In a token-based logical protocol, a token is passed around the network. If a node wishes to send data, it must get the token from the network. When the data arrives at its destination, the token is released and continues travelling around the network. The token method is most useful in a ring-based topology.

Sensor Network Applications

In the application domain, sensor networks are more commonly described by their application type than their network or logical topology. For example, a personal area network (PAN) transfers personal data, can be a star network or a point-to-point network, and can use any of a number of low-power, short-range radios to communicate. This section describes the most common applications of sensor networks in the health, wellness, and environmental-monitoring domains.

Personal Area Networks

Personal area networks connect computing devices, such as laptops, tablets, or smartphones, to each other or to other devices in proximity. These devices can be connected using wired (USB/serial cable) or wireless (infrared, Bluetooth, Bluetooth LE) interfaces. The data exchanged between devices on a PAN are typically of a personal nature (photos, files). It is therefore important to have some form of basic security to prevent unauthorized use of the network. Wireless personal area networks (WPANs) were originally developed as a cable replacement technology for personal electronic devices. WPANs can be categorized into one of three broad categories, according to their data throughput and power consumption (Misic et al., 2008):

> ***High data rate WPANs***: Real-time multimedia applications based on IEEE 802.15.3 (the IEEE standard for multimedia streaming over wireless personal area networks). The standard supports up to 245 wireless fixed and portable devices at speeds up to 55Mbps over distances up to 100 meters.

Medium data rate WPANs: The IEEE 802.15.1 Bluetooth standard was designed to be a cable replacement for consumer devices. Bluetooth supports data rates up to 3Mbps. This standard has been widely adopted for sensor-based WPAN applications.

Low data rate WPANs: These networks can be based on either Bluetooth or 802.15.4, which support data rates up to 250 Kbps.

The terms body area network (BAN) or wireless body area network (WBAN) are often used interchangeably with WPAN. WBANs are built on WPAN technologies to specifically implement communications on, near, or around the human body, as shown in Figure 4-5. A WBAN can include a number of sensor types depending on the requirements of the application. Wireless body area networks typically integrate pedometers, heart rate and respiration monitors, and so forth (see Chapters 9 and 10) with a smartphone or computing device. WBANs provide greater flexibility than wired PANs. This is particularly useful in diagnostic applications, where extended monitoring is required. WBANs are also very useful for supporting diagnostic protocols in which the sensors must not impact or limit patient performance during the course of a test. Smart clothing, which integrates sensors into clothing and textiles, provides accurate data as it is in direct contact with most body skin surface. Moreover, smart clothing is generally noninvasive and has minimal impact on the wearer; therefore, it is ideal for extended ambulatory health-monitoring applications (Fabrice et al., 2005). The use of sensors for smart clothing is discussed in more detail in Chapter 10.

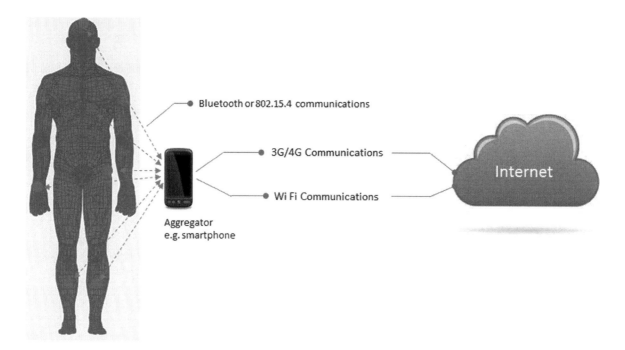

Figure 4-5. *Wireless body area network*

The FCC has approved a specific frequency for the implementation of medical body area network (MBAN) systems. Devices communicating on this protected spectrum allocation (between 2360–2400 MHz) experience less interference from ubiquitous unlicensed radio devices, such as Bluetooth, Zigbee, or Wi-Fi.

Ambient/Pervasive Home Sensor Networks

In the near future, homes will contain distributed networks of intelligent devices that will transparently sense the user and adapt the environment in an intelligent, personalized manner. To achieve this goal, each home must contain a large-scale distributed network of sensors, actuators, and display devices. This will require an intelligent backend, which can not only react to real-time events but also predict upcoming events and act accordingly. A simple example of pervasive sensing is a bed sensor that detects whether someone wakes in the middle of the night and activates low-level lighting along the path to the bathroom to ensure that he doesn't trip in the dark.

There are numerous challenges in implementing a pervasive sensor network, not the least of which are data interference, data mining, and data modeling. From a sensing and networking perspective, the communications protocol is a key question. Should all nodes in the home use the same Zigbee or Z-wave communication protocol? If so, an industry protocol must be defined to ensure that consumers have a wide range of sensors that can use that protocol. Alternatively, should the house be able to adapt to different communications protocols and allow wearable devices to seamlessly join the home network and upload their data to it? The communication network of a ubiquitous home system should meet certain requirements. In the first place it should support interoperability, so terminals are easy to add, replace, or remove. The sensor nodes must be self-describing and require minimal configuration by the user to install.

Wide Area Networks

A wide area network (WAN) is a network that covers a broad area (for example, any telecommunications network that links across metropolitan, regional, or national boundaries) using private or public network transports. Business and government entities utilize WANs to relay data among employees, clients, buyers, and suppliers from various geographical locations. In essence, this mode of telecommunication allows a business to effectively carry out its daily function regardless of location. The Internet can be considered a WAN as well, and is used by businesses, governments, organizations, and individuals for almost any purpose imaginable. WANs can be thought of as computer networking technologies used to transmit data over long distances, and between different local area networks (LANs), metropolitan area networks (MANs), and other localized computer networking architectures. This distinction stems from the fact that common LAN technologies operating at Layers 1 or 2 (such as the usual forms of Ethernet or Wi-Fi) are often geared towards physically localized networks, and thus can't transmit data over long distances. WANs do not just necessarily connect physically disparate LANs. A campus area network (CAN), for example, may have a localized backbone of a WAN technology, which connects different LANs within a campus. This could be to facilitate higher bandwidth applications or provide better functionality for users in the CAN.

WANs are used to connect LANs and other types of networks, so that users and computers in one location can communicate with users and computers in other locations (see Figure 4-6). Many WANs are built for one particular organization and are private. Others, built by Internet service providers, provide connections from an organization's LAN to the Internet. WANs are often built using leased lines. At each end of the leased line, a router connects the LAN on one side with a second router within the LAN on the other. Leased lines can be very expensive. Instead of using leased lines, WANs can also be built using less costly circuit-switching or packet-switching methods. Network protocols, including TCP/IP, deliver transport and addressing functions. Protocols including packet over SONET/SDH, MPLS, ATM, and frame relay are often used by service providers to deliver the links that are used in WANs. X.25 was an important early WAN protocol, and is often considered to be the "grandfather" of frame relay as many of the underlying protocols and functions of X.25 are still in use today (with upgrades) by the frame relay protocol.

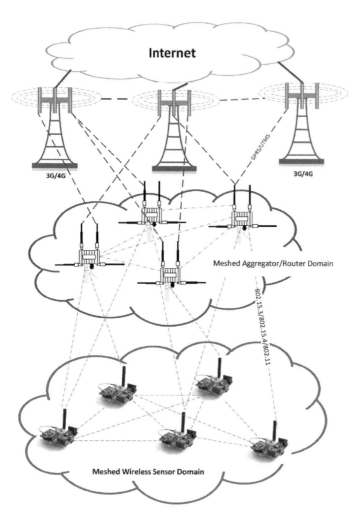

Figure 4-6. *A wide area wireless sensor network*

Sensor Network Features and Challenges

Software is pervasive at all levels of a sensor network, and the complexity of the software varies depending on which level of the sensor network the software is running and the capabilities of the microprocessor on that device. A solar-powered, wireless, environmental sensor node may simply capture data from the sensor, perform simple processing, and transmit to a higher-capability M2M device according to a predefined messaging protocol. An M2M device can aggregate data from multiple sensor nodes, store the data, perform more complex processing, and transmit data to another M2M device or a cloud server for additional aggregation and processing. Application services display the data from the aggregation devices on a computer application, web page, or smartphone app. Although the complexity of the software and the capability of the processor vary greatly at each level of a sensor network, the software on each device in the sensor network hierarchy contains the following features (Figure 4-7):

  Communications: Each device has the ability to transfer data to other devices in the sensor network hierarchy. The lowest order sink nodes in the network are usually wireless and battery-powered and must therefore implement a very low-power radio protocol. The software on sink nodes must manage power consumption by powering the radio off when the node is not transmitting. Aggregation devices, such as M2M devices or smartphones, are typically AC powered or regularly charged. These devices usually feature one or more radios to communicate with the sensor network and at least one method to backhaul the data to the Internet. The software on an aggregation device must be able to manage data transmitted over multiple radios. An application device can be an Internet-enabled device that interfaces with the aggregation device's API over the Internet, or the application and aggregation software may both reside on a single device, such as a smartphone.

Messaging: The traditional way to send a message between two devices is to agree on a message protocol and transfer data between the devices according to that protocol. If a different device type is added to the network, a new message protocol must be defined, and the gateway must interpret both protocols. This method is inefficient and costly, as it transmits data regardless of whether the gateway device is interested in the data. It is also not scalable to create a new protocol for each new device type. A number of protocols have been developed to address these inefficiencies and enable scalability. MQTT (`mqtt.org`), a lightweight publish/subscribe messaging transport, is becoming the de facto M2M connectivity standard for IoT and low-power or low-bandwidth sensor networks. All messages are sent to an MQTT message broker, which distributes messages to clients that have declared an interest in the message topic. The ability to subscribe to messages saves both processing and transport costs.

Processing: Data transmission and data storage are costly at every stage of a sensor network. It is therefore vital that sensor data is processed and reduced as close to where it is generated as possible. The processing capability of a device is dependent on the microprocessor and power constraints of the device. A low-power edge node on a wireless network may have limited processing capability but may perform basic processing, such as calculating the mean to reduce the volume of data to be transmitted. M2M devices are more powerful devices, capable of analyzing data from multiple sources, inferring trends and events from the data, and deciding which data can be discarded. In many M2M monitoring applications, the status of a system may be stable for several hours or days, so all data captured from these devices may be discarded. If an event is detected, the data used to generate that event can be held by the M2M device for additional analysis by a higher-capability device. The processing and data storage capabilities offered by cloud services allow the performance of complex analytics on big data using tools such as hadoop (`hadoop.apache.org`). Big data analytics and data visualization are discussed in more detail in Chapter 5.

Storage: The memory required on a smart sensor device is dependent on the sensor application. A sensor node in a WBAN that continually transmits raw data to a smartphone device requires minimal data storage. But a 3-lead electrocardiogram (ECG) Holter monitor, which captures data at 256Hz, requires significant storage to capture data for up to 48 hours. Smart sensors rarely contain the memory or processing capability to maintain an embedded database. Therefore, data is typically stored as flat files in the smart sensor's data memory or on an SD card. M2M devices have sufficient storage and processing capability to host an embedded transactional database such as Sqlite (`sqlite.org`). Most eLinux distributions contain the Sqlite application or at least the ability to download the software in a single command. The Sqlite database can be accessed natively on the console or using a Python, C++, or Java application library. The eLinux operating system and associated programming languages also contain libraries to query or write data to remote databases on other devices using SQL statements. There are many software options for data storage in the cloud, ranging from MySQL (`mysql.com`) for managing small to medium datasets, to distributed databases such as Cassandra (`cassandra.apache.org`) or MongoDB (`mongodb.org`) for managing "big data." The data in the databases can be queried or updated from the application device through APIs.

Manageability: Device manageability is one of the most critical tasks in a sensor network. The sensor network manager must be able to remotely configure the sensors in his or her network, upgrade software, run diagnostics, and be alerted if a sensor is unresponsive. A sensor network that can't be remotely managed is a non-scalable sensor network. A number of cloud-based services, such as Xively and Device Cloud, have emerged in recent years, to provide cloud-based device manageability. Both services offer libraries that can be installed on an IP-addressable sensor or gateway device, a method to register new devices on the cloud-based management console, and a manageability console that allows the sensor network manager to view status and remotely configure the devices on the network. These services also provide basic data storage, basic data analytics capabilities, and APIs for application devices and services to interface to the data and the network.

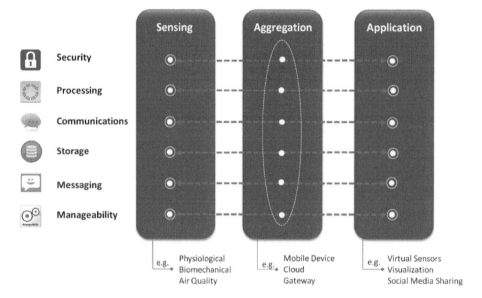

Figure 4-7. *Functional representation of software components in a sensor network*

Security

Security is a key requirement for many sensor applications. This is particularly true where the sensor must collect and forward sensitive health data. For wireless sensors, the question of whether someone can intercept the data is never far away. An in-depth analysis of sensor security is beyond the scope of this book, and many excellent texts deal with that topic in great detail. We will look at the key areas relevant to our application domains. Sensors have certain key challenges with respect to security as they are normally resource-constrained devices: they have limited computation, memory, and power resources, and limited communication speed and bandwidth.

Sensors can be used to provide security in a system by identifying individuals. This form of sensing is known as biometrics. In biometric security approaches, unique characteristics of individuals, such as the electrical characteristics of their hearts, can be used to identify them. This form of security is starting to appear in consumer devices, such as fingerprint identification on laptops and smartphones. In this way, sensors can be used to secure access to other sensor data sets.

Key Security Goals

The goal of security in a sensor network is to protect both the individual sensor node and the network from malicious attacks that may emerge either internally or externally. The key security requirements that are important in helping to maintain the integrity of a network are as follows:

> ***Data confidentiality***: This is normally the highest priority goal, and focuses on making the sensor inaccessible to unauthorized users through activities such as eavesdropping. This is particularly important for applications that utilize multiple sensor streams, such as WBANs. Attackers can infer information about an individual by correlating the data streams. The most common approach to protect the data is to use ciphers to encrypt the data.

> ***Data integrity***: The focus is on ensuring the data received has not been altered in any way, either by malicious action or by accidental communication errors during the transmission process. Integrity-checking is typically implemented by cryptographic hashes that are similar to cyclic redundancy checks (CRC). Common hashes include MD5 and SHA.

> ***Authentication***: Authentication enables either the sensor node or the aggregators to ensure the identity of the sensor or aggregator it is communicating with. Various mechanisms can be used for authentication, including the exchange of authentication keys or digital signatures. These approaches allow a party to prove its identity. They also protect against forgery or masquerading.

> ***Non-repudiation***: Non-repudiation ensures that a sensor node can't deny sending a message it previously sent. Digital signatures combined with public key infrastructures are a common mechanism for implementing non-repudiation.

> ***Authorization***: Authorization ensures that only approved nodes can access network services or specific destinations.

> ***Freshness***: Freshness-checking ensures that sensor data messages are current, ordered, and unduplicated. From a security perspective, this prevents the replay of old messages in an attack. Freshness is normally implemented through the use of sequence numbers and timestamps in the packets transmitted by the sensor.

Attacks on Sensor Networks

The key security issue for most sensors is a malicious attack. Wireless sensor networks are vulnerable to attacks such as message spoofing or message replays. Attacks can be categorized as either internal or external. An external attack can be either active or passive (Hongbo, 2011). Attacks can also be classified based on the network layer the attack attempts to exploit.

In a passive attack, unauthorized eavesdropping or listening to sensor messages occurs. This form of attack can be thwarted using encryption. An active attack on a network aims to disrupt the normal function of the network. Attacks using a denial-of-service (DoS) approach are commonly employed. Attacks of this type include signal jamming and repetitive queries to drain the sensor's battery (denial-of-sleep attack). Many attacks of this nature can be prevented with robust authentication mechanisms. Jamming is generally addressed through the use of spread-spectrum or frequency-hopping communications such as Bluetooth. Other forms of external attack include tampering, resulting in the physical capture of the sensor node. While it can difficult to prevent physical interference with sensors nodes, the nodes can react to the detection of tampering by erasing cryptographic keys and firmware/ programs from system memory (Chaos Computer Club, 2013).

An internal attack occurs when an attacker compromises the security of an individual sensor node and uses that node to disrupt or prevent the network from any useful function. Common attacks of this nature include Sybil, node-replication attack, Hello flood attack, selective forwarding, and sinkhole attack / black holes (Serbanati et al., 2011).

Security Approaches

Security for sensor networks can be divided into two broad categories: cryptography and intrusion detection. A variety of robust cryptographic implementations are available for WSNs, such as 128-bit AES-based encryption with multiple keys. But these solutions can have significant computational overhead and, as a consequence, significant power requirements. In additional, infrastructure may be required for key management, distribution, and authentication.

Intrusion detection focuses on detecting and responding to anomalies in the network, which may result from an attack such as a Wormhole or Sybil. Intrusion detection is referred to as second-line defense because it can't prevent an attack but only identify when one is occurring. Intrusion detection systems (IDS) are generally rule-based or anomaly-based. A rule-based IDS detects intrusions using predefined attack signatures. It can detect known attacks with great accuracy, but has difficulty detecting new attacks where a signature does not exist. An anomaly-based IDS detects intrusion by matching traffic patterns or resource utilizations. The anomaly detection approach can be useful at finding both known and new forms of attack. It can also suffer from high false positive and false negative rates (Drahanský, 2011).

Currently no truly end-to-end security solution exists for WSNs. Realizing a robust solution will be challenging due to the heterogeneous nature of the WSNs, varying node resource capabilities, usage models, and so forth.

As the importance of smartphone and tablets as sensor aggregators continues to grow, so do the associated risks. These devices have the potential to carry sensitive personal health data that requires protection. For applications that use discrete sensors that communicate with smartphones or tablets via a wireless connection, securing that connection between the sensor and smartphone is crucial. For example, Bluetooth implements confidentiality, authentication, and key derivation with custom algorithms based on the SAFER+ block cipher. For integrated sensors within the devices, a secure wireless link is not a concern. However, data stored on the device must be protected and remain secure at all times during its lifetime on the device, as well as during transmission of the data to another location such as a cloud service. Products such as AuthenTec MatrixDAR are available to support these requirements. However, in the future we are likely to see more security integrated directly into the hardware and operating system to deliver data features such as secure enclaves. Such features will be augmented with explicit user and platform environment policies to control sensor data access and processing. These features will also inform users when their data is or is not protected. The security platform will automatically manage data access requests by other applications and services, either local or cloud-based, depending on device policies.

Biometrics

Security for sensor applications typically focuses on securing sensor data during transmission from the sensor to an aggregator or from sensor to sensor in a multi-hop WSN. Sensors can also be used to provide security to a system in the form of biometric detection. Biometric techniques are used to identify an individual on the basis of a unique physical, physiological, behavioral, or biological characteristic. The robustness of biometrics as a form of security is based on the assumption that these characteristics are either impossible or at least very difficult to replicate or mask. Another key advantage of biometric security is that the identification process requires no passwords, ID cards, security fobs, and so forth. This can make it more convenient and potentially less costly than traditional security approaches. A variety of approaches exist, including facial recognition, fingerprinting, retinal scans, and DNA analysis. We will focus on approaches that require the use of sensors in the identification process.

> ***Fingerprint biometrics*** is one of the most widely used biometric approaches. It works by examining a finger's dermal ridges for verification or authentication. There are two main methods of fingerprint acquisition. The first approach involves a touch sensor on the user's fingertip to detect the peaks and valley of a fingerprint. The second approach is based on the use of a swipe sensor. The user places her finger on a designated starting point and in a continuous and smooth motion, swipes over a sensor. The sensor samples at a predefined frequency and then assembles the multiple readings into one image. Both approaches have the advantages of usability and acceptability. Additionally, the swipe sensor can be easily integrated into mobile form factors such as laptops or smartphones. Fingerprint sensors are

generally either optical or solid state. Optical sensing is based on imaging the fingerprint and using algorithms to process the image. Solid state sensors acquire the fingerprint using techniques such as capacitive, thermal, conductivity, and pressure measurements. In both methods, the acquired data is translated into a set of distinguishing features used to uniquely identify an individual. Fingerprint biometrics is not foolproof. A number of techniques have been demonstrated that can spoof a person's fingerprint using readily available household items, as highlighted by the iPhone 5S fingerprint hacking (Chaos Computer Club, 2013). The security of fingerprint biometrics can be enhanced by including a liveness indicator in the identification process to verify that the measured characteristics come from a live human being. There are a number of techniques to measure liveness in biometrics, including perspiration, blood oxygenation, and response to hot and cold stimulus (Drahanský, 2011).

EKG/ECG biometrics approaches use the heart's electrical impulses for user authentication. Distinctive characteristics such as the heart's position and size, chest configuration, and other features produce a unique ECG signal (Israel et al., 2005). An advantage of ECG-based authentication over other biometrics is the fact that an ECG signal can be extracted from the surface of the skin and measures the heart's activity, which makes ECG highly universal and easy to collect. Another key advantage is that it is non-trivial to spoof and can also be used as a liveness indicator. ECG biometrics is still in its infancy, with various research questions such as uniqueness, permanence, and scalability to be addressed before it can appear in consumer products.

Electroencephalogram (EEG) biometrics: An EEG provides a profile of brain electrical activity. It can potentially be used for biometric authentication because the human brain consists of neurons and synapses that are configured uniquely for each individual. EEG signals are typically broken into alpha (8-13 Hz), beta (14-30 Hz), and theta (4-7 Hz) rhythms. Features such as center frequency, maximum power, and sum power for each rhythm can be analyzed for identification purposes (Lin et al., 2011). A limitation of this approach, however, is the ability to produce cost-effective systems. Although consumer-level EEG readers are available, it is debatable whether this level of device can acquire EEG signals that are accurate enough to be used in biometric authentication. Also, sensors are currently too obtrusive for regular use, and the signals are sensitive to environmental noise.

Gait: Biometric identification of an individual based on walking style has been reported in the literature (Derawi et al., 2010). Gait is commonly measured using body-worn sensors or sensors integrated into a handheld device, such as a smartphone. In practice, this approach suffers from a variety of issues, including sensitivity to the sensor location on the body, foot injury, disease, intoxication, pregnancy, and weight loss or gain. Another approach is the use of floor sensors, which have the advantage of being unobtrusive and can provide accurate gait data for identification purposes. However, floor sensors can only be used in the physical locations in which they are installed, and the cost of these sensors can be prohibitive.

Challenges for Sensor Networks

There are a number of technical and domain-specific challenges in implementing and maintaining a sensor network. These range from power considerations for "deploy and forget" sensors that are used for environmental monitoring, to the biocompatibility of body-worn sensors used for health and wellness applications. The most common challenges are:

Power sources: Sensor nodes must be capable of harvesting or generating enough energy to meet their operational requirements. A sensor node that is not energy self-sufficient over a substantial lifetime (hours for an ingestible sensor, several days for a rechargeable, wearable sensor, or years for an environmental sensor) is not scalable. The power consumption and power generation challenges for sensor networks are being met on several fronts. First, battery technology is continually improving, providing longer battery life in smaller form factors. Second, power consumption due to data communication is improving as lightweight messaging protocols and low-power radio modules are introduced. Third, advances in processor technology have resulted in lower-power processors. Finally, advances in the power generated by, and the form factors of, solar cells, fuel cells, thermal cells, and biochemical cells mean that these are becoming increasingly practical ways to power sensor nodes.

Autonomic nodes and networks: The ability of sensor nodes and a sensor network to operate with minimal human interaction is essential for developing truly scalable large sensor networks. This is achieved by using predefined policies and rules that enable the individual nodes and the network to manage and configure themselves.

Reliability and security: Data security and reliable transport are key sensor network priorities, particularly in the health domain. However, these add high overhead in terms of data size, power consumption, and scalability to the system. Critical diagnostic health data must be protected and securely transferred, regardless of overhead. A balance may be found, though, by transferring less critical data. Can the data rate be reduced? Does anonymized fitness data require the same level of security as personal health records? These decisions will have to be made on an application-by-application basis, and appropriate hardware and software solutions will be required to meet these challenges.

Durability: Body-worn and ambient sensors are subject to numerous environmental challenges. Environmental sensors installed in an urban environment are subject to rain, wind, UV exposure, dirt, and perhaps vandalism. Body-worn sensors are subject to accidental or intentional submersion, friction with clothing, and scratching against other objects. The sensor must be durable enough to survive these conditions and able to operate reliably for extended periods, regardless of environmental conditions.

Biocompatibility: The effects of long-term sensor contact with the human body are yet not well understood. The biocompatibility of sensor materials is becoming increasingly important, as people begin to wear sensors for months or years at a time. For example, ECG electrodes must be replaced after 7 to 10 days of direct skin contact to minimize skin irritation. The topic of biocompatibility will become increasingly important as in-vivo sensing becomes more prevalent.

Privacy and data ownership: Personally identifiable data is a valuable commodity that must be protected whenever data is collected or transferred. Each country has legally enforceable data-protection guidelines, which must be complied with when collecting any data that includes personal information. Environmental sensors may unintentionally capture personal data, such as a conversation between individuals while recording traffic noise. Regardless of intent, such data must be protected and transferred using appropriate security measures. The issue of data ownership arises when data is sold or transported between different parties. In the health domain, data transfer and privacy are essential elements of any ethical-approval or device-regulation submission and should therefore be agreed on in advance of using any sensor technology.

Summary

This chapter introduced the topic of sensor networks and topologies by describing the hardware and software components of a sensor network and the various ways in which they may be configured. Common sensor network applications, including personal area networks, were described, and the challenges for current and future sensor networks were discussed.

References

Hongbo, Jiang, "Prediction or Not? An Energy-Efficient Framework for Clustering-Based Data Collection in Wireless Sensor Networks," *IEEE Transactions on Parallel and Distributed Systems,* vol. 22 (6), pp. 1064–1071, 2011.

Misic, Jelena and Vojislav Misic, "Prologue: Wireless Personal Area Networks," in *Wireless Personal Area Networks: Performance, Interconnection, and Security with IEEE 802.15.4,* Chichester, England, John Wiley & Sons Ltd, 2008, pp. 3–16.

Chaos Computer Club. *"Chaos Computer Club breaks Apple TouchID",* Last Update: November 2013, `http://www.ccc.de/en/updates/2013/ccc-breaks-apple-touchid`

Serbanati, Alexandru, Carlo Maria Medaglia, and Ugo Biader Ceipidor, *Building Blocks of the Internet of Things: State of the Art and Beyond,* 2011.

Drahanský, Martin, "Liveness Detection in Biometrics," in *Advanced Biometric Technologies,* Chetty, Girija, Ed., InTech, 2011, pp. 179–198.

Israel, Steven A., John M. Irvine, Andrew Cheng, Mark D. Wiederhold, and Brenda K. Wiederhold, "ECG to identify individuals," *Pattern Recognition,* vol. 38 (1), pp. 133–142, 2005.

Lin, Jia-Ping, Yong-Sheng Chen, and Li-Fen Chen, "Person Identification Using Electroencephalographic Signals Evoked by Visual Stimuli," in *Neural Information Processing.* vol. 7062, Lu, Bao-Liang, Liqing Zhang, and James Kwok, Eds., Springer Berlin Heidelberg, 2011, pp. 684–691.

Derawi, M. O., C. Nickel, P. Bours, and C. Busch, "Unobtrusive User-Authentication on Mobile Phones Using Biometric Gait Recognition," in *Intelligent Information Hiding and Multimedia Signal Processing (IIH-MSP), 2010 Sixth International Conference on,* 2010, pp. 306–311.

Conti, Mauro, Irina Zachia-Zlatea, and Bruno Crispo, "Mind how you answer me!: transparently authenticating the user of a smartphone when answering or placing a call," presented at the Proceedings of the 6th ACM Symposium on Information, Computer and Communications Security, Hong Kong, China, 2011.

Korotkaya, Zhanna, "Biometric Person Authentication: Odor", Lappeenranta University of Technology `http://www2.it.lut.fi/kurssit/03-04/010970000/seminars/Korotkaya.pdf`, 2003.

Gibbs, Martin D., "Biometrics: body odor authentication perception and acceptance," *SIGCAS Comput. Soc.,* vol. 40 (4), pp. 16–24, 2010.

Chigira, Hiroshi, Atsuhiko Maeda, and Minoru Kobayashi, "Area-based photo-plethysmographic sensing method for the surfaces of handheld devices," presented at the Proceedings of the 24th annual ACM symposium on User interface software and technology, Santa Barbara, California, USA, 2011.

Spachos, P., Gao Jiexin, and D. Hatzinakos, "Feasibility study of photoplethysmographic signals for biometric identification," in *Digital Signal Processing (DSP), 2011 17th International Conference on,* 2011, pp. 1–5.

■ ■ ■

CHAPTER 5

Processing and Adding Vibrancy to Sensor Data

Intelligence is the ability to adapt to change.

—Stephen Hawking, Physicist

The integration of sensors into many aspects of daily life will generate enormous volumes of data, and that will only increase as progressively more sensor output start to feed into "big data." The term "big data," which has received significant attention in recent years, is used to describe the voluminous amounts of unstructured and semi-structured data companies, governments, institutions, and individuals generate each day using information and communication technologies (ICT). Sensors are expected to be one of the largest generators of data, especially as the Internet of Things (IOT) gains traction in our everyday lives. Big sensor data will leverage capabilities such as cloud infrastructures for data storage, processing, and visualization. Access to this data will become pervasive, especially through mobile devices. We will also be able to combine other sources of data with sensor data in innovative ways to reveal new insights.

Intelligent processing of data and context-based visualization are critical to delivering meaningful, actionable information. Presentation approaches should strive to engage users by adding vibrancy to the data and allowing users to interact with the data in collaborative ways. Figure 5-1 shows the essential elements of data literacy. Collectively, these elements play an important role in helping to develop the kind of understanding that enables us to effectively utilize sensor data. In this chapter, we will look at the various methods to process, interpret, and display sensor data to end-users.

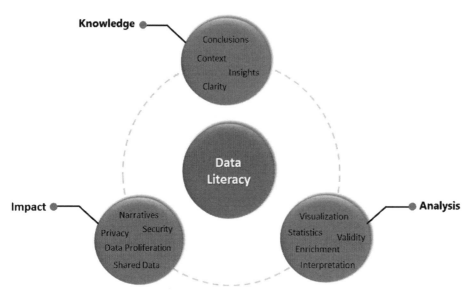

Figure 5-1. *The key elements in data literacy*

Data Literacy

Sensor data has value only if it allows us to do something useful with it, and we can't do that until we understand what the data is telling us. This process of understanding data is known as *data literacy* (Hart, 2011) and, from a knowledge perspective, it generally includes the ability to:

- correctly interpret visual representations of data, such as graphs

- accurately analyze the data and draw correct conclusions from the data

- utilize other datasets to add context

- know when the data is being interpreted in a misleading manner

- identify data that is inaccurate due to complete or intermittent sensor failure

The *New York Times* estimates that the United States will need 140,000 to 190,000 additional workers with strong data analytics expertise to deal with the abundance of data in areas ranging from science and public health to sports (Lohr, 2012). Data literacy needs to be the domain of more than just a few individuals; it must be embedded within an organization's culture to ensure that decision-makers understand data-driven insights and can act on them (Shelton, 2012).

Data literacy will become a more pervasive requirement, not only for specialists but also among the general population. Citizens will need to develop an understanding of mobile and ambient sensing and how this form can impact privacy, security, and risk. Casual technology users typically do not understand the security risks of data sharing. Therefore, it is increasingly important citizens become sufficiently data literate to grasp the implications of sensor-based data collection and the proliferation of shared data (Shilton et al., 2009).

Data literacy has three central themes, as shown in Figure 5-1: understanding the process of data analysis, understanding the impact of data, and gaining meaningful knowledge from the data. Clive Thompson, in his article *Why We Should Learn the Language of Data,* points out that many debates in the public domain, such as climate change or public health issues, often devolve into arguments over what the data means. In this context, he suggests that the new grammar is, in fact, statistics (Thompson, 2010).

Data literacy also enables individuals to utilize sensor data and other supporting data sources to provide contextualized observations and answers. Developing context may be as simple as knowing a sensor's expected range of measurement, which lets a person infer that measurements outside this expected range can indicate a malfunction. Alternatively, a clinician might be able to ignore a remotely acquired high blood-pressure reading if another data stream from a body-worn kinematic sensor shows that the patient engaged in physical activity before the measurement was taken, temporarily raising his blood pressure. Data structures, which provide contextual wrappers for healthcare-related sensor measurements, have also emerged in an effort to provide context for sensor measurements (Gonçalves et al., 2008). We can gain rich and meaningful insights into our health if we can ask the right questions from the data and understand the answers with a high degree of clarity. Without the clarity afforded by data literacy, we end up with "numerical gibberish, or data salad" (Bradshaw, 2012).

The Internet of Things

The IOT is a somewhat amorphous concept that continues to evolve along with the increased connectivity of a broad spectrum of technology devices. Early notions of the IOT focused on human-centric, Internet-enabled computing devices, such as smartphones, tablet devices, laptops, and so on. However, the IOT has grown to embrace a rich eco-system of devices including sensors, smart clothing, consumer electronics, utilities meters, cars, street lights, advertising signs, buildings, and more, all of which can now be connected to the Internet. One of the most salient definitions of the IOT comes from the US National Intelligence Council (Swan, 2012):

> The "Internet of Things" is the general idea of things, especially everyday objects, that are readable, recognizable, locatable, addressable, and controllable via the Internet—whether via RFID, wireless LAN, wide-area network, or other means.

The number of connected devices already exceeds the number of people on the planet, and Cisco estimated that the total number of connected devices will exceed 50 billion by 2020 (Cisco, 2011). A key driver of the IOT is sensors: discrete sensors, such as those for environmental monitoring; body-worn sensors, such as ECGs/EKGs; and sensors embedded into devices, such as accelerometers in smartphones. In fact, many devices feature multiple sensors. For example, a personal activity monitoring device may combine a kinematic sensor, such as an accelerometer; a physiological sensor to read heart rate; an ambient sensor to get the temperature; and a GPS to find the location. All these data streams can then be connected to the Internet via a smartphone.

Platforms like Xively (`https://xively.com/`), which allow hobbyists and companies to intuitively collect data from Internet-enabled devices, including sensors, are beginning to emerge. Xively supports secure sharing of data, builds collaborations around the data, and provides tools to visualize the data across multiple platforms. The platform has been applied in home environmental monitoring applications to gather and view sensor data streams, including barometric pressure, carbon monoxide, and temperature. New, innovative sensors for home environmental monitoring, such the Air Quality Egg (AirQualityEgg, 2013) are leveraging Xively to provide IOT capabilities. Popular platforms such as Arduino and Electric Imp (designboom, 2012) also provide the capabilities to connect sensors either directly to the Internet or via smartphones.

Realizing the potential of sensors to become the *"finger of the Internet"* will take a number of years. Several key factors still remain to be addressed in order to fully achieve this goal. These factors include reducing the cost of sensors; increasing battery life; developing reliable and powerful energy-harvesting capabilities; building more robust wireless data transmission capabilities; making wireless backhaul coverage ubiquitous (3G and 4G, for example); building data analysis and visualization tools capable of dealing with large scale, high-frequency sensor data streams; and, finally, understanding how to convert data streams into meaningful, real-time, personalized recommendations with appropriate context.

Beyond human-centric sensing utilities, machine-to-machine (M2M) applications, commonly known as ubiquitous or pervasive computing, will be a key driver of Internet-enabled sensing. It is estimated that by 2020 there will be 12.5 billion M2M devices globally, up from 1.3 billion devices in 2012. They will deliver a wide variety of applications for, among others, environmental monitoring and control (water management, smart cities, weather event monitoring, and more). Over time, M2M connectivity will change our daily experiences; altering how we interact with the world around us, from our home environments to the places in which we conduct our daily lives.

Sensors and the Cloud

Cloud computing has become one of the most active areas in information technology; it is already starting to transform how businesses manage and use their computing and storage infrastructure. The cloud-based model affords flexibility and scalability for computing, storage, and application resources, optimal utilization of infrastructure, and reduced costs. Cloud computing has the potential to provide storage, processing, and visualization capabilities for sensors and sensor networks, as shown in Figure 5-2. The sensors can be discrete or part of a geographically distributed network, and feature highly dynamic data throughputs. This cloud-based integration is able to accommodate dynamic loads and sharing of sensor resources by different users and applications, in flexible usage scenarios.

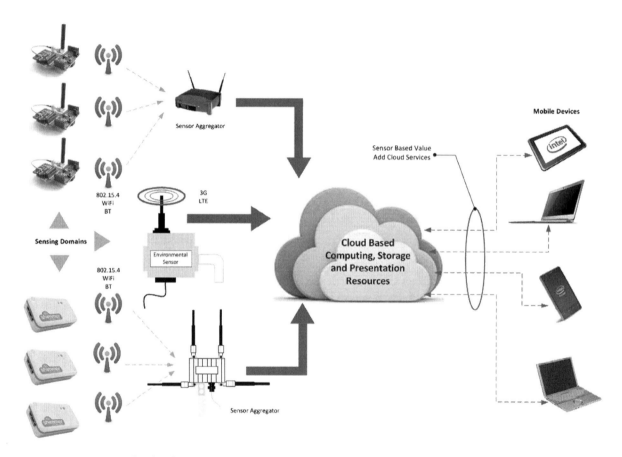

Figure 5-2. *A sensor cloud architecture*

Smart Cities is an application domain for which the use of sensor clouds has been proposed (Mitton et al., 2012). For example, a citywide environmental monitoring system would require significant computational and storage resources during an exceptional weather event, but would return to standard requirements at the end of that event. A cloud-based approach has the potential to reduce overall cost in a sensor deployment, as it can easily support elastic consumption of resources. Clouds are typically based on usage models, allowing application developers to optimize frequency and resolution of data against cost. Commercial software as a service (SaaS) solutions for sensor data are already starting to emerge, including the SensorCloud system from MicroStrain (MicroStrain, 2013) and sensorcloud from temperature@lert (temperature@lert, 2012).

Vast amounts of sensor data can be processed, analyzed, and stored using computational and storage resources of the cloud. Once the sensor data is stored in the cloud, novel applications based on aggregated data sets can be created from different organizational resources or from crowd sourcing. Essentially, the cloud can be used to create virtualized sensors that can be accessed by any user or application. This breaks down the siloing that currently exists with many sensor applications. There are number of efforts to realize this goal, including Sensor-Cloud from IBM (Yuriyama et al., 2010), Cloud@Home from ANR (Recherche, 2011), and SensorCloud from Aachen University (Hummen et al., 2012).

Users and applications do not need to be concerned about the physical location of sensing resources when using cloud-based functions, because they are essentially virtualized. End users can dynamically provision and group virtual sensors based on need, and terminate them easily when no longer required. New physical sensors can usually be added to the cloud through a registration process. This process includes a mechanism to register sensor characteristics, in a format similar to TEDs as described in Chapter 3, as well as a way to describe the sensor's data type in an XML format, such as SensorML.

Data Quality

The success of any sensor application depends on the quality of the data. Without trust in that quality, the value of the data is significantly undermined, and it's observational, diagnostic, or actionable value is limited. It is important, therefore, to ensure that data quality is an integral part of any sensor application development process. A variety of issues can affect the data quality during the application lifecycle, in all of its phases:

- Sensor system design, development, and validation

- Deployment

- Protocol design

- Data processing and visualization

Some issues can be mediated through careful design of the sensor system. A tightly controlled deployment process or active management strategy can proactively identify issues that affect data quality. Key factors to be considered include data consistency, measurement accuracy, and reliability during data collection, processing, storage, and transmission. The primary objective should be to minimize, or ideally eliminate, both the general and application-specific data deficiencies. A risk matrix can be useful in prioritizing data-quality impacts. In this matrix, priority is normally allocated to both high-impact and high-frequency risks. The rationale for this prioritization is based on propensity for significant impact. These are then followed in order by lesser influences, such as outlier detection. The key factors affecting data quality are outlined in Table 5-1 (Puentes et al., 2013).

Table 5-1. *Factors That Affect Sensor Data Quality*

Factor	Impact
Sensor limitations	*Operational limitations*—such as over-sensitivity to environmental influences. *System-design limitations*—such as data-throughput constraints, processing bottlenecks, reliability of communications.
Calibration error; drift	Incorrect calibration for the required operational range, or frequent recalibration needed to maintain accuracy. Accuracy deteriorates over time.

(continued)

Table 5-1. (*continued*)

Factor	Impact
Environmental influences	Performance variation due to temperature, humidity, ingress of moisture, and the like.
	Degrading of sensor materials.
	Malicious damage to the sensor or the measurement environment.
	Damage from wildlife.
	Damage from vehicles.
Malfunctioning sensor	Sensor ceases to function correctly, resulting in erroneous output.
Incorrect Values	Incorrect sensor measurements can arise due to external influences such as noise.
Unsuitable Protocol	Measurement protocol cannot be utilized correctly due to its complexity. Unclear how to use the sensors correctly. Protocol does not acquire data at required periodicity or range.
Human Influences	Skewed results due to location of humans in the measurement environment.
	Incorrect use of the sensor: for example, incorrectly attached electrodes a body-worn application.
Pertinence	Data collected is irrelevant or has no utility.
Incorrect installation	Inaccurate sampling.
Trust and repudiation	Inability to guarantee origin of data limits value of data, particularly for diagnostic purposes. Data traceability and robust security need to be established.

Addressing Data Quality Issues

Identifying and addressing quality issues in sensor applications are important. A wide variety of potential influences and impacts can affect the accuracy of sensors readings, but checking manually is extremely tedious and time-consuming and does not scale to accommodate larger sensor deployments. Automated methods represent the most pragmatic approach to monitoring data. Statistical modeling, machine learning, and other data mining techniques can be utilized to identify anomalous or outlier data in real time or during post-processing. It may even be possible to eliminate the outlier or anomaly and replace it with an appropriate calculated value. Some of the common approaches to monitoring data quality are discussed in the next section.

Outlier Detection

Outlier detection, also known as anomaly or deviation detection, is commonly used to monitor data quality and improve robustness in wireless sensor networks. This approach identifies malfunctioning sensors or malicious network attacks from external parties by detecting measurements outside the expected range. A number of methods exist to deal with outliers. Visual inspection can be used to spot erroneous data, which can be removed manually.

Another approach involves plotting data in histograms or scatter plots to help identify outliers. However, these approaches are time-consuming and not very scalable. For greater efficiency, model-based approaches are commonly utilized. Here are five useful approaches (Zhang et al., 2010):

- *Statistical modeling*: This method is based on the normal probability distribution of the data under standard operational conditions. Actual data is evaluated against this model to determine whether it fits correctly. Data identified as low probability by the model is classified as outliers.

- *Nearest neighbor*: This method compares the data value with respect to its nearest neighbors. The distance (such as Euclidean distance or a similarity measure) between the new sensor measurement and previous measurements is calculated. Too much distance from neighbor measurements results in the measurement being identified as an outlier.

- Clustering: In this approach, data instances are grouped into clusters that have similar behavior or characteristics. Instances of data are identified as outliers if they do not fit into a predefined cluster or if they generate a cluster that is significantly smaller than other clusters. Euclidean distance is often used as the dissimilarity measure between two data instances.

- *Classification*: This approach is based on the development of a classification model that is then trained using representative data sets. Once the model has been taught the expected data distributions, it can classify unseen data into either a normal or outlier class. As new data is collected or the operational parameters of the sensor or sensor system change, the classifier can be updated to reflect new instances of normal data. Popular approaches for developing the classifier include support vector machines (SVM) and Bayesian networks.

- *Spectral decomposition*: Principal component analysis (PCA) is used to reduce the number of dimensions within a dataset to those, such as variability, that capture the expected behavior of the data. Data whose components fall outside these structures are considered to be outliers.

When dealing with outlier data, it is vital to have an informed and objective decision-making process regardless of the techniques used. Without such a process, there is always the risk of introducing unintentional bias into the outlier removal process. It is also important to ensure that the integrity of any processed data is maintained by clearly identifying that outliers have been removed along with information on the process utilized. And it is essential to maintain the raw data (at least for a defined period of time) should access to it be required for clarification purposes.

Automated Data Cleaning

Automated data cleaning builds on outlier detection by using techniques like machine learning, artificial neural networks (ANN), and clustering techniques such as k-nearest neighbors (KNN). These techniques predict the value of a sensor reading based on the readings from a set of related sensors. The sensor measurement can simply be rejected or substituted with another value, based on the predicted value (Ramirez et al., 2011). The obvious downside to this approach, particularly where the true accuracy of sensed value is of critical importance, is the rejection of a true outlier sensor measurement. There is also a significant computational overhead associated with this approach, which makes it more suitable for post-processing than real-time implementation.

Plausibility Testing

A plausibility framework can test whether a received sensor reading is credible based on predefined validity checks. The expected ranges or thresholds for the characteristics utilized are defined using statistical models designed to capture the natural variations under normal operational circumstances. The test data are generally updated dynamically to account for expected temporal variations. Characteristics such as range, persistence, and stochasticity in the measurement data are interrogated for agreement with expected limits under a given set of conditions. Each test produces a simple binary pass/fail output. Plausibility testing has found application in the environmental monitoring domain (Taylor et al., 2012).

Fusing Sensor Data

Single sensors can't always be relied on to produce the measurement of interest. Measurements often contain noise, are incomplete, or lack context. In some cases, it may not be possible to measure the data of interest directly, and other approaches will be required. Sensor fusion and virtual sensors are two such approaches, which are widely used to improve the informational value of sensor data.

In the sensor fusion process, the sensor data or the derived sensor data is combined with data from other sensors or sources. The resulting information is superior to what could be achieved using the sensor data or other resources in isolation. In some applications, multiple sensors may be required to either fully quantify the measurement of interest or provide context sensitivity or situational awareness for the measurement. For example, non-contact measurement of gait velocity requires multiple sensors at fixed distances in order to calculate the velocity of people as they move past. Sensor fusion can also provide context for remote physiological measurements. In this case, kinematic sensors can identify whether a person was active prior to a physiological measurement such as ECG/EKG or blood pressure (Klein, 2004).

The way sensor data streams are fused depends on the application's requirements, sensor resolution, and available processing resources. The fusion process can occur at the sensor-system level if the microcontroller (MCU) has sufficient computational capabilities. This is particularly useful if real-time measurements are necessary. Alternatively, if real-time measurements are not necessary, the fusion process can occur on the data aggregator or on the backend IT infrastructure during post-processing of the data.

An important application of sensor fusion is motion analysis. 3D-accelerometer, 3D-gyroscope, and 3D-magnetometers have been utilized for motion-related applications, such as falls detection. When used in isolation, these sensors have some limitations that can impact accuracy and sensitivity. For example, accelerometers are sensitive to on-body position or might generate a signal when a subject is at rest. To compensate for individual sensor limitations, a sensor fusion approach combines the 3D-accelerometer, 3D-gyroscope, and 3D-magnetometer signals to deliver a 9-DoF (degrees of freedom) motion-capture solution. Such systems can provide accurate motion analysis capabilities, which are significantly cheaper and more flexible than standard optical systems (See Chapter 9). Sensor fusion is also used in compass applications, enhanced navigation, and 3D-games (Ristic, 2012). The growth in sensor fusion applications is likely to continue. Devices such as smartphones, tablets, and ultrabooks with dedicated sensor hubs that can support a wide range of sensing capabilities will enable delivery of new and exciting applications.

As discussed in Chapter 4, virtual sensors are software-defined sensors, as opposed to physical sensors. The function of a virtual sensor is to provide an indirect measurement of an abstract quantity or measurand that can't be measured directly. This measurement can be consumed by an application or user without reference to or knowledge of the contributory sensor streams (Kabaday, 2008). Virtual sensors and sensor fusion are related, as the sensor fusion process is required to create a virtual sensor. However, virtual sensors fuse data from real sensor data streams only. In smartphones, the device orientation is determined using the virtual sensor output, generated by fusing accelerometer, magnetometer, and gyroscope data. As outlined earlier in this chapter, the growth in cloud computing will result in the proliferation of virtual sensors, creating rich data sets that can be virtualized to generate novel observations. These virtual sensors will lead to new commercial and new public domain applications, created by both hacktivists or interested citizens.

Data Mining

Extracting useful and actionable knowledge from raw sensor data is a nontrivial task. Data mining is an important tool that can be applied to the knowledge-discovery process on sensor data. Effective for modeling relationships among sensor measurements, data mining is used to reveal non-obvious patterns among the data and to determine data quality issues, such as outliers. Data mining leverages a wide range of techniques, from traditional statistical analysis and nearest-neighbor clustering to more modern techniques, such as ANN, decision trees, and Bayesian networks.

Before data mining can be applied, the data typically requires some form of preprocessing to address issues such as noise, outliers, missing data, or data from malfunctioning sensors. In some applications, particularly those that require real-time or near real-time performance, data reduction may also be required. The high volumes of data generated by some sensor applications make it extremely challenging to maintain the entire data set, which is required to achieve optimal algorithm performance, in memory. This is also an issue for applications that utilize in-memory databases to achieve improved application performance (Tan, 2006). Preprocessing of sensor data typically incorporates one or more of the following activities:

- Data cleaning or filtering, such as noise reduction.

- Outlier detection and removal or replacement of outlier data.

- Reducing the data set size by removing redundant values using techniques such as statistical sampling.

- Reducing the number of dimensions within the data using methods such as principle components analysis (PCA).

- Feature extraction such as event detection; for example, identification of R-wave maxima (QRS point) in an EKG/ECG signal.

Preprocessing of data can occur in a distributed manner at the sensor node or at an aggregator node, or in a centralized manner on the backend aggregator or sensor cloud. If the sensor node has sufficient computational capabilities and energy budget, initial data processing should occur there to reduce the size and frequency of transmissions. This also helps to improve the performance of the data-mining algorithm, by reducing the data set, which is particularly important for real-time processing.

Although a wide variety of mining techniques can be applied to sensor data, they can be rationalized into four broad categories (Duda et al., 2001):

- *Classification* is based on a machine-learning approach and uses methods such as decision trees and neural networks. The basic principle is to classify a measurement into one of a predefined set of classes, based on a feature vector. Classification performs well on sensor measurements that do not contain significant feature variability.

- *Clustering* combines groups of similar sensor values together based on a set of common characteristics. Two main types of measures are used to estimate the relationship to a group: either distance (such as Euclidean distance) or similarity measures. Clustering defines the classes into which a measurement should be added as opposed to classification which adds measurements to predefined classes. Common clustering methods include: *k*-Means, fuzzy clustering and single linkage (nearest neighbor).

- *Regression* identifies a functional description of the data that can be used to predict further values for measurements. The most commonly used implementation of regression is linear regression, where the function is linear with respect to the input variables.

- *Rule induction* identifies all possible patterns in a systematic manner. Accuracy and significance are added to indicate how robust the pattern is and the probability that it will occur again. This is probably the most common form of knowledge discovery in unsupervised learning systems.

The ultimate goal of these methods is to provide a model that can be used to interpret existing data and, if necessary to predict future sensor values in an automated manner. Due to the variety of available methods, a key step is determining the most appropriate approach for modeling a given data set. With practice, experience, and some expert guidance, this selection process should become somewhat intuitive. For most applications, an iterative process will be required to optimize the particular technique being utilized. In some cases, more than one method may be needed to achieve the desired result, especially where the output of one model forms the input to another.

Standard visualization techniques, such as typical 2D or 3D bar charts and line graphs, may not be successful due to screen size constraints on mobile devices, human visual limitations, and restrictions on available computational resources. Visual data-mining approaches address these limitations by applying techniques like geometrically transformed displays (such as scatter plot matrices), dense pixel displays, stacked displays, or icon displays to the inspection and interpretation of very large data sets. Visual data exploration serves three general purposes:

- Presenting data in a graphical form that allows users to gain insight into the data.

- Confirmatory analysis that lets users confirm or reject hypotheses based on insights gained through direct interaction with the data.

- Exploratory analysis, resulting in the development of new hypotheses.

Presenting the data under scrutiny in an interactive, graphical form can facilitate new insights into a data set. It can provide a deeper understanding that is not readily discernible using standard data-mining techniques. This approach has been used in a variety of domains, including the oil industry and IT forensics, and is being applied with large-scale sensor data (Rodriguez et al., 2012). The key requirement is a presentation tool to generate initial views, navigate data sets with complicated structures, and to deliver the results of analysis. Many analytical methods don't involve visualization or have limited visualization capabilities. As the application of visual data mining continues to mature, it will evolve beyond current limitations into a highly functional and flexible tool.

Both healthcare and environmental sensor applications are areas where data mining can have meaningful utility. Sensors used to monitor a patient's condition, both in the hospital environment and outside of it, have the potential to generate significant volumes of data. These data sets will likely continue to grow unabated. However, such data sets are vastly under-utilized, despite their potential to deliver insights into the future well-being of patients, particularly for time-critical scenarios (Sow et al., 2013). And various sensor types are already being used to track the environment. Again, tremendous amounts of sensor data are being generated through air, water, climate, soil, and ecology monitoring. These data sets, if harnessed correctly through the careful application of data mining, have the potential to determine both short- and long-term trends in our environment and climate. By detecting events and revealing cause-and-effect relationships, such data will enable us to be more responsive and proactive in situations where the environment, and consequently our health and well-being, is under threat (Karpatne et al., 2013). But, as outlined in Chapter 11, significant challenges remain before this vision can be fully realized. For example, the Argo project has deployed a global array of 3660 floats containing temperature and salinity sensors in the oceans. The purpose of the project is to provide real-time data for use in climate, weather, oceanographic, and fisheries research (Argo, 2013). The challenge is how to expand the available sensing, including other measurements of interest such as pH, oxygen, and nitrate levels. Developing sensors that can operate autonomously, reliably, and accurately in this harsh environment is technically challenging and costly (West, 2011).

Mining of sensor data can involve significant overhead costs, including IT infrastructure, software tools and licenses, and networks and staff to maintain and grow the infrastructure over time. Therefore, it is important to continually question whether the correct data is being collected at the correct sampling rate. There is little point in collecting and mining data if it can't be used to drive meaningful actions. The question of whether the data mining and associated costs are delivering a return on investment must also be continually asked. Vast quantities of sensor data mined in a variety of sophisticated ways may have limited impact if the resulting information has no real predictive value. The output of the data-mining process should also be used to validate any subsequent actions taken on the basis of the analysis. It should also help determine the utility of these actions on a continual basis. Collecting more sensor data is useful only if it supplements and strengthens the quality of the analysis process. It becomes counter-productive if used as a substitute for informed analysis.

Data Visualization

Generally, people prefer graphics and visuals to pages of numeric values or text. Visual representations help address issues such as information overload or *data glut*. They allow people to more easily see the patterns and connections that are meaningful and important. If used appropriately, data visualization is a key component in the value-add chain of sensor data processing because it adds vibrancy to the data. It supports pattern recognition and can act as a primary catalyst in changing the manner in which sensor data is acted upon, either at an organizational level or by affecting the behaviors of individuals (for example, to initiate and maintain a sufficient level of physical activity). As the visualization process enables us to bring various information sources together, including non-sensor sources, context can be added that informs the interpretive process. Ultimately, visualization lets us create designs that tell a story about the data (McCandless, 2013). Good design, particularly in the health and wellness domains, often utilizes relative data, which connects the sensor data to peer data sets or to values that generate a fully rounded and qualified picture, rather than one based on absolutes, which could be misleading. The ability to visualize sensor data in a compelling manner allows individuals to evaluate the utility of a decision or to identify personal benefit to their health and wellbeing (as shown in Figure 5-3).

Figure 5-3. *Mobile app visualization of a personal activity record on a temporal basis with supporting lifestyle targets*

The kinds of visualizations that are effective differ according to the context. For example, 3D visualizations typically require higher resolution, which may impose certain restrictions on their use in small form factor displays. It is therefore important to match the visualization wishes of the user—for example, differing views depending on specified context (the viewing device)—while addressing a meaningful real-world problem (Richter, 2009). There are seven potential classes of visualizations that can be used depending on the composition of the underlying dataset (Shneiderman, 1996), as shown in Figure 5-4.

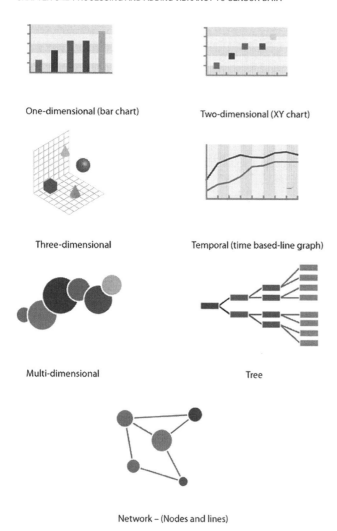

One-dimensional (bar chart)

Two-dimensional (XY chart)

Three-dimensional

Temporal (time based-line graph)

Multi-dimensional

Tree

Network – (Nodes and lines)

Figure 5-4. *Seven classes of visualization based on underlying data type*

1-, 2-, and 3-dimensionalrepresentations are common ways of organizing sensor data sets based on combinations of characteristics, such as temporal or spatial components along with properties such as frequency, amplitude, and so forth. Visualization of multidimensional data sets may require modifying the dimensions in some manner, either reducing the number of dimensions for display or separating dimensions into different components for display. This approach is particularly advantageous when dealing with high-dimensional data sets that must be transposed into 2 or 3 dimensions for visualization (Rodrigues et al., 2010). Temporal representations are one of the most familiar methods of visualization because the data contains definite start and end times and can be represented by a timeline.

When the dimensionality of data can't be reduced without loss of information, a multidimensional visualization approach is required. This often involves the creation of virtual sensors or other information sources to add context for sensor measurements. These forms of visualization are often customized for a particular application. For example, visualizations could fuse environmental sensor data with geospatial and cartography data in a hierarchical structure in the form of a tree. These are very useful for demonstrating the whole evolution of an aggregated value or virtual sensor reading or the relationships between groupings of similar sensors. Networks have similarities to trees in how they connect sensor measurements, but do so in a non-hierarchical manner.

As sensor deployments grow in scale, the need to visualize distributed sensor networks, such as wireless sensor networks (WSNs), will increase. A number of efforts to address this requirement have been reported. HiperSense is designed to provide scalable sensor data visualization with the ability to handle up to 6200 independent stream of data (Chou et al., 2009). In the environmental sensing domain, Teris et al. discusses an environmental monitoring system based on MicaZ motes that was used to monitor soil temperature and moisture. The resulting data was visualized using Microsoft Research SensorMap, which enabled the geographic coordinates of the motes to be accessed via a web service interface. This allowed users to find specific sensor locations and to drill down into that location for both current and historical measurements, providing both a micro and macro view of the data with geographical context (Terzis et al., 2010).

Another popular tool for visualizing sensor data is Google's Fusion tables. Fusion is a web-based application that allows users to gather, visualize, and share large data tables (Bradley et al., 2011, Fakoor et al., 2012). Once the data has been collected, the user can apply filters and create summaries across rows, up to hundreds of thousands. The user can visualize the data using charts, maps, or custom layouts and embed the visualization in a web page to share it with others. The tool enables citizens to upload a variety of environmental data sets, such as air and water quality data and contextual metrological data. It has also been used by researchers, such as those at the Waterbot program at the Create Lab in Carnegie Mellon University (CMU), to visualize data from water-quality sensors (temperature and conductivity sensing) deployed at the Nine Mile Run watershed in Pittsburgh, as shown in Figure 5-5. The researchers used Google Fusion tables to present their sensor data against a reference sensor (Solinst) with geographical sample mapping. They have been able to identify conductivity spikes that corresponded to sewage overflow events from heavy rainfall. In a blog post on the Climate Code, Professor Illah Nourbakhsh at CMU described Google Fusion tables as a key enabler of citizen science. He outlines how access to web-based data collection and visualization enables democratization of data, and in doing so empowers citizens to make informed decisions about their environment (Nourbakhsh, 2012).

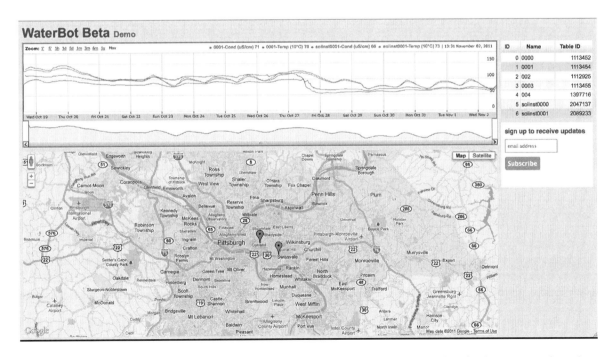

Figure 5-5. *Visualization of water quality sensor measurements using Google Fusion tables (with permission from the Create Lab, Carnegie Mellon University)*

In the health and wellness domain, the ability to mine and visualize longitudinal data sets, such as behavior patterns at home, can provide early indications of abnormal behaviors and health-related issues (Lotfi et al., 2012). Visualization designs for this domain should accommodate both individual- and peer group-level norms as appropriate. Keep in mind that we are all individuals with our own unique biology, so adopted designs must be carefully selected in order to prevent "loaded" representations that yield narrow and restricted representations and do not reflect individual complexity.

Visualization can provide the tools for driving awareness in domains of interest. But, ultimately, its usefulness is determined by the ability to build accurate and relevant models that produce correct answers. Visualization is a powerful and effective tool for adding texture to sensor data sets and providing a mechanism to compress significant amounts of knowledge into an intuitive visual metaphor. However, visualization can only provide answers and insights to properly constructed questions. It is not a magic tool that can make sense from data chaos. It requires careful guidance to ensure data is correctly interpreted. In the future, data visualization will move beyond the current static modes of interactions to more interactive modalities, which will enable individuals to interact with data. Augmented reality solutions, such as Google Glass, will enable real-time delivery of visualized data that enhances our perception of the world and its impact on us. Ultimately, visualization is about adding vibrancy to sensor data so we can make connections to it and to tell meaningful stories about it.

Big Sensor Data

Big data is a catchphrase that has gained considerable traction in the business analytics world. Big data is said to be the "new oil." Of course, this is something of a misnomer. Data is not a finite resource like oil. In fact the opposite is true, with new reserves of data being created on a daily basis (Thorp, 2012). It is hard to avoid the fact that we are generating ever increasing amounts of personal and systems-based data each day from connected devices. According to IBM, mankind and its supporting infrastructure generate a massive 2.5 quintillion bytes of data daily (IBM, 2013). Whether "big data" is truly a new phenomenon or just a part of the continuous evolution of a technological society is likely to remain a point of contention among the business intelligence analytics vendors and industry veterans and academics (Few, 2012).

The proliferation of sensors into all aspects of our lives—including smartphones, body-worn sensors, homes, and monitoring future smart cities—is often used to illustrate how sensors are and will be a key contributor to big data growth. It is important to realize that collecting data from new sensors may not involve collecting new data types. Instead, it will simply add to the overall cumulative effect of existing sensor data. Sensors will slowly add incremental data sources only as new technologies emerge. They will, though, add increasing volumes of the same measurement types and become more pervasively used. Most big data sources typically generate data in an automated manner without human intervention. Automated sensing does occur in the health and wellness domain (such as home-based activity monitoring). At the same time, a significant human interaction element remains in the sensing process, for example, physiological sensing like blood pressure or blood chemistry monitoring (for diabetes control, for example). Despite the large "manual" element in health- and wellness-related sensing, the volumes of data generated continue to grow. Another characteristic of data in these domains is the high levels of interaction and participation it engenders. People often feel a strong sense of personal ownership of the data and can be highly motivated to interact with it and compare their "numbers" with either peer groups or other sources of aggregated data.

The distinct category of "big sensor data" has started to emerge with the advent of sensor-enabled smartphones and tablets, coupled with cloud-based services, which enables persuasive user feedback (Lane et al., 2010). In the healthcare domain, large-scale data sets, such as those that can be generated by smartphone sensors, do present challenges—particularly with respect to the manner in which the data is mined. Population-level data can often have the effect of degrading the differences among people, which is particularly problematic for classification-based systems. This issue is commonly called the "classification diversity problem." As mentioned in the preceding section, the uniqueness of an individual's biological and biomechanical composition makes creating highly generalizable models extremely difficult. Generalized models typically afford only indicative value, as opposed to diagnostic value, which require highly granular models tailored to small population groups with common epidemiology (Campbell et al., 2012).

The value of big sensor data is only as good as the information you can extract from it. The ability to interpret the data correctly is also critical and dependent on the data literacy of citizens as discussed earlier in this chapter. A lack of awareness can result in confusion among the public and lead to misinformed debate. New methods of analysis may not necessarily be required. Enhancements to current tools will be necessary to handle and analyze the large sensor data volumes in order to deliver the performance muscle needed, especially if real-time analytics are required. Existing analytics solutions can process temporal sensor measurements but have difficulty in correlating data sets with other data sources quickly. The new generation of big data analytics tools, including NoSQL databases, Hadoop, and MapReduce, are designed to address these requirements. Hadoop's open-source stack uses a simple programming model to enable distributed processing of large data sets on clusters of computers. The Hadoop stack includes utilities, a distributed file system, analytics and data storage capabilities, and an application layer. These features support distributed processing, parallel computation, and workflow and configuration management. MapReduce, the software programming framework in the Hadoop stack, simplifies processing of large data sets by giving programmers a common method for defining and orchestrating complex processing tasks across clusters of computers.

Big data analytics remains an area of active and growing research. For example, in Ireland the national research body Science Foundation Ireland recently announced the Insight Centre at a cost of over 75 million euros. The focus of this center is to develop a new generation of data analytics technologies focusing on key application areas, such as healthcare and the sensor web(Insight, 2013). It is the biggest ICT R&D investment in the history of the country, demonstrating the strategic importance of big data analytics to the national economy. Within the research domain, active topics include algorithmic techniques for modeling high-dimensional data, knowledge discovery for large volume dynamic data sets, and methods for automated hypothesis generation. In data storage research, the focus is on data representation, data storage, data retrieval, and new parallel data architectures, including clouds.

The value of big sensor data can only be systematically realized by a bottom-up approach. That approach starts with basic tenets: What do we want to measure and how do we measure it? Scaling data collection to large sample sizes will then enable us to see the patterns and connections that are important. This process will move us into data-driven discovery, which in turn will lead to an accelerating pace of innovation.

Summary

In this chapter we looked at the importance of data literacy and the steps required to extract new knowledge about our environment and our health and well-being. The process of turning sensor data into actionable information includes: data preparation, mining, and visualization. But to realize the value of this process, people need be sufficiently data literate to understand the information sensors can provide. We also saw how the visualization process is a key element in adding vibrancy to data. That process can help turn data into stories that enable individuals, groups, and organizations to make a connection to a data set. We have seen that the amount of sensor data is growing through the emergence of a connected world and the Internet of Things, leading to the phenomenon of 'big sensor data.' The value of these large scale data sets is dictated by its quality and whether it is measuring something of interest in an accurate and contextualized manner.

References

Hart, Robert V. "*Data Information Literacy?*," Last Update: July 26th, 2011, http://esciencecommunity.umassmed.edu/2011/07/26/data-information-literacy/

Lohr, Steve. *The Age of Big Data*, The New York Times, New York, http://www.nytimes.com/2012/02/12/sunday-review/big-datas-impact-in-the-world.html?pagewanted=1&_r=1, 2012.

Shelton, Steve. "*Building a Big Data workforce: how can we get started?*" [Blog]. Last Update: 17th August, 2012, https://www.baesystemsdetica.com/news/blogs/building-a-big-data-workforce-how-can-we-get-started/

Shilton, Katie, *et al.*, "Designing the Personal Data Stream: Enabling Participatory Privacy in Mobile Personal Sensing," presented at the 37th Research Conference on Communication, Information, and Internet Policy (TPRC 2009), Arlington, Virginia, 2009.

Thompson, Clive, "Why We Should Learn the Language of Data". *Wired Magazine,* (May), 2010

Gonçalves, Bernardo, José G. Pereira Filho, and Giancarlo Guizzardi, "A Service Architecture for Sensor Data Provisioning for Context-Aware Mobile Applications," presented at the ACM Symposium on Applied Computing (SAC '08), Fortaleza, Ceará, Brazil, 2008.

Bradshaw, Leslie. "*Data Dreaming*," Last Update: December 14th, 2012, `https://medium.com/american-dreamers/4ee4351f8aab`

Swan, Melanie, "Sensor Mania! The Internet of Things, Wearable Computing, Objective Metrics, and the Quantified Self 2.0," *Journal of Sensor and Actuator Networks,* vol. 1 pp. 217-253, 2012.

Cisco. "*The Internet of Things*," Last Update: 2011, `http://share.cisco.com/internet-of-things.html`

AirQualityEgg. "*AirQualityEgg*," Last Update: 2013, `http://airqualityegg.wikispaces.com/AirQualityEgg`

designboom. "*Electric Imp for the Internet of Things*," Last Update: May 17th 2012, `http://www.designboom.com/technology/electric-imp-for-the-internet-of-things/`

Mitton, Nathalie, Symeon Papavassiliou, Antonio Puliafito, and Kishor S. Trivedi, "Combining Cloud and Sensors in a Smart City Environment," *EURASIP Journal on Wireless Communications and Networking,* vol. 2012 (247), 2012.

LORD MicroStrain, "SensorCloud," `http://www.sensorcloud.com/`, 2013.

temperature@lert. "*Temperature@lert Sensor Cloud Tour*," Last Update: 2012, `http://www.temperaturealert.com/Remote-Temperature/Sensor-Cloud/Sensor-Cloud-Tour.aspx`

Yuriyama, Madako and Takayuki Kushida, "Sensor-Cloud Infrastructure - Physical Sensor Management with Virtualized Sensors on Cloud Computing," in *Network-Based Information Systems (NBiS), 2010 13th International Conference on*, 2010, pp. 1-8.

Agence Nationale De La Recherche, "Clouds@Home," `http://clouds.gforge.inria.fr/pmwiki.php?n=Main.HomePage`, 2011.

Hummen, René, Martin Henze, Daniel Catrein, and Klaus Wehrle, "A Cloud Design for User-controlled Storage and Processing of Sensor Data," presented at the IEEE CloudCom, Taipei, Taiwan, 2012.

Puentes, John, Julien Montagner, Laurent Lecornu, and Jaakko Lahteenmaki, "Quality Analysis of Sensors Data for Personal Health Records on Mobile Devices," in *Pervasive Health Knowledge Management*, Bali, Rajeev K., Indrit Troshani, and Steve Goldberg, Eds., New York, Springer, 2013, pp. 103-134.

Zhang, Yang, Nirvana Meratnia, and Paul Havinga, "Outlier Detection Techniques for Wireless Sensor Networks: A Survey," *IEEE Communications Surveys & Tutorials,* vol. 12 (2), pp. 159-170, 2010.

Ramirez, Gesuri, Olac Fuentes, and Craig E. Tweedie, "Assessing data quality in a sensor network for environmental monitoring," in *Fuzzy Information Processing Society (NAFIPS), 2011 Annual Meeting of the North American*, 2011, pp. 1-6.

Taylor, Jeff R. and Henry L. Loescher, "Automated Quality Control Methods for Sensor Data: A Novel Observatory Approach," *Biogeosciences,* vol. 9 (12), pp. 18175-18210, 2012.

Klein, Lawrence A., *Sensor and Data Fusion - A Tool for Information Assessment and Decision Making*. Bellingham, Washington: SPIE Press, 2004.

Ristic, Lj. "*Sensor fusion and MEMS for 10-DoF solutions*," Last Update: 3rd September, 2012, `http://eetimes.com/design/medical-design/4395167/Sensor-fusion-and-MEMS-technology-for-10-DoF-solutions`

Kabaday, Sanem, "Virtual Sensors: An Intuive Programming Abstraction," in *Enabling Programmable Ubiquitous Computing Environments: The DAIS Middleware*, Ann Arbour, Michigan, ProQuest LLC, 2008, pp. 36-57.

Tan, Pang-Ninh. "*Knowledge Discovery from Sensor Data*," Last Update: March 1st, 2006, `http://www.sensorsmag.com/da-control/knowledge-discovery-sensor-data-753?page_id=1`

Duda, Richard O., Peter E. Hart, and David G. Stork, *Pattern Classification*, 2nd ed. New York: Wiley-Interscience, 2001.

Rodriguez, Claudia C. Gutiérrez and Anne-Marie Déry-Pinna, "Visualizing Sensor Data: Towards an Experiment and Validation Platform," in *Human-Centred Software Engineering*, Winckler, Marco, Peter Forbrig, and Regina Bernhaupt, Eds., Heidelberg, Springer-Verlag, 2012, pp. 352-359.

Sow, Daby, Deepak S. Turaga, and Michael Schmidt, "Mining of Sensor Data in Healthcare: A Survey," in *Managing and Mining Sensor Data*, Aggarwal, Charu C., Ed., New York, Springer US, 2013, pp. 459-504.

Karpatne, Anuj, *et al.*, "Earth Science Applications of Sensor Data," in *Managing and Mining Sensor Data*, Aggarwal, Charu C., Ed., New York, Springer US, 2013, pp. 505-530.

Argo. "*Argo - part of the integrated global observation strategy*," Last Update: 2013, `http://www.argo.ucsd.edu/About_Argo.html`

West, Amy E. *"Widespread floats provide pieces of the oceanic productivity puzzle,"* Last Update: October 28th 2011, `http://www.mbari.org/news/homepage/2011/johnson-floats/johnsonfloat.html`

McCandless, David. *"Information is Beautiful,"* Last Update: 2013, `http://www.informationisbeautiful.net/tag/health/`

Richter, Christian, "Visualizing Sensor Data - Media Informatics Advanced Seminar on Information Visualization," University of Munich, Munich, `http://www.medien.ifi.lmu.de/lehre/ws0809/hs/docs/richter.pdf`, 2009.

Shneiderman, B., "The eyes have it: a task by data type taxonomy for information visualizations," in *Visual Languages, Proceedings., IEEE Symposium on*, 1996, pp. 336-343.

Rodrigues, Pedro P. and João Gama, "A Simple Dense Pixel Visualisation for Mobile Sensor Data Mining," in *Knowledge Discovery from Sensor Data: Second International Workshop, Sensor-KDD 2008*, Vatsavai, Ranga Raju, Olufemi A. Omitaomu, João Gama, Nitesh V. Chawla, and Auroop R. Ganguly, Eds., Heidelberg, Springer, 2010, pp. 175-189.

Chou, Pai H., Chong-Jing Chen, Stephen F. Jenks, and Sung-Jin Kim, "HiperSense: An Integrated System for Dense Wireless Sensing and Massively Scalable Data Visualization," presented at the Proceedings of the 7th IFIP WG 10.2 International Workshop on Software Technologies for Embedded and Ubiquitous Systems, Newport Beach, CA, 2009.

Terzis, Andreas, *et al.*, "Wireless Sensor Networks for Soil Science," *International Journal of Sensor Networks*, vol. 7 (1), pp. 53-70, 2010.

Bradley, Eliza S., *et al.*, "Google Earth and Google Fusion Tables in support of time-critical collaboration: Mapping the deepwater horizon oil spill with the AVIRIS airborne spectrometer," *Earth Science Informatics*, vol. 4 (4), pp. 169-179, 2011.

Fakoor, Rasool, Mayank Raj, Azade Nazi, Mario Di Francesco, and Sajal K. Das, "An Integrated Cloud-based Framework for Mobile Phone Sensing," presented at the Proceedings of the first edition of the MCC Workshop on Mobile Cloud Computing, Helsinki, Finland, 2012.

Nourbakhsh, Illah, *"Citizen Science for Watershed Action: Big Data Meets Fusion Tables,"* The Climate Code, Last Update: March 13th 2012, `http://www.theclimatecode.com/2012/03/guest-post-citizen-science-for.html`

Lotfi, Ahmad, Caroline Langensiepen, Sawsan M. Mahmoud, and M. J. Akhlaghinia, "Smart Homes for the Elderly Dementia Sufferers: identification and Prediction of Abnormal Behaviour," *Journal of Ambient Intelligence and Humanized Computing*, vol. 3 (3), pp. 205-218, 2012.

Thorp, Jer. *"Big Data Is Not the New Oil,"* Last Update: 2012, `http://blogs.hbr.org/cs/2012/11/data_humans_and_the_new_oil.html`

IBM. *"What is big data,"* Last Update: 2013, `http://www-01.ibm.com/software/data/bigdata/`

Few, Stephen, "Big Data, Big Ruse". *Visual Business Intelligence Newsletter*, vol. July/August/September, 2012, `http://www.perceptualedge.com/articles/visual_business_intelligence/big_data_big_ruse.pdf`

Lane, Nicholas D., *et al.*, "A survey of mobile phone sensing," *IEEE Communications Magazine*, vol. 48 (9), pp. 140-150, 2010.

Campbell, Andrew and Tanzeem Choudhury, "From Smart to Cognitive Phones," *Pervasive Computing*, vol. July-September, 7-11, 2012

Insight. *"The Insight Centre for Data Analyticsn*, Last Update: 2013, `http://www.insight-centre.org/about/mission`

CHAPTER 6

▦ ▦ ▦

Regulations and Standards: Considerations for Sensor Technologies

All sensor-based devices, particularly healthcare devices, require a degree of regulation to ensure that they are electrically, chemically, biologically, and physically safe for the end user. The degree of regulation required depends on the level of risk associated with the device. Implantable devices, such as pacemakers, require more stringent regulation than a noninvasive thermometer. When developing or using health, wellness, or environmental devices, it is important to be aware of the regulations that pertain to that device and ensure that your device is compliant. In fact, because of the potential risks posed by certain medical devices, it is illegal to market or sell a medical device without putting it through the appropriate regulatory processes. Geographical and domain-specific standards provide benchmarks against which the compatibility, interoperability, safety, or quality of a device can be measured. Given this broad scope, it would be impossible to describe, or even list, all the standards that pertain to health, wellness, and environmental sensors within a single chapter. Rather, this chapter will provide an example-based introduction to the topics of regulation and standards, referencing some of the most common standards and regulations applied in these domains.

Sensors are the key component of any medical device that has a measuring purpose. As discussed in Chapter 3, sensors can be stand-alone discrete devices (such as home testing kits) or can interface with devices such as smartphones. Most sensor-based medical devices operate by making physical contact with the user. It is therefore critical that the device does not harm the user physically, chemically, or electrically. Sensors generate medically sensitive data, which must be protected or shared in a secure manner. Sensor data also informs clinical and nonclinical decisions, making accuracy a key requirement. Given the risk associated with even the simplest sensor-based device, compliance with standards and regulations is essential.

The level of regulation differs depending on whether a device is for research or manufacture. For example, CE (Conformité Européene) marking is not required for investigational devices but is necessary for devices that are to be sold. Investigational devices must be labeled "Exclusively for Clinical Investigation." Ethical review should always be sought for a clinical investigation of a non-CE medical device, and informed consents should be obtained from end users.

Regulation of Medical Devices

Before discussing standards and regulations for medical devices, it is helpful to understand the differences between both terms. The International Organization for Standardization defines a *standard* as follows:

> *A document, established by consensus and approved by a recognized body, that provides, for common and repeated use, rules, guidelines or characteristics for activities or their results, aimed at the achievement of the optimum degree of order in a given context.*

And a *regulation* is defined as follows:

> *A document providing binding legislative rules that is adopted by an authority*

In effect, a regulation has a legal status, but a standard does not. Therefore, medical devices must comply with the regulations in the geographical area in which they are sold.

The term *medical device* can be used to describe a broad range of items, ranging from a simple bandage to implantable pacemakers. Despite the broad scope of the term, medical devices are regulated by a single set of regulations. The process of medical device regulation is managed by national or international regulatory bodies, such as the United States Federal Food and Drug Administration (U.S. FDA) or a notified conformity assessment body in the European Union (EU). Although the regulatory requirements for medical device safety and manufacture are similar in most countries, they are not identical. Therefore, to market or sell a device in a specific jurisdiction, a device must undergo the regulatory process for that jurisdiction. This section will provide an overview to medical device regulation, using the U.S. FDA process and European Union Medical Device Directive as examples.

CE Marking

CE marking indicates that a product complies with EU legislation and can be sold within the European Economic Area (EEA), which are the 27 member countries of the EU plus Iceland, Norway, Liechtenstein, and Turkey. A CE mark is the manufacturer's declaration that the product meets the requirements of the applicable EU directives. It can be found on everything from toys to lightbulbs to PCs. CE marking does not indicate that the product is made in the EEA but simply that it has met all the requirements to be sold there. In the EU, all medical devices must be identified with the CE mark. To achieve a CE mark, the medical device must comply with one of the following directives:

- Directive 90/385/EEC regarding active implantable medical devices

- Directive 93/42/EEC regarding medical devices

- Directive 98/79/EC regarding in vitro diagnostic medical devices

The EU Medical Device Directive (also known as MDD or 93/42/EEC (EU 1993) is the most commonly applied directive for sensor-based devices. The MDD is a complex document, consisting of 23 articles, 12 annexes, and 18 classification rules. It is therefore highly recommended to work closely with your national "notified body" or regulatory agency to ensure all criteria of the directive are met. At a high level, obtaining CE certification for a medical device can be summarized as a six-step process (EC Enterprise and Industry):

1. ***Directives***: Verify that your device is a medical device, as defined in Article 1 of the MDD and that none of the exclusion criteria in this article applies. Ensure that your device is not an active medical device (in which case Directive 90/385/EEC applies) or an in vitro diagnostic medical device (in which case Directive 98/79/EC applies).

2. ***Verify requirements***: The essential requirements that the device must meet are listed in Annex I to the MDD. Compliance with these requirements must be demonstrated by a clinical evaluation in accordance with Annex X to the MDD. Note: it is possible that more than one directive applies to the same product (such as horizontal legislation on chemicals or environment); therefore, the requirements for these directives must also be met.

3. ***Need for notified body***: A notified body is required to certify a device's compliance if a device is classified as a Class II (medium risk) or higher or as a Class I (low risk) device, which is placed on the market in a sterile condition. Device classification is defined in Annex IX of the MDD. The role of the notified body is defined in Article 16 of the MDD.

4. ***Check conformity***: The conformity assessment procedure(s) depends on the class of the medical device. These procedures are listed in Annexes II to VII of the MDD, and the manufacturer can choose which procedure to apply. The conformity procedures address both the design and manufacture of the device. The manufacturer must provide objective evidence of how the design of the device meets with the essential requirements, described in Annex I of the MDD. A documented quality system must be in place to ensure that the devices continue to comply with the essential requirements. For Class IIa, IIb, and III devices, a notified body must verify and certify that the quality management of the manufacturer assesses the device's compliance with the essential requirements. Class I devices that are not placed on the market in a sterile condition can be self-certified. Regardless of the certification method, the manufacturer must declare its sole responsibility for the conformity to the MDD in a Declaration of Conformity (DoC).

5. ***Technical documentation***: Technical documentation (called a *design dossier*) must describe how the device conforms with the MDD requirements. This documentation must be provided by the manufacturer before submitting an application to the notified body or, at the latest, before placing the device on the market. The manufacturer must keep copies of the technical documentation for at least five years after the last product has been placed on the market.

6. ***Affix CE marking***: Once the necessary steps have been successfully completed, the CE marking must be visibly placed on the medical device. If this is not possible, it must be placed on the packaging and on the accompanying documentation. The identification number of the notified body must also be displayed if it was involved in the conformity assessment procedure.

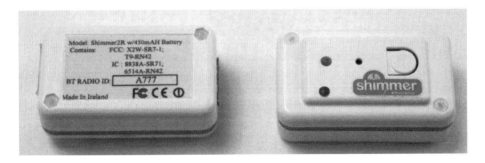

Figure 6-1. *CE marking on a Shimmer device (reproduced with permission from Realtime Technologies Ltd)*

Obtaining CE certification is only part of the process. Once the device is on the market, the facilities in which the device will be manufactured will be subject to annual ISO 13485 audits by the national competent authorities. Any incident pertaining to the device must be reported to the competent authority, who will decide the appropriate action to take. This EU regulatory framework for the device lifetime is well illustrated by Eucomed in Figure 6-2.

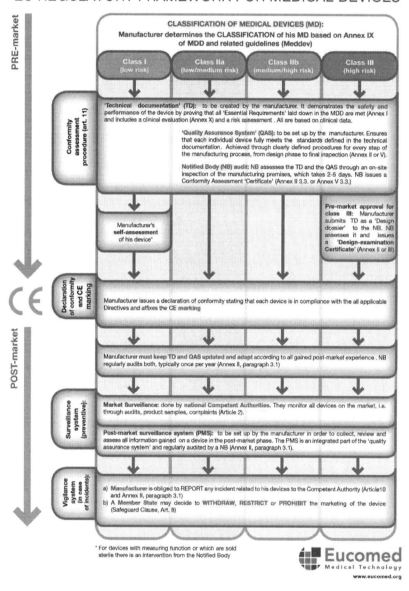

Figure 6-2. *EU regulatory framework for medical devices (reproduced with permission from Eucomed (www.eucomed.org/uploads/_key_themes/mdd/EUCOMED_infographie_03.jpg)*

U.S. FDA

The Food and Drug Administration's Center for Devices and Radiological Health (CDRH) is responsible for regulating firms that manufacture, repackage, relabel, and/or import medical devices sold in the United States (www.fda.gov/MedicalDevices/). It is also responsible for regulating medical (for example, X-ray systems) and non-medical (for example, color televisions) radiation-emitting electronic products. All medical devices are subject to the general controls of the Federal Food Drug & Cosmetic (FD&C) Act. These controls, which are contained in Title 21 Code of Federal Regulations Part 800-1200 (21 CFR Parts 800-1200) (FD&C Act, 2010), are the baseline requirements for marketing, labeling, and monitoring the postmarket performance of all medical devices. Technically, the U.S. FDA does not "approve" medical devices; it "clears" them for sale. The U.S. FDA marketing clearance process for medical devices can be described in three steps (U.S. FDA, 2013):

1. **Ensure the product is a medical device**, as defined by section 201(h) of the FD&C Act. Products that do not meet this definition (for example, drugs) may be subject to different U.S. FDA regulations. Some medical devices (for example, radiation-emitting devices) may also require additional regulation.

2. **Identify the risk-based device classification** (see Table 6-1), as described in 21 CFR 860. The classification will determine the level of regulatory controls required to ensure the safety and effectiveness of the device. It will also determine the marketing process (premarket notification or premarket approval [PMA]) required for the device to obtain U.S. FDA clearance. A device for which there is no substantially equivalent device is automatically classified as a Class III (high risk) device, regardless of the risk it poses. A "de novo" petition may be submitted to the U.S. FDA to request a re-classification from Class III to a Class I or II, if appropriate.

Table 6-1. *FDA Device Classes*

Device Class	Description	Risk Level
Class I: General controls	Class I devices are subject to the least regulatory control. Class I devices are not intended to help support or sustain life or be substantially important in preventing impairment to human health and may not present an unreasonable risk of illness or injury.	Low
Class II: General controls with special controls	Devices in Class II are held to a higher level of assurance than Class I devices and are designed to perform as indicated without causing injury or harm to the patient or user. Examples of Class II devices include powered wheelchairs, infusion pumps, and surgical drapes.	Medium
Class III: General controls and premarket approval	Class III devices are usually those that support or sustain human life, are of substantial importance in preventing impairment of human health, or present a potential, unreasonable risk of illness or injury.	High

3. **Develop data and/or information necessary to submit a marketing application**. The premarket notification process, which is also called the 510 (k) process, applies to most Class II (medium risk) and some Class I (low risk) and Class III devices (high risk). In this process, the device manufacturer must demonstrate that the device is safe and effective by proving "substantial equivalence" to a legally marketed "predicate device." The 510 (k) process rarely requires clinical trials. Premarket approval (PMA) is required to evaluate the safety and effectiveness of Class III (high risk) medical devices. PMA is the most stringent type of device marketing application required by U.S. FDA and is similar to the new drug approval process. Some 510(k) and most PMA applications require clinical trials to obtain clearance to market. Clinical trials must be performed in accordance with the U.S. FDA's Investigational Device Exemption (IDE) regulation.

The U.S. FDA reviews most 501(k) applications within 90 days and PMA applications within 180 days. If a 510(k) application is cleared, the U.S. FDA will mail the manufacturer a letter, with an assigned 510(k) number that says they "have determined that your device is substantially equivalent to legally marketed predicate devices." If a PMA device is cleared, the U.S. FDA audits the quality system regulation (QSR) of all major suppliers involved in the design, development, and manufacture of the device. If successful, a PMA approval letter is issued. On receipt of a 510(k) or PMA approval letter, the device is clear to sell, once the U.S. FDA device listing and establishment registration is completed on the U.S. FDA web site. The U.S. FDA will conduct random inspection to ensure compliance with the Quality Systems Regulation (QSR), 21 CFR Part 820.

Other Medical Device Regulators

According to the 2010 World Health Organization Baseline Country Survey on Medical Devices (World Health Organization, 2010), only 65 percent of 145 responding countries have a national authority responsible for implementing and enforcing medical device regulations. Many of those governments that have drafted regulations have made little progress in implementing them. The WHO is supporting countries that do not have regulations to develop and implement such regulations.

Medical device regulations differ among the 65 percent of countries that have implemented regulations. The WHO is an official observer of International Medical Devices Regulatory Forum (`www.imdrf.org`) and also supported its predecessor, the Global Harmonization Task Force (GHTF). The IMDRF is a voluntary group of medical device regulators (including the EU, U.S. FDA, and Australia) that have come together to "accelerate the international medical device regulatory harmonization and convergence." Their initial tasks include the following:

- Defining a path to implementing a globally harmonized approach to the uniform device identification system, previously defined by the GHTF

- Developing a standard set of requirements for auditing organizations that perform regulatory audits of medical device manufacturers' quality management systems

- Creating a list of international standards used for medical device regulatory purposes that are recognized by IMDRF Management Committee members

Standards for Medical Devices

Standards can serve different purposes. They can do all of the following:

- Provide reference criteria that a product, process, or service must meet

- Provide information that enhances safety, reliability, and performance of products, processes, and services

- Assure consumers about reliability or other characteristics of goods or services provided in the marketplace

- Give consumers more choice by allowing one firm's products to be substituted for, or combined with, those of another

Standards apply across many aspects of sensor-based devices, including radio standards (previously discussed in Chapter 3), industry standards, quality standards, and clinical standards. This section describes the standards and industry groupings most applicable to the health, wellness, and environmental domains.

Industry Standards and Certification

The healthcare industry, like many other industries, has developed a number of standards and guidelines where regulation does not exist. These standards were agreed upon by industry leaders to enable interoperability between devices and to ensure that a certain quality was maintained. Compliance with standards is voluntary, but compliant devices and software are more appealing to consumers because they are interoperable with other devices.

Continua

The Continua Health Alliance (`www.continuaalliance.org/`) is a nonprofit, open industry organization of more than 240 healthcare and technology companies collaborating to improve the quality of personal healthcare. Continua is not a standards body; rather, it identifies and resolves gaps in standards bodies so that personal telehealth solutions are interoperable and contribute toward improved health management. The alliance creates and updates design guidelines on standards to ensure interoperability between devices and manufacturers. Continua has created a product certification logo program with a consumer-recognizable logo signifying the promise of interoperability with other certified products. Continua is the only certification group in the personal connected healthcare domain.

Integrating the Healthcare Enterprise (IHE)

Like Continua, IHE (`www.ihe.net`) is a collaborative effort between healthcare professionals and the industry to promote the coordinated use of established standards, such as DICOM and HL7. The goal of the IHE is "to improve the quality, efficiency and safety of clinical care by making relevant health information conveniently accessible to patients and authorized care providers." To achieve this goal, every year the IHE brings together users and developers of healthcare information technology (HIT) to select and optimize established standards into "IHE Profiles" for HIT systems. The vendors can then test their systems against these profiles at "Connectathon" events to ensure they comply with the new profiles. The IHE focuses on total end-to-end interoperability of a system, not just one piece of it (as is the focus with most standards bodies). The IHE focus is primarily on medical imaging devices, radiology, cardiology, and HIT systems.

Happtique Health App Certification Program (HACP)

The Happtique Health App Certification Program (`www.happtique.com/app-certification/`) is a voluntary program developed to help healthcare providers and consumers easily identify medical, health, and fitness apps that do the following:

- Deliver credible content

- Contain safeguards for user data

- Function as described

Both federally regulated and unregulated medical, health, or fitness apps can be awarded a Happtique certification seal if they meet the operability, privacy, security, and content standards defined by HACP. The standards were developed under the direction of domain experts and relevant private organizations (for example, the American Medical Association). Federal agencies (for example, U.S. FDA, FCC) provided feedback during the development process. Compliance with the "technical standards" (Operability, Privacy, Security) is assessed by a third-party company (Inertek). Compliance with "content standards" is evaluated by the Association of Medical Colleges, CGFNS International, and appropriate clinical specialists. The HACP certification program, launched in February 2013, applies only to apps that are written in English and run natively on iOS, Android, BlackBerry, or Windows devices.

Quality Management System Standards

A quality management system (QMS) is a structured systematic approach to process and product quality management. It consists of organizational structure, responsibilities, processes and procedures, and resources. The most common QMS, the ISO 9001, is applicable to all business sectors. In many nonmedical device industries, creation and compliance with a QMS standard are simply methods to ensure quality and to promote continuous process and product improvement. A QMS standard can provide a competitive advantage over companies without QMS certification. In the medical device industry, demonstrating compliance with a QMS is a key part of the regulation process. The most common QMS for medical devices are ISO 13845 and 21 CFR 820. ISO 13845 and related standards.

ISO 13845 is an International Organization for Standardization (ISO) standard that defines the requirements for a comprehensive quality management system for the design and manufacture of medical devices. ISO 13845 is generally harmonized with ISO 9001, which sets out the requirements for a quality management system. They differ in one key area: ISO 9001 requires the organization to demonstrate continual improvement, whereas ISO 13485 requires only that a quality system is implemented and maintained. ISO 13485 is closely linked to the EU medical device directives, and demonstrating conformity with ISO 9001 and/or ISO 13485 and ISO 14971 is often seen as the first step in achieving compliance with European regulatory requirements. ISO 13485 is now considered to be an inline standard and requirement for medical devices. The International Medical Devices Regulatory Forum is currently working on the Medical Device Single Audit Program (MDSAP), which will align with the current ISO 13485 revision to achieve a harmonized standard among its members.

ISO 14971 is an ISO standard that establishes the requirements for risk management to determine the safety of a medical device during the product life cycle. This standard is required by higher-level regulations and other quality standards, including the ISO 13485 standard.

The U.S. FDA quality system requirements (21 CFR 820) were created many years before ISO 13485. As a result, they differ. The U.S. FDA does not recognize ISO 13485 certification, and the EU does not recognize 21 CFR 820. An integrated quality management system that meets the requirements of both the U.S. FDA and international regulatory bodies must be used if a medical device will be marketed within and outside of the United States. The differences between the EU and U.S. FDA QMS auditing processes are discussed later in this chapter.

Clinical Research Standards

Clinical research trials evaluate the efficacy of a clinical protocol, device, or drug. They are an essential part of the medical device approval process, and it is therefore essential that they are conducted safely and ethically and their results are reported accurately. Clinical research standards were developed to protect the patient and their data during clinical trials. The most commonly applied standards are the Declaration of Helsinki and Good Clinical Practice.

Declaration of Helsinki

The Declaration of Helsinki (WMA, 2013) is a set of ethical principles developed by the World Medical Association (WMA) to provide guidance to the medical community in research involving human subjects. This includes research on people, identifiable human material, or identifiable data. Although not a legally binding instrument in international law, it is considered a fundamental document in the ethics of healthcare research. As a result, the principles have been embodied in or have influenced national and regional legislation and regulations. The declaration was first adopted in 1964 in Helsinki, Finland, and has since undergone six revisions and two clarifications to accommodate advances in medical science and ethical problems. The declaration has 35 paragraphs, including principles on safeguarding research subjects, informed consent, minimizing risk, and adhering to an approved research plan/protocol.

The U.S. FDA rejected the 2000 and subsequent revisions of the declaration, and in 2006 announced it would eliminate all reference to it. In October 2008, the U.S. FDA replaced references to the Declaration of Helsinki with Good Clinical Practice.

Good Clinical Practice (GCP)

Good Clinical Practice (ICH, 2006) is a set of internationally recognized ethical and scientific quality requirements that must be observed for designing, conducting, recording, and reporting trials that involve the participation of human subjects. The GCP includes standards on how clinical trials should be conducted and defines the roles and responsibilities of clinical trial sponsors, clinical research investigators, and monitors. This standard ensures that the rights, safety, and well-being of trial subjects are protected and that the clinical trial data are credible. The unified clinical data standard provided by the ICH GCP guideline is accepted by the European Union, Japan, and the U.S. regulatory authorities. The guideline may also be applied to other nonregulatory clinical trials that involve human subjects.

Data Interoperability Standards

Data interoperability standards are essential to deliver better health and fitness data more quickly, safely, and at a lower cost. Without interoperability standards, data is either captured manually, captured using custom equipment, or not captured at all. Manual data capture is both labor-intensive and prone to errors. Custom equipment is invariably more expensive to run and maintain. The purchaser may be obliged to purchase all equipment from a single manufacturer to achieve end-to-end data connectivity rather than network the best (or cheaper) individual items to achieve the same goals. Lack of interoperability also hinders delivery of care. If individual devices are simultaneously capturing data from a single patient but cannot communicate with each other or with a centralized system, alarming trends or correlations may not be noticed.

CEN ISO/IEEE 11073

The CEN ISO/IEEE 11073 is an internationally adopted family of standards developed to enable complete connectivity between medical, healthcare, and wellness devices. These standards describe connectivity from the physical levels (cable or wireless connectivity) up to the abstract representation of data and the services to be exchanged with external computers. The standards are targeted at both personal health and fitness devices (including pulse oximeters, medication dispensers, and activity monitors) and hospital-based devices (including ventilators and infusion pumps). The goals of the standards are to do the following:

- Provide real-time plug-and-play interoperability for citizen-related medical, healthcare, and wellness devices

- Facilitate efficient exchange of care device data, acquired at the point of care, in all care environments

The ISO/IEEE 11073 Personal Health Device (PHD) standards are a subgroup of the ISO/IEEE 11073 family; they address the interoperability of personal health devices. These standards leverage existing IEEE11073 standards but apply a simpler communication model because they are designed for personal rather than hospital use.

Health Level 7 (HL7)

Health Level 7 (www.hl7.org/) describes both a nonprofit international standards organization and the interoperability standards it creates. HL7 specifies a number of flexible standards, guidelines, and methodologies that enable the different computer systems in hospitals and other healthcare organizations to communicate with each other. Specifically, HL7 develops the following standards:

Messaging standards: The HL7 v2.x and v3.0 messaging standards define how data is packaged and transferred from one party to another.

Conceptual standards: The HL7 Reference Information Model (RIM) standards represent the HL7 clinical data and life cycle of the message(s).

Document standards: The HL7 Clinical Document Architecture (CDA) standard specifies the XML-based encoding, structure, and semantics of clinical documents for the purposes of exchange.

Application standards: The HL7 Clinical Context Object Workgroup (CCOW) standard allows a clinical user to access a single patient's data across multiple applications using a single username and password.

Regulation of Environmental Sensors

As we become increasingly aware of our health and our environment, we become increasingly interested in quantifying the interactions between them. Environmental monitoring allows us to measure the quality of the air we breathe, the water we drink, any changes in weather, and the noise around us. These parameters can be measured using highly calibrated specialized devices or using off-the-shelf hobbyist devices. These devices report parameters that can have a serious impact on our lives; thus, it is vitally important that the sensors we rely on to warn us about unsafe water or dangerously high levels of carbon monoxide report accurately, consistently, and in a timely manner. A number of standards and regulations have been developed to quantify what parameters should be measured, how they should be measured, and how these data should be reported. Understanding both the standards and the ability of the sensors to meet these standards is a key part of application design: there is no point having a low-cost carbon dioxide sensor in an office environment if it cannot accurately measure carbon dioxide levels in the range set down by the indoor air quality standards. In many cases, low-cost sensors cannot perform to the specification required by the standards, but there is a research interest in understanding if a number of less accurate sensors can compensate for each other and collectively provide as much useful information as a single regulated sensor. This research question has yet to be answered, and until it is answered, it is best to comply with existing standards and regulations for critical applications or to indicate from the outset that the device has limitations.

Regulations for environmental noise, air quality, water, and weather have many subregulations—typically one regulation per parameter to be regulated. It is outside of the scope of this section to describe, or even list, every subregulation pertaining to these topics. However, this section will describe the overarching regulation covering each topic and the body responsible for regulating these environmental parameters.

Environmental Noise

Environmental noise pollution is the term used to describe excessive, unwanted, or disturbing outdoor sounds levels that affect the quality of life of people or animals. Unwanted noise can cause annoyance and aggression, increase stress levels, disturb sleep, and in severe cases damage hearing. Traffic, construction, industrial, and some recreational activities are the most common sources of outdoor environmental noise. Noise pollution can also occur indoors, but the sources of indoor noise are different (house alarms, music, home appliances, animals, and family conflict). Indoor noise pollution may also be subject to different regulations, depending on the use of that indoor location (for example, occupational health and safety). Noise regulations restrict the amount of noise, the duration of noise, and the source of noise. The permitted noise level can also be dependent on the time of day and the location of the noise: at nighttime or in very quiet locations the permitted noise levels are much lower than during the daytime in other areas.

Sound level meters are used to measure noise. These devices sense changes in pressure because of sound and amplify and filter this signal to provide a decibel reading. These devices must be calibrated in the field before every series of reading using a calibrator. Both the sound level meter and calibrator must comply with ISO standards and must be calibrated in a laboratory annually. The key standards describing the measurement of environmental noise are ISO 1996-2 and ISO 9613. Both these standards describe how to quantify noise from various sources. The most common measures used to describe noise are the equivalent continuous sound level ($L_{Aeq,T}$), which describes fluctuating noise from all sources in terms of a single noise level over the sample period (T); and the rated noise level ($L_{Ar,T}$), which adds a penalty to the $L_{Aeq,T}$ for more annoying tonal and impulsive noise. These levels can be measured continuously throughout the sample period or can be calculated by taking a number of representative samples for a prescribed duration during the sample period. Modern sound meters are capable of measuring other relevant statistical, maxima/minima, and 1/3 octave band data, which are also relevant to the assessment of noise. Information on these measures can be found in the ISO standards referred to earlier. As with many environmental measures, it is important not to overlook the time aspect of these measures. These standards describe an average value over a period of time, which can range from a few seconds to a day. Single samples of a pollutant, taken intermittently, may be interesting to an individual but is not comparable to the legislated values.

In Europe, the Environmental Noise Directive (2002/49/E, 2002) was created to map areas affected by noise pollution levels and to act upon it both at the member state and EU level. It defines a common approach to avoiding, reducing, and preventing the harmful effects due to exposure to long-term environmental noise. The directive deals mainly with noise due to major roads, railways, airports, and agglomerations. The World Health Organization recently published the Night Noise Guidelines for Europe (WHO, 2009), which presents details on the impact of nighttime noise on health. These guidelines recommend that the annual average outdoor noise at night should not exceed 40 decibel (dB). The WHO Guidelines for Community Noise (WHO, 2010) provides guideline exposure levels for community scenarios (Table 6-2). In the United States, individual states and local governments are responsible for addressing noise issues. However, the Environmental Protection Agency (EPA) investigates and studies noise and its effect, disseminates information to the public regarding noise pollution, responds to inquiries relating to noise, and evaluates the effectiveness of existing regulations for protecting the public health and welfare.

Table 6-2. *WHO Community Noise Guidance (Source: WHO Guidelines for Community Noise)*

Environment	Critical Health Effect	Sound Level dB(A)*	Time (Hours)
Outdoor living areas	Annoyance	50 to 55	16
Inside bedrooms	Sleep disturbance	30	8
School classrooms	Disturbance of communication	35	During class
Industrial, commercial, and traffic areas	Hearing impairment	70	24
Music through earphones	Hearing impairment	85	1
Ceremonies and entertainment	Hearing impairment	100	4

Ambient Air Quality

Humans can be adversely affected by exposure to solid particles, liquid droplets, or gases in the air. There is a wide range of air pollutants, which can occur naturally (radon gas) or be man-made (carbon monoxide from a vehicle exhaust). These pollutants come from stationary sources, such as manufacturing facilities, refineries, and power plants; and mobile sources, such as cars, heavy goods vehicles, and airplanes. Many regulations exist to manage all these sources. For example, in Europe there are regulations for paint emissions (the Paints Directive), Industrial Emissions (the IPPC Directive), and Emissions from Maritime transport (Directive 1999/32/EC), among many others (EU, 2013). The Clean Air For Europe (CAFE) Directive (2008/50/EC) is the most relevant European regulation for this book. This directive provides both limits (Table 6-3) and target values for air quality pollutants. Like noise pollution, these limits and targets apply over differing periods of time. This is because the health impacts associated with each pollutant can occur over different exposure times. The individual member states in the EU are responsible for implementing this directive in their own countries. They must assess air pollution levels in zones across their country, prepare an air quality plan for when a limit is exceeded, and disseminate air quality information to the public.

Table 6-3. *Limit Values of CAFE Directive (Source: http://ec.europa.eu/environment/air/quality/standards.htm)*

Pollutant	Concentration	Averaging Period	Permitted Exceedences Each Year
Fine particles (PM2.5)	$25 \, \mu g/m^3$	1 year	n/a
Sulfur dioxide (SO_2)	$350 \, \mu g/m^3$	1 hour	24
	$125 \, \mu g/m^3$	24 hours	3
Nitrogen dioxide (NO_2)	$200 \, \mu g/m^3$	1 hour	18
	$40 \, \mu g/m^3$	1 year	n/a
PM10	$50 \, \mu g/m^3$	24 hours	35
	$40 \, \mu g/m^3$	1 year	n/a
Lead (Pb)	$0.5 \, \mu g/m^3$	1 year	n/a
Carbon monoxide (CO)	$10 \, mg/m^3$	Maximum daily 8 hour mean	n/a
Benzene	$5 \, \mu g/m^3$	1 year	n/a
Ozone	$120 \, \mu g/m^3$	Maximum daily 8 hour mean	25 days averaged over 3 years
Arsenic (As)	$6 \, ng/m^3$	1 year	n/a
Cadmium (Cd)	$5 \, ng/m^3$	1 year	n/a
Nickel (Ni)	$20 \, ng/m^3$	1 year	n/a
Polycyclic Aromatic Hydrocarbons	$1 \, ng/m^3$ (expressed as concentration of Benzo(a)pyrene)	1 year	n/a

The Clean Air Act was introduced in 1970 to protect the health and environment in the United States from air pollution. This act gives the EPA the authority to set and revise national ambient air quality standards (NAAQS), based on the latest science. The Clean Air Act refers to two standards: primary standards are the standards for public health, and secondary standards are for the protection of crops, the environment, and property. The EPA currently regulates six "criteria pollutants": sulfur dioxide, carbon monoxide, particles, nitrogen dioxide, ozone, and lead (Table 6-4). These pollutants can damage health, the environment, and property. Each of these pollutants is regulated by a different code of federal regulation (CFR). Each U.S. state is responsible for implementing its own air pollution regulations, programs, and policies, but they cannot have weaker limits than those set by the EPA. Each state can also grant and enforce operating permits to major pollution sources that contain emission standards and limitations.

Table 6-4. *U.S. National Ambient Air Quality Standards (Source: http://epa.gov/air/criteria.html)*

Pollutant	Primary/Secondary	Averaging Time	Level	Form
Carbon monoxide	Primary	8-hour	9 ppm	Not to be exceeded more than once per year
		1-hour	35 ppm	
Lead	Primary and secondary	Rolling 3-month average	$0.15 \, \mu g/m^3$	Not to be exceeded

(*continued*)

Table 6-4. (*continued*)

Pollutant		Primary/Secondary	Averaging Time	Level	Form
Nitrogen dioxide		Primary	1-hour	100 ppb	98th percentile, averaged over 3 years
		Primary and secondary	Annual	53 ppb	Annual mean
Ozone		Primary and secondary	8-hour	0.075 ppm	Annual fourth-highest daily maximum 8-hour concentration, averaged over 3 years
Particle pollution	PM2.5	Primary	Annual	12 $\mu g/m^3$	Annual mean, averaged over 3 years
		Secondary	Annual	15 $\mu g/m^3$	Annual mean, averaged over 3 years
		Primary and secondary	24-hour	35 $\mu g/m^3$	98th percentile, averaged over 3 years
	PM10	primary and secondary	24-hour	150 $\mu g/m^3$	Not to be exceeded more than once per year on average over 3 years
Sulphur dioxide		Primary	1-hour	75 ppb	99th percentile of 1-hour daily maximum concentrations, averaged over 3 years
		secondary	3-hour	0.5 ppm	Not to be exceeded more than once per year

An air quality index is a simple method to represent air quality status as a single value on a scale. Different countries have created different scales by weighting the inputs differently. The EU air quality index, the Common Air Quality Index (CAQI), is a 5-level scale, ranging from 0 (very low) to >100 (very high). This scale (Elshout et al., 2012) is based on 3 pollutants (PM10, NO_2, O_3) and is applied to provide air quality status in the previous hour, the last day, and the last year. This scale is applied by several EU countries and allows nonexperts to quickly compare air quality between locations without understanding the underlying data. The EPA implemented a 6-level AQI (U.S. EPA, 2009) based on 5 of the "criteria pollutants." This data is gathered from around the United States and is represented using color-coded levels on the live AirNow air quality website (`www.airnow.gov/`).

Indoor Air Quality

While outdoor air quality and industrial air quality are well regulated at a federal level, there are few regulations for indoor air quality. This is surprising considering how much time we spend indoors, sleeping, working, traveling, or engaging in indoor sporting or leisure activities. Indoor air quality (IAQ) is the term used to describe the concentrations of air pollutants that are known or suspected to affect people's comfort, health, or performance at work or school. In serious cases, poor IAQ can spread airborne infections, such as Legionnaire's disease; cause cancers, such as lung cancer from radon exposure; or cause death due to severe acute respiratory syndrome (SARS) or carbon monoxide (CO) poisoning. There as several sources of air pollution, with corresponding standards and regulations.

Most indoor air pollutants come from topical chemical sources, such as cleaning products, air fresheners, and pesticides; or emissions from construction materials, heating, and cooking. The impact of these pollutants can be overcome by adequate ventilation. Ventilation is increasingly becoming an issue in Western countries. As we strive to achieve airtight energy-efficient homes and workplaces, we overlook the importance of natural or mechanical air flow in and out of a building. Global warming also has a part to play; extreme weather encourages us to shut all the windows and sources of natural ventilation, thus leading to a buildup of chemicals, pathogens, and allergens. Good building and ventilation design are therefore essential factors in ensuring IAQ. The American Society of Heating, Refrigerating, and Air-conditioning Engineers (ASHRAE) publishes a well-recognized series of standards and guidelines relating to HVAC systems and issues, such as ASHRAE Standard 62-2001, "Ventilation for Acceptable Indoor Air Quality" (ANSI/ASHRAE). These standards are widely applied in industry but are not legally enforceable. However, the EPA has adopted some of these recommendations in its regulations. Poor thermal conditions and inadequate ventilation can encourage the growth of microorganisms on building surfaces and the survival of airborne infectious pathogens and dust mites. Outdoor sources of air pollution can also impact indoor air quality.

From a sensing perspective, the ISO/TC 146 Air Quality Technical Committee (ISO/TC 146, 2013) is responsible for standardization of tools for air quality characterization of emissions, workspace air, ambient air, and indoor air and for meteorological parameters. It describes measurement methods for air pollutants (particles, gases, odors, and micro-organisms), measurement planning, procedures for Quality Assurance/Quality Control (QA/QC), and methods for the evaluation of results including the determination of uncertainty. This technical committee is responsible for a total of 140 ISO standards in the IAQ sensing domain. The WHO Guidelines for Indoor Air Quality Selected Pollutants (WHO, 2010) provides scientific-based guidelines for a number of chemicals commonly present in indoor air. The chemicals described in this guideline are commonly found indoors and are demonstrated to be hazardous to health. These chemicals are benzene, carbon monoxide, formaldehyde, naphthalene, nitrogen dioxide, polycyclic aromatic hydrocarbons, radon, trichloroethylene, and tetrachloroethylene. The guideline describes the scientific evidence, which demonstrates the risk posed by each of these chemicals. As with outdoor air quality regulations, the exposure limits of each chemical is described according to an average exposure time.

The most commonly sensed chemicals, from a consumer perspective, are carbon monoxide and radon. Carbon monoxide (CO) is a byproduct of heating, cooking, and combustion engines and is therefore often found at low levels in both indoor and outdoor environments. Inadequate ventilation or damaged appliances can cause a lethal buildup of this tasteless, colorless, odorless gas. It is therefore recommended that all homes install and maintain a CO alarm. In Europe, in-home CO sensors must comply with the European Standard EN50291, which states that an alarm should be triggered at the following levels:

- Not before 120 minutes for a concentration of 30 ppm

- Between 60 and 90 minutes at a concentration of 50 ppm

- Between 10 and 40 minutes at a concentration of 100 ppm

- Before 3 minutes at a concentration of 300 ppm

These standards are safer than the U.S. standards for CO (Underwriters Laboratories, 2005). It should be noted that CO alarms are designed to prevent acute poisoning (one-time accidental poisoning). They are not designed to prevent chronic poisoning (multiple low-level poisonings), which also poses a health risk.

Radon is a naturally occurring radioactive gas that results from the decay of uranium in rocks and soils. Like CO, it is colorless, odorless, and tasteless and can be measured only using special equipment. It is the leading risk factor for lung cancer in nonsmokers. In open air, radon is quickly diluted to harmless concentrations. However, in enclosed spaces, such as a house, radon levels can build up to dangerous concentrations. National radiological monitoring agencies map locations of high radon risk. Building regulations state that mitigation methods should be employed to protect the building from radon from the ground during the construction phase of a building. These measures include fully sealed, low permeability membranes, or radon sumps. However, these membranes can be damaged, and radon may still leak into the building. Radon sensors can be purchased from national radiological agencies levels for a nominal fee. These sensors measured radon over a three-month period to allow for temporal fluxations in radon levels. Radon levels are described by regulation agencies in terms of action level and reference levels. As the name implies, an action level is the level at which action should be taken to mitigate against radon exposure, whereas a reference level is a warning of unacceptable levels. The WHO (WHO, 2010) recommends a maximum acceptable annual average level of 100 Bq/m^3 for radon in dwellings. European countries (EU, 2009) have references levels between 200 and 400 Bq/m^3; the EPA recommends action be taken at levels of 74 Bq/m^3 (US EPA, 2013).

Drinking Water

Drinking water is essential to sustain life, and access to an adequate, safe, and accessible supply is a basic human right. However, drinking water may contain microbial, chemical, or radiological constituents that are unsafe. Drinking water standards are defined and implemented on a national or regional level. The WHO publishes guidelines (WHO, 2011) on the minimum standards that should be achieved, and these standards are applied in countries in which there are no existing standards. The WHO guidelines contain guideline levels for chemical and microbial pollutants, as well as describing how to apply these guidelines. However, these standards are not legally enforceable. In Europe, drinking water is regulated by the European Drinking Water Directive (98/83/EC). In the United States, the EPA regulates drinking water according to the Safe Drinking Water Act (42 U.S.C. 300f). Both the EU and U.S. regulations are legally enforceable. These standards and regulations describe the parameters of a substance in terms of a concentration (30 mg/l of iron) or a population count for microbial contamination. The maximum accepted concentration for each parameter varies according to the regulation body. For example, the maximum contaminant levels (MCL) for cyanide in the EU is 0.05 mg/l, but the MCL for cyanide is 0.2 mg/l in the United States(SWDF). Drinking water standards and regulations not only describe the MCLs but also the context (sampling location, sampling methods, and sampling frequency) of the sample acquisition and the interpretation of the sample (analytical methods, and laboratory accreditation). This context is important if an individual wants to personally monitor water quality using a sensing device. It is also important to be aware of the parametric range at which pollutants are unlikely to have any impact on health.

Regulation and Allocation of Radio Spectrum

Radio spectrum is the term used to describe the part of the electromagnetic spectrum used for radio frequencies (the full frequency range from 3 kHz to 300 GHz). The radio spectrum is used for a wide range of applications, including government communications (defense, public safety, transport); commercial services for the public (voice, data, TV and radio broadcasting); and industrial, scientific, and medical use (cordless telephone, baby monitors, Wi-Fi). This wide variety of applications requires careful management to ensure the spectrum is best used for the benefit of all. Radio spectrum management is the role of government authorities in each nation, although it is closely aligned with regional and global authorities. The radio spectrum is broken into different nonoverlapping frequency ranges, called *bands*, to prevent interference and allow for efficient use of the radio spectrum. Similar services are grouped in the same bands, and these bands are described according to their frequency (for example, Very High Frequency [VHF]) or their application (for example, marine). Each band has a basic set of usage rules, which ensures compatibility between receivers and transmitters and avoid interference between different sources.

Radio spectrum is a valuable commodity, which is typically owned by the government of a country. The government-appointed regulators can license parts of the spectrum for exclusive use by radio, television, and cellular phone companies in a given geographical area. A broadcasting license gives the commercial entity exclusive rights to broadcast their services in the band(s) that they were allocated. Entities that broadcast their services in the licensed spectrum without a license are called *unlicensed* broadcasters and are breaking the law. Fortunately, there are also bands of the spectrum that have been allocated for individuals to use for local communications. The most common of these bands are located at 900 MHz and 2.4 GHz and are called the industrial, scientific, and medical (ISM) bands. These bands are unlicensed; therefore, the user is free to use them without having to register or to pay for an individual license from the telecommunication regulatory authorities. The ISM radio bands were originally reserved for electromagnetic radiation produced by ISM equipment. However, in recent years these bands have also been used by license-free, error-tolerant, communications applications such as cordless phones, Bluetooth devices, near field communication (NFC) devices, and wireless computer networks. Low-power communication devices operating in this band must accept interference from licensed users of the frequency band and must not cause interference to licensed users.

The term *unlicensed* ISM radio devices does not imply they are unregulated; the device itself must usually meet strict regulations and be certified by the appropriate regulatory authorities. In the United States, the Federal Communications Commission is responsible for ensuring that low-power communication devices comply with Title 47 of the United States Code of Federal Regulations Part 15 (47 CFR Part 15). This regulation applies to most electronic equipment because it describes the regulations under which intentional, unintentional, or incidental radiators that can operate without an individual license. 47 CFR Part 15 requires that most electronic devices are either verified to not cause harmful emissions or certified to not cause harmful emissions. The verification process is typically used for receivers and unintentional transmitters and involves the creation of a declaration of conformity, which states that the emissions limits are within the FCC Part 15 rules. An accredited test laboratory must test a sample device and produce a test report and Declaration of Conformity for the manufacturer to submit to the FCC. All intentional transmitters must receive FCC certification. To obtain certification, an accredited test laboratory must request a FCC Grantee Code, test the device, and submit a detailed test report to the FCC. If the FCC deems that the device meets with its regulation, it will certify the device and issue an FCC identification number for the device. The vendor must attach this FCC identification number and the FCC logo to each transmitter device it sells.

In Europe, ISM band devices are referred to as *short-range devices* (SRD). These devices are low-power wireless devices, which have low capability of causing interference to other radio equipment. In Europe, the regulations governing low-power wireless devices are defined by two separate bodies:

- The European Conference of Postal and Telecommunication Administration (CEPT) defines the frequency, allocation, and use of short-range radio device (SRD) frequency bands in document ERC/REC 70-03 (CEPT, 2013)

- The European Telecommunications Standards Institute (ETSI) defines the procedure required to bring SRD wireless equipment to the EU market in the Radio and Telecommunications Terminal Equipment Directive (1999/5/EC)

The European process for achieving radio compliance is similar to the FCC process, in that receivers can simply create a declaration of conformity and establish technical documentation to support their application, whereas transmitters must undergo radio testing to establish compliance with harmonized standards. If harmonized standards are not applicable, the radio device must also be assessed by a notified body. A number of harmonized standards may apply to any given radio. Therefore, it is best to seek the advice of a qualified laboratory when developing and applying for certification.

The FCC and EU bodies perform a number of other vital nonregulatory roles, which are outside of the scope of this chapter. These include advancing the introduction of new wireless technologies, rationalizing and optimizing the use of RF spectrum, and collaborating with other governmental bodies for the good of citizens. The FCC, for example, formed a mobile health (mHealth) task force in 2011, which investigates methods in which the FCC can facilitate adoption of mHealth technologies to improve health outcomes and lower healthcare costs. As a spectrum regulator, it was able to define and allocate spectrum for a new class of devices, called medical body area networks (MBANs); investigate and plan for improved rural broadband healthcare networks; and provide input to the FDA on its mHealth regulations.

Challenges

There are a number of challenges in the standards and regulation space; the most pressing of which is the limited regulation of mobile phone applications. Developing standards and regulations can be a slow process requiring consensus across many parties. The difficulty in achieving consensus for mHealth regulation is further exacerbated by the lack of consensus in international regulatory processes. Yet again, there is widespread agreement that an international standard for medical device regulation would be beneficial for both device manufacturers and consumers, but progress toward achieving this goal has been slow. The lack of international guidelines for data privacy and data sharing could have a significant impact on the development of personalized health solutions. Large quantities of data are required to investigate and develop personalized health solutions; for particularly rare diseases, it may not be possible to gather a statistically significant dataset within the geographical region controlled by an individual regulatory body. Finally, the ability for citizen scientists to generate, store, and report data from their own experiments is an exciting prospect. However, it may also be risky if people place faith in lower-quality sensors from nonrigorous experiments. As low-cost sensors become more readily available, there may be a requirement for light-touch regulation or disclaimers for such data.

Country-Specific Regulatory Processes

Safety, quality, performance, equitable access, and cost effectiveness of medical devices are common goals of all device regulators. However, it can be argued that the variety of regulatory agencies and differing regulatory requirements (see Table 6-5) can impede these goals.

Table 6-5. *Selected International Medical Device Regulatory Authorities*

Geographical Location	Regulatory Authority
Australia	Therapeutic Goods Administration (TGA)
Brazil	Agência Nacional de Vigilância Sanitária (ANVISA)
Canada	Health Canada
China	State Food and Drug Administration (SFDA)
India	Central Drugs Standard Control Organization (CDSCO)
Japan	Pharmaceuticals and Medical Devices Agency, Japan (PMDA)
Russia	Roszdravnadzor

The most obvious example of this is the lack of compatibility between U.S. FDA and EU medical device regulations, which differ in three significant ways (COCIR/MITA, 2013):

- *Auditing of medical technology manufacturer quality management systems*: The EU conformity assessment bodies and U.S. FDA do not mutually accept reports of each other's audits of QMS. As a result, manufacturers must be audited by both bodies, despite having similar requirements. Both authorities are members of the IMDRF and could resolve this issue by implementing a common audit process or single quality system.

- *Marketing application format*: Although a common dataset is accepted by both authorities, the submission methods and application formats differ greatly. This leads to further regulatory burden for manufacturers, which could be eliminated by adopting the harmonized premarket submission format developed by the GHTD.

- *Unique device identification (UDI)*: Development of a UDI database is an international objective to facilitate traceability and interoperability. However, a UDI or common labeling requirements have yet to be implemented in Europe, and the FDA is in the process of developing a database.

The members of the IMDRF, overseen by the WHO, are collaborating to create regulatory harmonization and convergence. However, despite years of harmonization talks, the debate continues on which is the best regulatory model. The U.S. FDA applies a centralized model, in which it is responsible for all aspects of premarket and postmarket regulation of medical devices. The EU applies a decentralized model, in which national "notified bodies" review the safety and performance of new medical devices. Critics of the centralized model (www.dontlosethe3.eu) complain that it is slow and bureaucratic and delays patient access to devices by three to five years (see Figure 6-4). Those who advocate a centralized model cite the PIP breast implant incident as an example of the failure of the distributed model. Research (BCG 2011) has demonstrated that both systems are equally safe. The members of the IMDRF will continue to align various aspects of medical device regulation. Whether they will ever be able to answer the centralized versus decentralized model debate remains to be seen.

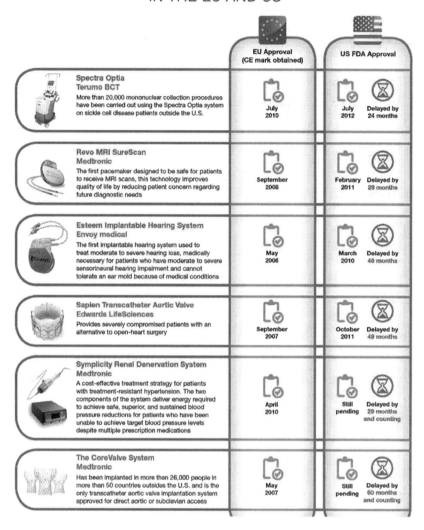

Figure 6-3. *Patient access to medical technology in the EU and United States (reproduced with permission from Eucomed www.eucomed.org/uploads/images/_key_themes/mdd/visuals/patient_access.jpg)*

Mobile Health Applications

Mobile medical applications (mHealth apps) are a rapidly increasing market, with more than 38,000 apps categorized as healthcare and fitness apps and 24,000 apps categorized as medical apps in the iOS app store in 2013. In an era in which doctors are increasingly prescribing health apps, it is extraordinary that the mHealth app market is still largely unregulated. Although the majority of apps are wellness or health monitoring apps, a small but increasing number of apps claim to diagnose or recognize disease. Developers of apps that made unsubstantiated claims were recently fined by the Federal Trade Commission, but a proactive rather than a reactive approach is urgently required.

In 2012, in the absence of clear guidelines as to how current regulations apply to mHealth, a private company, Happtique, developed a certification system (HACP, 2012) for mHealth apps. The HACP, described earlier in this chapter, uses independent third parties to assess compliance with content, privacy, performance, and operability guidelines.

Regulating for mHealth applications is a complex task. New regulations must allow for rapid innovation while ensuring safety, and they must consider the end-to-end application rather than a single device or module. In the United States, the U.S. FDA issued guidelines on mobile medical applications in 2013 (U.S. Food and Drug Administration, 2013). In these guidelines, a mobile medical app is defined as follows:

> *a mobile app that meets the definition of "device" in section 201(h) of the Federal Food, Drug, and Cosmetic Act (FD&C Act); and either: is used as an accessory to a regulated medical device; or transforms a mobile platform into a regulated medical device. The intended use of a mobile app determines whether it meets the definition of a "device."*

According to these guidelines, the FDA will focus its regulatory oversight on a subset of mobile medical apps that present a greater risk to patients if they do not work as intended. Therefore, the majority of mHealth applications, which are low-risk applications, will not be subject to regulation. The Federal Communications Commission has set up an mHealth taskforce to consider the implications of mHealth on the communications industry. In 2010, the U.S. FDA and FCC signed a memorandum of understanding on regulation, which is indicative of the cross-disciplinary nature of mHealth.

Personalized Medicine

The emergence of personalized medicine will have significant implications for regulatory and standards bodies. Personalized medicine promises to move healthcare from the "one size fits all" medical approach to a "right intervention to the right person at the right time" approach. However, to achieve this goal, patients must be subdivided into groups according to their biological makeup, lifestyle, and environmental factors. By stratifying patients into groups, interventions can be identified that are most effective for individual groups. Each person's unique genetic disposition, lifestyle, and environment factors must be understood, and integrated data profiles must be created and maintained for large populations. As diseases are reclassified into smaller and smaller subtypes, transborder sharing of data will be necessary to achieve sufficient numbers in each study group. Transborder sharing will pose several challenges to the regulatory bodies. A consistent, international, regulated approach to data capture, data protection, data use and reuse, and data lifetime must be developed that balances citizens' rights and public good will be required.

Data literacy will become increasingly important. Patients must understand the choices available to them so that they can make informed decisions about their health. Data privacy laws will have to change from a "data protection" to a "data sharing with controls" mentality. Commercial use of genetic/genomic data must be closely monitored and regulated to prevent discrimination between patients. From a sensing perspective, electronic health records will have to be amended to allow for lifelong data capture from personal health and wellness devices, as well as traditional medical records. The context and quality of personal health and wellness device data will require careful consideration if it is to be associated with clinical data.

Citizen Science

Easy access to health, wellness, and environmental sensors and aggregation platforms has enabled a generation of citizen scientists to capture, interpret, and disseminate data. Crowd-sourced data can provide a level of geographical granularity that more expensive regulated devices cannot provide. The Asthmapolis mHealth application (`http://asthmapolis.com`) is a good example of crowd-sourced data. This app is synchronized with an asthmatic's inhaler, and every location where the inhaler is used is geotagged. This data can be shared with the wider community to identify asthma "hotspots" where inhaler use is high. Similarly, the Air Quality Egg (`http://airqualityegg.com/`) allows anyone to collect readings of NO_2 and CO concentrations outside of their home and share this data with the wider community. These are just two examples of Internet of Things (IoT) applications, which contribute to public knowledge and well-being.

However, there are limitations to data captured by citizen scientists: the sensor resolution of the devices may not be comparable to regulated devices. The data may be unintentionally biased by untrained volunteers applying incorrect data capture protocols. Further, data may be incorrectly interpreted by nonexperts. In personal health, incorrect application of regulated devices such home blood pressure monitors also leads to invalid data. Highly accurate weather and pollution stations can give misleading data if they are placed in the shade or too close to a road. Trusting citizen data gathered using a highly accurate regulated device without considering context may cause unnecessary alarm, which could have serious implications in crowded locations such as subways. Regulations apply to ensure the safe use of the device, but should there be guidelines pertaining to the safe use and interpretation of data? Should data be curated, according to a lightweight hobbyist standard? Or is it safe to assume that invalid data will simply be an outlier within a larger grouping of data sources? Would education on research methods and existing standards ensure more accurate data? Or should the data consumer simply be willing to accept the risks of using data from unregulated sources? In the next chapter, we will examine the social relationships that create opportunities and barriers for widespread, consumer-based biosensing. Citizen-led science is driving a shift from sensor technologies of "should" to sensor technologies of "could." These technologies facilitate new understandings of the body and its environment and drive new methods and practices of personal data sharing. For this reason, citizen science will be an area of significant focus in the EU Horizon 2020 research program (EU, 2013).

Summary

This chapter introduced the topics of standards and regulations as they apply to sensor-based health, wellness, and environmental domains. The complex medical device regulation process was described, using the U.S. FDA and EU MDD as examples. The topic of standards was introduced, using a representative sample of the most common standards that apply to sensor applications in the domains of concern. The regulations and standards bodies that regulate environmental sensors and radio spectrum were also introduced. Finally, the challenges facing regulatory and standards bodies, in an era of rapidly evolving science, technology, and user demands, were discussed.

References

European Standards, "Council Directive 93/42/EEC of 14 June 1993 concerning medical devices," 1993.

European Commission Enterprise and Industry. "*CE marking for professionals: 6 steps for manufacturers*", Last Update: November 2013, http://ec.europa.eu/enterprise/policies/single-market-goods/cemarking/professionals/manufacturers/directives/index_en.htm

Underwriters Laboratories, "Single and Multiple Station Carbon Monoxide Alarms," vol. UL 2034, ed 2, 2005.

United States, "Federal Food Drug & Cosmetic (FD&C) Act," in *Title 21 Code of Federal Regulations Part 800-1200*, 2010.

U.S. Food and Drug Administration. "*Medical Devices: How to Market Your Device*", Last Update: November 2013, http://www.fda.gov/medicaldevices/deviceregulationandguidance/howtomarketyourdevice/default.htm

World Health Organization, "Baseline country survey on medical devices", http://whqlibdoc.who.int/hq/2011/WHO_HSS_EHT_DIM_11.01_eng.pdf, 2010.

World Medical Association. "*Declaration of Helsinki*", Last Update: November 2013, http://www.wma.net/en/30publications/10policies/b3/

International Conference on Harmonisation of Technical Requirements for Registration of Pharmaceuticals for Human Use (ICH), "ICH Harmonised Tripartite Guideline. Guideline for Good Clinical Practice E6(R1)," 1996.

European Standards, "Directive 2002/49/EC of the European Parliament and of the Council of 25 June 2002 relating to the assessment and management of environmental noise," 2002.

World Health Organization, "Night Noise Guidelines for Europe", 2009.

World Health Organization, "WHO guidelines for indoor air quality: selected pollutants", 2010.

European Commission. "*Air Quality Legislation*", Last Update: November 2013, http://ec.europa.eu/environment/air/legis.htm

European Standards, "Directive 2008/50/EC of the European Parliament and of the Council of 21 May 2008 on ambient air quality and cleaner air for Europe," 2008.

Elshout, Sef van den, Hans Bartelds, Hermann Heich, and Karine Léger, "CAQI Air quality index. Comparing Urban Air Quality across Borders", http://www.airqualitynow.eu/download/CITEAIR-Comparing_Urban_Air_Quality_across_Borders.pdf, 2012.

U.S. Environmental Protection Agency Office of Air Quality Planning and Standards Outreach and Information Division, "A Guide to Air Quality and Your Health," 2009.

American Society of Heating Refrigerating and Air-Conditioning Engineers, "Ventilation for Acceptable Indoor Air Quality," vol. ANSI/ASHRAE 62-2001, 2003.

ISO/TC 146 Air quality Technical Committee. Last Update: November 2013, http://www.iso.org/iso/home/standards_development/list_of_iso_technical_committees/iso_technical_committee.htm?commid=52702

European Environment and Health Information System, "Radon Levels in Dwellings: Fact Sheet 4.6," in http://www.euro.who.int/__data/assets/pdf_file/0006/97053/4.6_-RPG4_Rad_Ex1-ed2010_editedViv_layouted.pdf, ed, 2009.

United States Environmental Protection Agency, "Basic Radon Facts," in http://www.epa.gov/radon/pdfs/basic_radon_facts.pdf vol. EPA 402/F-12/005, 2013.

World Health Organization, "Guidelines for drinking-water quality - 4th ed.", http://www.who.int/water_sanitation_health/publications/2011/dwq_chapters/en/index.html, 2011.

European Standards, "Council Directive 98/83/EC of 3 November 1998 on the quality of water intended for human consumption," vol. 98/83/EC, 1998.

"Safe Drinking Water Act," in *Title 42 - The Public Health and Welfare. Chapter 6a - Public Health Service. Subchapter XII - Safety of Public Water Systems* vol. 42 U.S.C. 300f, 1996.

Safe Drinking Water Foundation. "*Comparison Chart of Drinking Water Standards from around the World*", Last Update: November 2013, http://www.safewater.org/PDFS/resourceswaterqualityinfo/RegulationsGuidelinesComparisons.pdf

Code of Federal Regulations, "Title 47-Telecommunication Chapter I--Federal Communications Commisions Subchapter A--General Part 15--Radio Frequency Devices," vol. Title 47 CFR Part 15.

European Conference of Postal and Telecommunication Administration, "ERC Recommendation 70-03 (Tromsø 1997 and subsequent amendments) relating to the use of Short Range Devices (SRD)," in *ERC/REC 70-03*, 2013.

European Standards, "Directive 1999/5/EC of the European Parliment and of the Council of 9 March 1999 on radio equipment and telecommunications terminal equipment and the mutual recognition of their conformity," vol. 1999/5/EC, 1999.

COCIR/MITA Joint Contribution, "EU and US call for input on regulatory issues for possible future trade agreement," 2013.

Boston Consulting Group, "EU Medical Device Approval Safety Assessment. A comparative analysis of medical device recalls 2005-2009", 2011.

U.S. Food and Drug Administration, "Guidance for Industry and Food and Drug Administration Staff - Mobile Medical Applications," 2013.

European Union. "*Horizon 2020 Funding Programme*", Last Update: November 2013, http://ec.europa.eu/research/horizon2020/index_en.cfm

CHAPTER 7

■ ■ ■

The Data Economy of Biosensors

Dawn Nafus, Senior Researcher, Intel Labs

Biosensing does not take place in a void. It always has a social context of some kind, and that context has profound implications for the types of things that biosensors can and cannot do. The social context is, however, not as obvious as it might at first seem. There are some design considerations that must be tied to specific situations. For example, what one might build to enable professionals to care for an older person with chronic obstructive pulmonary disease (COPD) is very different from the monitor that tracks an athlete's activity levels or what a citizen science group might use to look for better assessments of local air quality. What works well in fully privatized healthcare systems may not find much demand in single-payer systems. Even within single-payer systems, what works in the Netherlands may not work well in the United Kingdom. There are also differences that need attending to, based on not just the population of end users but on a whole range of other actors involved. The way we represent data to professionals must be very different from the way it is represented to epidemiologists or civil society groups.

Not every design consideration, however, applies at the level of these specific contexts of interaction. Larger-scale social transformations are happening that change how people encounter biosensing in everyday life. This chapter discusses those changes, which have to do with who interprets data and to whom data circulates. The point of view from which I offer these reflections is as an anthropologist who contributes to the relevant scholarship and as a person working in the information and communication technology (ICT) industry whose job it is to distill and translate that scholarship into concrete design and strategy decisions. Although this may appear somewhat unusual in a technical volume such as this, anthropologists now frequently work in the technology industry and regularly inform decisions regarding technology design and market strategy (refer to Cefkin, 2010, for an overview). Given my anthropological background, this chapter will flow somewhat differently than the other chapters, and its subject matter will be different as well. I leave it to the other chapters to focus on the material affordances of various sensors and suggest possible uses based on those affordances. Instead, I will draw on the relevant social science to discuss the social arrangements that make some uses more valuable than other uses. I cannot parse every social situation in which biosensing occurs, but I do address some aspects of what it is these situations have in common.

There are patterns in how the industry and engineering research tends to approach biosensing, and these patterns have social as well as technical origins. The usages that at first seem to be the most likely usages seem that way because of a social history that ties sensing technologies to institutional use. These most obvious usages may not ultimately prove to be the most valuable to end users. I have confidence, however, that it is possible to see past the first port of call. Indeed, there is good reason to do so. The evidence shows that applications that at first seem most plausible are also the same applications that lead to biosensors falling into disuse and that have troubling societal effects. Some of that evidence is presented here. Once we can identify the commonalities in how today's biosensors are conceptualized, we can develop additional approaches. In this chapter, there are pointers to new kinds of use models and applications; however, these are intended to be suggestive of a broader underlying approach.

Biosensing for the purposes of this chapter includes both sensors that sense what is on or in the body and sensors that sense things in the environment that affect the body. Biosensors are already part of a larger data economy. By "data economy", I mean the everyday circulation of data between devices, people, and institutions. Regardless of device, use case, user group, or institution, data is most useful when it moves around. If it goes nowhere, the data can fall flat or fall into disuse. If it has an extended biography, either by moving between different kinds of people or as one data stream providing context for another data stream for a single person, it can be said to have a life of sorts—an extended set of social and cultural meanings. As it moves around, it acquires different valences (Neff and Fiore-Silfvast, 2013). That is, we will not all agree on what the meaning of "5,000 steps" is or what kind of action the measurement calls for. For some, it is an indicator of good health, and for others it is considered medically useless. For some, it means that more steps should be taken, while for others, it is a low level of activity across a week. That we use "steps" at all is the result of previous circulations; for example, early product demos gave examples of fitness indicators calculated in "steps," and through use, "steps" became adopted, understood, and accepted.

Whether through differences in perspective or through the way that standard metrics begin to emerge, when data is part of an exchange or circulation, that is where we see its value.[1] Whether that exchange looks like a market or, as in the exchange of open source code, a gift economy, or whether it takes yet another form, depends on particular circumstances. Indeed, when data moves between family members and a person being cared for, the economy of data is not at all like a market. But a circulation it nonetheless is, and circulation is one aspect of biosensor data that makes it so deeply social. Kenner (2013) provides a helpful classification of different kinds of data economies for mobile asthma technologies (see Table 7-1). These examples show clearly that when the participants change, so do the social effects of data.

Table 7-1. *Data Economies for Mobile Asthma Technologies*

	Type	Examples	Economy Participants	Social Relationships and Data Flow
Class I	One-way information delivery	Asthma Signal	Patients	Patient receives alerts to take medicine based on action plan.
			Doctors	Doctors provide information about patient's condition.
			App developer	
			Environmental data providers	Patient receives health information from app developer.
Class II	Compliant care	My Asthma Asthma Check Asthma Tracker	Patients	Patient receives alerts based on action plan.
			Makers of national standards of asthma care	Patient enters observations of symptoms.
			App developer	Little information available about who looks at those observations.
Class III	Environmental health	AsthmaSense AsthmaWin	Patients	Patients record observations of symptoms.
			Makers of national standards of asthma care	Patient receives environmental data.
			App developer	Combination of health and environmental data makes it possible for patient to make sense of triggers.
			Environmental data providers	
Class IV	Participatory epidemiology	AsthmaMD Propeller Health (Formerly Asthmapolis) Breathe Easy	Patients	Patients record observations of symptoms.
			App developer	Patients generate location data for where symptoms occur.
			Third-party data collectors	Patients opt in to third-party data collectors to conduct research on sources of asthma triggers.

---

[1] Anthropologists will see that here I am drawing on notions of circulation and exchange derived from Tarde (Latour and Lépinay, 2009), not neoclassical economics.

Each system is designed to support asthma sufferers, and each takes a different approach. Class I apps treat data exchange as an extension of the current medical system; data moves out from that system and to the patient but not the other way. The patient is there to be managed by experts. In Class II apps, the patient has the opportunity to record observations about symptoms. Note that this recording is done largely by user input, but we might imagine that with an extended availability of biosensors on the market this might not be the case in the future. It is unclear whether this information is for the patient's own consumption or whether it is intended for medical practitioners to look at it. In my own research among Quantified Self participants (refer to the "Evidence Base" section for details), it is rare that a doctor has the patience or inclination to look at patient-generated data. It forces doctors to parse what is and is not medically relevant, as opposed to relevant for self-care. In the context of a busy clinic, that parsing is also not likely to take priority (Neff and Fiore-Silfvast, 2013). A connection between medical system and patient where the patient has the opportunity to speak to the medical professional may be intended, but it also may not succeed. In Class III apps, the addition of environmental data brings in additional data providers and also affords possibilities for patients to make sense of their condition, as opposed to simply being told when to take their medicine. In Class IV apps, the circulation of data is yet again different. The patient is both a consumer and generator of data, and epidemiological research is enabled. Because these apps are so new on the market, it is impossible to tell how the power relations between the actors work in practice, but the flow of data is designed to create relationships between participants and epidemiological research, not clinical care.

Declining costs mean that biosensing is no longer confined to medical institutions. Now that it is more popularly accessible, the exchanges in which biosensor data circulate are also diversifying in surprising ways. A generic example is provided in Figure 7-1 for an electronic pedometer. The chain of data exchange in Figure 7-1 demonstrates that who has access to what data, and who ultimately benefits from that data, is different in a consumer market than it is in the earlier asthma example. Note first the actors: social media companies are not traditionally considered actors in the healthcare space, nor are they subject to monitoring by health regulators. Then note the distributed nature of who or what makes sense of the data. The data is not sent to an expert who validates it or invalidates it. The beneficiaries of the data exhaust do not necessarily share institutional goals or incentives. They also do not benefit by creating connections with careers or relationships between careers and patients. They benefit by creating correlations that can be achieved only through large, complex datasets that may or may not have anything to do with health.

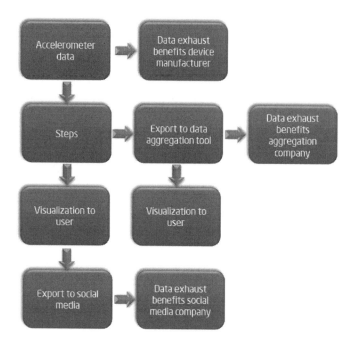

Figure 7-1. *Example of a simple data economy for an electronic pedometer. "Data exhaust" refers to that which can be inferred from a dataset that the creator of that dataset did not originally intend to collect*

Looking at sensor data in this way—in other words, tracing its movements across different actors—also allows us to ask questions of how data moves around: What social processes are really at stake in these arrows? Are all the actors involved equals, or are there power relationships that shape these relationships? Here I am drawing on a longstanding methodology within the social sciences to analyze the social meaning of objects by looking at their biographies as they are exchanged (Kopytoff, 1986). Although it would be foolish to expect data to do the same thing it once did in clinical or scientific environments, thinking in terms of a data economy helps us see that it is not a complete free-for-all either. Patterns form based on social arrangements and cultural assumptions that make some uses, designs, and business models more plausible than others.

The shift from expensive biosensors in labs to relatively inexpensive biosensors in the hands of many has consequences for the kinds of use models and designs that are appropriate for a consumer market. The first section of this chapter will examine how biosensors have been socially shaped through their origins as devices that institutions use. This institutional history has created a preoccupation with controlling the behavior of others, based upon population-based science from which beliefs about what is normal and healthy have been derived. This history gives rise to the use models that appear most obvious to technology designers: to set and track progress toward the goal of higher activity levels so that people lose weight, monitor someone's blood pressure and deliver tips on reducing it when it is high, and so on. The history of biosensors is so rooted in institutional use, yet the devices are rapidly expanding into the consumer domain. The data economy of today's biosensing has changed much more slowly and is underwritten by a set of assumptions that do not necessarily hold when developing a consumer product.

There is reason to believe that the limitations of this early ethos of "behavior modification" have been reached and that early adopters of biosensing at the consumer level have found a different set of preoccupations altogether. The second half of this chapter will document cases of early adopters, where a notion of biosensing is forming that is centered on the ways that biosensing can help people make sense of the world around them and rely on their own knowledge about personal context to make appropriate decisions. This shift is happening primarily among early adopters, but others are well positioned to take part in this transformation. The underlying approach is that personal context is always, ultimately, a matter of human interpretation. These early adopters consider machine recording of certain phenomenon to be useful, but ultimately how people come to understand their own context will always take into account more than machines will ever be able to do. This perspective generates debates about how much automation is valuable in what circumstances. Whereas Chapter 9 addresses context as a type of data that people who are out of context would need in order to make sense of that data (for example, a healthcare provider trying to understand a patient), here context is something a person has and can draw on. Data can be contextual data to the extent each data stream sheds new light on the other; however, when the user is at the center of the sensemaking, there is no need to separate "contextual" data as a particular kind of data.

Let me be clear that I am not talking about "personalized medicine," or "personalized health" as it is commonly understood. I am making an argument for changing our underlying reflexes about the kinds of problems we choose to solve. The shift is away from predefining problematic behavior and using technology in an attempt to control it remotely and toward supporting people and communities to make sense of data for themselves—and to act based on what is normal or appropriate for them. This requires designers to not only make clearer choices about what is and is not a design for healthcare, or will be subject to health regulation, but to innovate well beyond these frameworks. This shift also brings with it implications for the kinds of sensing capacities necessary to maximize the overall value that biosensors bring. That is, the sensors are hardly enough. Better analytics tools, data exploration tools, and innovations in the technical and social pathways through which data circulates are all necessary.

The Evidence Base

I make this argument by drawing on longstanding and recent scholarship in anthropology, sociology, science, and technology studies (STS) and media studies. There are three components of that research I am drawing from:

- Longstanding social theories shared by all the previously mentioned disciplines. Although they will be new to many readers of this book, they form the underlying conceptual framework of much qualitative social scientific research today. In particular, I have used the following:

    - Approaches to government and social control derived from Foucault (1977)

    - Approaches to responsibilization derived from Giddens (1990)

    - Poststructural approaches to how societies perceive what is natural (Strathern, 1992; Haraway, 1991)

- My own scholarship on how people make sense of sensor data. There are three studies that have informed the present argument:

    - Ongoing research in the Quantified Self movement (Nafus and Sherman, forthcoming), which is a group of 20,000+ lead users and makers of sensing technologies. They meet monthly in major metropolitan areas to discuss their biosensor data and other data relevant to their mental and physical well-being.

    - Past research on users of home energy monitoring systems (Nafus and Beckwith, forthcoming).

    - Past research in the United States, Bulgaria, and Portugal in which researchers showed large, complex datasets of computer use to the people who generated those datasets (Rattenbury, Nafus, and Anderson 2008).

- Recent publications from Intel's Biosensing in Everyday Life Program (see Table 7-1 for details)

The Biosensors in Everyday Life research program is sponsored by Intel's University Research Office. This program involves projects at four universities over three years, ending in December 2013. I serve as the program's technical manager. Table 7-2 contains details of these projects and principle investigators (PIs). While not all the researchers on this program will agree with every component of my argument, they have deeply informed my thinking. In this chapter, I have deliberately limited my comments about their work to what they have made public at the time of writing and do not draw on private communication or reports to Intel, unless the researcher has given me explicit permission, in which case I have noted it explicitly. Where I do draw on the research coming from that program, I corroborate it with other work in the social sciences more broadly.

Table 7-2. *Research Projects within the Biosensors in Everyday Life Program*

Institute: Researchers	Focus Area and Goal	Case Studies	Methods
Lancaster University: Celia Roberts, Maggie Mort, Adrian Mackenzie, Mette Kragh-Furbo, Joanne Wilkinson	Focus: Risk perception Understand the practices of using health information, relation to risk and anxiety, notions of personal/institutional responsibility, and uses of social networking and health advocacy groups	Pregnancy and conception practices Direct-to-consumer genomics practices	Ethnographic field research Citizen panels
Goldsmiths College: Nina Wakeford, Sophie Day, and Celia Lury (now Warwick University)	Focus: The new numeracy Understand how everyday, informal practices of numeracy and calculation are emerging	Weight Watchers Biobanks Fine-art practices	Ethnographic field research Theoretical enquiry Speculative design
University of Washington: Gina Neff and Brittany Fiore-Silvfast)	Focus: Institutional systems of healthcare Understand how healthcare systems might (not) adapt to patient-generated biosensor data	U.S. primary-care clinics Heath practitioners Biosensing Technology firms	Ethnographic field research
State University of New York at Buffalo: Marc Böhlen, Joe Atkinson and students	Focus: Challenging the scope of biosensing applications Explore additional uses of biosensing that are excluded from current market framing	Sites of public water use (swimming and drinking) in the United States and Indonesia	Designing, building and evaluating working prototypes

All scholarship reflects the epistemic cultures in which the researcher is embedded, and this work is no exception. I have largely not chosen to engage with the human-computer interaction (HCI) literature on the topic because on the whole it has not addressed the underlying social dynamics I address here; Leahu, Schwenk, and Sengers (2008) and Böhlen et al. (2012) are important exceptions. I also have not extensively examined the relevant psychological literature because this lies beyond my expertise.

Why Building Technologies for "Should" Rarely Helps

Chapter 9 situates consumer-based biosensing within the broader transformations of healthcare delivery systems and links consumer-based biosensing to healthcare in an institutional context. In a similar vein, Chapter 10 is optimistic about the current trajectory of biosensor design for wellness: "Technology is now having a positive effect on individuals by helping them to manage their physical wellness. This trend will continue to grow in the future as sensing and supporting technologies are seamlessly integrated into our daily lives." Indeed, as I have witnessed in both public talks and private conversations throughout the industry, there is an overwhelmingly common narrative surrounding biosensors' role on the consumer market that coheres with this claim. The narrative is that preventable diseases such as obesity, diabetes, and high blood pressure are now overwhelming healthcare systems, and biosensors designed for consumer use are a low-cost way of monitoring patients. They are seen as a way of ensuring patient involvement in disease management and a way to shift to an emphasis on prevention. Chapter 9 lays out this approach more fully, though it is useful to note that this particular framework is in widespread circulation and thoroughly pervades industry conferences and workshops on mobile health.

Usually, however, this narrative rarely includes specific reference to how people actually use the devices that are already on the market. It is one thing to elucidate the affordances of biosensors that could contribute to solving certain problems in healthcare delivery and another thing to look at actual practice. If we look at how biosensors are used in practice, there are more reasons to be cautious than if we based our judgments on affordances alone. First, a seamless integration of technology is not something that is desirable in all cases (Ratto, 2007). Second, it would be fair to say that there is no comprehensive, authoritative impact assessment that assesses whether the effects have truly been positive and for whom. Usually with any technical change, there are both winners and losers, and those have not been exhaustively identified. Indeed, the research program I manage is but one attempt at filling in the picture. More work would be needed to dig deeply into both the kinds of technologies that do or do not successfully help people manage their physical wellness and also into cases where even if there were a medical consensus on what constituted physical improvement, what the long-term social consequences would be. Sometimes physical improvement is not the same thing as happiness or well-being, particularly if it creates power imbalances between people in the process.

In fact, the limited quantitative and qualitative data that we do have to support or refute the claim that technology is helping people manage their physical wellness suggests healthy skepticism is warranted. For instance, Mort, Roberts, and Callen (2012) show how telehealth technologies are not being used in the way their designers intended. They show how elderly people who are being monitored by telehealth technologies are not enjoying the "independent living" promised by the makers of telehealth technologies. Instead, they often creatively misuse the technology in order to access the kind of care they do want—the kind provided by a human. They also sometimes "fail" to use the technology in order to avoid suffering the indignity of living under surveillance. In other domains, quantitative work has shown extensive nonuse of biosensors or apps working in the space that biosensors are slated to occupy. Mobile health and wellness applications have a 67 percent user drop-out rate in the first six months if the app relies on manual entry and a surprising 74 percent drop-out if data entry is automated (EIU, 2012). If, as is often claimed, biosensors are to be used to alleviate diseases of industrialized living that play out over the long term (diabetes, obesity, hypertension, and so on), then a six-month usage cycle is not likely to solve the problem the industry is claiming to solve. My own ethnographic evidence from the Quantified Self community suggests many of those who stick it out do so only with significant adaptation. Steps, for example, stop serving as an indicator of whether one has successfully exercised for the day and become contextual data for making sense of other phenomenon such as sleep quality or stress levels. Such a high drop-out rate should serve as an occasion to question what design approaches have in common that contribute to it.

There are many conceivable reasons for nonuse. One contributing factor is the prevalence of a "problem-solution" approach to design. In this approach, user needs are framed in terms of problems that can be solved by technologies. While this is the most common approach, it is not by any stretch of the imagination the only way to conduct user-centered design (Dourish, 2006; Dunne and Raby 2001; DiSalvo, 2009). However, more importantly for the present argument, there is an implicit assumption that both the problem and the solution can be tidily contained within the frame of the technology. The result of this problem-solution approach is that today's biosensing technologies are largely designed to recommend some sort of action or to facilitate achieving a goal in a narrow way. For example, a user might be shown growing flowers on a display or given points in a game if he or she is engaging in more exercise. Such design strategies seem obvious enough and are intended to help by identifying a discrete problem and creating opportunities for discrete solutions. In practice, however, they create an overdeveloped confidence with which designers predefine a problem and an under-recognition of the complexity of solutions necessary in practice. These may involve key components well outside of the user's control.

This approach can be seen in many biosensor systems, including ones that address lifestyle diseases and beyond. The overall effect is a large number of devices on the market that too often facilitate feelings of failure and discourage people from developing their own expertise about the phenomenon being sensed. To demonstrate how this overall effect is created, I will offer examples from weight monitoring and ovulation monitoring. In the context of ovulation monitoring, Wilkinson (2012) shows how ovulation monitors are sold as tools to aid "natural" conception by pointing out likely fertile days. Ovulation monitoring can happen though either body temperature monitoring,[2] testing saliva, salts on the body, or hormones in urine. In the case of body temperature, the device reads body temperature either as a continuously worn sensor or as temperature taken intermittently throughout the day. Before it even gets to the user, there has already been an "exchange" in the data economy of ovulation: temperature is changed into the device's inference of fertile days. That inference is represented as the word *fertile* or even a smiley face. That ovulation merits a smiley face makes clear that its intended use is when people are trying to conceive children, rather than avoid them. The data economy here is between device manufacturer and user, between user and partner (if partnered), between users in online forums discussing fertility, and occasionally between doctors and patients. Interestingly, it is often in online forums, not doctors' offices, where interpretations of the meaning of the word *fertile*, or the actions that ought to happen, based on that reading are made.

In the exchange between device and user, the focus on inferred fertility days gives the false impression that there is a "normal" body that cycles in normal ways. While this is true across a population, when brought to the individual, it has the added effect of framing the deviations from "normal" that must occur by definition as problematic or even as failures. All bodies are different. In fact, more people are "abnormal" than "normal" in one way or another, and basal temperature varies individually. There can be basal temperatures that are normal for one person but not normal for others. By designing devices around notions of a normal range, designers give users the false impression that somehow theirs is the odd one out. Over time, device users do develop a sense of what is normal for them, but as much despite the interpretive frames offered by technology as because of them.

Abnormal readings do stoke users' anxieties, but the problem is more than just raised anxiety levels in an already anxious situation. By extension, the impression is given that outcomes other than conception through sexual intercourse are not normal and are undesirable (Wilkinson, 2012). In the vast repertoire of reproductive technologies, including ovulation monitoring technology, "natural" cannot plausibly describe a state of being devoid of technological mediation or assistance. There is no such thing. Humans have been building tools for thousands of years, and there is no body that remains free of any technology whatsoever. Indeed, earlier technologies such as pasteurization and improved agricultural production have all shaped what is today considered "natural" and "normal" fertility rates. The marketing of ovulation monitoring as "more" natural hides the basic fact that measurement is itself a technical intervention. Therefore, we should not understand claims to "naturalness" as a straightforward, naïve claim but a claim that stokes and manipulates fears, desires, and anxieties about what is "natural."

While the point may seem theoretical, the consequences are very real. There is a long history of scholarship that shows how claims to "naturalness" both in terms of beliefs about "natural" conception (Strathern, 1992) and, more broadly, about what is and is not natural about the body (Haraway, 1991) carry cultural and moral weight about what is supposed to be desirable. There are many, many people who do not fit the mold of what is considered desirable. The framing of these devices as enabling "natural" conception creates culturally loaded distinctions between people who reproduce through sex and the people who do not. There are many people who start out using an ovulation monitor and end up adopting, using in vitro fertilization, miscarrying, co-parenting, or remaining childless. That's too many people to brush off as abnormal or as people who failed to act in "natural" ways.

As with many sensor system designs, the line between information and action is not made clear in the design. Designers want their devices to be useful, not merely informational, and therefore have every incentive to encourage their users to take action based on that information. In this case, as is true in many biosensing cases, this puts unfair burdens on device users when the ultimate outcome is not limited to the action related to that information. Here the sensor designs have created the illusion that the body is somehow "fixable" with enough knowledge about

---

[2]The effectiveness of these various methods of ovulation monitoring is contested.

its workings when in reality conception comes down to phenomenon in the body the user does not control. The user cannot control whether sperm meets egg or whether that egg is implanted in the uterus, or any number of compounding factors that make conception a complex biological process. Ultimately, no amount of temperature sensing will change the vagaries of the body. While intended to surface a probability of conception, that probability is, in practice, vague (Guyer, 2012); it is not cleanly connected to the desired result of conception. In these ways, not only do ovulation monitors contribute to false norms, but they also contribute to a sense that simply "trying harder" could change a situation that it cannot.

When device manufacturers create frames that have negative social consequences, they also leave opportunities on the table in doing so. People who take alternative paths in reproduction may in fact abandon the importance of "naturalness" and seek other frames to understand their circumstances. The device manufacturers, however, remain wedded to notions of naturalness, and that in turn constrains the data economy they could actually be in. For example, "natural" flattens and hides the myriad social practices people in fact have around ovulation (Wilkinson, pers. comm.). It makes ovulation one thing—fertile or not—where in fact there is more diversity to how people are experiencing the process as a whole. As time goes on, the cycles of what people do with that data change. There is also an extended social media apparatus that helps people make meaning out of the data, and people's roles in that social media change over time, too, as they become more expert in the topic. Companies could extend their markets by paying closer attention to these nuances and evolutions in how their customers use their devices. If they abandoned "natural conception" as their value proposition, they could also develop partnerships with other actors with whom their users ultimately engage. This would enable them to provide information about the full range of options could be tabled earlier in the process. In essence, the data economy of ovulation monitoring could be more nuanced than it already is, both in terms of the stakeholders to whom the data is shuttled and how the data is framed and reframed through time.

The consequences of ovulation monitoring might at first blush appear extreme, but there is a much longer history of biosensor data working in similar ways. For the overweight, scales, manually entered food diaries, and pedometers have been measuring devices used to lead an intensified war on fat (Greenhalgh, 2012). Berlant (2007) calls this war on fat a "cruel optimism," in which "raising awareness" about fatness[3] is a cultural activity that does little to solve the actual problem at hand and in fact gets in the way of people leading meaningful and productive lives. According to the EIU data previously mentioned (2012), technologies designed for weight management are not being used in the ways that they were intended. At least in terms of obesity management, they have not secured prevention or ensured patient involvement in that management (although in the case of mobile health apps, the users are rarely patients). Here the current data economy in which data is trafficked between health professionals, insurers, device manufacturers, and device users sets a frame that forces inappropriate conclusions. If we hold on to the premise that biosensors are a way to enable people to manage their health independently, stay out of the healthcare system, and yet continue to think about users as essentially patients, then we would be forced to conclude that the high drop-out rate is a function of a lack of compliance or self-control. In reality, much more is going on.

Compliance is a tricky term if biosensors are truly consumerizing. It is notable that in most spheres of life within Western societies, and particularly in the United States, people who are not "compliant" are the ones who are celebrated. It is notable, too, that the expanding waistlines of industrialized countries correspond with major shifts in geographical arrangements, car reliance, food manufacture and distribution, changes in work types, and distribution of paid and unpaid labor. And yet in our enthusiasm for technical solutions, these factors are acknowledged only as other parts of the puzzle out of the control of the technologist. Personal fitness monitoring is often acknowledged as a contribution, not a total solution, but it is problematic to downplay the significant matters of social structure that cannot be managed through technology. The issue is not a lack of "compliance." The issue is that people are compliant with other, more powerful forces. Put differently, if Westerners did not suddenly and consciously decide to put on massive amounts of weight as a series of individual decisions, then the plausibility that we can individually consciously decide to lose that weight as a matter of individual self-control, enhanced by technology, is thin at best. As with ovulation monitoring, the "problem-solution" design approach is at the root of the problem. It insufficiently acknowledges the factors that are outside the control of the technology or the user. The limitations of personal monitoring to solve these large problems need to be acknowledged more robustly if we are to build truly useful technologies.

---

[3]Fatness is the term Greenhalgh (2012) uses in order to avoid using the medical terms (*obese, overweight*) that she convincingly argues *inflict* shame. This chapter follows her usage.

If fitness monitoring technologies are able to contribute only one piece of the puzzle, then when the rest of the puzzle starts to exert its power, these other social forces start to change the effects that the technology has on the user's practices, habits, and beliefs. Behind those high drop-out rates are cycles of initial enthusiasm followed by disappointment. Ultimately, the sheer amount of headwinds one has to fight in order to stay fit leads most people to give up. Through the course of this process, the valence of the information communicated by devices changes. Two thousand steps in a day starts as progress toward a goal and ends as a way to tell people with great authority and precision exactly how much they failed to exercise. There is even evidence that the cultural connection of these devices with institutionalized healthcare and healthcare experts is itself a significant source of the problem. Greenhalgh (2012) has shown that the framing of fatness as a health problem (that is, speaking in terms of "obesity") exacerbates the human suffering involved. Historically, fatness was not popularly thought of as an issue of health, but now we say that people should lose weight because it is healthy and that others should lose weight because we are concerned for their health. Politeness now dictates we keep our aesthetic concerns to ourselves. Greenhalgh's study documents the fact that this change has not softened the blow but made it worse. The notion that fat is unhealthy in all cases—and changeable with diet and exercise for anyone willing—is a topic of an ongoing debate in scientific communities. Little is known conclusively about how bodies metabolize, so even if were the case that it is in fact biologically changeable, what one person's body responds to is likely to be very different than another person's. The consequences of fatness vary individually, too. What is true in the aggregate—a correlation between widening waistlines and various health problems—may or may not be the case close-up, for an individual person.

This debate, however, is rarely discussed outside of research communities. Only the aggregate is presented, and it is presented as if all the relevant mechanisms were not just known but as if each factor were known to be of equal importance for each individual. This rounding up to the aggregate makes some intuitive sense, but the consequences for end users are enormous given the significant cultural baggage that fatness carries. Greenhalgh (2012) demonstrates that the medicalization of fatness results in people overidentifying with being "the fat person" because it has become a matter of authority figures saying so, not just because of impolite comments from peers. She shows how the shame only deepens the more it is connected to a "health" issue and how the sense of being the "fat person" becomes all-encompassing. Greenhalgh shows how people internalize the sense of fatness and make it the dominant part of their individual identity, rather than reaching out to social movements or seeking political change that would address the underlying structural issues. Many then take drastic measures, such as extended periods of near starvation and excessive exercise, that can do serious physical and psychological damage.

Indeed, this propensity to internalize negative feelings about the body, or to interpret negative information as a much more worrying indication of a deeper character flaw, is a propensity that expands beyond issues of body size. Much sociology has documented the ways that Western cultures have shifted to cultures of responsibilization (a voluminous literature that began with Giddens, 1990). In cultures of responsibilization, individual choice is seen to be both the only possible cause and the only possible solution to a problem, regardless of the broader social forces that may in fact be in play. In cultures of responsiblization, the preferred solutions to problems are framed as individual, but they are never really individually devised. They have been designed by experts and are implemented by individuals who are supposed to internalize the knowledge of experts (refer to Cheney-Lippold, 2010, for a discussion of how this social dynamic works in the context of big data). This means that the control supposedly offered to the individual as a newly active participant in their healthcare is often not in fact real empowerment. It is not an expansion of that person's agency but an expansion of the power of experts and institutions who defined and specified the problem to be solved. This cultural shift pervades the current biosensor market, but it is worth noting that it is also much larger than that market or even healthcare. For example, it was clearly at work in the 2008 Great Recession. The newly unemployed were perfectly aware of the larger economic forces happening and attributed other people's unemployment to be a function of those larger forces. Still, they attributed their own unemployment to their personal failings and not the wider social phenomenon. Predictably, books, blogs, and even new technologies claiming to help people make themselves more employable continued to flourish and prey upon self-doubts (Gregg, forthcoming).

The pervasiveness of the framework that claims biosensor technologies can solve a widespread social problem like lifestyle diseases through individual responsibility for management and monitoring (but without individual control over what to monitor) echoes the broader cultural shift toward responsibilization too strongly, and too consistently, to be mere coincidence. When our sense of personal responsibility goes so far that we can no longer see or address what else is at work, it becomes a hindrance rather than a help. While we must design for the cultural context we are in, when we can see its workings more clearly, we can choose to draw on other aspects of that culture that are more constructive.

Once we can see how cultures of responsibilization work, we can start to see that there is a world of difference between an athlete (or someone who is generally enthusiastic about technology using one of the myriad of devices that record bodily activity) and the fantasy that these devices will solve the obesity crisis. In the fantasy that obesity can be resolved with accelerometers and gamification, the technologies do find market demand, but it is demand that takes shape in the context of cycles of drastic measures and subsequent despair. That is not the same thing as meaningful support for making major changes to one's body. Instead, as with ovulation monitoring, technologies for fitness and weight loss are designed to create an awareness of something predefined as a possible problem, and that predefinition creates its own need for action regardless of whether the right problem has been identified.

There are examples of current fitness devices that show how, specifically, their design choices play into the wider culture of responsibilization I have been discussing. In Figure 7-1, which is an abstracted synthesis of how many accelerometer-based fitness devices work, note the reduction of data that takes place in the first three steps before it ever gets to the end user. Designers make decisions about what is and is not relevant data to their target user group. For example, some device manufacturers only show steps taken per day. But what if the user were attempting to cultivate the habit of taking walks in the morning? When those steps took place is relevant information. It could have been a high concentration of steps in the morning followed with a sedentary job or a day that had mild activity. For that purpose, some steps do count more than others. Even before the data is cleaned up and binned into "steps," it is entirely possible that an end user could find the data as it comes from the accelerometer useful in ways that the designer cannot anticipate ahead of time. It is nearly impossible for end users to get access to data beyond "steps per day." This suggests that designers of devices like these are doing more than just making choices about what to emphasize as a normal part of the design process. By not leaving the door open for other calculations and interpretations of that data to flourish, they have made a much stronger assumption that it is the designer who has the privilege of predefining both problem and solution. They leave very little room for their users to adapt these devices to their own situation.

Many fitness devices, including the JawboneUP, Fitbit, Fuel, and BodyMedia, emphasize daily targets. I have provided an example of one such device—BodyMedia—in Figure 7-2. The example is not intended to call out any one manufacturer but to illustrate a much broader approach shared by many systems designers.

What Devices Display

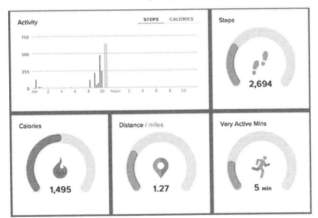

What Devices Communicate

- There is a known ideal
- Most of the time you fall short of it
- The ideal is equally appropriate every day
- The day is the unit of time that matters most
- These are the only possible relevant factors

Figure 7-2. *What user interfaces (UIs) communicate*

On the right side of Figure 7-2 there is a composite of how many people interpret numbers like this. There can in fact be many interpretations of these numbers, but these are the themes that commonly arise in the research. For example, it is possible in many systems for users to set their own goal number of steps or calorie deficit they want to create, but there are few systems that provide good resources to even figure out what these goals should be, given the wild variation from person to person in terms of physiology, enabling geography, and constraints in terms of family and work commitments. The design choices made about what and how to measure already imply there is an ideal even before anyone has the faintest idea of what that ideal is. This can be motivating for a little while, but when the realities of life start to kick in, they stop becoming motivating and start becoming demoralizing. It becomes a reminder of just how much the user falls short. There is also a tremendous emphasis on the day in current designs, whereas people with heavy travel schedules will need to manage their exercise and calorie consumption across the course of a week or month. The emphasis on the day is almost entirely unworkable for many people, but it is what is cleanly imaginable from afar—the epitome of the ordered person (see also Gregg, forthcoming). When we see things close-up and in context, people make all sorts of temporal trade-offs, compositions, and rearrangements that are highly complex (Darrah et al., 2007).

What is most concerning about these designs is the way they act as a frame that implicitly makes claims about what is and is not relevant to fitness. There is a narrow repertoire of measures that have been deemed relevant. Most devices do not ask their users to take measures of the amount of time spent in sloth-inducing artificial lighting, assessments of microbiome, exposure to poor air quality, weather conditions, or responses to certain foods but not other foods. Some of these are technologically far more difficult, and indeed politically and scientifically controversial, but regardless of what we can or cannot scientifically say actually contributes to fatness, it would be hard to disagree with the proposition that fatness is likely to be more complicated than calories and exercise. As Chapter 10 observes, calorie expenditure is technologically difficult to sense and can deliver a false sense of accuracy. Calories consumed, on the other hand, is notoriously difficult to track according to the Quantified Self participants I have been studying. It is complex because portions are tedious to estimate, and specific nutritional contents are difficult to specify without significant labor. That labor is somewhat reduced if one is prepared to eat manufactured foods, but many find eating manufactured foods problematic from a dietary, environmental, and economic perspective. And yet, calories and activity levels are the main focus of devices currently on the market. By emphasizing the day, narrowing the choice of relevant information, and creating an impression of ideal states, these technologies fit squarely in the wider culture of responsiblization where controlling the behaviors of others is done remotely so as to appear as if it were an individual solution.

The Consequences of Designing for "Should"

What do these examples have in common? They tell us that the first generation of biosensors took at face value the medical model of what sensing and measurement are for. This first generation too easily took for granted that the underlying science is well established in all cases and that it scales easily down to the individual level, such that whatever is good on the whole must be good for the individual person. They retained legacies from their origins in medical systems that privileged experts' control over patients' behavior, and experts' control over what to measure, even though users are no longer patients. We can see it readily in the data economies currently in play: medical knowledge, device manufacturers, and end users are in a tight loop. The communication primarily happens between device manufacturer and user, possibly including a clinician or insurance company, depending on the business model. Medical knowledge frames what data ought to be collected, either directly to the extent medical practitioners design devices or indirectly in the sense that medical framings shape which problems are seen as appropriate problems to address. That data is sent to end users who are left with narrow ways of interpreting that data, but with the impression that the problem is theirs alone to solve and solvable only within the bounds given by the device. To the extent there are "social" components, such as the ability to share data with others either to compete against them or to motivate one another, these components primarily do not open new ways the data could be interpreted for end users. Possibilities do open for data brokers and advertisers, of course, but does not substantively change the user experience.

The consequence has been that sensor measurements appear more authoritative than they are, and technology designers have become empowered as a kind of extension of medical authority at discerning what is and is not beneficial. This comes at the expense of people actually learning about their own bodies. The problem with "should" is that it creates more guilt, shame, and dependence on experts than it does actual support. Current devices afford little opportunity for people to investigate for themselves what the significance of the measurement could be for them and afford limited opportunity for people to participate in the creation of new knowledge, scientific or otherwise. This is of major societal significance: the apparently authoritative answer to a problem either may be bogus to begin with or may became obsolete as new knowledge emerges. In a limited data economy, data-sharing practices are limited to motivational concerns, and users are not given the opportunity to learn from one another. If we all already know what a "good number" is—more activity, low glucose, low weight—then there is little to be gained by sharing, beyond asking for encouragement or outright bragging. The data falls flat, quickly becoming uninteresting.

There are cases where sensors telling people what they should and should not do is absolutely appropriate. In fact, Böhlen et al. (2012) note an important tension between voluntary and involuntary biosensing and essential and nonessential biosensing practices. Similarly, athletes are not deeply shamed by negative feedback, and running or cycling coach technologies help people adjust their movements in ways that do not feed a broader cultural dynamic of shame and blame. While the social costs described earlier should be reason enough to change design strategies, there is a very real business cost for device manufacturers and service providers. The high churn in the user base might be an opportunity for more disruptive hardware innovators, but it should concern service providers who have costs associated with acquiring customers.

Why Designing for "Could" Matters

There are clear areas where what a person "should" do cannot be defined *a priori*. Allergies are an example. Many people have allergies, and responses to allergens are deeply individual. Different people's bodies respond differently not just to different allergens but to different combinations of allergens and circumstances. In my own research, one woman told me about how she thought that she was allergic to "Chinese food." She had no idea which actual substance in Chinese food she was allergic to, but the precise chemical cause mattered less than the ability to avoid it being ingested. In her case, she had a strong weekly pattern of going to the gym on Fridays and eating Chinese food afterward. On the rare days when she did not go to the gym but did have the Chinese food, there was no reaction. Because she had a distinct, human-discernible pattern, the underlying issue became clear: her allergy had something to do with the combination of the gym and the food.

In cases like these, people do not need a system with predetermined goals for them to meet. They need a way of developing their own hypotheses about what could be going on. Most are not lucky enough to have such a distinct pattern that we would notice a combination like the gym and Chinese food. Machines, however, are remarkably good at picking up on patterns. If the daily pattern were not as distinct, machines could help spot the potential pattern amid the noise. A system does not necessarily have to provide a conclusive answer. It can suggest possible pathways—practices that are changeable or exposures that are avoidable. The researchers in the Biosensors in Everyday Life program found a range of human experiences along these lines: sleep, headaches, fatigue, mood, and asthma all share the characteristics of being rooted in patterns of everyday life that are complex enough to make human detection of the pattern hard. Health systems are largely not helpful in these circumstances, and the resolution is largely nonmedical. These problems also do not carry the cultural baggage and feelings of shame associated with traditional biosensor interaction design strategies. For one person, headaches may be related to air quality. Another might try sensing air quality, having heard of the first person's experience; if it seems not to correlate, they may try sensing sleep or caffeine intake. Moving from one sensor to the next is a known practice. People involved in the Quantified Self movement rarely stick with one sensing practice. They move on to the next when they develop new areas they want to explore, sometimes for fun and sometimes for practical need. For example, one man I interviewed had been tracking his sleep using a Zeo and found that the data became boring and not useful after a few weeks. During that period, he also began tracking his mood. He found the Zeo data to be excellent contextual data to help him discern whether his mood indicated the beginnings of a mental health issue he had experienced in the past—or if he just needed a good night's sleep. This suggests a much more productive role for churn in the marketplace. Instead of abandoning a sensor out of a sense of failure, long-term self-trackers evolve their understanding of how their particular bodies work by composing together different sensor technologies as necessary, effectively doing their own ad hoc sensor fusions.

Today, doing these evolving sensor fusions is tedious and laborious, but it need not be. Figure 7-3 shows how a data economy for biosensor data might work if the emphasis were more on exploration and sensemaking. While this is still hypothetical, mapping it in this way shows important differences from Figure 7-1. In this scenario, the end user begins suspecting that air quality or something in her diet might be triggering her allergies. She begins tracking these two but does not find a relationship to her allergies. Although the initial hypothesis that air quality might be related to an allergic response was proved wrong in this case, it inspires greater use of location tracking that then makes it possible for her to decide to adjust her jogging route to avoid other possible effects. In this hypothetical scenario, the location tracking becomes a basis on which to test her new suspicion that travel might have something to do with it.

This new hypothesis came because her data is better connected to a community forum that helps her make sense of it. Because she is continuing her practice of photographing what she eats, she can now see her diet in relation to location and can work out that her allergy is related to alcohol consumption, which she tends to do more of on trips.

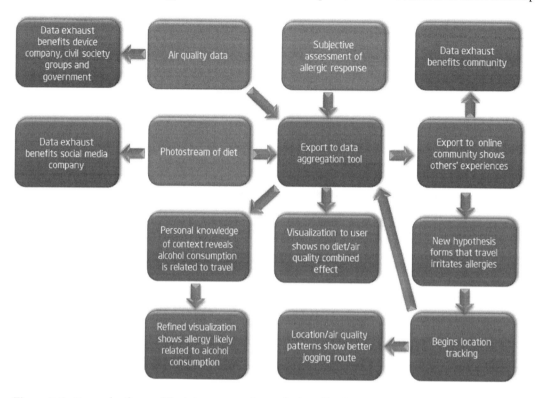

Figure 7-3. *Example of a possible data economy for exploring allergies*

In this scenario, the end user benefits twice—she finds a better jogging route and works out the cause of her allergy problem. The ability for machines to find patterns and synthesize them supports end users in making their own decisions and developing their own hypothesis. It stops short of presuming to know what the answer is; instead, the problem the user is trying to resolve shifts over time, and her use of biosensors and other data shifts with that evolution. Within this scenario, different designers might make different decisions about how much automation is useful. Some end users will want to see more of the granular data, while other end users might want a system to alert them to what other people have also tried to collect. No air quality monitoring system manufacturer will be able to anticipate all the uses to which that data could be put, but the ability to compose data in ways designers cannot anticipate makes it possible for end users as well as companies to benefit from data exhaust—the flow does not go one way. With improved data security technologies that would allow people better control over their data exhaust, it is possible that the balance could be evened up even more. Another difference is that the institutional beneficiaries of the data are more heterogeneous, which opens up the possibility for additional solutions should it prove impossible to simply avoid poor air quality by changing one's route through the city. It is entirely possible, of course, that the various actors involved in this scenario may have poor relations or conflicting incentives and might not want to see data exchanged in this way. But by emphasizing exploration, we open up the possibility to create alignment or otherwise manage conflicting incentives and decrease the probability of the data simply falling into disuse.

Once we shift from thinking of technologies as machines that tell us what we should do to machines that tell us what could be going on, the role of pleasure and fun changes. In the mobile health space, there are many attempts at "gamification," also noted in the foreword and Chapters 10 and 11 of this book. In gamification, developers use Skinneresque reward systems to entice people into doing what has been pre-ordained to be good for them. Some designers are having success with these techniques, but people are more than Pavlov's drooling dogs hoping for the next treat. Already in this space we see plenty of examples of people adapting the sensors currently on the market for fun and creative endeavors. Indeed, I interviewed a man who wore a continuous heart monitor out of sheer curiosity and happened to get into a car accident while wearing it. The data stream from that moment holds a particularly poignant memory for him. The monitor is hardly there for diagnostic or disease management reasons, and "pleasure" would not be the best word to describe his relationship to that data, but it nevertheless has personal significance for him. He sees it as an occasion to remember what it is he is thankful for and shares that with his family.

Similarly, genomics used to be only about establishing risks for disease. People often deem this information useless, inasmuch as there is often no action to take other than eating healthy and engaging in exercise, which we are all told we must do in any case (Bietz, 2013). That same "useless" data has another life as people turn to DNA to examine their heritage. There is nothing utilitarian about looking at one's heritage genetically, but some find it interesting to do nevertheless. In some domains, these more entertainment-oriented practices can once again get caught up in the cycle of shame and guilt. Ultrasound is a well-researched example (Roberts, 2013). Turning an ultrasound of a fetus into a three-dimensional picture might at first appear entertaining or endearing, and in fact it is so commonplace that it is possible to purchase such an image in shopping malls. The cultural politics of doing so are at best thorny. There are many people who would use those images to fuel the culture wars around abortion, or, in parts of the world experiencing high rates of female infanticide, they could be used to select the sex of the fetus either before or after birth. In this way, what at first appears to be a game becomes far too serious.

We know from the anthropology of numeracy (Lave, 1988; Verran, 2001; Guyer, 2004) that people are much better adapted to dealing with complex numbering systems than the technology industry usually gives them credit for. Gerlitz and Lury (2012), for example, have showed how people's enjoyment in measurements of their social media impact is rooted in its complexity, not simplicity. For people who pay attention to their social media presence, the game is one of ongoing recalibration. Metrics companies that do this well, given both highly impactful people and people who do more listening than talking, have a continued role to play. The role is one not rooted in their "failure" to be as influential as those more famous. Indeed, in a study on computers and time use (Rattenbury, Nafus, and Anderson, 2008) computer users in three countries were shown vastly complex multivariate datasets that showed their second-by-second computer usage—applications, keystroke frequency, location of computer, and so on—and had no trouble whatsoever parsing the information and telling stories about what else was happening in that time period and why the computer use data was the way it was. In the world of "should," the ethos is about making the sensor readings as simple as possible in order to get a specific message across. This fails to take advantage of the extraordinary levels of numerical complexity humans of all education levels and backgrounds are capable of.

Sometimes people do want sensors to "tell the truth" as straightforward empirical knowledge, and other times what is "real" is neither here nor there. Some other form of human creativity takes over. Leahu, Shwenk, and Sengers (2008), for example, see possibilities for how people might relate to machine-inferred states not in terms of whether the machine inferred correctly or incorrectly the emotional state of the user but in terms of a playful unfolding of the relationship between machine and person. Indeed, it is notable that the measurement of "fuel" used by the Nike FuelBand is entirely made up. There is no real meaning of "fuel." It has something to do with the accelerometer, of course, but the accelerometer is not measuring "fuel" per se because there is no such thing. This tells us that we need not constrain biosensor measurements to what is *a priori* understood. No one cared about "fuel" before Nike brought it into existence. Fuel users start to care in varying degrees, depending on how they are using the FuelBand. Sometimes they game it and shake it in full knowledge that they are increasing the number without any actual exercise, and sometimes the inadvertent gyrations from sitting in a vehicle on a bumpy ride can create disappointment in having accidentally stumbled into more points. In this way, there is more "could" in sensor numbers than we anticipated. Not only does this open up new physical paths to walk down, but it can enable new kinds of pleasurable fictions about how we can quantify our world.

The Quantified Self movement has been the most visible in terms of supporting practices and discourses around "could." In Quantified Self meetings, people share with one another the hypotheses they have about what is happening to their bodies, why they track what they track, and what they learn. They also suggest to each other what else could be going on, learn appropriate phenomenon to track, and come to understand the technologies available to track it. There is a social basis on which "could" could become much bigger than Quantified Self. Marc Böhlen and team (2012) are showing what "could" could look like from a design point of view (refer to `www.sirebi.org` for an extensive portfolio of concepts and literature). For example, one of these concepts suggests taking environmental data and wearable sensors of bodily response to that environment and suggesting different places to take a stroll (refer also to Chapter 11). These are recommendations to be sure, but it serves up new choices rather than scolds the user. It facilitates the enjoyment of new spaces and enables the serendipitous exploration of finding oneself in a new part of the city. With biosensors on a hike, combined with topological maps and the knowledge of how much water the person is carrying, a system could help a person assess which hikes are realistic for them. All of these things expand people's horizons in new and compelling ways.

Requirements for a Data Economy of "Could"

When we start from a place of enabling exploration and pleasure rather than self-management and compliance, we help people create and capture value from their interactions with data. The usages of biosensors in the world of "could" require a better way for people to combine different kinds of data and use each other's data to collaborate, corroborate, and identify new pathways.

For data to be more useful to end users, there needs to be more heterogeneity in the actors who participate in the data economy of biosensors. The allergies example makes clear the need to combine different kinds of data and enable people to fold in new data sources as they explore. This in particular requires the ability to make connections between environmental sensing and bodily sensing. Consumer-level environmental sensors are only just getting off the ground, which makes folding into the environmental picture a hard if necessary job. Those data may at first not appear relevant to health or be provided by traditional healthcare stakeholders. Similarly, the beneficiaries of data aggregation also need to expand. That is, instead of sharing one's individual data with chosen friends, end users do in fact have interest in the aggregated data too. Indeed, the Asthmapolis project (now a commercial company called Propeller Health) creates a mapping system where a location-tracking asthma inhaler records the location of asthma attacks and enables people to make sense of potential irritants through the lens of geography. This suggests that sharing data when trying to discern the sources of one's asthma triggers becomes a valuable exercise in collaboration and mutual benefit.

Currently, wearable technologies are designed to make building a picture with multiple sensors difficult; making a Fitbit talk to a sleep sensor like the Zeo is at best heavy lifting, let alone making it talk to an Air Quality Egg. Exporting data into common formats is difficult for users without coding skills, and widespread awareness of what can and cannot be obtained from device providers is lacking. Even active participants in the Quantified Self movement sometimes do not know, for example, that it is impossible to export raw data from the FuelBand, unless they are developers with a business relationship to Nike. No single biosensor manufacturer can predict every possible use case, but we currently have a system of nominally open APIs whose characteristics in terms of the amount of data that can be obtained, and by whom, is at best patchy. At the time of writing, however, many start-up companies and projects, such as Singly, Quantify.io, and Human API, are filling this important gap in the market (refer to Franzen, 2013). In the medical devices space, the Continua Alliance has made significant progress in increasing medical device interoperability, but not every biosensor device is medical, and not every data stream relevant to what users want to understand comes directly from a biosensor (for example, lead users often use location data to understand their dietary habits). In the consumer space, the supply of data can be less stable than one would like as companies decide to turn on or off data services.

While there are trade-offs in terms of data sampling rates and aggregation in any technical system, it is also clear that better data granularity opens up new uses than any single designer can design for. Some subset of end users will find value in this data, provided they have access to it and provided they have robust ways of controlling where it goes and who else has access to that data. Data use controls (DUCs) (Maniatis et al., 2011) are likely to be an important technology that allows users to travel these waters more securely. DUCs wrap data in user-controlled permissions, such that even if a Facebook user uploads a photograph onto Facebook, they can control who sees its contents— including whether Facebook itself can conduct facial recognition in it. This makes it possible to benefit from data aggregation in a secure way, without giving up one's raw data.

We will also need forms of analytics and machine learning that place a greater emphasis on helping people develop hypotheses and take advantage of what they know about their own context, while also taking advantage of a machine's ability to recognize the patterns difficult for humans to detect. It might be that no single sensor or product will be able to help my research participant discern whether it is the gym or the Chinese food causing her allergic reaction. However, the ability to easily compose data sources in a human-interpretable way so that she can develop the hypothesis that it might be a combination of the two is an important capability. Early indications from the Quantified Self research suggest that simply categorizing data according to simple temporal cycles (i.e., good sleep quality tends to happen on Thursdays) and being able to visualize data in ways that make cumulative effects more visible (i.e., a stacked graph showing sleep quality and weight might not surface the relationship if it takes two weeks of poor sleep to have an effect on weight) are two simple ways to take advantage of machines' pattern recognition advantages over human perception. These are often processing steps taken on the way toward building more sophisticated machine learning capabilities. But if the goal is to have humans do the sensemaking rather than the machines make the inference, knowing when to stop predicting is often just as important as knowing what to predict.

There is currently a large gap between the limited functionality that device manufacturers currently provide for the sake of ease of use and generic statistical packages such as R or Matlab, which require full statistical fluency. Most people are perfectly capable of asking quantitative questions in lay ways or asking about recurring patterns, but today's tools do not occupy an appropriate middle ground that would enable them to do so. At the time of writing, Intel Labs is building a tool to support data literacy in order to test some of the ideas developed in the course of the research within the Quantified Self community. Figure 7-4 shows how this tool works to support people trying to make sense of their data. This is but one tool that can fill a large gap in only a small way.

Thinking differently about analytics tools and data processing will go a significant way toward supporting more widespread data literacy. Data literacy is not simply the ability to perform mathematics. Data literacy is the ability to answer questions with data and critically interpret those answers. This may or may not involve mathematical skills. Not everybody wants to have, or can have, the statistical skills that would be required to use data to answer the questions they have, given the tools available to us. People with high levels of mathematical skill can also be data illiterate and either ask the wrong questions or fail to critically interpret the answers they receive from data. Indeed, a public scandal erupted in 2012 that involved Target, a large U.S. retailer sending advertisements to a pregnant person based on inferences from her shopping patterns when that person had not told other members of her household about her pregnancy. In this instance, sophisticated mathematical skills were required to put her in the "pregnant person" box, however, and poor data literacy skills were also at work in the failure to critically interpret the meaning of that box.

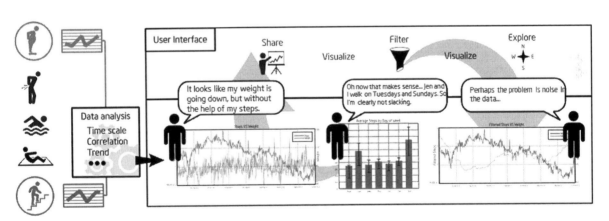

Figure 7-4. *Schematic diagram of Intel Labs data processing tool for the Quantified Self community. (Image courtesy of Pete Denman)*

Improved APIs needs to be supplemented by other ways of bringing data together for nontechnical people. This is crucial to creating a vibrant economy of biosensor data. A vibrant data economy is one that enables people to calibrate and contextualize their data, as well as build new hypotheses together rather than just individually. Without sharing data, people have few ways of discerning whether it is their body that works differently or if, as so many of our research participants are inclined to believe, they "just aren't doing it right." Again, we can do this incrementally.

Even comparing two people's Fitbit data streams would enable them to understand whether the devices are working. There are some cases in the research in which people confidently use sensors to buck the norm of what they are told they should do. One person told us, "I don't get migraines like most diabetics. Most diabetics get migraines when their glucose is really high; I get the opposite." Although people who can do this on their own are still the exception rather than the rule, with better ways of sharing data, more people will be able to come to similar conclusions with confidence. They will know what to try, and why.

This means, however, that "sharing" in a data economy of "could" requires some retooling. Appropriate sharing here is one that preserves the context that each person is grappling with. For example, it is not useful to see an aggregate statistic on the prevalence of migraines or whether an individual's migraines are more severe than on average. What is useful to see, and what must be done in a privacy-preserving manner, is more about the context of another person's experience so that the user can assess whether it is an appropriate comparison and to learn from that person's experience. A user will want to know, did that person also have sleep disturbances? Did that person have the same dietary issues that I do? To the extent that there are clusters of similar people, that is helpful and even comforting to know, but on the whole what matters is what people are capable of imagining, not the abstractions that can be derived. There can be overlap, but they are not the same thing. This must be done in a way that reveals the main components of that person's data such that another person can make sense of it but does not share the raw data or other identifying data.

Finally, in cases where something like a recommendation is in order, we need these recommendations to be designed in ways that lay out surprising and pleasurable options beyond gamified points. Such combinations and associations between data must be incremental from a user's point of view. They must enable people to move along a path of A to B to C in their own way. Sensor systems can show them roads they may not choose to take, but what developers should not do is wait for data to pile up into a single, central system with all the conclusive answers. It needs to deliver immediate, personal value. Even enabling simple comparisons across two data streams would do that, yet that is surprisingly difficult from an end user's point of view.

Summary

This chapter has shown how the industry's current thinking about the uses of biosensors has been shaped by their legacy as objects for institutional use. Their movement into the consumer space has been accompanied by design choices that make biosensors extensions of institutional or expert control over people. This choice has constrained adoption and has negative societal effects. However, the ethnographic record shows plenty of examples where end users are perfectly capable of making meaning from biosensor data and benefit from an expanded ability to pick and choose what to keep track of and how. This modality involves a more exploratory ethos—a sense of what "could" be at stake rather than what one "should" do. It also creates more value for data within the ecosystem.

This does not suggest that any particular sensor is more crucial than the other but that people will want to create an ensemble of them so that each sheds light on the other as new hypotheses emerge. It does suggest the need for improving, and making available for alternative uses, higher levels of data granularity. There are also additional requirements beyond sensor design itself that are likely to support a thriving biosensor ecosystem organized in this way. They are more stable, expanded APIs, end-user facing security technologies that enable people to manage their data exhaust more meaningfully, applications of machine-learning capabilities that refrain from putting people into machine-inferred boxes, interfaces that support greater data literacy, and design strategies that support experiences of pleasure beyond Pavlovian responses to gamification.

References

Berlant, Lauren. 2007. Cruel Optimism. Raleigh, NC: Duke University Press.

Bietz, Matthew. 2013. Personal Genetic Code: Algorithmic Living, Genomics, and the Quantified Self. Society for the Social Studies of Science 2013 Annual Meeting.

Böhlen, Marc, Ilya Maharika, Paul Lloyd Sargent, Silvia Zaianty, Nicole Lee, Angelica Piedrahita Delgado, Nevena Niagolova, and Fabian Vogelsteller. 2012. Prototyping Ubiquitous Biosensing Applications through Speculative Design. 8th International Conference on Intelligent Environments (IE), pp. 198–205. IEEE.

Cefkin, Melissa. (Ed.). 2010. Ethnography and the Corporate Encounter: Reflections on Research in and of Corporations. New York: Berghahn Books.

Cheney-Lippold, John. 2011. A New Algorithmic Identity Soft Biopolitics and the Modulation of Control. Theory, Culture & Society, 28(6), 164–181.

Christensen, Clayton. 1997. The Innovator's Dilemma: When New Technologies Cause Great Firms to Fail. Cambridge, MA: Harvard Business Press.

Darrah, Charles, James Freeman, and June Anne English-Lueck. 2007. Busier Than Ever!: Why American Families Can't Slow Down. Stanford: Stanford University Press.

DiSalvo, Carl. 2009. Design and the Construction of Publics. Design Issues, 25(1), 48–63.

Dourish, Paul. 2006. Implications for design. In Proceedings of the SIGCHI Conference on Human Factors in Computing Systems (pp. 541–550). ACM.

Dunne, Anthony, & Fiona Raby. 2001. Design Noir: The Secret Life of Electronic Objects. London: Springer.

Economist Intelligence Unit, Price Waterhouse Cooper. 2012. Emerging mHealth: Paths for Growth. www.managementthinking.eiu.com/sites/default/files/downloads/Emerging%20mHealth.pdf

Foucault, Michel. 1977. Discipline & Punish. New York: Random House.

Franzen, Carl. 2013. Free Your Fitbit: Can a 'Human API' Liberate Your Health Data from Corporate Overlords? Retrieved from http://www.theverge.com/2013/6/4/4392996/fitness-tracker-data-platforms-launch-giving-users-control.

Giddens, Anthony. 1990. The Consequences of Modernity. Cambridge: Polity Press.

Gerlitz, Caroline, and Celia Lury. 2012. Self-Evaluating Media: Acting on Data. Paper presented at "The new numeracy? A conversation about numbers and numbering practices." Goldsmiths College, London.

Greenhalgh, Susan. 2012. "Weighty Subjects: The Biopolitics of the U.S. War on Fat." American Ethnologist, 39:3, pp. 471–487.

Gregg, Melissa. (Forthcoming). Getting Things Done*: Productivity, Self-Management and the Order of Things. submitted to Networked Affect, Ken Hillis, Susanna Paasonen and Michael Petit (eds) MIT Press.

Guyer, Jane. 2012. Percentages and Perchance: Archaic Forms in the 21st Century. Public lecture given at Goldsmiths College, London, February 15.

Guyer, Jane. 2004. Marginal gains: Monetary Transactions in Atlantic Africa. Chicago: University of Chicago Press.

Haraway, Donna. 1991. Simians, Cyborgs, and Women: The Reinvention of Nature. London: Routledge.

Kenner, Alison. 2013. Diagnosing Data: Tracking Asthma Through U.S. Agencies and Beyond. Society for the Social Studies of Science 2013 Annual Meeting.

Kopytoff, Igor. 1986. The Cultural Biography of Things: Commoditization as Process. In Appadurai, Arjun (Ed.). The Social Life of Things: Commodities in Cultural Perspective. Cambridge: Cambridge University Press.

Kragh-Furbo, Mette. 2012. Living Data: Genetic Data Travels to an Online Forum. Society for the Social Studies of Science Annual Meeting, Copenhagen, Denmark.

Lave, Jean. 1988. Cognition in Practice: Mind, Mathematics and Culture in Everyday Life. Cambridge: Cambridge University Press.

Latour, Bruno, and Vincent Lépinay. 2009. The Science of Passionate Interests: An Introduction to Gabriel Tarde's Economic Anthropology. Chicago: Prickly Paradigm Press.

Leahu, Lucian, Steve Schwenk, and Phoebe Sengers. 2008. "Subjective Objectivity: Negotiating Emotional Meaning." In Proceedings of the 7th ACM Conference on Designing Interactive Systems, 425–434. DIS '08. New York, NY, USA: ACM.

Maniatis, Petros, Devdatta Akhawe, Kevin Fall, Elaine Shi, Stephen McCamant, and Dawn Song. 2011. "Do You Know Where Your Data Are? Secure Data Capsules for Deployable Data Protection." In Proc. 13th Usenix Conf. Hot Topics in Operating Systems.

Nafus, Dawn and Jamie Sherman. (In press). This One Does Not Go Up to Eleven: The Quantified Self Movement as Soft Resistance. International Journal of Communication.

Nafus, Dawn and Richard Beckwith (forthcoming). Number in Craft: Situated Numbering Practices in Do-It-Yourself Sensor Systems. In Clare Wilkinson and Alicia De Nicola (eds). Taking Stock: Anthropology, Craft and Artisans in the 21st Century.

Neff, Gina. and Brittany Fiore-Silfvast. 2013. What We Talk About When We Talk about Data: Metrics, Mobilization and Materiality in Performing Digital Health. Theorizing the Web Conference, March 6. Ratto, M. 2007. Ethics of seamless infrastructures: Resources and future directions. International Review of Information Ethics, 8, 12.

Roberts, Julie. 2013. The Visualised Foetus: A Cultural and Political Analysis of Ultrasound Imagery. London: Lund Humphries Publishers. Strathern, Marilyn. 1992. Reproducing the Future: Essays on Anthropology, Kinship, and the New Reproductive Technologies. Manchester: Manchester University Press.

Verran, Helen. 2001. Science and African logic. Chicago: University of Chicago Press.

Wakeford, Nina. 2012. The New Numeracy. Retrieved from https://vimeo.com/56148680.

Wilkinson, Joann. 2012. Matter of Bits: Articulations of Reproduction through Ovulation Technologies. Society for the Social Studies of Science Annual Meeting, Copenhagen, Denmark.

CHAPTER 8

■ ■ ■

Sensor Deployments for Home and Community Settings

In this chapter, we will outline the methodologies that have been successfully developed and utilized by Intel and Technology Research for Independent Living (TRIL) Centre researchers in the design, implementation, deployment, management, and analysis of home- and community-based research pilots. Translating research from the confines of the laboratory to real-world environments of community clinics and people's homes is challenging. However, when successful, applying that research correctly can deliver meaningful benefits to both patients and clinicians. Leveraging the expertise of multidisciplinary teams is vital to ensuring that all issues are successfully captured and addressed during the project life cycle. Additionally, the end user must be the center of focus during both the development and evaluation phases. Finally, the trial must generate data and results that are sufficiently robust to withstand rigorous review by clinical and scientific experts. This is vital if any new technology solution is to be successful adopted for clinical use.

■ **Note** The TRIL Centre is a large-scale collaboration between Intel and research teams at University College Dublin (UCD), Trinity College Dublin (TCD), National University of Ireland (NUI) Galway, and St James's Hospital in Dublin. It is a multidisciplinary research center focused on discovering how technology can be used to facilitate older people living independent lives in the location of their choice. TRIL research encompasses identifying, understanding, and accurately measuring clinical variables to predict health, prevent decline, and promote well-being and independence. The driving principles are to facilitate the measurement of critical clinical variables and test technology-enabled clinical assessments and interventions in a nonclinical environment, with validation in both environments. This is combined with a technology design and development process that is person-centered and informed by ethnographic research. Many of the insights presented in this chapter were collected during the course of TRIL research activities. The case studies outlined were carried out collaboratively by Intel and TRIL researchers.

You can find additional information at www.trilcentre.org.

Healthcare Domain Challenges

Technology is used during the course of everyday practice in hospital clinics to identify and measure the extent of gait issues, cardiovascular health, sensory impairments, cognitive function, and so on. However, technologies are rarely used in community settings for a variety of reasons, including cost, usability, and the necessity for specialized facilities and/or expert personnel. Additionally, the value of monitoring data sets over the long term within the clinical domain is subject to debate, with critics seeking evidence of impact on healthcare outcomes, costs, and efficiencies (Alwan, 2009, McManus et al., 2008, Tamura et al., 2011). Although sensor technologies for singular or short-term measures, such as EKGs/ECGs or 24-hour ambulatory blood pressure monitoring, has achieved acceptance in the diagnostics process, there has been slow progress in embracing prognostics-oriented technology. The use of prognostics originated in the engineering domain, where it is used to predict, within specified degrees of statistical confidence, whether a system (or components within a system) will not perform within expected parameters. Of course, the human body is a complex biological system, which makes it difficult to model as a system because of the subtle interactions between physiological, biomechanical, behavioral, and cognitive parameters. Therefore, frequent assessments, long-term monitoring, or both are required to develop an understanding of what indicates a significant trend from an individual's own normal limits. Large population data sets that enable the creation of groupings with strongly related epidemiological characteristics are also critical. Normative values or ranges can be established that identify how an individual differs from other similar individuals. The population sizes within these data sets are critical because larger sample sizes support the development of more granular models, which are reflective of groups with shared physiological, cognitive, and biomechanical ranges.

Collecting high-quality sensor data sets in a reliable, robust, and low-cost manner over long periods of time, with minimal clinical oversight, poses enormous challenges. To successfully meet these challenges, new thinking is required into the way biomedical research is conducted. A broader perspective of sensor based applications is required, which includes all stakeholders in the research process, and is not just limited to the engineering-doctor interface. Clinicians, scientists, biomedical engineers, social scientists, designers, information and communication technology (ICT) engineers, and others need to work collaboratively in the development, deployment, and evaluation of technologies that will facilitate new paradigms of health and wellness management, as illustrated in Figure 8-1.

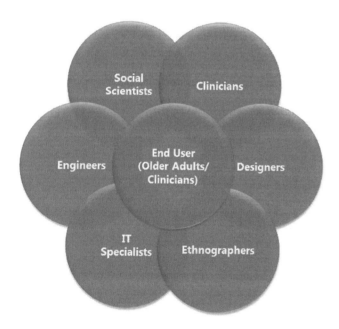

Figure 8-1. *TRIL's multidisciplinary technology research approach*

Because health and wellness applications are human-centric in nature, insights collected directly from end users play an important role in the development process. By using this information to inform the design of the sensor solution, it will have a higher probability of being successfully used in clinical practice or people's daily lives. The science of ethnography is a highly effective tool for developing the insights required to deliver a successful application or product. The ethnographic process helps to develop an understanding of how people live, what makes them live the way they do, and how technologies, including sensors, can be acceptable and beneficial. Ethnographers often spend extended periods of time with people, getting to know them and understanding their day-to-day lives. This helps identify opportunities to put technologies in place that are both unobtrusive and effective in supporting the health of the people that researchers and clinicians are studying.

A consistent finding of much aging research is that older adults want to stay in their own homes as they age, and not in care institutions. Homes are symbols of independence and are a demonstration of people's ability to maintain autonomous lives. Homes are full of personal possessions and memories and help maintain continuity in people's relationships with their past and their hopes for the future. Homes evoke and support autonomy, independence, freedom, and personal space. However, homes by their very nature are uncontrolled environments, which make both the deployment and utilization of sensor technologies challenging.

Study Design

The design and execution of any research study is a multiphase process, as shown in Figure 8-2. The steps should be followed in a sequential manner to minimize study design issues and to maximize the quality of the research outputs.

Figure 8-2. *The project life cycle*

1. The obvious starting phase of any research project is defining the research question, and in some cases the technology questions, to be addressed.

2. The cohort size required to generate statistically significant results is assessed during the power analysis phase. Cohort sizing is particularly important for any sensor applications that are required to demonstrate statistically significant diagnostic capabilities.

3. Protocol design focuses on the data to be collected. Careful design of the protocol is critical to ensure data quality. Data quality can be achieved by observing the data collection (in other words, a supervised protocol) or by having very rigid measurement methods, although both these methods may be unacceptable for large-scale deployments.

4. The utility and acceptability of the sensor system is determined during the user evaluation phase. Based on the information collected during this process, the system design may be refined or completely redesigned to make it more acceptable to end users.

5. The deployment phase focuses on the successful installation of the sensor system. The goal is to collect the necessary data required to answer the research question set out at the start of the study design. Technical issues that were not identified during laboratory testing may also be found. The deployment will also highlight usability issues that were not found or prioritized during the user evaluation phase.

6. The final phase of the life cycle is data analysis, where many of the data mining and visualization techniques as described in Chapter 5 can be applied to reveal interesting patterns in the data.

Setting the Research Questions

A clear research question supports the identification of what data must be collected to address the research hypothesis, which in turn defines the cohort size by means of a power analysis. Participant inclusion/exclusion criteria will be determined based on the research question and the data to be examined. The clinical protocol will be determined by the type of data and the personnel required for data collection. The presence of a clinician may be legally or ethically required if blood samples are required or if the cohort is vulnerable in any way. Trained psychologists may be required to administer and interpret psychological assessments, and engineers may need to install and maintain technologies and validate data as it is collected.

The clinical protocol should be documented accurately as part of the ethical approval process required by most institutions. The protocol document will be referred to during the data collection phase and should be strictly adhered to. This document will be invaluable during the data analysis phase of the study, providing context to the data and its interpretation.

When working in a multidisciplinary environment, as is common during clinical studies, it is appropriate to create a clinical requirements document (CRD) as well as a prototype requirements document (PRD). A CRD is developed by clinicians to document their requirements for the study. This document extends the protocol document to specify what the clinician requires from the sensor technology and personnel to achieve the study aims. The PRD is a technical document, developed by engineers, that describes the hardware and software choices made to meet the clinical requirements. Both of these documents are shared and debated among the multidisciplinary team members until agreement is achieved on the requirements for the initial prototype. Sometimes these documents raise questions that necessitate further research or focus groups to answer. Although creating (and maintaining) documents such as the PRD and CRD is time-consuming, these documents are invaluable in preventing the misinterpretation of requirements, which can arise in multidisciplinary teams. Ultimately, these structured requirement capture processes can result in significant overall time savings and can minimize potential disagreements between the team during the evaluation phase of the project.

Clinical Cohort Characterization

Clinical cohorts are a pivotal component in any health- and wellness-oriented research. Considerable cost and effort are required in the recruitment of cohorts. However, the up-front investment in characterizing a cohort can pay significant dividends. These dividends include helping to inform the analysis of the research data and revealing interesting and novel relationships between parameters during the analysis.

One of the first issues to be addressed is cohort size. A power analysis should be conducted to establish the ideal cohort size required to enable accurate and reliable statistical analysis (Cohen, 1988). Power analysis is used to calculate the minimum sample size required to detect an effect of a given size. This prevents either under- or over-sizing of the cohort. If the sample size is too small, the data will not be accurate enough to draw reliable conclusions on predefined research questions. If the sample size is too big, time and effort will be wasted. The power of a study is dependent on the effect size, the sample size, and the size of type I error (e.g., $\alpha = 0.05$, meaning incorrect rejection of a true null hypothesis, in other words, incorrectly identifying a relationship between parameters when none exists). The effect size should represent the smallest effect that would be of clinical significance. For this reason, it will vary with the measure under consideration. If the effect size and alpha are known, then the sample size becomes a function of the power of the study. Typically, statistical power greater than 80 percent is considered adequate, and a sample size corresponding to 80 percent power is used as the minimum cohort size. The size of the recruited cohort should always be larger than the size calculated by a study power analysis to account for drop-outs. This buffering factor depends on the cohort demographics and the nature of the protocol.

Where feasible, the cohort should be given a generalized assessment to establish their baseline health and to identify any risks that must be immediately addressed and would preclude them from participating in a study. This will be a requirement of most ethics committees dealing with clinical studies. For example, an elderly cohort may undergo a falls risk assessment, cognitive functional tests, and physiological testing to establish their baseline health.

Protocol Options: Supervised vs. Unsupervised

The selection of a supervised or unsupervised protocol is contingent on the specifics of the research question under investigation. A clinician or researcher is present during a supervised protocol, recording the data, ensuring that the protocol is followed correctly, and ensuring the safety of the participant. For these reasons, a supervised protocol is usually suited to trials where sensor data quality is critical. However, when long-term sensor measures are of interest, it is not always practical to conduct a supervised study. It may be inconvenient for a participant to visit a clinic/lab every day for a number of months; similarly, it may not be convenient for a researcher to visit the home of a participant on an ongoing basis. In such cases, an unsupervised protocol may provide the best option. During an unsupervised study, issues such as remote sensor management, data management, and data context are important. Remote management tools may be used to monitor data as it is collected (see the section "Home Deployment Management"). These tools allow researchers to monitor data quality, protocol adherence, and equipment status as the trial is conducted. If data is not monitored using a remote management infrastructure, participants may be required to complete a diary on every day of the study to provide context to the sensor data collected, as described in Case Study 3.

Clinical Benefit

Technological solutions can often be more costly and time-consuming than "care as usual." However, financial and temporal costs are surmountable if the clinical benefit of using a sensor technology can be demonstrated. Technology—which is simply a lower-cost, more portable version of existing clinical solutions—can leverage the existing research for the clinical device, provided that the new sensor technology is validated against the clinical device. Such a sensor will be readily accepted by those who already have experience in using and interpreting data from the existing clinical device.

The burden of proof is much higher for technologies that do not have a clinical equivalent. First, the economic and health benefit of using the new measures must be compared to "care as usual" through costly longitudinal trials, such as randomized control trials (RCT). Second, results of these studies must be published in clinically accepted, internationally peer-reviewed journals. Finally, the burden of interpreting the data is higher for a new technology/ assessment than for an existing measure that the community-based practitioner has experience in interpreting. This interpretation must be provided by the new technology or by additional training.

Home Deployment Elements

The development of sensor systems suitable for home settings, and to a lesser extent community settings, creates significant challenges, including cost, reliability, sensitivity, practicality of installation, and aesthetic considerations. The relative weight of these factors will vary from application to application. In this section, we focus on the considerations that apply to the development of body-worn or ambient sensing solutions.

Home- and Community-Based Sensing

The availability of low-cost, reliable, and intuitive technologies is critical in enabling community- and home-based solutions. While these technologies may not have the ultra-high resolution of systems found in hospital clinics, they can provide the community-based clinicians with a strong indication of whether an issue exists or whether the patient is trending significantly in a manner that warrants referral to a specialist facility for further investigation.

Geriatric medicine makes extensive use of subjective or largely subjective tools to assess the patient. The ability to add insights obtained from patient observation to the result of the tests requires years of specialized training by the clinician. Even if the clinician has the ability to provide an accurate assessment of the patient's condition, there is no comprehensive quantitative record of the tests. This impacts the ability of the clinician to accurately track whether a prescribed intervention is working appropriately. Sensor systems provide a means to fully capture the spectrum of data available during the tests. Objective measures enable the repeatability and reproducibility of tests, which are important in enabling long-term patient monitoring.

Sensors can play a key role in providing objective cost-effective measurements of patients. New clinical sensor technologies will enable public health policy to move from a reactive to proactive healthcare model. These solutions must process the sensor data, present the data in a manner that enables intuitive interpretation, demonstrate whether and how the patient's data differs from their comparative population, and allow the clinician to compare the patient's previous test results. Collectively, these elements can give local health professionals capabilities that have up to now been the preserve of specialist clinicians in specialized clinics. Consequently, the cost of patient treatment should be reduced. Early intervention and proactive patient treatment are often less expensive than reactive treatment in a hospital following a health event.

The current sensor-oriented approaches fall into two broad categories:

- Body-worn applications are primarily used in either assessment and/or monitoring applications.

- Ambient applications are typically used to passively monitor a subject's behaviors and activity patterns or to trigger actuators to initiate actions, such as switching on lights when a bed exit sensor is triggered during the night.

Although both approaches can utilize common technology elements, they will have differing design considerations and constraints such as contact requirements with the human body, long-term deployments, and data processing requirements.

Body-Worn Assessment Applications

Body-worn sensors (BWS) have been used in a wide variety of physiological and kinematic monitoring applications (Catherwood et al., 2010, Ghasemzadeh et al., 2010, Aziz et al., 2006, Greene et al., 2010). BWS have the potential to support the clinical judgment of community-based practitioners through the provision of objective measures for tests, which are currently administered in a qualitative manner. Because of their small form factor, BWS can provide on-body measurements over extended periods of time. They can also support flexible protocols. Data-forwarding BWS can stream data up to distances of 100 meters from the sensor to the data aggregator. Data logging BWS can record data to local data storage, thus allowing location-independent monitoring (Scanaill et al., 2006). However, the design of the on-body sensor attachments is extremely important. The sensors used to capture the data must ensure that the data collected is of sufficient resolution to prevent motion artifacts corrupting the signal. The method of attachment should also be intuitive and prevent incorrect positioning and orientation of the sensor on the body. Because of these various interrelated requirements, a sensor systems approach will be the most effective method to ensure integrated end-to-end capabilities (see Chapter 3).

For applications that require long-term monitoring, compliance can be challenging. The patient must remember to reattach the sensor if it has been removed at night, during showering, or for charging. In physiological-sensing applications, the electrode must be carefully designed to minimize skin irritation and ensure good signal quality. Given these considerations, body-worn sensors must be carefully matched to the application. Short-term measurements—such as 24-hour EKG/ECG monitoring or a one-off measurement for diagnostic tests—provide good use cases for BWS. Such applications are supervised in some manner by a healthcare professional, ensuring that the sensor is correctly attached and the data is of the required quality.

Kinematic sensors are increasingly used by research groups for supervised motion analysis applications because their size has no impact on the gait pattern of the subject being tested. They can also provide location-independent monitoring by storing data to an onboard memory card. Gait and balance impairment, one of the most prevalent falls risk factors, can be accurately measured using low-cost kinematic sensor (in other words, accelerometer, gyroscope, or magnetometer) technology. Despite the low-cost of these technologies, they are rarely used outside of a research or clinical environment. There are a few reasons for this. First, many existing technologies do not provide sufficient context for the results they produce and therefore require a level of expertise to interpret. Second, community-based clinicians do not have the time to set up the technology and perform complex protocols as part of their routine examinations. Finally, these technologies are not developed for, or marketed toward, the community clinician. Therefore, most are unaware of the existence of such technologies. Case Study 1 describes a body-worn kinematic sensing application that was designed and developed with these considerations in mind.

Ambient Sensing

Noncontact sensing systems provide 24-hour monitoring of subjects in their home by connecting various sensing technologies, such as passive or active infrared sensors, to a data aggregator. The data aggregator can provide simple storage of the data for offline analysis or can process and forward the data to a back-end infrastructure. Once data is transferred to a back end, it can be processed in application-specific ways. For example, in an activity of daily living (ADL) application, the data can be used in an inference engine (for example, Bayesian and Markov Models) to determine the subject's ADLs. The determination is based on the interactions detected between the subject and their home environment. Alternatively, the data could be used to identify a change in personal routine, which may indicate an onset of disease. For example, diabetes may be diagnosed by identifying more frequent visits to the bathroom during the night, or dementia may be diagnosed by increasingly erratic movement patterns during the day or night. Other noncontact solutions include the following:

- Activities of daily living (Wood et al., 2008)
- Safety (Lee et al., 2008)
- Location determination (Kelly et al., 2008)
- Gait velocity (Hagler et al., 2010, Hayes et al., 2009)
- Cognition/dementia (Biswas et al., 2010)

Ambient sensors can also be used to provide inputs into actuators or other forms of integrated systems. Pressure sensors can be used in a bedroom to detect when someone exits their bed. They can trigger an action such as lighting a path to the bathroom to prevent accidental trips.

From a user perspective, ambient sensing can engender mixed reactions. On one hand, the systems can provide people with a sense of security, especially those who are living alone. However, they also generate strong negative responses, especially if the person associates the sensor with being monitored by a camera. Good form-factor design can make the sensor less obvious, which helps reduce people's awareness of them. Battery-powered sensors afford great flexibility in placement and can be placed in unobtrusive locations, unlike mains-powered sensors, which must be placed near a power socket.

User Touch Points

The user touch point is playing an increasingly important role in the design and deployment of monitoring and assessment tools, as solutions are no longer limited to large PCs and laptops. There is increasing interest in exploiting the growing capabilities of smartphones and tablets in a variety of domains, including healthcare (Middleton, 2010). More than 80 percent of doctors now use mobile devices such tablets and smartphones to improve patient care (Bresnick, 2012). Leveraging the capabilities of these low-cost devices for healthcare applications is a logical next step to enable greater access at lower cost to previously silo' d applications. However, significant focus must be given to the appropriate design of the user interfaces to ensure that applications can be used effectively on smaller screen sizes. Smartphones are already being used by clinicians and medical students to manage e-mails, access online resources, and view medical references. However, for clinical applications, such as viewing lab results or instrumented tests such as ECGs, and electronic prescribing, usage is significantly less (Prestigiacomo, 2010). Despite the sensing, processing, and data storage capabilities of smartphones, they are also not yet commonly applied as clinical data capture/ assessment devices.

Smartphones and tablets provide intuitive user interaction, integrated sensing, low-power processing, low-cost data acquisition and storage, and wireless connectivity. Another key advantage of smartphones is the ability to extend the functionality of a device by downloading software applications from online app stores or creating custom applications using the software development kit (SDK) provided by the manufacturer.

The tablet form factor provides a natural and intuitive interaction model for older adults and individuals who have some form of physical or cognitive disability (Smith, 2011). The ability to use a tablet requires little or no training. Applications for older adults such as reminiscing (Mulvenna et al., 2011), language translation (Schmeier et al., 2011), and toilet locations (Barnes et al., 2011) have been recently reported in the literature. The design of the interaction model for the application should be given appropriate attention. The benefit of a simple physical interaction with the device quickly evaporates if the application navigation and interaction are not of equivalent simplicity.

One application focus area that benefits from the easy user interaction, location independence, and large screen size afforded by a tablet is cognitive functional testing. Some cognitive tests simply require the subject to re-create a displayed pattern using a pen and paper. Replicating such a test using a standard computing device, such as a laptop or desktop computer, could present significant usability challenges. Those challenges make it difficult to separate the ability to perform the test from the ability to use the laptop/desktop effectively. Tests built on tablets can address many of these usability issues and also allow the participant to take the test in their preferred location in their own home. The integrated sensors on a pad can also be utilized to improve usability. The pad's built-in light sensor, for example, can be used to ensure a consistent visual presentation baseline, by detecting the ambient light conditions and automatically adjusting the screen brightness.

Most smartphones are augmented with integrated inertial sensors, including accelerometers and gyroscopes. The availability of this integrated kinematic sensing capability has led to the development of smartphone applications for biometric detection (Mantyjarvi et al., 2005), activity detection (Khan et al., 2010), and motion analysis (LeMoyne et al., 2010). However, there are some limitations to using the integrated sensors in a tablet/phone device, particularly for applications that require consistent sampling rates. Smartphone devices cannot guarantee a consistent sampling rate or sensor sensitivity. In applications where control of these parameters is essential, interfacing the smartphone/tablet device to a known discrete sensor is a more appropriate design choice than using integrated sensors. The development of an Android-based application with discrete body-worn sensors is described in Case Study 1. Stand-alone sensor hubs for smartphones, operating independently of the phone's CPU, address many of the current deterministic performance limitations.

Televisions have received interest for a number of years as a potential healthcare touch point. Commercial assisted-living products, such as Philip's Motiva (Philips, 2013) have emerged that are focused on chronic disease management (CDM). Until now, CDM solutions have required the use of a set-top connected to the TV. The emergence of web-enabled televisions containing integrated CPUs and network connectivity from manufacturers such as Samsung, LG, Sony, and Panasonic will provide a new platform for healthcare content consumption in the future. As health-related devices connect to the cloud, data and other analytics-derived information could potentially be consumed through a "smart TV" web interface. However, it is likely to be a number of years before this platform is sufficiently mature to be a viable health platform (Blackburn et al., 2011). Although the user experience on this platform is improving, it is still far from seamless, and significant challenges still remain in delivering a high-quality user interaction experience.

Participant Feedback

The provision of feedback to the end user raises some interesting questions and conflicts, especially if the technology deployment is primarily research oriented. Participants in a trial generally look for feedback on their performance and context for any results obtained and ask questions such as "Does that mean I did well?" Feedback and the manner in which it is delivered to a participant can provide a critical hook in maintaining participant engagement. However, the advantages of providing feedback must be offset against the potential negative influence on the data set acquired during the course of the study. Users who receive feedback may bias the data by over-engaging with the technology or adapting the way they perform the experiment to improve their scores. Ultimately, whether feedback is provided or not, the type of feedback provided will be defined by your research questions.

Home Deployment Management

There are two key overheads in any home-based sensor technologies. First, *truck roll* means the time and resources required to physically install, maintain, and uninstall the technology in the participant's home. A clearly defined process should be developed to minimize truck roll time and ensure that the participant is happy with the technology. The process documentation should be continually updated to reflect new insights as they arise. Second, the ability to manage remote sensor deployments is a key requirement to a successful deployment (see Figure 8-3). This includes ensuring that data is collected as defined by the experimental protocol and transported and managed in a secure and reliable manner. It should also be possible to remotely debug and update the sensors and any associated technology as required. Remote management tools enable the deployment to be managed in an efficient and proactive manner. Automated monitoring identifies issues at the earliest juncture, thus minimizing the potential for data loss. The system design should allow for the loss of remote connectivity and provide local buffering of data until connectivity can be restored.

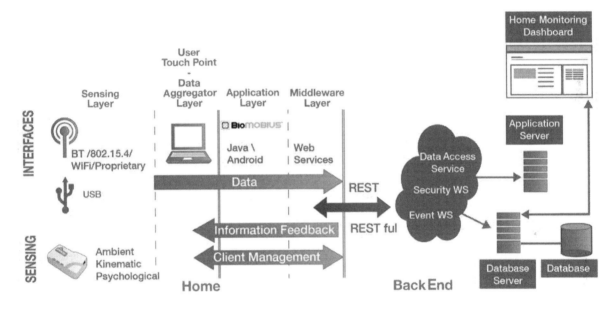

Figure 8-3. *System architecture for home deployment data and client management*

Finally, the remote management tools should provide data quality checks. Automated processes can be put in place to interrogate the validity of received data packets/files before the data is committed to the central data repository. These processes often take the form of scripts that can check the file/packet for errors such as missing data, null data, and outliers.

The ability to remotely manage computer equipment is standard practice in enterprise environments, where it significantly improves operational efficiencies and reduces costs. The heterogeneous nature of home and community technology deployments makes delivery of this type of functionality more challenging than in the controlled and homogenous enterprise environment. However, many of the existing technologies available in the enterprise environment can be adapted successfully to this domain if an appropriate understanding of the issues involved is developed and assumptions are continuously challenged.

Various sensor data management frameworks have been reported. These frameworks have been proposed to manage various aspects of the network, such as data accuracy (Ganeriwal et al., 2008), data coordination (Melodia et al., 2005), and data queries (Li et al., 2008). However, these efforts have been focused between tier 1 (sensor) and tier 2 (aggregator) with little focus on external data transfer. Balazinska suggests that most sensor network researchers have paid too much attention to the networking of distributed sensors and too little attention to tools that manage, analyze, and understand the data (Balazinska et al., 2007).

Remote data transport from sensor networks normally requires management frameworks, which are generally bespoke in nature, and consequently require significant development time, cost, and support overhead. These frameworks typically do not provide management tools to support the remote administration of the data aggregator, back-end management reporting, and configuration and management of exceptions. Online tools such as Xively (xively.com) and iDigi (www.idigi.com), which allow users to remotely manage their sensor deployment from sensor to the cloud, may prove to be significant.

Remote Deployment Framework

The remote deployment framework (RDF) (McGrath et al., 2011) is an effort to address these issues based on lessons learned during the deployment of remote sensor technologies by TRIL researchers. The primary function of the RDF is to provide a generic framework to collect, transport, and persist sensor data in a secure and robust manner (Walsh et al., 2011). The RDF has a service-orientated architecture and is implemented using Java enterprise technologies. The framework enables secure and managed data collection from remotely deployed sensors to a central location via heterogeneous aggregators. The RDF also provides a full set of tool to manage any home deployment including remote client monitoring, data monitoring, remote client connectivity, and exception notification management.

The RDF is based on the realization of the five key requirements for a home deployment management framework:

- *Platform independence*: The framework should work on a range of hardware platforms and operating systems including Windows and Linux. Programmable interfaces should support C/C++, .NET, Java, and scripting languages. This ensures that a sensor system architect has a wide range of design options available.

- *Interoperability*: The framework supports open standards (such as WS-I) where possible to ensure future compatibility, integration, and security.

- *Data independence*: The RDF is data agnostic; its data model can support a variety of usage models.

- *System scalability and extensibility*: The framework supports variable numbers of sensor nodes, data volumes, and the seamless addition of new functionality. A single instance of the RDF should support multiple discrete sensor trials.

- *Security*: The framework must support data confidentiality at both the transport and application layers. It should also offer multiple authentication/authorization mechanisms and a secure audit trail to ensure full traceability from the sensor node to the data store and subsequent data retrieval.

The RDF embraces the philosophy of open standards and the use of nonproprietary technologies to ensure the ease of integration for third parties and research collaborators. The RDF was applied by TRIL for ambient home monitoring and the remote monitoring of chronic obstructive pulmonary disease (COPD) patients.

The Prototyping Design Process

In TRIL, ethnographers spend time in the homes and communities of end users to understand their lives and experiences. The information gathered during this fieldwork is distilled and presented to multidisciplinary teams to inspire concept development and inform the development of research prototypes. These brainstorming data downloads are typically led by designers and/or ethnographers, and the teams include clinical researchers, engineers, and research scientists. The best concepts from these sessions are explored further using design tools, such as storyboards and low-fidelity models, before they are presented to potential end users during focus groups. Feedback from the focus group is presented back to the multidisciplinary team and applied to further refine the concepts. This refinement and feedback loop may be repeated several times, with increasingly sophisticated prototypes, until a final prototype is developed for deployment into the home or community.

This design process is dependent on gaining an understanding of both the user and their environment and then applying this knowledge, along with the collective knowledge of multidisciplinary stakeholders, to develop an appropriate technology for the purpose.

Design for and with the End User

Understanding the end user is critical to developing technology they will be motivated to use and interact with. Physical and cognitive abilities/limitations of the user, their daily routine, and the user's previous experiences with technology all need to be known. In understanding end users, it is important to recognize that no two users are the same. Therefore, individuals within the target grouping should be examined in depth. The larger grouping to which they belong should be broadly examined as well. Figure 8-4 shows an example of interaction testing results with target users to confirm design choices and usability.

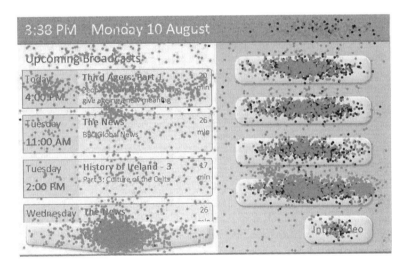

Figure 8-4. *Visualization of the participants' ability to use the touchscreen menu using a log of all user interactions*

Unfortunately, some designers and engineers have little understanding of the unique needs of their target user. For example, some of the early generation of the insulin pens had a small liquid crystal display (LCD) that was difficult for diabetics to read (Burton et al., 2006). The product designers had failed to consider that diabetics often suffer from poor eyesight. As result, these early version of devices had to be redesigned at significant cost with larger displays featuring improved contrast that were easier for diabetics to read. Therefore, strategies such as ethnographic fieldwork and engaging end users in the design process are necessary to get to know the end users. In TRIL, projects encompass an iterative participatory design process, actively involving older adults in "co-designing" technology for older adults. Designing technology in this way contributes to a higher probability of usable technology and fosters compliance in long-term usage by addressing specific needs.

There are also challenges in co-designing technology with nontechnical end users. These end users can struggle to understand the potential benefits of new technology. That struggle can limit their ability to actively contribute to a discussion on technological requirements. We found that using storyboards, scenarios, and personas in focus groups can address this issue by shifting the focus from the technology itself to what the technology can provide in terms of benefitting the individual. These techniques facilitate open discussion among participants and ultimately help the design team identify key features of the technology. We have also found it necessary to educate users to be critical in their feedback. Ethnographers are experts in getting beyond the overly positive, superficial level of feedback and "setting the stage" for critical feedback.

Design with Multidisciplinary Team Members

The tenet of assessment and intervention technologies is that they address a clinical need, whether physical, social, or cognitive. Technology should not be developed for the sake of technology. As such, the design process must begin with expert input from health professionals to determine clinical requirements. In designing Case Study 1, for example, the process began with a geriatrician, who had expertise in falls of older adults, outlining the desired outcomes of the project. These outcomes were then translated into design and engineering requirements through a series of workshops with multidisciplinary team members.

In multidisciplinary teams, each team member brings their own expertise and experiences to the project. The research scientists typically ensure that the scientific integrity of the study is maintained. The ethnographic researchers ensure that any solution will be practical and fit into an end user's life. The engineers and designers will identify and develop a technology to answer the research question. As a multidisciplinary team works together on more and more projects, these roles may evolve and overlap. These overlaps can be beneficial as team members gain confidence in providing feedback on not only their domain of expertise but also the domains of others. There are often disagreements within multidisciplinary teams because of the differing priorities of team members. For example, the most sophisticated technology may not be the most appropriate for the user, the research question cannot be answered using technology alone, or the proposed protocol may be too restrictive for the user. In addressing such disagreements, the needs of the user are always the priority. Solutions that prioritize sophisticated technology or strict study protocols over a user's needs risk noncompliance. That in turn impacts the quantity and quality of the data captured during the study (Bailey et al., 2011).

Data Analytics and Intelligent Data Processing

The process of examining, processing, and modeling data to uncover clinically meaningful patterns and relationships is essential to the success of any clinical research trial. The topic of data analytics and intelligent data processing (reviewed in Chapter 5) is complex and diverse. A brief overview of commonly used techniques in biomedical data analysis is provided in this section.

As previously described in Chapter 5, an important step preceding data analysis is removing noise and unwanted artifacts due to movement or electronic equipment. Data should be filtered to remove frequency components outside the active bandwidth of the signal. For example, in gait analysis, the kinematic data of interest are typically at frequencies below 100 Hz. The data should be low-pass filtered to remove the influence of higher frequency artifacts. Similarly, when looking at physiological data such as the electromyogram (EMG), where the frequency range of interest would be 20–450 Hz, data should be band-pass filtered to remove the low-frequency movement artifacts and high-frequency noise.

To interpret clinical data, it is necessary to extract relevant features. These features are dependent on the type of data and the protocol under which it was collected. Typically, features would be computed that have clinical relevance. For example, in gait analysis, features are determined that may relate to the timing of strides, the distance traveled during each stride, or the coordination of left and right legs during gait. In EMG, the median frequency of the power spectrum could be examined to provide insight into muscle fatigue over the duration of an experiment. In electrocardiography, the Q, R, and S wave (QRS) events may be detected for each heartbeat and used to examine heart rate variability.

Relatively simple statistical techniques may be used to examine differences in a specific feature for subgroups of a cohort. For example, you may be interested in differences between men and women, between young and old participants, or between healthy and pathological participants. Simple t-tests, analysis of variance (ANOVA), or rank sum tests could be used for this investigation.

Alternatively, if the study aims to classify participants by subgroups, it would be more appropriate to combine a selection of features using regression or discriminant analysis. If the dependent variable is numerical (e.g., age), linear or nonlinear regression analysis would be most appropriate. On the other hand, if the dependent variable is categorical (e.g., gender), either logistic regression or discriminant analysis could be employed, depending on the nature of the predictive features. If a large number of features relative to cohort size are available, it may be necessary to reduce the number of features to avoid overfitting and to produce a more robust model that will generalize to unseen data. This may be achieved using either feature extraction or feature selection. Feature extraction methods, such as principal component analysis (PCA), transform the feature set to a smaller number of uncorrelated components that describe as much variance in the data as possible. Feature selection methods, such as forward feature selection, sequentially add features and evaluate model performance at each step, continuing until model performance does not further improve. Model performance should be cross-validated to test robustness. A commonly used technique is k-fold cross-validation (Kohavi, 1995, Han et al., 2000). Using this technique, data is divided into k subsections or folds, the model is trained using k-1 folds, and its performance is tested on the remaining fold. The process is repeated k times with the model being tested using a different fold each time.

Machine learning techniques can be split into three categories: supervised, unsupervised, and reinforcement learning. The previous paragraph primarily deals with supervised learning, where the identities of each feature and dependent variable are known. This technique has clinical applications in identifying physical, cognitive, or psychological pathologies based on clinical or sensor-derived features. In unsupervised learning, the aim is to extract hidden trends and predictive information from large databases of unknown variables using a range of methods, including clustering. Applications of unsupervised learning range from medical image processing to genome mapping to population analysis. In reinforcement learning, feedback is provided to a classifier model on whether a decision was correct or incorrect, and this feedback is used to train the model over time.

Ultimately, many different approaches will provide clinically insightful results, and your choice should be determined by the research objectives of the study. The method used to analyze a data set must be carefully chosen based on the nature of the dependent variables as well as the predictive features and must always consider the research objectives of the study. In choosing the most appropriate method, you will achieve scientifically valid as well as clinically relevant results.

Case Studies

Over the last number of years, the TRIL Centre has deployed a variety of technology platforms into several hundred homes. We present three representative case studies here that demonstrate the application of sensor technologies and techniques already described. The case studies describe sensor-based applications either for assessments or for interventions.

Case Study 1: Quantified Timed Get Up and Go (QTUG) Test

The standard Timed Get and Go (TUG) test is a quick and popular clinical assessment used to assess the basic mobility skills of older adults. The test requires the subject to get up from a seated position, walk 3 meters (approximately 10 feet), turn, return to the chair, and sit down—as quickly and safely as possible. This test challenges several aspects of a subject's gait and balance control, but only a single measure—time to complete the test—is objectively measured. The exact timing thresholds can vary with cut-off values of 10 to 30 seconds to distinguish between fallers and non-fallers (Beauchet et al., 2011). For example, in the United States the Centers for Disease Control and Prevention (CDC) specifies that a test time of greater than 12 seconds indicates a high falls risk. TRIL researchers focused on developing a clinical tool that used data captured from body-worn kinematic sensors on a subject that was undertaking the TUG test in an effort to quantify their falls risk, as shown in Figure 8-5. The new test was called Quantified Timed Get and Go or QTUG.

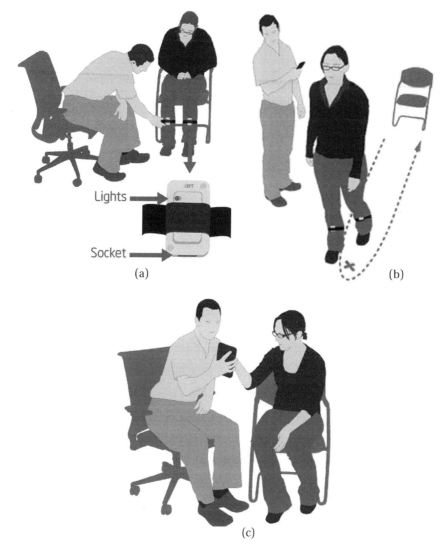

Figure 8-5. *The QTUG test: (a) attaching kinematic sensors to the front of lower leg shanks, (b) performing QTUG test, and (c) reviewing falls risk estimation on an Android tablet*

Initially, a PC application was developed to collect data from the sensors as patients completed the TUG test. This data was used to develop algorithms that could extract features of interest from the kinematic signals. The algorithms generate a variety of features (greater than 45)—for example, stride time and so on—that were used to build statistical models that could provide a prospective estimation of falls risk within a two-year period.

Algorithm Development

The first phase in the development of the QTUG prototype was the implementation of an adaptive threshold algorithm in Mathlab that was used to reliably identify the initial and terminal contact points in the data stream (in other words, heel-strike and toe-off events) from the body-worn kinematic sensors (located on the front of the lower shank on each leg), as shown in Figure 8-6.

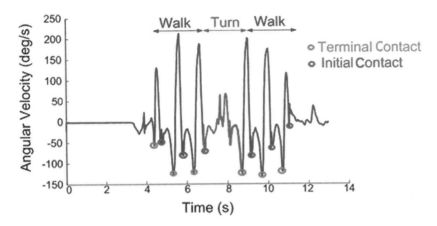

Figure 8-6. *Gyroscope-based gait pattern collected by body-worn kinematic sensor*

The algorithms developed were used to identify the following parameters from the gait cycle:

- Temporal gait parameters
- Spatial gait parameters
- Turn parameters
- Tri-axial angular velocity parameters

Model Development

The data was then stratified by gender and age into three separate groups: males, females younger than 75, and females older than 75 years. Sequential forward feature selection combined with regularized discriminant (RD) classifier models were used to generate each of the three predictive classifier models (males, females<75, and females ≥75) for estimating the risk of future falls in older adults. A grid search was used to determine the optimum feature set and classifier model parameters for each of the three classifier models.

Models were validated using tenfold cross-validation to provide a statistically unbiased estimate of performance. The output is the probability of a fall for each patient. The models developed were validated using a cross-selection study based on the falls history collected over a five-year period in the TRIL clinic where the sample size was as follows: N=349 (103 male, 246 female), mean age 72.4±7.4. 207 of the subjects had a self-reported history of falling (Greene et al., 2010). Additionally, a prospective study was conducted using data collected in the clinic (two-year falls follow-up data). The sample size was as follows: N=226, mean age 71.5±6.7 years, 164 female, 83 fallers. Results obtained through cross-validation yielded a mean classification accuracy of 79.69 percent (mean 95 percent CI: 77.09–82.34) in prospectively identifying participants who fell during the follow-up period. The results obtained were significantly more accurate than those obtained for falls risk estimation using two standard measures of falls risk (manually timed TUG and the Berg balance score (Bogle et al., 1996), which yielded mean classification accuracies of 59.43 percent [95 percent CI: 58.07–60.84] and 64.30 percent [95 percent CI: 62.56–66.09], respectively) (Greene et al., 2012).

Prototype Development

The algorithms and statistical models were then converted into an Android application than ran on a 7" tablet. The application had an intuitive and easy-to-use interface that steps the user sequentially through the process of running the QTUG test.

The kinematic body-worn sensors stream data via Bluetooth to the application running on the Android tablet where it is displayed (as shown in Figure 8-7a). The data is processed using the algorithms and models to calculate a falls risks estimate for the subject under test (as shown in Figure 8-7b).

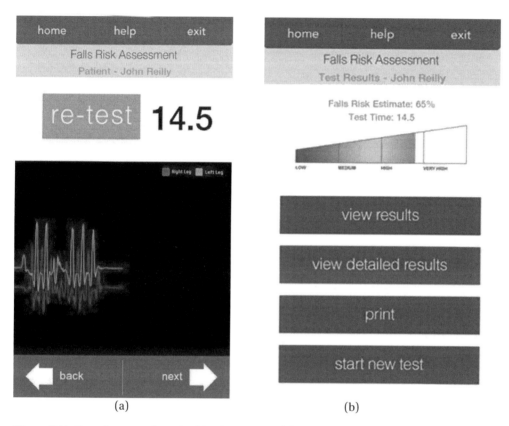

(a)   (b)

Figure 8-7. *Sample screens from the QTUG prototype: (a) real-time display of the gyroscope signals from sensors positioned on the front shank of the left and right legs with the TUG completion time, (b) graphical representation of the subject's falls risk*

Ethnographic researchers ran focus groups with various types of clinical professionals to collect feedback throughout the prototype design and evaluation process. The focus groups revealed that clinical falls experts preferred a tool that provided the details of all the parameters so that they could combine this data with other data from their supplementary assessments and apply their expertise to determine a subject's falls risk. As a result, the application was modified to provide user access to detailed parametric data that can be used to develop an understanding of the underlying cause of a falls risk. Community-based practitioners preferred a tool that interpreted the data for them. This feedback was incorporated into the prototype to provide a percentage-based score for community practitioners and an option for clinicians to view details of each measure.

The prototype demonstrated the implementation of a falls risk assessment tool that is simple, portable, and low cost. Findings from clinical focus groups have shown that the prototype could form the basis for a screening tool for community-based falls risk screening because of its ease of use and intuitive presentation of results. The QTUG prototype encapsulated how a standard clinical test can be enhanced through the use of technology and how user-centered design can be applied to develop technology suitable for community use (Greene et al., 2010). The success of the QTUG prototype has led to the formation of a TRIL start-up company that is planning to bring the technology to market.

Case Study 2: Ambient Assessment of Daily Activity and Gait Velocity

Gait velocity has long been correlated with falls history, and many studies indicate that fallers tend to walk slower than nonfallers. However, gait velocity may have been recorded in a clinical setting days, weeks, and sometimes months after a fall. It is difficult to establish whether this is the same velocity at which the person walked at prior to the fall occurring or whether this is a new velocity adopted by the faller following the fall. The purpose of this study was to determine whether gait velocity changes prior to a fall event. If so, could a change in gait velocity predict an increased risk of falling?

Daily measurement of velocity was a key requirement for this project; therefore, an in-home ambient sensing approach was selected to ensure long-term compliance. A home-monitoring system was developed using PIR wireless sensors and an Internet-enabled aggregator (see Figure 8-8). Velocity was measured in two ways in the home. First, a velocity rail was developed to measure the time taken to walk a fixed distance in the home. Second, sensors were placed in multiple doorways to measure time taken to pass through the doorway. The PIR sensors measured velocity by measuring the difference between the time in which the person was first detected and the time in which the person was last detected. The sensors transmitted their data via an 802.15.14 radio to a laptop-based data aggregator, which forwarded data to a remote server. Data was collected from eight (one male, seven female) older adults (aged 67–87) for an average 36-day period per participant. No significant correlations were found between health status, as recorded in the bi-daily diaries and gait velocity measurements. However, a longer trial with a larger number of homes may reveal such correlations.

Figure 8-8. *Fixed-distance, wall-mounted PIR sensors measuring in-home gait velocity*

Context is critical in any assessment. The inability of PIRs to distinguish between different people was a key consideration in planning the trial and analyzing the trial data. Various strategies were used to overcome these issues, including recruiting only those people who lived alone, developing physical maps of the participant's home and temporal maps of their routines within the home, and asking participants to keep diaries rating how well they felt and if they had visitors.

Deploying ambient technology into unsupervised settings for even short periods of time required significant planning, preparatory work, and maintenance by the deployment teams. There was also a high demand on the participants to be available for predeployment visits, installation visits, and uninstall visits, as well as completing their bi-daily diaries. This high overhead made it difficult to manage more than ten homes at any given time, and the demands on the participants made deployments longer than eight weeks difficult. In working through the challenges in the study, key improvements were identified and applied in subsequent home deployments. Uploading data to a remote server allowed the home deployment teams to detect sensor and data issues within 24 hours of faults occurring. The ability to remotely log in to the in-home data aggregator significantly reduced the time spent in the home troubleshooting. Finally, participant information booklets reassured the participants about the study's goals, what was required of them, and who the members of the home deployment team were (Walsh et al., 2011). Because of the overhead and difficulties in deploying ambient monitoring solution in people's home, there has been interest in utilizing other sources of data within homes to provide ambient intelligence monitoring. The rollout of smart meters for monitoring energy and other utilities is an area that researchers have been actively looking at to provide a data stream that provides insights into regular life behaviors without the need to deploy additional sensors (see Chapter 9).

Ambient monitoring applications irrespective of whether the user deployed sensors in the home, smart meters, or other forms of data raise issues of ethics, privacy, and security. A clear legal framework within which the data and access to it is controlled will be required before potential innovation in this area can be exploited.

Case Study 3: Training for Focused Living

The Alertness: Training for Focused Living project aimed to raise awareness of the concepts of alertness and attention and their importance in our everyday lives. The project was a four-week, self-administered, home-based training program that taught older adults a technique to modify their alertness at will. The program was developed through an iterative participatory design process with older adults. The first iteration of this study involved deploying a low-cost version of existing clinical technology into the homes of older adults. Users were taught to perform the alertness technique and shown how to use the technology in a clinical setting before the technology was installed in their homes. This technology—a laptop and a handheld galvanic skin response (GSR) sensor—gave the user biofeedback via a graph on the laptop screen. Ethnographic evaluation of this approach discovered that participants found using a laptop and interpreting graphs difficult, and they applied the technique only when they had the technology. These findings demonstrated that the project aim of improving everyday alertness was not being achieved.

A new revision of the system was developed in which participants received an Alertness Training Kit in the mail, consisting of the biofeedback device, audio CD, and guidebook that provided education about alertness, reflective questions, and instructions for the self-alerting technique (see Figure 8-9). On receipt of the home deployment kit, participants were encouraged to use the guidebook to explore their perception of alertness. The following week, they used the audio CD, along with the guidebook, to learn the self-alerting technique. On the third and subsequent weeks of the trial, participants were given the new biofeedback device consisting of a SHIMMER GSR sensor to provide real-time feedback on how well they were performing the technique. The biofeedback device had a user-friendly cushion-like form factor, a single on-off switch, and a built-in LCD display to provide feedback to the user on how well they were performing the technique. Data from this study was saved to a built-in micro-SD card on the device and analyzed after the study was completed.

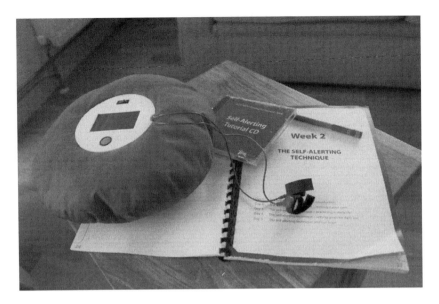

Figure 8-9. *Training for focused living cushion and support materials*

In adopting the ethnographic findings and re-imagining both the technology and the study methodology, a more reliable, user-friendly system was developed. The new technology allowed participants to quickly and easily practice their self-alertness technique whenever they had time. The new methodology led to participants who were more aware of their alertness and who were both willing and able to raise their alertness in their everyday lives—thus achieving the research aims. The low cost of the technology and the mail-drop deployment technique enabled researchers to deploy systems into many more homes than would have been possible using a PC-based technology and a home deployment team (Greco et al., 2011).

Lessons Learned

Because of the heterogeneous nature of most homes, deploying sensor-related technologies that are either ambient or require direct participation with a subject are challenging for variety reasons. Planning and preparation are instrumental to success. When each deployment or set of deployments is completed, carefully capturing what worked and what did not work is important. Insights into both the positive and negative aspects of any deployment will help ensure higher probable success in the future. The following sections discuss some of the key insights collected by researchers both at Intel and the TRIL Centre over many years of home- and community-based sensor deployments.

The Installation Process

Technology installation must be as expeditious as possible. After about 90 minutes, participants can tire, become impatient, or have to leave for other appointments. Even simple installations can easily exceed this threshold. Therefore, advance preparation by the engineer is critical to minimizing the *in situ* installation time. Complex installations involving the calibration of sensors can take well over two hours and are generally not appropriate. Photographic documentation or mapping of the pre- and postinstallation areas is important, especially when addressing issues that may arise after the uninstall process.

Key Sensor Findings

Sensors must respect the privacy and security of subjects and users. Unencrypted wireless sensors are open to potential eavesdropping outside the home. The sensor should avoid transmitting personally identifiable information. Ideally, an eavesdropper should not be able to gain any information about the users or their behavior. This is of particular concern when a sensor is deployed in the home or worn for an extended period of time.

In applications where the sensor system measures human behavior, it must minimally disturb that behavior. Sensor maintenance must also be considered: body-worn sensors that require daily recharging require the wearer to remember to take the device off, charge it, and put it back on. That can be challenging for many people. Paradoxically, remembering to charge a device every other day may be much more difficult than remembering to charge it daily.

Design can play a key role in the success of home-based sensor systems. The design of the sensor should not cause needless privacy concerns to users. Designs that feature a blinking LED may result in a study participant worrying that there is a camera in the room, even if the sensor doesn't behave anything like a camera. Design is particularly important for body-worn sensors, which have to worn for extended periods of time or are externally visible to others. Older adults are resistant to any visible indications of dependency or failing health. Aesthetic considerations are not as important for single-use or ambient sensors, but design for usability is important. Usability includes considerations such as how the sensor is attached to the person's body (see Chapter 10). For example, if a strap is required to attach a sensor to a limb for a motion analysis application, that strap must be designed to securely hold the sensor in the correct orientation throughout the assessment/monitoring period, while still allowing for ease of attachment and comfort. The design of the sensor can have a direct impact on the comfort level for the subject. For example, sensors designed for wearing to bed must be particularly comfortable to avoid disturbing the wearer's sleep. Ambient sensors should be designed with as few placement restrictions as possible. Wall-mounted sensors have to share space with existing photos, paintings, bookcases, tapestries, vases, and other wall decorations and must visually co-exist, both in form and in color, with the room decor. Light, pastel-colored devices have a better chance of blending in than those with darker or highly saturated colors.

The deployed system should have a minimal requirement for site visits by the deployment engineer. Poor battery life of wall-mounted sensors can mean regular visits by the deployment engineer. These visits cause disruption to participant lives and can remind the users that they are in a study, reducing the invisibility of the sensors and consequently the validity of the data.

The industrial, scientific, and medical (ISM) 2.4 GHz radio frequency band is crowded with various radios, such as Bluetooth devices, some Digital Enhanced Cordless Telecommunications (DECT) phones, home networks, microwave oven, baby monitors, smart TVs, and so on. Some of those can cause serious interference with sensor transmissions. Resistance to potential inference sources depends on radio choice. For example, the Bluetooth and 802.11 protocols can frequency-hop to avoid bands that experience interference. Similarly, Ultra Wide Band (UWB) radios find unused bands to work in. In contrast, 802.15.4 does not have a frequency-hopping protocol, making it susceptible to interference sources. If a non-frequency-hopping protocol is used, manual selection of the channels may be required to avoid local sources of ISM interference. It is important that any deployed technology can co-exist not only with environmental interference, as just described, but also with other instances of the deployed technology. This is particularly important in deployments in which two households or two clinical systems are within radio range of each other.

Radio messages are often the largest consumer of power in a sensor. Duty cycle designs should therefore focus on minimizing the number and frequency of communications. However, in designs that feature very low messaging rates, it can be difficult to differentiate between a failed sensor and a sensor that simply has not needed to say anything. To avoid this problem, each sensor should periodically send a "heartbeat" or "keepalive" message. This data can be used by the back-end monitoring system, such as an RDF, to generate an alert for a failed sensor when a predefined window for receipt of a "heartbeat" message is exceeded.

Data Quality

From a technology perspective, data quality is influenced at the sensor layer, application layer, aggregation/transport layer, and analysis layer. Most sensors use low-power radios, which suffer frequent interruptions in service. For this reason, the data sent to and from sensors must either be transferred reliably (for example, via a positive-acknowledgement-and-retransmit protocol) or be transmitted redundantly (for example, via a fixed number of retransmissions per message, without acknowledgment). The sensor protocol should also enable the receiver to detect errors. Packet checksum or Cyclic Redundancy Check (CRC) bytes are generally adequate to detect common transmission errors.

For applications such as an assessment carried out in a doctor's office, automated checking of the data quality received from a sensor is important. Any quality issues detected—such as significant dropped packets, temporary loss of communications with the sensor, or an incomplete test time—should force a retest situation. Any variability in the data that is not a result of the subject's test performance can result in an incorrect result, the magnitude of which will depend on the type of data analysis technique being used. Applications such as the falls risk estimation application described in Case Study 1 are sensitive to data variability. As such, these applications must have rigorous checks in place to ensure data quality.

Early detection of sensor/aggregator failures or missing data in the back-end database is important. The aggregation/transport layer should provide this early detection of equipment issues. The layer should also provision robust transport protocols to prevent data loss between the aggregator and the back end. The robustness of the solutions implemented will depend on data loss sensitivities and temporal constraints.

To ensure data quality during the data processing phase, it is important to filter data correctly, avoiding over- and under-filtering. Ideally, data should be recorded in an electrically "quiet" environment, and body-worn sensors should be securely fastened in place. These measures will reduce the need for excessive filtering. The appropriate calibration of data is essential when interpreting inertial and physiological signals, and gravity correction should be considered when examining accelerometer data. As features are extracted from the processed data, it is advisable to check that they are within published ranges and that they make intuitive sense.

User Engagement

Maintaining user engagement is a requirement for home-based assessment and interventions. A poor experience in using the technology will engender negative feelings and may result in the technology being abandoned. Good design and reliable technology are essential to creating a positive user experience and increasing the user's confidence in the technology. Another key aspect in developing sensor technology for the home and community is user engagement in the design process. Technologies designed by representative members of the end user's peer group are more likely to be accepted by the end user and will ensure that their day-to-day lives are not negatively impacted. Engaging users in the design process will increase the probability of capturing and successfully addressing potential usability issues.

One area of user engagement that can be problematic is the provision of user feedback. Feedback is provided to the end user to motivate the user and maintain engagement with the technology. Visualization of data in an engaging and intuitive form is therefore necessary. Technical feedback, comprising endless trend charts with control limits, while intuitive to engineers, may not be appropriate for all users. Simple and clean design that is dynamic in nature and adds vibrancy to the data is important in helping maintain user engagement over time. Such design can include a social networking element, where participants can compare themselves to their peers. However, information of this kind should be presented with appropriate context to ensure that participants are not unduly worried if they differ significantly from their peers. There is also growing interest in using computer gaming technologies to provide feedback, such as avatars that represent the subject of the study within a virtual rendering of the home environment. These techniques are finding application in sports and fitness sensing applications where there is a focus on using gaming techniques to introduce an element of competition. The inclusion of a competitive element is designed to maintain long-term user engagement in physical activity (see Chapter 10).

Summary

In this chapter, we have outlined how a multidisciplinary team approach can be applied to develop and deploy innovative assessment and intervention technologies for home and community settings. The use of wireless sensors, mobile form factors, and intelligent data analytics is enabling the migration of capabilities that were previously the preserve of specialized clinics into these settings. The TRIL Centre has demonstrated that successful technology solutions require a structured approach to ensure the members of the multidisciplinary teams are correctly aligned and that the end user is at the center of the design process.

References

Alwan, Majd, "Passive in-home health and wellness monitoring: Overview, value and examples," in *IEEE Annual International Conference of the Engineering in Medicine and Biology Society (EMBS '09)*, Minneapolis, Minnesota, USA 2009, pp. 4307–4310.

McManus, Richard J, *et al.*, "Blood pressure self monitoring: questions and answers from a national conference," *BMJ*, vol. 337 2008.

Tamura, Toshiyo, Isao Mizukura, and Yutaka Kimura, "Factors Affecting Home Health Monitoring in a 1-Year On-Going Monitoring Study in Osaka. ," in *Future Visions on Biomedicine and Bioinformatics 1*, Bos, Lodewijk, Denis Carroll, Luis Kun, Andrew Marsh, and Laura M. Roa, Eds., Heidelberg, Springer 2011, pp. 105–113.

Cohen, Jacob, *Statistical Power Analysis for the Behavioral Sciences*, 2nd ed. Oxford, England: Routledge Academic, 1988.

Catherwood, Philip A., Nicola Donnelly, John Anderson, and Jim McLaughlin, "ECG motion artefact reduction improvements of a chest-based wireless patient monitoring system," presented at the Computing in Cardiology, Belfast, Northern Ireland, 2010.

Ghasemzadeh, Hassan, Roozheb Jafari, and Balakrishnan Prabhakaran, "A Body Sensor Network With Electromyogram and Inertial Sensors: Multimodal Interpretation of Muscular Activities," *IEEE Transactions on Information Technology in Biomedicine,* vol. 14 (2), pp. 198–206, 2010.

Aziz, Omer, Benny Lo, Ara Darzi, and Guang-Zhong Yang, "Introduction," in *Body Sensor Networks*, Yang, Guang-Zhong, Ed., London, Springer-Verlag, 2006, pp. 1–39.

Greene, Barry R., *et al.*, "An adaptive gyroscope-based algorithm for temporal gait analysis," *Medical and Biological Engineering and Computing*, vol. 48 (12), pp. 1251–1260, 2010.

Scanaill, Cliodhna Ní, *et al.*, "A Review of Approaches to Mobility Telemonitoring of the Elderly in Their Living Environment," *Annals of Biomedical Engineering*, vol. 34 (4), pp. 547–563, 2006.

Wood, Anthony D., *et al.*, "Context-aware wireless sensor networks for assisted living and residential monitoring," *IEEE Network,* vol. 22 (4), pp. 26–33, 2008.

Lee, Byunggil and Howon Kim, "A Design of Context Aware Smart Home Safety Management using by Networked RFID and Sensor Home Networking." vol. 256, Agha, Khaldoun Al, Xavier Carcelle, and Guy Pujolle, Eds., Springer Boston, 2008, pp. 215–224.

Kelly, Damien, Sean McLoone, Terrence Dishongh, Michael McGrath, and Julie Behan, "Single access point location tracking for in-home health monitoring," in *5th Workshop on Positioning, Navigation and Communication (WPNC 2008)*, 2008, pp. 23–29.

Hagler, Stuart, Daniel Austin, Tamara L. Hayes, Jeffrey Kaye, and Misha Pavel, "Unobtrusive and Ubiquitous In-Home Monitoring: A Methodology for Continuous Assessment of Gait Velocity in Elders," *IEEE Transactions on Biomedical Engineering*, vol. 57 (4), pp. 813–820, 2010.

Hayes, Tamara L., Stuart Hagler, Daniel Austin, Jeffrey Kaye, and Misha Pavel, "Unobtrusive assessment of walking speed in the home using inexpensive PIR sensors," in *Annual International Conference of the IEEE Engineering in Medicine and Biology Society (EMBC 2009)*, Minneapolis, Minnesota, USA, 2009, pp. 7248–7251.

Biswas, Jit, *et al.*, "Health and wellness monitoring through wearable and ambient sensors: exemplars from home-based care of elderly with mild dementia," *Annals of Telecommunications,* vol. 65 (9), pp. 505–521, 2010.

Middleton, Catherine, "Delivering services over next generation broadband networks: Exploring devices, applications and networks," *Journal of Australia Telecommunications* vol. 60 (4), pp. 59.1–59.13, 2010.

Bresnick, Jennifer. "*HIMSS survey: 80% of clinicians use iPads, smartphone apps to improve patient care*", Last Update: December 4th 2012, http://ehrintelligence.com/2012/12/04/himss-survey-80-of-clinicians-use-ipads-smartphone-apps-to-improve-patient-care/

Prestigiacomo, Jennifer. "*Dialing Into Physician Smartphone Usage*", Last Update: August 3rd 2010, http://www.healthcare-informatics.com/article/dialing-physician-smartphone-usage

Smith, Ken, "Innovations in Accessibility: Designing for Digital Outcasts.," presented at the 58th Annual Conference of the Society for Technical Communications, Sacramento, CA., 2011.

Mulvenna, Maurice D., *et al.*, "Evaluation of Card-Based versus Device-Based Reminiscing Using Photographic Images," *Journal of CyberTherapy & Rehabilitation,* vol. 4 (1), pp. 57–66, 2011.

Schmeier, Sven, Matthias Rebel, and Renlong Ai, "Computer assistance in Bilingual task-oriented human-human dialogues," in *Proceedings of the 14th international conference on Human-computer interaction: interaction techniques and environments*, Orlando, FL, 2011, pp. 387–395.

Barnes, Ian, Elizabeth Brooks, and Grant Cumming, "Toilet-Finder: Community co-creation of health related information," presented at the 3rd International Conference on Web Science (ACM WebSci'11), Koblenz, Germany, 2011.

Mantyjarvi, Jani, Mikko Lindholm, Elena Vildjiounaite, Satu-Marja Makela, and Heikki Ailisto, "Identifying users of portable devices from gait pattern with accelerometers," presented at the IEEE International Conference on Acoustics, Speech, and Signal Processing (ICASSP '05), Philadelphia, Pennsylvania, USA, 2005.

Khan, A. M., Y. K. Lee, S. Y. Lee, and T. S. Kim, "Human Activity Recognition via an Accelerometer-Enabled-Smartphone Using Kernel Discriminant Analysis," presented at the IEEE 5th International Conference on Future Information Technology (FutureTech), Busan, South Korea, 2010.

LeMoyne, Robert, Timothy Mastroianni, Michael Cozza, Cristian Coroian, and Warren Grundfest, "Implementation of an iPhone as a wireless accelerometer for quantifying gait characteristics " in *Annual International Conference of the IEEE Engineering in Medicine and Biology Society (EMBC '10)* Buenos Aires, Argentina, 2010, pp. 3847–3851.

Philips Electronics N.V. "Motiva - Improving people's lives", http://www.healthcare.philips.com/main/products/telehealth/products/motiva.wpd., 2013.

Blackburn, Steven, Simon Brownsell, and Mark S Hawley, "A systematic review of digital interactive television systems and their applications in the health and social care fields," *Journal of Telemedicine and Telecare,* vol. 17 (4), pp. 168–176, 2011.

Ganeriwal, Saurabh, Laura K. Balzano, and Mani B. Srivastava, "Reputation-based framework for high integrity sensor networks," *ACM Trans. Sen. Netw.,* vol. 4 (3), pp. 1–37, 2008.

Melodia, Tommaso, Dario Pompili, Vehbi C. Gungor, and Ian F. Akyildiz, "A distributed coordination framework for wireless sensor and actor networks," in *Proceedings of the 6th ACM international symposium on Mobile ad hoc networking and computing*, Urbana-Champaign, IL, USA, 2005, pp. 99–110.

Li, Lily and Kerry Taylor, "A Framework for Semantic Sensor Network Services," in *Service-Oriented Computing – ICSOC 2008*. vol. 5364, Bouguettaya, Athman, Ingolf Krueger, and Tiziana Margaria, Eds., Springer Berlin / Heidelberg, 2008, pp. 347–361.

Balazinska, Magdalena, *et al.*, "Data Management in the Worldwide Sensor Web," *IEEE Pervasive Computing,* vol. 6 (2), pp. 30–40, 2007.

McGrath, Michael J. and John Delaney, "An Extensible Framework for the Management of Remote Sensor Data," in *IEEE Sensors*, Limerick, Ireland, 2011, pp. 1712–1715.

Walsh, Lorcan, Barry Greene, and Adrian Burns, "Ambient Assessment of Daily Activity and Gait Velocity " in *Pervasive Health 2011 AAL Workshop*, Dublin, 2011.

Burton, Darren and Mark Uslan, "Diabetes and Visual Impairment: Are Insulin Pens Acessible?", *AFB AccessWorld Magazine*, vol. 7 (4), 2006, http://www.afb.org/afbpress/pub.asp?DocID=aw070403

Bailey, Cathy, *et al.*, "ENDEA": a case study of multidisciplinary practice in the development of assisted technologies for older adults in Ireland," *Journal of Assistive Technologies,* vol. 5 (3), pp. 101–111, 2011.

Kohavi, Ron, "A study of cross-validation and bootstrap for accuracy estimation and model selection," in *14th International Joint Conference on Artificial Intelligence (IJCAI'95)*, Montreal, Quebec, Canada, 1995, pp. 1137–1143.

Han, Jiawei and Micheline Kamber, *Data Mining: Concepts and Techniques*, 1st ed. San Francisco, CA: Morgan Kaufmann, 2000.

Beauchet, Olivier, *et al.*, "Timed up and go test and risk of falls in older adults: A systematic review," *The journal of nutrition, health & aging,* vol. 15 (10), pp. 933–938, 2011.

Greene, Barry R., *et al.*, "Quantitative Falls Risk Assessment Using the Timed Up and Go Test," *IEEE Transactions on Biomedical Engineering,* vol. 57 (12), pp. 2918–2926, 2010.

Bogle, Linda D, Thorbahn, and Roberta A Newton, "Use of the Berg Balance Test to Predict Falls in Elderly Persons," *Physical Therapy,* vol. 76 (6), pp. 576–583, 1996.

Greene, Barry R., *et al.*, "Evaluation of Falls Risk in Community-Dwelling Older Adults Using Body-Worn Sensors," *Gerentology,* vol. 58 pp. 472–480, 2012.

Greco, Eleonora, Agnieszka Milewski-Lopez, Flip van den Berg, Siobhan McGuire, and Ian Robertson, "Evaluation of the efficacy of a self-administered biofeedback aided alertness training programme for healthy older adults " presented at the 8th Annual Psychology, Health and Medicine Conference, Galway, Ireland, 2011.

■ ■ ■

CHAPTER 9

Body-Worn, Ambient, and Consumer Sensing for Health Applications

There has been increasing momentum, particularly in the last decade, for new healthcare sensing and monitoring devices, driven in part by advances in sensor and sensor system technologies, which are delivering greater capabilities at economically viable costs. Moreover, global demographics are driving a significant rethink in the way we deliver healthcare. The cost of healthcare will continue to rise unabated, to economically unaffordable levels, unless we change our current approach. Technology affords greater flexibility in clinical protocols and enables the new consumer healthcare market. Sensing and sensor technologies play a key role at the center of healthcare innovation, and will continue to enable that innovation into the future as they integrate with a range of other information and communications technologies (ICT) to deliver exciting new capabilities.

As new sensing technologies, such as microelectromechanical systems (MEMS), biochemical, and immunological sensors continue to emerge, their proliferation into healthcare will continue to accelerate. Sensing will enable regular or continuous monitoring of health status, which will in turn enable the delivery of new proactive models of care. In the longer term, patient outcomes should improve, because issues will be identified earlier, when interventions can be more effective and less costly. Continuous monitoring solutions have already emerged in the telehealth space for monitoring chronic conditions, such as chronic obstructive pulmonary disease (COPD), congestive heart failure (CHF), and diabetes. Such monitoring provides continuous observation of disease state, which is valuable for anticipating and avoiding the physical and financial cost of acute episodes. Treating patients after an acute episode—which is the current reactive model of care—can result in catastrophic and irreversible changes in a person's health and well-being and lead to accelerated decline. Over time, sensing will also be applied to screening the general population as part of national healthcare programs to improve public health. Individuals, particularly the increasing number of "worried well" individuals (those who are healthy but are worried about becoming ill and seek reassurance by visiting their doctor, testing themselves, or taking medication when there is no medical reason to do so), are also likely to utilize sensing technology to proactively monitor and maintain their own health.

As pervasive sensing becomes the norm in healthcare, it will significantly increase our knowledge about disease risk and the effectiveness of interventions. Existing technology-based solutions are currently helping us to better understand the aging process, including identifying early signs of cognitive decline, frailty, motor and neurological issues. Sensor technologies enable a fresh look at healthcare at the individual level by building a detailed understanding of changes in a person's health status. This data provides the early warning signs for issues that most affect health and well-being.

Changing the Way We Do Healthcare

Currently, healthcare is delivered using a doctor-centric model. While this model was appropriate for its time, it is not be scalable into the future. The world's population is getting older. In 2010, there were approximately 0.5 billion people over the age of 65; this is projected to increase to over 1.5 billion by 2050 (Suzman et al., 2011), due to increases in life expectancy. The prevalence of lifestyle diseases, like hypertension, diabetes, and obesity, are also increasing significantly. Consequently, the amount of money spent on healthcare continues to rise and is fast approaching the point where western economies can no longer afford healthcare. In 2010, the US spent a total of 2.6 trillion US dollars (17.92 percent of GDP) on healthcare, as shown in Figure 9-1. This contrasts worryingly with 5.2 percent of GDP spent on healthcare in 1960. The Congressional Budget Office has estimated that healthcare spending will reach 25 percent of GDP by 2025, 37 percent by 2050 and 49 percent of GDP by 2082, if healthcare spending continues to follow current trends (Fodeman et al., 2010).

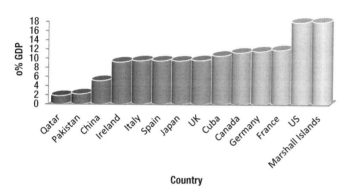

Figure 9-1. *Expenditure on healthcare in 2010 as percentage of GDP (source: WHO)*

Demands on healthcare resources will continue to grow: the longer we live, the higher the incidence of age-associated chronic diseases such as COPD and cognitive decline. Scientific advances will allow conditions such as cancer, previously considered to be acute or terminal, to be treated as chronic diseases instead. Without changes to the way healthcare is delivered, some 25 percent of a typical western country's population may have to be involved in healthcare delivery by 2040 (Vavilis et al., 2012). Therefore, there is a pressing need to invent a different way of delivering care while reducing the already unsustainable healthcare costs that plague virtually every major Western government.

Modern lifestyles are seen to play an ever-increasing role in people's health. Non-communicable diseases such as coronary heart disease, hypertension, diabetes, and some cancers (such as lung cancer) have clinically proven correlations with lifestyle choices. These "lifestyle diseases" are becoming the most significant causes of death (Colvin, 2012). Factors that influence lifestyle diseases include sedentary lifestyles, obesity, stress, high fat/sugar/salt/processed meal diets, cigarette smoking, and high levels of alcohol consumption. People are looking to technology, primarily in the area of activity monitoring, to provide more awareness of our sedentary lifestyles. Sensing technologies and supporting software can be used to encourage people to develop habits that predispose them to better health in later adult life (Corocoto, 2011). A wide variety of products, including Nike Fuel and Fitbit, already aim to make people more active, and provide mechanisms to keep them engaged in fitness over the longer term. We discuss the sports and recreational sensing area in more detail in Chapter 10.

Incidences of disease, whether lifestyle-related or due to aging, are forcing us to look at the way we currently deliver healthcare, and to consider how it should be done in the future. Modifying the healthcare delivery model will embrace a multi-faceted approach and require changes such as the following:

- Using screening and assessment technology in home and community settings to reduce pressure on hospitals.

- Moving from a reactive model to a preventative model.

- Personalizing healthcare to individuals, including risk factor identification, preventative intervention, and treatment.

- Involving individuals to a greater extent in monitoring and maintaining their health and wellness.

- Using technology to enable better management of clinical workloads and to allow health professionals to prioritize the patients of greatest need.

However, healthcare is an extremely conservative market in terms of ICT adoption, especially when it comes to large-scale systematic change. It is also a market that requires equipment to be proven and certified before adoption, which translates into a long process for new products coming to market (the regulation and certification process is discussed in Chapter 6). Finally, it is an industry that demands a lot from suppliers, including the ability to provide product liability in key healthcare situations.

The healthcare management business has long been an activity-driven or fee-for-service model that incentivizes activity over outcome (Chase, 2012). As the costs of hospital admissions continue to grow rapidly, a new emphasis on patient outcomes has started to emerge (Porter, 2010). Governments (Scher, 2011) and the private insurance industry are now starting to focus on the quality of patient outcomes, with hospitals not being reimbursed for patients who are readmitted within a specified period for the same problem. Sensing will play an important role in realizing this new model of care by providing quantitative measures of patient status in the clinical environment prior to discharge, and in the home after discharge. Insurance companies are also getting more interested in sensing, which can be used in the home to maintain the health and wellness of patients on a longitudinal basis, thus preventing or minimizing costly hospital admissions for acute events.

In the longer term, the use of health-related sensor data by insurance companies and similar organizations will undoubtedly raise significant social debate. Insurance companies already use sophisticated statistical models to estimate the future risk of clients based on their previous medical history and that of their families. The increasing availability of sensor data, especially genetic information, has the potential to quantify the impact of an individual's genetics and behavioral risks. In principle, certain individuals could have premiums that are prohibitively expensive, or they could even become uninsurable. There is likely to be significant resistance ethically to using genetic factors to load insurance premiums, especially on the basis that people can't do anything about the DNA-related risks they inherited from their parents. The real battle to be fought is likely to be related to modifiable behavior, for example, compliance with therapeutic regimes. If someone's behavior negatively impacts the predicted cost, should others bear the burden through higher premiums? Sensed information will be central to this debate as it will enable behavior and compliance to be tracked.

With the availability of over-the-counter (OTC) diagnostic tests, direct-to-consumer genetic testing kits, physiological monitoring sensors, and fertility monitoring, there is a rapidly growing online trend toward the phenomenon of the "quantified self" and "life-logging." Individuals may be driven by various motivations, such as endeavoring to stimulate discussion, seeking a cure, or experimenting with preventative measures for a known disease risk. They may choose to share this information socially, either in person or through online forums. These individuals are highly motivated to understand what the data is telling them and to utilize the data to improve their health outcomes. Part of that process is changing the conversation with an individual's doctor, as outlined in Chapter 7. The extent of these data-driven discussions is somewhat limited. In areas such as fertility, the use of sensor data is becoming the norm, and is seen by the both the patient and clinicians as adding significant value to the consultation process. However, it will take time before the use of personal sensing information provided by individuals will be accepted in the clinical community. Issues such as data quality, duty of care, and relevance must be addressed to gain acceptance. Still, the first tentative steps in shifting this dynamic have started, driven in part by the use of sensors.

Healthcare is on the cusp of a significant change in the way we understand and treat disease in individuals. We are beginning to move away from empirical, "population-based" medicine to precise, "personalized" medicine. Driven by advances in "omic" technologies—namely genomics, transcriptomics, proteomics, and metabolomics—disease pathology is now starting to be defined at a molecular level. This molecular-level classification will mean that the optimum treatment can be selected according to the both the molecular behavior of the disease and the DNA of the individual. Sensing will play a key role in personalized medicine. Companion tests, based on biosensors, will determine if a patient can benefit from a genetically targeted drug treatment. And sensors will monitor the patient during the course of the treatment (for example, monitoring biochemical by-products associated with a drug's targeted metabolic pathway). There is significant potential to radically alter our approach to disease diagnosis, prognosis, and therapeutic interventions over the coming decades.

Sensing Context in Health Applications

Context plays an important role in determining the value of sensor data. For example, some sensor readings, taken in isolation, can have limitations. These limitations can be addressed at least in part by collecting supporting contextual information. What was the person doing when the measurement was collected? Where was she located? What were the local environmental conditions that could influence the measurement? Contextual information is particularly important when capturing physiological measurements, such as activity levels prior to heart rate measurements. Context can typically be gleaned using additional sensors, accelerometers, for example, to determine if the person is moving when a physiological measurement is taken.

Qualitative approaches, such as weekly health questionnaires, can also prove useful. This is commonly used in chronic disease management systems. However, the quality of self-reported information is dependent on the accuracy of response by the patient, which is difficult to determine. When collecting contextual data to support a clinical sensor reading or observation, it is also important to ensure that any data has the appropriate temporal resolution and spatial characteristics. If not matched correctly, additional information can add ambiguity rather than clarity. Contextual sensing information can generally be used in three ways:

- The most common approach is for a clinician to manually review the contextual sensor information on an ad hoc basis to support the interpretation process.

- Alternatively, contextual information can be overlaid with the sensor measurements of interest in the same graphical representation or in an adjacently chart. This overlapping of data visually can be very helpful in the interpretative process.

- Finally, the most sophisticated approach is the intelligent and automated fusion of contextual data with the data source of interest. Algorithmic data fusion can be very useful in reducing the dimensionality of data and inferring higher-level information. It can also be useful to determine whether the context of measurement is valid based on a defined measurement protocol.

Context can also play an important role in determining the security, privacy, performance, and accessibility requirements of sensor networks. This continues to be an area of active research, exemplified by new solutions such as AlarmNet from the University of Virginia (Stankovic et al., 2011).

Sensors can also be used to provide context to the success or failure of a treatment protocol. By knowing what happens between outpatient visits, a clinician can optimize an existing treatment protocol or develop a new protocol. Data from ambient and body-worn sensors can also be combined with context-detection algorithms to generate support messages. Such messages are generated at appropriate times to support a patient on a specific treatment protocol, for example to prompt to take medication, remind about exercise, or advise about the consumption of food and drink.

Hospital and Community-Based Sensing for Assessment and Diagnosis

Sensing is pervasive in every aspect of hospital-based care, from the simplest digital thermometer to complex laser-guided surgical tools. Imaging sensors, such as x-ray, magnetic resonance imaging (MRI), computed tomography (CT), positron emission tomography (PET), and ultrasound provide doctors with non-invasive insight into the human body and how it operates. These sensors have radically transformed diagnostic medicine. In general medicine, these images allow doctors to pinpoint areas of injury or abnormality, perform minimally invasive surgery, and evaluate the success or failure of a procedure. In obstetric care, ultrasound allows doctors to monitor the developing fetus and identify any fetal or other abnormalities that could impact the health of the mother or baby.

Complex sensing devices are used by clinical pathologists in hospital laboratories every day to perform hematology, biochemistry, immunology, histopathology, and microbiology functions. These large, non-discrete sensors require careful sample preparation by skilled professionals to ensure optimum results. Sensors also play an important role in treatment technologies. They can sense events, such as missed heartbeats, that can be acted upon by clinicians or actuators. They can optimize drug delivery devices by identifying the optimum time to administer a drug. And they can continuously track a patient's vital signs to ensure that a treatment, such as dialysis, is delivered safely. Imaging, implantable, and drug-delivery devices are all rich sources of sensor application, worthy of entire chapters in their own right. Given our space limitations, though, this book focuses on discrete, non-invasive monitoring and assessment technologies that can, or will soon, be applied in a home or community setting.

Monitoring Vital Signs

The most familiar hospital sensors are those that measure vital signs. A patient's vital signs describe the status of their main body functions—typically body temperature, pulse rate (or heart rate), blood pressure, and respiratory rate. But other measurements may be included, depending on the context. For example, in a first-aid situation, skin, pupils, and level of consciousness are also examined. In intensive-care or post-operative units, blood pressure, heart rate, blood oxygenation, and many other variables are continuously monitored using sensing technology. In lower-dependency units, these variables are intermittently monitored by nursing staff, who manually measure these variables using portable monitors. Disposable, wearable vital sign sensors are beginning to emerge that permit personal, low-cost, continuous monitoring of vital signs for all patients, regardless of health status or location. ABI Research estimates that 5 million of these sensors will be sold by 2018 (Comstock, 2013). Similarly, sensor technologies that target both elite athletes and ordinary individuals, such as body-worn pulse-rate monitors or smart clothing with integrated sensing capabilities, are also emerging to determine performance and fitness levels (see Chapter 10).

Heart Rate

Heart rate refers to the speed of the heartbeat. It is typically measured in beats per minute. Heart rate is measured to detect bradycardia (slow heart rate), tachycardia (fast heart rate) or arrhythmia (irregular heart rate and rhythm), any of which can indicate illness. Like many vital signs, heart rate is age-dependent: an infant's heart rate is fine between 130 and 150 beats per minute, whereas an adult's should fall between 50 and 80 beats per minute. Heart rate is also highly dependent on context: it is raised following exercise and at times of stress, and the resting heart rate of an endurance athlete is much lower than a non-athlete. Given the context, neither measure would be concerning. The non-technical method to measure heart rate is to feel artery pulsations at a pulse point (such as the wrist) using the index and middle fingers. The number of pulsations is counted to find the heart rate. In a hospital setting, heart rate is measured continuously using an electrocardiograph (called an ECG or an EKG).

An ECG measures the electrical activity of the heart, using electrodes attached to the surface of the skin, filtering circuitry, and a data logger. The heart rate can be determined by measuring the interval between one R-wave and the next R-wave of the ECG signal, called the R-R interval. Variability in heart rate can also be predictive of many issues, including congestive heart failure. The timing between different points of an ECG signal (see Figure 9-2) can indicate a number of conditions, including hypocalcemia (indicated by a shortened QT interval) or coronary ischemia (indicated by flattened or inverted T waves). In a hospital setting, 12-lead ECGs are used for diagnostic purposes, and 5-lead and 3-lead ECGs are used for continuous monitoring. The number of leads describes the number of electrodes attached to the body. Each electrode is connected using cables to a data-filtering and logging circuit. Expertise is required to attach the ECG electrodes correctly and interpret the resulting ECG strip.

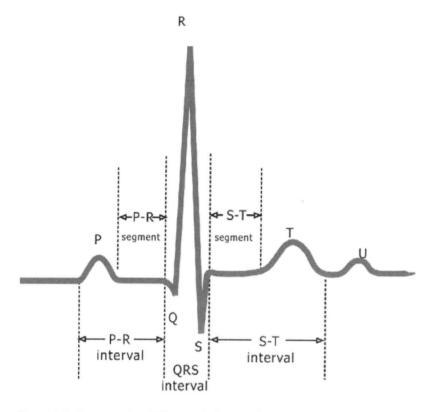

Figure 9-2. *Segment of an ECG trace, indicating the various markers and intervals of interest*

Fitness and in-home heart-rate sensors are beginning to move toward integrated wireless ECG devices, which simplify the placement of electrodes and interpretation of data. Doppler fetal monitors measure fetal heart rate using a hand-held ultrasound transducer that detects the heartbeat and produces an audible simulation of it. These devices are used by obstetric and community clinicians, but are increasingly being sold for personal use. Heart rate can also be measured using pulse oximeters or body vibrations (seismocardiography).

Blood Pressure

Blood pressure is the pressure exerted by the blood on the walls of the large arteries, such as the brachial artery in the arm. High blood pressure is a risk factor for stroke, heart attack and chronic renal failure; therefore, it is essential to not only diagnose it but also to continuously monitor the impact of treatment. Low pressure can be problematic if it results in fainting or dizziness. Blood pressure is typically described as a systolic value over a diastolic value, and is measured in millimeters of mercury (mm Hg). Systolic pressure is the peak pressure in the arteries during the cardiac cycle and the diastolic pressure is the lowest pressure at the resting phase of the cardiac cycle.

The blood pressure of a resting, healthy adult human is approximately 120 mm Hg systolic and 80 mm Hg diastolic (written as 120/80 mm Hg). Arterial blood pressure (BP) is the most accurate method to measure BP. This invasive method involves placing a cannula into a blood vessel and connecting it to an electronic pressure transducer. It is typically used only in intensive care medicine, anesthesiology, and for research purposes. Non-invasive methods are simpler and quicker and require less expertise, but are slightly less accurate. These methods measure the pressure of an inflated cuff at the points when it just occludes blood flow (systolic pressure), and again when it just permits unrestricted flow (diastolic pressure). There are three non-invasive methods commonly used for routine examinations and monitoring or blood pressure:

- The auscultatory method requires a clinician to manually compress the artery in the upper arm using an inflatable cuff. The clinician listens to the artery using a stethoscope to recognize when the blood just begins to flow back in the artery (systolic blood pressure) and when no sound can be heard (diastolic blood pressure). The blood pressure at both of these points can be read from the mercury or aneroid manometer that is connected to the cuff. This method is considered the gold standard by many, despite its high reliance on human hearing and interpretation.

- Oscillometric methods are used in long-term measurement, home measurement, and sometimes in general practice. The equipment is functionally the same as for the auscultatory method, but with an electronic pressure sensor (transducer) fitted in the cuff to detect blood flow, instead of using the stethoscope and the expert's ear. These devices use a method, called mean arterial pressure (MAP) to calculate blood pressure. The accuracy of the algorithms can vary greatly among different devices. It is therefore essential to confirm worrying home readings with a clinician, who will have a more accurate BP device.

- Continuous noninvasive arterial pressure (CNAP) is used in research, critical care, and anesthesia to understand blood pressure at a more granular level than can be achieved using auscultatory or oscillometric methods. There are three common methods to do this: arterial tonometry is a technique for measuring blood pressure in which an array of pressure sensors is pressed against the skin over an artery. The second method, pulse transit time (PTT) is the time it takes a pulse wave to travel between two arterial sites. Blood pressure can be determined from the inverse of the PTT. In the final method, which involves clamping the finger, blood volume in the finger is measured using a light transmitter and receiver. The pressure of a finger cuff is adjusted to maintain constant blood volume in the finger. This pressure corresponds to the patient's blood pressure. CNAP methods were traditionally expensive and limited to hospital settings, but community-based PTT devices are currently available, and home-based devices, such as the Scandu Scout (`www.scanadu.com`), will soon be available.

While annual blood pressure measurements in a doctor's office may be appropriate for healthy young adults with no cardiovascular risk factors, there are many situations in which blood pressure requires more detailed or long-term investigation. Older adults with impaired blood pressure regulation may experience sudden drops in blood pressure when they go from sitting to standing. This is a known risk factor for falls, and can be diagnosed only using beat-to-beat CNAP techniques in a clinical setting. There are also situations in which the blood pressure reading in a doctor's office is not representative of the patient's actual blood pressure. "White coat hypertension" can cause a rise in some patients' blood pressure while they are in a clinical setting. This is a very common occurrence and may lead to clinician's prescribing blood pressure medicine to those who do not need it. Circadian variations in blood pressure can also result in incorrect prescription of medication. Some patients, who have high or normal blood pressure during the day, may have low blood pressure at night. Prescription of blood pressure-reducing medication to manage the high blood pressure measured in the doctor's office during the day could drop the patient's blood pressure to dangerously low levels overnight. Ambulatory blood pressure monitoring, using a wearable oscillatory device for a 24-hour period, is the only way to identify circadian blood pressure rhythms. As form-factor and interpretation technology evolve, it is expected that monitoring this valuable vital sign outside of a hospital setting will become increasingly smaller, cheaper, and more accurate.

Temperature

The body employs several strategies to maintain body temperature. When the body is too hot, the blood vessels in the skin dilate (expand) to carry the excess heat to the skin's surface, where it is removed through perspiration. When the body is too cold, it conserves body heat by vasoconstricting (narrowing) blood vessels to reduce blood flow to the skin and generates heat by shivering. An abnormally low (hypothermia) or high (hyperthermia) body temperature can be serious and even life threatening. Temperature sensors are therefore an essential, low-cost, reliable method to indicate health status. Body temperature can be measured in many locations on the body, including the mouth, ear, armpit, rectum, forehead, bladder, skin, and esophagus, as outlined in Table 9-1. The traditional method to measure temperature, the mercury thermometer, has been replaced by sensor-based contact and non-contact sensors. Contact temperature sensors reach thermal equilibrium with any object they are in contact with. They can measure the temperature of that object by measuring their own temperature. Noncontact temperature sensors measure radiated heat from the measured brightness or spectral radiance of an object.

Table 9-1. *Current Temperature Sensing Methods in Humans*

Location	Sensor	Advantages	Disadvantages
Rectal temperature probe	Flexible catheter with thermistor on top or mercury thermometer	Accurate measure of core temperature	Slow to change Slightly higher (up to 0.3 °C) than other measures Potential to spread contaminants Potential to perforate rectum
Oral thermometer	Mercury thermometer or digital thermometer	Easily accessible Less prone to operator error Quickly reflects changes in core body temperature	Influenced by the ingestion of food or drink and by mouth breathing
Axillary (armpit) thermometer	Mercury thermometer or digital thermometer	Easily accessible Repeatable temperature measurements without significant discomfort	Time needed to record the temperature (3-4 minutes)
Esophageal temperature	Flexible thermistor-type probe	Accurate and precise estimate of core temperature	Invasive (only used during anesthesia) Placement too close to trachea could result in lower readings
Pulmonary temperature	Thermistor	Gold standard temperature	Invasive (restricted to critically ill patients who already have a pulmonary artery catheter)
Bladder temperature	Thermistor-tipped catheter	Correlates highly with rectal, esophageal, and pulmonary arterial temperatures	Invasive (only suitable for those requiring bladder catheter) Accuracy dependent on urinary output
Tympanic temperature (contact)	Small thermocouples or thermistor probes	Considered gold standard due to proximity to hypothalamus	Difficult to position correctly without otoscope Inaccurate if incorrectly positioned Risk of perforation and bleeding of eardrum

(continued)

Table 9-1. (*continued*)

Location	Sensor	Advantages	Disadvantages
Tympanic temperature (non-contact)	IR emission detectors (thermopile sensor or pyrosensor)	Reasonable estimate of core temperature within 1-2 seconds Suitable for awake patients	
Temporal artery (head) thermometry	IR emission detectors	Easily accessible Poses no risk of injury for the patient	Measuring temperature at head, which is not the same as core temperature (algorithm required to compensate)
Skin thermometry	Thermocouples or liquid crystals enclosed in adhesive pads	Safe Accurate to +/- 0.1 °C Useful for screening older children	Difficult to interpret Not reflective of core temperature
Pacifier thermometry	Thermocouple inserted in heat conductive nipple of pacifier	Accurate Convenient Non-distressing for babies	
Ingestible thermometry	Quartz crystal temperature sensor	Direct measure of core temperature	Currently expensive Works only for 1–2 days

Respiratory Rate

Respiratory rate is the number of breaths taken in one minute. Like heart rate, normal respiratory rate depends on several factors, including age, emotional state (for example, crying or agitation) and sleeping. Abnormally high respiratory rate is called tachypnea. Abnormally low respiratory rate is called bradypnea. Tachypnea can be caused by something as simple as exercise, or as serious as carbon monoxide poisoning. Bradypnea can indicate issues such as damage to heart tissue or high blood pressure. Respiratory rate is most commonly used to diagnose pauses, shallow or infrequent breathing during sleep, a condition known as sleep apnea. This condition affects both adults and children and can result in daytime sleepiness, as well as attention and memory issues. Sufferers are typically unaware that they have the condition, and require technology to detect and monitor the extent of the condition (see Chapter 10). Sleep apnea can be diagnosed during an overnight sleep study in a hospital sleep lab, during which respiration, brainwaves, muscle movement and eye movement are monitored. Inability to breathe without life support machines is one of the three key indicators of brain death (the others are being in a coma and having no brainstem reflexes). Naturally, the criteria for detecting apnea in this situation are more stringent.

The non-technical method of measuring respiration rate is to count the number of times the chest rises and falls during a fixed period. This method is prone to error. Chest straps and smart clothing can measure respiration by measuring changes in tension on the fabric as the chest expands and contracts. Contact and non-contact acoustic and optical methods have also been developed to measure respiration. Pressure-sensitive mattresses have been used to measure the respiration rate of sleeping babies or at-risk adults. These sensors detect respiration by measuring changes in pressure on the mattress as the monitored person inhales and exhales. Contactless bedside sensors, such as the SleepMinder from BiancaMed (biancamed.com), enable hospital-grade respiration-sensing in the comfort of the patient's own home. In a hospital setting, respiration rate can be derived from an existing ECG signal or from the electrodes used to measure ECG.

Blood Oxygenation

The body needs a certain level of oxygen in the blood circulating to cells and tissues in order to function correctly. When the oxygen level falls below a certain point (hypoxia), a person may experience shortness of breath. The amount of oxygen traveling in an artery can be measured by testing a sample of blood from an artery. It can also be estimated non-invasively using a pulse oximeter, a small device that clips on the finger, earlobe or across a baby's foot. Pulse oximetry is a non-invasive method for monitoring a patient's O_2 saturation. It is used throughout the healthcare domain, particularly for assessing patients with respiratory complaints or in respiratory-related procedures. Normal pulse oximeter readings range from 95 to 100 percent. Values under 90 percent are considered low.

Transmissive pulse oximeters measure the saturation of oxygen in the blood, which is a proxy measure of blood oxygen levels. They operate by passing light of two wavelengths from one side of the clip, through the patient, to a photodetector on the other side of the clip. The pulsing arterial flow can be determined by measuring the changing absorbance at each of the wavelengths. This method can be used to measure both oxygenated and deoxygenated hemoglobin at the peripherals. Reflectance pulse oximetry can be used on the feet, forehead, and chest. In this method, the detector lies adjacent to the light source on a flat surface such as the forehead. A number of situations can cause an erroneous SpO_2 reading, especially with the use of transmission probes. These include skin pigment, nail polish, motion, ambient or excessive light, hypoperfusion, cardiac arrest, hypoxia, malposition of the probe, and intravenous dyes. These variables must be considered and blood tests should be used to confirm hypoxia if an erroneous pulse oxygenation reading is suspected.

Community-Based Sensing

As mentioned, shifting demographic patterns are making the current reactive models of care unsustainable and compel several dramatic changes in the way healthcare is delivered. First, healthcare must become proactive and predictive to prevent costly acute health episodes. Second, healthcare must become individualized, rather than population-based, to ensure the optimum treatment is delivered. Third, the delivery of care must be decentralized from hospitals to the community and the home. Technology will play a key role in all these shifts. The first and second healthcare model shifts will be discussed later in this chapter, and this section will discuss the current and future state of community-based sensing.

Community care refers to the general practice doctor, the clinic, and nursing services in a community. In most Western countries, doctors and community clinics are the first point of contact with the healthcare system for normally healthy people. Community doctors and clinics provide routine medical services. They also act as triage services that refer those requiring further care to specialist clinics in hospitals. Community-based nursing provides hospice and long term care for people in their own homes. Nursing services can be privately or publically funded and the level of care provided is dependent on the patient's condition and the payer's resources.

A typical consultation with a community doctor lasts approximately 10 minutes, during which the doctor must listen to and record patient history, measure vital signs, and make a diagnosis. Given the time constraint, technology must be quick and easy to use. Currently, the only technology in a typical doctor's office is an electronic health record (EHR) system, a digital thermometer, a digital blood pressure cuff, and various disposable test kits. This is very much in keeping with the reactive diagnostic model of care. Technology can be used more holistically to improve the quality and throughput of community care services:

- Technology can be used in the home, in the form of clinical applications and self-care diagnostic kits to capture vital signs and other biomedical metrics. Such data can be shared with a doctor in person or using teleconsultation, to make a diagnosis. In the future, diagnosis may even be automated, thus removing the need to visit the doctor for simple illness, such as colds, flu, earache, and the like. These technologies are discussed later in this chapter.

- In the doctor's office, point-of-care tests can reduce the time to diagnosis by eliminating the need to send samples away to be tested. Automated testing, such as with blood pressure cuffs and digital thermometers, allow the doctor to take a patient history while a measurement is being taken.

- The doctor's office also has a role in reducing the burden on hospitals. The falling cost of sensor technology permits many hospital out-patient services, such as blood-coagulation monitoring, to be carried out in the community. The community practice could also be a point of contact for attaching and removing diagnostic devices, such as Holter monitors and ambulatory blood pressure monitors. Data from these devices could be shared with hospital-based specialists using secure data-sharing techniques, and face-to-face hospital visits can be arranged, if required.

- Sensor and non-sensor technologies, including electronic health records, can give patients ownership of their own health. Patients will be able to shop around for a doctor, as they can move their complete patient histories and sensor data between doctors. Patients will also be able to acquire healthcare services from retail health clinics. Such clinics can provide health services in nontraditional environments, like pharmacies, big box stores, and other non-medical locations

- Community doctors are expected to be experts in many disciplines and to keep up to date with continually changing illnesses, diagnostic methods, and treatments. Analyzing multiple sensor and non-sensor inputs and cross-referencing these inputs against specific criteria to derive a result are tasks ideally suited to computers. Community doctors could leverage these devices to diagnose an illness, thus freeing them to elicit the appropriate information, provide care, and deliver diagnoses.

- Community nurses visit patients in their own homes to provide care and monitor their health status. A community nurse carries lightweight vital sign monitors to determine the patient's weight, heart rate and blood pressure. Many of these measurements can currently be taken with home-based clinical devices or telemonitoring devices without the presence of a nurse. This allows community nurses to optimize their schedules to visit those most in need of care first, and eliminate visits to check that people are well.

- Community-based nurses provide hospice and long-term care to a very small number of patients. The technology used in these situations varies according to the patient's condition. A patient requiring dialysis, but who is too ill to travel, may have a hospital-quality dialysis machine in their home. On the other hand, a nurse caring for someone following a fall may not use any technology at all.

Home-Based Clinical Applications

Home healthcare delivery has been an area of significant effort over the last decade, both from commercial and research perspectives. This work has primarily focused on chronic disease management for conditions such as COPD, CHF, and diabetes. However, the initial focus has expanded to include additional areas, such as post-operative care, stroke rehabilitation, and well-being monitoring and alerting (with, for example, body-worn fall detectors). Clinical-grade sensing plays an important role in delivering reliable physiological and biometric monitoring of patients.

Clinically oriented home-care technologies can be classified into two groups: patient monitoring sensors and patient mobility sensors, as shown in Table 9-2. Patient monitoring sensors measure the physiological and biometric attributes of an individual and store or react to the data, as required by a supporting application. This form of sensing requires either direct contact with a human body or the collection of a sample, such as blood, for testing. Patient motion sensors, such as passive infrared (PIR) motion sensors (which can detect an individual entering or exiting a room) and pedometers (which count steps taken) observe actions. Behavioral patterns can be inferred from this data, and abnormal patterns can be used to trigger an alert. Mobility data can be sensed through direct contact with the human body, as for example, with a pedometer; or by using ambient sensors, such as PIRs, attached to the subject's environment. Wearable motion sensors are in direct contact with the person and can therefore accurately measure the motion of that person regardless of location or the presence of others. Ambient solutions are ideal for situations in which the person may forget to attach a sensor, or attach it incorrectly. However, ambient sensors are mounted in fixed locations and can't sense a person if that person is in a different location.

Table 9-2. *Sensors for Home Use in Clinical Applications*

Patient Monitoring	Measurand	Patient Mobility	Measurand
IR thermometer	Body temperature	Radio frequency identification (RFID)	Object interaction—activities of daily living
Lung function - Spirometer - Peak flow meter	FVC (forced vital capacity), FEV (forced expiratory volume), PEF (peak expiratory flow)	Pressure sensors	Bed occupancy
Pulse oximeters	Blood oxygenation	Accelerometers	Acceleration—falls detection Limb movement—rehabilitation Step counting—pedometer
Blood pressure	Systolic/diastolic	Gyroscopes	Angular velocity—falls detection Limb movement—rehabilitation
ECG	Electrical activity of the heart	Magnetometers	Body position—falls detection
Glucometer	Blood-glucose levels		
Body fat analyzer	Percentage body fat	PIR	Room occupancy
Weighing scales	Weight		
Hemoglobin Photometer	Hemoglobin concentration—measurement of anemia		
PT/INR meters	Prothrombin time (PT) and its derived measures of prothrombin ratio (PR) and international normalized ratio (INR); Long-term use by warfarin users		
Nebulizers/Drug delivery aerosols	Inhalation patterns Drug delivery via controlled aerosols		

The focus on developing telehealth with clinical-grade sensing has been driven by the expected benefits these technologies could provide in terms of support and supervision, without requiring a clinical professional to be present. This in turn would lessen healthcare costs for both providers and individuals by reducing the time associated with in-person consultations, redundant doctor's visits, and providing early detection and reaction to adverse health events. Additionally, sensor technologies may also have the ability to notify caregivers to changes in behavior patterns or physical state that may go unreported or unnoticed by the patient but that may represent early warning signs of an impending health event. Despite the expected benefits, remote patient monitoring through telehealth remains an area of continuing debate. Studies show inconsistent results in patient benefits, expected cost savings, and so forth. For example, some studies have shown measurable improvements in patient outcomes (Miguel et al., 2013); others have been neutral (Cox et al., 2012); while others reported no meaningful impact (Cartwright et al., 2013). The area of telehealth is still relatively immature and will continue to evolve over the next decade. As we embrace and better understand personalized medicine, knowledge of how and which patients will benefit from this technology will improve. So will our understanding of when it is not appropriate for an individual. Realization of the actual benefits will also require structural changes within the healthcare domain. With a data-driven approach to remote patient monitoring, it will take time to realize the benefits and to identify weakness in the granularity, scope and context of patient measurements. Despite the on-going debates on telehealth, its use is projected to increase six-fold to 1.8 million by 2017. In 2012, it was estimated that, globally, 308,000 patients with chronic disease utilized telehealth solutions. These were primarily post-acute patients who had been discharged from hospitals to their own homes. The expected rise in telehealth users by 2017 will be driven by the following factors:

- Government health bodies, who want to reduce readmission rates after hospital discharge.

- Provider-driven demand to improve the quality of patient care.

- Insurance companies, who want to reduce the cost of care.

- Patient-driven demand, as patients slowly embrace the concept of personal monitoring stemming from the increasing penetration of personal-fitness sensing devices (InMedica, 2013).

The availability of affordable, clinical-grade sensing for home use continues to grow. An important enabler has been the continued miniaturization and decreased power consumption of MEMs sensing devices, coupled with the integration of either wired or wireless standards-based interfaces. MEMs-based pressure sensors, for example, can be found in a variety of blood pressure monitors. They are also found in applications that require drug absorption by inhaling aerosols through positive-pressure ventilation. Delivery aerosols are increasingly being used for the treatment of cancers, AIDS, diabetes, and asthma in home environments. The key to successful operation of these devices is the ability of the MEMS pressure sensors to detect inhalation pressures as low as 0.018 psi and to accurately and rapidly switch the delivery mechanism on and off in response. In addition, MEMS pressure sensors can be used to sense the person's inhalation patterns and in turn adjust the pattern of delivery to maximize the benefit.

Body-temperature sensing is another area that has benefitted from the availability of low cost and accurate infrared sensors. The most common form of this sensor is the tympanic ear thermometers, shown Figure 9-3. These sensors work on the principle that the eardrum emits infrared radiation. Using an algorithm, the amount of received IR radiation is converted into a temperature that can be displayed via a digital display. This form of temperature sensing has proven very popular due to its ease of use, relatively low cost, and accurate results.

Figure 9-3. *Tympanic thermometer*

Chronic Disease Management

Until now, telehealth has primarily focused on chronic disease management. Chronic diseases, such as diabetes, heart disease, COPD, and asthma account for 70 to 80 percent of healthcare expenditure. The costs of these diseases is projected to reach USD 4.3 trillion by 2023 (Versel, 2012). Chronic diseases cause around 70 percent of deaths each year in the United States, with about 133 million Americans (approximately 1 in 2 adults) living with at least one chronic illness (NCCDPHP, 2009). The majority of patients who had telehealth systems deployed in their homes suffered acute symptoms requiring hospitalization and were subsequently released after stabilization of their condition. CHF is currently the dominant condition in telehealth deployments, followed by COPD. However, it is projected that diabetes will replace COPD as the second largest grouping of telehealth users. In-home telemonitoring of diabetes will support a more structured approach to monitoring and data management. Caregivers and patients can access the data any time and any place across a variety of devices, including smartphones. They can access historical data to better understand how lifestyle choices are positively or negatively influencing the readings, in an effort to better manage their condition (Mearian, 2013).

From a sensing perspective, there are a number of challenges with chronic disease management. The sensors must be able to monitor the vital signs of the patient dependably and with a high degree of precision. Measurements must be transmitted reliably on a wired or wireless connection. There should be fully traceability of the sensor readings from the source of measurement to the point of storage. The sensors should be low-powered, and must be capable of running for months or years with standard alkaline batteries. While using rechargeable batteries is possible, it adds a layer of complexity that is undesirable given the target population. These characteristics are currently fulfilled by standard semi-mobile, discrete sensors currently found in clinical environments. Many of the clinical sensors used for chronic-disease monitoring require the patient to actively engage with the device during the measurement process and in some cases to log the data to a recording device, such as a smartphone (as with diabetes measurements).

The emergence of smaller, cheaper sensors and smartphone technology is already beginning to provide new, more flexible telehealth solutions for chronic-disease management. Emerging trends in this domain include the following:

- Smart clothing solutions, which enable simple and accurate continuous monitoring of biometric parameters. For example, the EU Chronius project has developed a smart t-shirt to monitor patients with COPD and chronic kidney disease (CKD). This t-shirt features heart-, respiration-, and activity-monitoring sensors, which are connected to a smartphone for data aggregation, processing, and transmission. The system has been successfully demonstrated in two trials with COPD and CKD patients in Spain and the UK (Pasolini, 2012).

- Intelligent, disposable sensor patches, such as the prototype developed by Sano Intelligence that sticks to the skin and continuously monitors blood parameters for seven days. This patch eliminates the need for blood tests by measuring parameters, such as glucose and potassium levels, that would usually require a full blood panel to obtain. The data is wirelessly transmitted to a smartphone for analysis, long-term monitoring, and alert detection (Schwartz, 2012). A number of continuous glucose monitors (CGM) are now commercially available, such as the Medronics Guardian REAL-Time CGM System and the Dexcom SEVEN Plus. Additionally, the Freestyle Navigator from Abbot Diagnostics was launched in 2009. However, the product was withdrawn from the US market in 2010 due to reported issues with an inconsistent supply chain, according to Abbot. The product continues to be sold in seven countries outside the US (Gilles, 2011). CGM systems are more expensive than conventional glucose monitoring, costing in the region of $1,000 to $2,000 USD for measurement units plus the additional monthly cost of sensors that may run to a couple of hundred dollars. These are not intended for day-to-day monitoring or long-term self-care, but to track trends in blood-sugar levels. The data should be used by the patient's health care team to modify the treatment plan when necessary to better optimize glucose control (WebMD, 2012). The CGM device is regarded as a niche market; however, in Europe and the US, the market for the devices is growing at a significant pace and is estimated to reach several hundred million dollars by 2018 (SBWire, 2013).

- Sensing new measurands, as demonstrated by Podimetrics, a startup company that focuses on the complications of diabetes rather than blood sugar measurement. The Podimetrics insole technology will detect the beginning of diabetic foot ulcers, which are a leading cause of lower-limb amputations. The sensor insole is placed in the patient's shoe and collects data about blood flow in their feet. This data is transmitted to a cloud-based service for processing. Alerts on potential issues are sent to both the individual and their clinician (Podimetrics, 2013).

Investigative and Episodic Monitoring

This type of sensing is designed to capture specific physiological (blood pressure, EKG/ECG) or biochemical parameters (blood-glucose level) for defined periods of time. It is used for investigative purposes, to track the progress of a disease, or to monitor recovery from a specific health event. In the cardiovascular monitoring domain, Holter monitors (or ambulatory electrocardiography devices) have been commonly used for diagnostic purposes, particularly for individuals with arrhythmias and older adults presenting with possible cardiogenic syncope (blackouts due to irregular heart rates). The monitors usually provide the ECG signals in two or three channels, via electrodes attached to the chest area. The aggregation unit (or monitor) records the ECG signal and stores it in flash memory for analysis after the monitoring period. Many Holter monitors also feature a "patient button" that enables the patient to mark the recording by pressing the button at significant points, such as feeling unwell, being dizzy or short of breath, taking medication, and so on. This allows doctors to quickly identify these areas of interest when analyzing the signal. Normal monitoring periods are 24 to 48 hours. While the form factor of the Holter monitor is relatively compact (approximately the size of a smartphone) and it can be worn around the neck using a lanyard or placed in a shirt pocket, it is still somewhat inconvenient.

The next generations of cardiac monitors are based on the concept of epidermal sensing in a patch-type configuration (a "smart band-aid"). Corventis has developed a mobile cardiac telemetry system called Nuvant, which features a single patch that can measure heart rate, respiratory rate, temperature, motion, and interstitial fluid levels around the heart. The patch has a Bluetooth radio that connects to gateway for transmission to a monitoring center for arrhythmia detection. The sensor can also be used to monitor COPD patients, due to its ability to measure interstitial fluid levels. Similarly, the zensor product offering from Intelesens provides vital signs monitoring, as shown in Figure 9-4. This compact patch device provides integrated data capture, from a diagnostic-grade, 3-lead ECG; and integrated data processing that can detect arrhythmias. Data is wirelessly transmitted via Wi-Fi to a remote database. A key feature of the Intelesens system is the biocompatibility capabilities of the patch, which allows patients to wear it for up to seven days before changing (Intelesens, 2013).

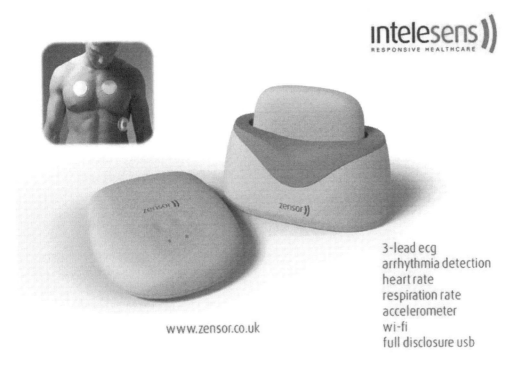

3-lead ecg
arrhythmia detection
heart rate
respiration rate
accelerometer
wi-fi
full disclosure usb

www.zensor.co.uk

Figure 9-4. *The Intelesens zensor provides ambulatory vital-signs monitoring (with permission from intelesens)*

Sphygmomanometers are increasingly being used as a noninvasive method of obtaining ambulatory blood pressure (ABPM) readings over a 24- or 48-hour period, in a patient's own home. Many studies have demonstrated that blood pressure measured over a 24-hour period gives a more accurate reflection of blood pressure than one-off measures in a clinical setting. Apart from the detection of hyper and hypo tension, ABPM can also be used to detect organ damage, such as left ventricular hypertrophy, episodic dysfunction, and autonomic dysfunction (Rull, 2010). There are two techniques for measuring ambulatory blood pressure: intermittent measurement over 24 hours, and continuous waveform analysis. The original devices were large, cumbersome, and difficult to wear, particularly for older adults, but current devices are similar in size to an EKG/ECG Holter monitor with an arm cuff. Many now feature Bluetooth connectivity for data transfer after the monitoring period. More recently, a number of devices that can measure blood pressure from the wrist have appeared on the market. Some studies report that the accuracy of the readings is comparable to those obtained with upper-arm ambulatory monitoring (Uen et al., 2009). However wrist blood-pressure measurement is controversial and is not currently recommended by the European Society of Hypertension or the American Heart Association. Certain issues related to these devices have the potential to cause inaccuracies, such as incorrect position in relation to the heart and measurement of BP in two arteries—radial and ulnar, and peripheral pulse wave distortion (Parati et al., 2010) (Anderson, 2010).

Mobility and Behavioral Monitoring

The concept of ubiquitous sensing is based on distributed and networked sensors that monitor user activities while remaining transparent to the users (Ning, 2013). For behavioral monitoring, wireless sensors and other methods such as RFID are used to detect interactions between humans and their environment. Behavioral monitoring has garnered attention due to its potential for providing clinicians and care givers with an unbiased view of patients in their home environments on a longitudinal basis. Behavioral information could allow a clinician to determine if an individual is capable of living independently by tracking his ability to complete the activities of daily life (ADLs). This data could also be used to identify early signs of diseases, such as dementia or diabetes, through changes in behavior patterns. Reliable and accurate behavioral information will allow family doctors or public health professionals to ask questions informed about the patient's recent history, thus optimizing patient visits. Sensors can also be used to enable supporting technologies. For example, PIR sensors deployed in a kitchen environment can detect when the person is there; and RFID tags and readers can identify what objects they are using. The data can be used to actuate cues (audio, video, or visual) to support users through each step in a task such as preparing a meal (Stanley et al., 2011).

Another approach to behavioral monitoring that does not require the installation of application-specific sensors is based around the use of smart meter data. The data can be used to identify patterns such as cooking, sleeping, when the home is unoccupied, and so forth. The ability to detect these events has the potential for smart meters to act as basic wellness monitors, particularly for older adults. As smart meters become more ubiquitous over the next five years there is significant potential to exploit the data for wide-scale behavioral monitoring applications (Lisovich et al., 2010). However, issues such as privacy, data protection, and the like will need to be addressed before such capabilities can be rolled out (McKenna et al., 2012).

■ **Note**   Smart meters are generally electric, but they can be water or gas meters as well. They have embedded intelligence that enables them to record consumption of electric energy at defined intervals (say, every 5 minutes) and communicate that information back to the energy supplier for monitoring and billing purposes. Many smart meters can also communicate wirelessly with a home display unit that allows the home owner to monitor energy consumption in near real-time.

A significant downside to this type of sensing is the loss of privacy. Other sensing systems, such as those used for chronic-disease management, provide information on health status, which, of course, does raise some privacy considerations. But that is not as invasive as tracking the number of times you go to the toilet during the night or whether you decided to stay in bed until the afternoon. It therefore important that such sensing systems are deployed on a voluntary basis and that access to the data is strictly controlled and managed. Of course, loss of privacy has to be offset against the potential loss of independence and the financial cost that a move to an assisted-living community would bring. For many, the controlled loss of privacy is a price worth paying to remain in their own home.

A significant number of small-scale demonstrations of assisted-living technology solutions incorporating wireless sensors in the research domain have been carried out. But large-scale, longitudinal studies with numbers in the high hundreds or thousands have not been realized to date. The barriers to achieving large deployments are a complex mixture of the technical and financial, as well as organizational structures and medical conservatism. One key limitation that must be addressed is that of electronic health records (EHRs) for patients. These are critical in connecting assisted-living data sets to the traditional hospital and community records. An integrated view of these diverse data sets is vital in establishing a complete picture of a patient's healthcare at any moment in time. Only then can the health delivery strategy ensure maximum patient benefit. There are number issues associated with the use of EHR's. Key among them is the issue of who owns the data (Stafford, 2010). We need answers to questions such as:

- Does the patient, the doctor, or the hospital own the data?

- Who has the right to access the data? Do insurance companies and national health authorities?

- Can the records be moved from one hospital to another, from one country to another?

- What types of data should be stored and in what formats? Are the records interoperable between access systems?

These are challenging questions that will require answers before EHRs can become more ubiquitous. Population-level data that can be harvested for EHRs has the potential to deliver enormous benefits, particularly in the areas of personal healthcare. Organization such as the European Alliance for Personalized Medicine are working with policy makers to develop regulatory frameworks to enable researchers and doctors to realize the value of these records when they are eventually fully implemented and are accessible on both a national and cross-border basis (euapm.eu).

For assisted-living technologies to succeed in the long term, they must demonstrate an ability to drive a "closed-loop" system. Closed-loop means data extracted from the home environment drives an appropriate response from a clinical decision support system, which results in improvements in well-being, patient outcome, and cost reduction. That goal is very much a work in progress and will take many years of trial and error to realize tangible, quantifiable, and sustainable benefits.

Apart from activity-tracking, other types of applications include fall detection, medications tracking, physical activity, and social engagement. Fall detection, through the use of body-worn sensors, is a well-established market. Initial fall-detection products relied on a single sensing modality, such a triaxial accelerometer. They suffered from high false-positive rates due to poor selectivity, for example, difficulty in distinguishing between sitting down rapidly and falling on the floor. Current products employ a multisensory approach, with some combination of accelerometers, gyroscopes and magnetometers, to reduce the false-positive rate. Some devices also feature mobile phone network connectivity to automatically alert a call center when a fall occurs. This feature is particularly useful if the fall results in a loss of consciousness. The use of walking aids, such as canes and walking frames, is common among older adults and has attracted the attention of researchers. The addition of inertial sensors to walking frames has been reported in the literature with a high degree of sensitivity and specificity for key gait characteristics, such as heel strike and toe events. Poor stability of the walker likely indicates poor stability of the subject (Alwan, 2009).

Mobility-tracking is starting to play a role in dementia care. GPS tags worn by patients allow caregivers to track their location via a web-based application, if required. In 2012, the GPS smart shoe from GTX Corp was launched; it tracks patients who wander away from the confines of their home. These devices are not only useful to caregivers but can be beneficial in supporting the patients themselves. The systems can be used to define areas within which the patient should remain, and trigger alarms when the patient leaves this area. This form of monitoring can allow sufferers increased levels of freedom, mobility, and independence.

Mobility monitoring can also play a role in post-surgery support. Body-worn sensor solutions, containing inertial and/or physiological sensors can be useful in helping to quantify recovery status. Continuous in-home behavioral data is more useful than one-off measures in a clinic, where patients may "put on a performance" for the doctor that does not give a true reflection of their progress. Mobility-sensing is useful, whether the person's mobility is impaired, is recovering, or has returned to normal. It can be used to quantify whether the patient has returned to normal patterns of walking, sleeping, exercise, and so forth. Abnormal activity patterns may indicate issues with the recovery process. The e-AR sensor was developed by Imperial College London to assess postoperative gait impairment. The sensor module contains a triaxial accelerometer, weighs only 7.4g, and is worn on the ear. It is used for functional recovery monitoring in patients in their own homes (Atallah et al., 2013). Other approaches include balance and stability monitoring using pressure-sensitive floor sensors (Taylor et al., 2012); and mobility trend monitoring using ultrasonic sensors to monitor bed exits or sit-to-stand transitions (Pouliot et al., 2012).

Biomechanical Rehabilitation

The use of body-worn sensors for in-home rehabilitation is an emerging healthcare application domain (Patel et al., 2012). These virtual reality applications typically consist of body-worn sensors, interactive software, and real-time representations of the patient. This modern approach to rehabilitation is fun for the patient and has psychological as well as physical benefits. Providing biofeedback to the patient is both a motivation and a reward for the user, and encourages compliance with the program. As well as monitoring biomechanical performance during the virtual reality session, sensing can also be used to quantify activity levels, rate of recovery, and physiological well-being outside of the sessions. This provides a more holistic view of the patient's status and can be used to detect potential complications at an early stage. Demand for these types of sensor applications will increase over time with the increase in global aging and obesity. Sensor-based rehabilitation is typically used in the following situations:

- Monitoring post-operative recovery, such as range of motion, following a joint replacement.

- Monitoring patient performance and progress in a rehabilitation program; for example, a post-stroke or post-fall program.

Post-operative applications are typically based on one or more inertial body-worn sensors:

- The Telefonica "Rehabitic" product uses SHIMMER inertial sensors to enable knee-replacement patients to perform their post-operative rehabilitation regimes in the comfort of their own home. The patient simply attaches the SHIMMER sensors to both sides of the affected knee. The sensor data is transferred wirelessly to an application on a touch screen PC that visually instructs the patients through a predefined therapy session. Visual feedback is provided to the patient in the form of an onscreen avatar, which displays the movement in real-time and indicates performance against targets. Clinicians can remotely follow the therapy sessions in real time or review the data offline (Smith, 2012).

- Smart Step, from Canadian company Motion Health, is an inertial sensor unit that is worn on the ankle to monitor and provide guided therapy sessions after orthopedic surgery. The sensor unit can provide auditory feedback, based on the identification of correct or incorrect gait patterns. It is also used in stroke rehabilitation and diseases such as Parkinson's (Motion Health, 2013).

Approximately 16 million first-time strokes occur annually on a global basis, resulting in 5.7 million deaths (Carlo, 2009). In the US, it is estimated that 795,000 people experience a stroke annually, at an estimated cost of USD 38.6B (CDCP, 2013). Stroke is the leading cause of long-term disability, with about half of stroke survivors being left with some degree of physical or cognitive impairment. The use of sensors for home-based stroke rehabilitation has been an area of research in both in academia and industry for many years. Efforts have focused on the use of body-worn inertial sensors both for upper (Chee Kian et al., 2010) and lower limb rehabilitation. Recent research efforts have included sensing technologies, such as flex sensor and force sensitive resistors that have the potential to be integrated into clothing (Bin Ambar et al., 2012):

- The Philips Research Stroke Rehab Exerciser coaches the patient through a series of prescribed exercises using a touch-screen PC. Body-worn wireless inertial sensors record patient movement and stream the data to the PC. Data is analyzed for deviations from a required movement target and feedback is provided to the patient. A physiotherapist can also review the patient remotely and update the targets for the exercise program.

- A recent development in stroke rehabilitation is based around the availability of low-cost games platforms, which integrate inertial sensors in the controller. Studies have shown that game-based therapies are enjoyable and comparable in delivering patient improvement to conventional therapy without any significant safety risks (Joo et al., 2010).

Aggregation and Management

As outlined in Table 9-2, there are a variety of sensing options to monitor patient health and activities in the home. These sensors can be used in discrete, standalone devices with no external connectivity, as well as in connected devices. Connected sensor devices are linked into a larger patient care system using wired (USB, for example) or wireless (Bluetooth, Wi-Fi, or Zigbee) interfaces. These care systems typically consist of an in-home aggregator, which can process, display, contextualize, and securely transfer the sensor data and other qualitative data to a remote back end, for clinical access and review. The architecture of a patient-care system is shown in Figure 9-5. These multifunctional aggregation devices were initially customized personal computers, such as the Care Innovations Guide and Bosch Health Buddy System; or customized set-top boxes for use with a television, such as Motiva from Philips Healthcare. More recently, product software elements (such as the Care Innovations Guide) have been decoupled from the custom hardware, allowing them to run on standard, off-the-shelf laptops or tablets. In this mode, the patient management software takes complete control of the computing device, thus preventing any accidental or intentional user modifications to the software. This gives the end user or care provider the freedom to repurpose unused computing devices as health aggregators, or to select new form factors, such as smartphones or tablets, as they become available. The emergence of health communication standards, such as Continua, guarantees that any compliant sensor device can be seamlessly interchanged with another sensor of the same type.

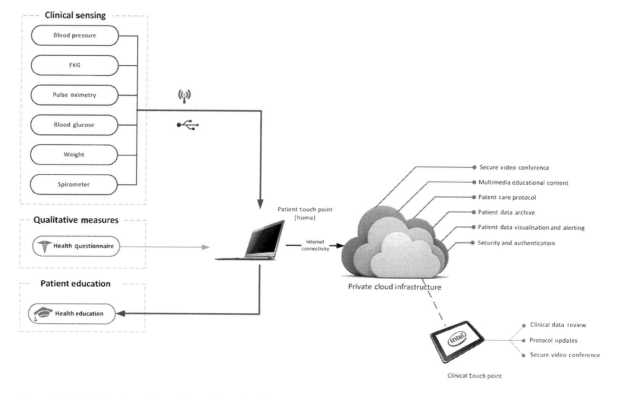

Figure 9-5. *Architecture of home-based chronic-disease management system*

Qualcomm has developed a different approach to the aggregation of clinical sensor data. Its 2net Hub is a stationary telehealth hub or gateway that plugs into an electric socket. The device incorporates Bluetooth, ANT+, Wi-Fi, and USB connectivity and can communicate wirelessly with clinical sensors and other peripherals. The hub also features cellular connectivity, allowing it to transmit data to the 2net Platform, a cloud-based system. The 2net Platform provides interoperability with different medical devices and applications. It also enables end-to-end wireless connectivity for sensors and medical devices, and provides secure access to biometric data for patients and their physicians. A 2net gateway for embedded form factors can be directly built into a clinical sensor. Additionally, a software module is available for mobile devices, such as smartphones and tablets, to serve as gateways to the 2net Platform. When combined, the 2net gateways and 2net Platform provide building blocks that allow companies to build home health-monitoring services without having to deal with major integration and data management tasks. Similarly, Verizon has collaborated with Entra Health Systems to develop its own cloud-based platform that facilitates the connection of medical devices to a common diagnostic database (Fitchard, 2011).

The Smartphone as a Healthcare Platform

Smartphones are commonly used as sensor aggregation platforms for wellness applications, as discussed in Chapter 10. This functionality is now being extended into the healthcare domain for the provision of in-home health monitoring services. Smartphone apps have a number of common components: wired or wireless interfacing to a health sensing device, and facilities for data storage, analysis, and display, as well as data forwarding to a clinician or a server.

As discussed in Chapter 4, smartphones enjoy many advantages over custom aggregators. Many, if not most, people already own a smartphone, so the patient only pays for the health sensor device and any cloud-based data services. Smartphones inherently feature Internet connectivity, processing, and display capabilities, and they can interface to internal and external sensors to provide contextual data for health related data measures. Sensor and contextual data can be archived locally on the smartphone, on a cloud-based service, or shared with family, friends, or clinicians. Individuals can use the software application to see micro and macro trends in their health readings.

Initially, customized healthcare apps were developed to interface to individual devices, but there is an increasing trend towards apps, such as the ZephyrLIFT app (`www.zephyr-technology.com`), that interface to multiple sensor devices. Similarly, sensor manufacturers are opening their communication interfaces to external app developers, providing consumers with a choice of free or paid apps for their health sensor devices. Healthcare apps are most commonly found in the following domains, although this list is likely to change as both health sensors and smartphones continue to evolve:

- *Blood pressure monitoring*: iHealth Labs, for example, has an innovative range of product offerings for blood pressure monitoring using a smartphone or tablet. One option is the wireless blood pressuremonitor that is placed around the upper arm. Data from the cuff is streamed wirelessly to the patient's iPhone running iHealth's mobile app, as shown in Figure 9-6 (a). The app displays your current systolic and diastolic readings, heart rate, pulse wave, and measurement time. The app also lets users compare daily results against their historical averages, as well as World Health Organization (WHO) classifications to provide context for the readings. There is also an integrated cloud service, where the user's data can be backed up and stored securely, giving the user access to his data regardless of location.

  Another option is a wrist cuff with wireless connectivity to a smartphone running the iHealth app as shown in Figure 9-6 (b). The cuff unit also features a motion sensor to improve the accuracy of the measurements by detecting the optimal wrist position, which helps users take a more accurate blood pressure reading. There is also an upper arm cuff that connects to a blood pressure dock as shown in Figure 9-6 (c). An iOS-based device (smartphone or tablet) is then connected to the dock, turning the device into a blood pressure monitor. Similar blood pressure dock and smartphone combinations are available from companies such as Withings and Verdian Healthcare. Blood pressure monitoring is one of the application domains that benefits from the contextual data provided by smartphones, as taking a blood-pressure reading immediately following strenuous activity, for example, will result in misleading data.

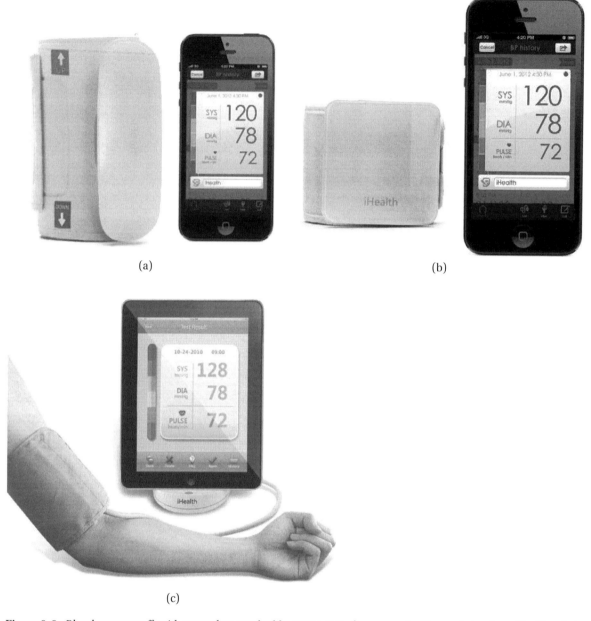

(a)

(b)

(c)

Figure 9-6. *Blood pressure cuffs with smartphone and tablet connectivity (image used with permission from iHealth Labs)*

- *Heart rate monitoring:* The ZephyrLIFE iOS app, for example, provides data processing and remote data transmission services. The app interfaces to the Zephyr BioPatch module over Bluetooth to provide heart monitoring measurements, including heart rate, R-R interval, respiration rate, and EKG/ECG. The app can also interface wirelessly to other medical devices, including pulse oximeters, weighing scales, blood pressure cuffs and glucometers. The Zephyr

BioPatch differs from basic heart rate sensors, used in fitness applications, in the number and quality of the cardiovascular parameters it provides. It is likely that smartphone apps and external, health-grade cardiovascular sensors will replace the discrete Holter monitor devices as diagnostic devices in the near future.

- *Diabetes monitoring:* Smartphones are ideal for diabetes management, which requires frequent entry of both diary and sensor-based information, display of micro and macro trends, and data aggregation for sharing with clinicians. Various hardware solutions have been proposed for monitoring blood-glucose levels using a smartphone. These include manually entering glucometer readings into an app, connecting standard glucometers to a smartphone using the Glooko MeterSync Cable, creating smartphone glucometer accessory devices, such as the Sanofi iBGStar, or creating a smartphone device with integrated glucometer functionality, such as the LifeWatch V smartphone. The apps associated with these hardware interfaces feature the data storage, analysis, display, and data-sharing capabilities previously described for other apps.

Home health monitoring is an exciting use of smartphone technology, and the practice will keep on growing as the computational capabilities of smartphones continue to increase, external sensors become increasingly easy to integrate, the performance and range of on-board sensors and sensor hubs grow, and the capabilities of mobile networks continue to develop.

Self-care Diagnostic Test Kits

As we have already discussed, individuals have a growing interest in proactively managing their own health. This is leading to increased adoption of self-care diagnostic test kits for home use. Various motivations drive the utilization of test kits, including self-empowerment of individuals, convenience, privacy, anonymity, the "worried well" effect, and financial considerations. A proactive consumer philosophy has developed over the last few decades and is now percolating into the personal health domain, driven in part by easier access to test kits that are available off-the-shelf at pharmacies and online. In-home diagnostic test kits have been available for less than four decades. In 1977, the first over-the-counter early-pregnancy test appeared. At the time, there was significant professional and public controversy surrounding the test (Pray, 2010). Many were concerned about potential societal impacts, particularly on younger women. That discussion has now been largely confined to the history books and has moved on to debates about the availability of tests for disease, infection, and blood chemistry.

As the popularity and general availability of self-care health test kits have grown, voices of concern or even alarm have increased. If used correctly, FDA-approved test kits should be as accurate as a laboratory tests, which are conducted under controlled conditions. However, the manner in which the test is performed at home can vary significantly, due to poor instructions related to sample collection and data interpretation. This variability can result in misleading readings, false positives (such as for the prostate specific antigen, or PSA), and give a false sense of security (for example, with a colon cancer screening). Experts argue that home tests can often be a waste of money. Clinicians will most likely repeat the tests an individual has carried out at home once they present themselves at the doctor's office (NHS, 2011).

Cholesterol-level kits are among the most popular home test kits currently on the market. However, results vary significantly, especially if subjects are not fasting when they take the test. Another common problem is poor adherence to the sampling instructions. In cholesterol testing, people tend to squeeze or "milk" a finger to get blood onto the test strip or into the well, which may affect the accuracy of the results.

In some circumstances, the scientific value of particular tests is highly debatable. Food allergies may cause life-threatening shock reactions, such as severe breathlessness and tongue swelling, while symptoms of food intolerances range from mild discomfort to diarrhea. An allergic food reaction results in an immunological response in the form of IgE antibody production. Food allergy test kits are designed to detect and quantify this antibody-based immunological response. Some experts argue that these results are questionable and are often dependent on the intensity of the allergic reaction. Food intolerance test kits are also available, which apply the same immunological response principle to identify food intolerances, although food intolerance does not elicit a full-blown allergic reaction. There is little or no scientific support for this form of testing. A simple trial and error approach with the suspected foods is the normal course of action prescribed by most experts for identification of food intolerance.

Home testing suffers from a lack of legislation and corresponding regulation, as discussed in Chapter 6. In the US, only some tests have FDA clearance. Some tests can be certified by other professional bodies. For example, cholesterol tests can be certified by the Cholesterol Reference Method Laboratory Network (CRMLN). Other tests have no certification or peer-reviewed science to back them up. The lack of regulation and consistent quality assurance will continue to bring confusion and uncertainty to the area of home monitoring for many years to come. In the interim, some de facto certification of tests will occur on an ad-hoc basis or through utilization of crowd-sourced determination of efficacy.

Some experts believe that affordable tests don't provide enough information to be truly useful. Others think this is a limited and somewhat vested view by the medical establishment. As we head down the road of patient-centric healthcare, it can be argued that considerations valued by patients, such as convenience and privacy, will gain greater weight—especially when it comes to people having basic access to healthcare. The value of any testing, despite potential flaws, has to be weighed against no testing and no understanding of potential risks (Carrell, 2012).

There are three sensing techniques commonly used for home testing kits:

- Enzymatic/immunological assays

- Enzymatic test strips (Clinistrip)

- Chromatic wet chemistry

Enzymatic/Immunological Assays

The immunoassays used in home test kits are based around the enzyme-linked immunosorbent assay (ELISA) The test uses antibodies and color change to identify the presence of a substance in a liquid sample (blood, urine, or saliva). Monoclonal antibodies, which are single-specificity antibodies, are typically used in these tests. The substance to be detected is usually an antigen, which evokes the response of one or more antibodies. In a direct immunological assay, an antigen that has been coated to the "wells" in a plastic well plate (also known as a microtiter plate, a flat plate with one or more depressions, or "wells," that can act as small test tubes) is detected by an antibody that has been directly conjugated (attached) to an enzyme (such as horseradish peroxidase (HRPO), urease, or alkaline phosphatase (AP)). This can also be reversed, with an antibody is coated to the "wells" in the plate and a labeled antigen used for detection. When the enzyme-labeled conjugated antibody is added to the sample, the test antigen reacts and prevents the antibody from binding to the antigen on the solid phase—the walls of the well. The added antigen in the sample (liquid phase) and solid phase antigen compete for the labeled antibody. The higher the concentration of the liquid-phase antigen, the greater the competition between the two phases. Unbound antigen and antibody enzyme conjugate is removed in a washing step. Upon the addition of the enzyme substrate, the intensity of color is inversely proportional to the concentration of antigen of interest in the sample (BIO-RAD, 2013). Chemiluminescent or fluorescent signals are alternative optical approaches to determining antigen concentrations, but are generally unsuitable for home use, due to the cost of detectors. Variations on the direct ELISA approach include Indirect Elisa, Sandwich Elisa (as shown in Figure 9-7) and Competition or Inhibition ELISA. This form of sensing is highly sensitive, with typical detection ranges of 0.01 to 0.1ng, with sensitivities of 99.7 percent (Jordan, 2005).

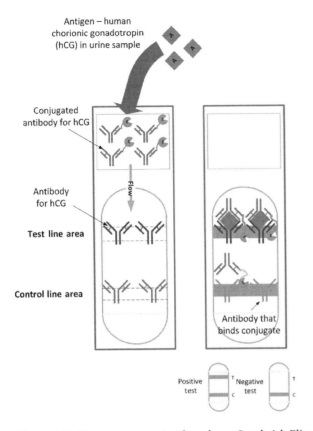

Figure 9-7. *Home pregnancy test based on a Sandwich Elisa*

Enzymatic Test Strips

Test strips or "dip sticks" are a very common approach to home test kits and are also commonly found in doctors' offices. They offer a quick and cheap mechanism to screen for a variety of conditions, and may be either biological or chemical. Clinistix sticks, which first appeared in the 1950s, are commonly used to test for the presence of glucose in urine. The sticks contain two enzymes, glucose oxidase and peroxidase, which are immobilized onto a cellulose fiber pad. The pad is fixed onto a plastic strip approximately 5 to 10mm in width and in 70 to 80mm in length. The sample is applied to the pad, where the reaction between glucose and oxygen is catalyzed by the glucose oxidase, producing gluconic acid and hydrogen peroxide. The peroxidase in turn catalyzes the reaction between the hydrogen peroxide and an indicator pigment, resulting in a visible color change. The intensity of this color change is proportional to the concentration of glucose present in the sample.

Chromatic Wet Chemistry

Chromatic wet chemistry test strips can detect a wide range of analytes in urine and saliva samples. They consist of a plastic strip approximately 5 to 10mm in width that is impregnated with various chemical compounds. The chemicals react with one or more analytes present in the sample being tested, normally producing a color change proportional to the concentration of the analyte of interest. For example, ketones in the form of acetoacetic acid and acetone in a urine sample are detected by the reaction with sodium nitroprusside, which forms a purple color, as shown in Figure 9-8 (Chronolab, 2009).

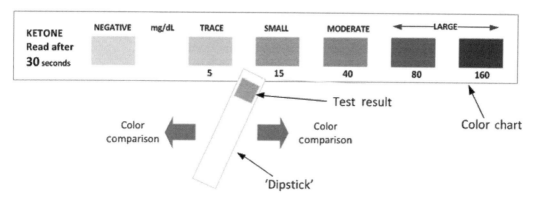

Figure 9-8. *Ketone detection in a urine sample using a dip stick*

The Home Test Market

The self-diagnostic home test-kits market is volatile and continually changing. New tests are introduced while others disappear as their efficacy or utility is disproven by the scientific community or they become outdated as the technology moves on. The market continues to grow at around 7 to 8 percent annually, with sales in 2013 expected to reach USD 5.68B. Revenues are currently dominated by pregnancy and cholesterol test kits, which account for about 85 to 90 percent of sales; however, that share will change over time as other tests gain traction among consumers (Kelleher, 2009). Table 9-3 outlines the home test kits that are currently available to consumers over the counter or via the Internet. A variety of kits also provide home sampling in which analysis is carried out by a laboratory and results are returned to the customer. Those tests are not included in Table 9-3 because they do not provide "sensing" capabilities. The FDA recently approved the first home test for the HIV, which raised significant debate about the lack of appropriate support structures and access to counseling if a positive test result occurs. Clinical support would be valuable for this and other tests, in case of false positives due to improper context.

Table 9-3. *Consumer Home Health Test Kits*

Category	Type	Condition	Description
Infection	Fungal	Yeast infection (Candidiasis)	Changes in urine pH
	Bacterial	Cystitis (Bladder) Pyelonephritis (Kidney) Helicobacter pylori (Stomach) Chlamydia	Measurement of protein, nitrites or Leukocytes (esterase) in urine—chemical reagent-based test strips with interpretation based on color intensity Immunological assay for bacterial antibodies in blood sample.
	Virus	HIV	Immunological assay for HIV antibodies in saliva.

(*continued*)

Table 9-3. (*continued*)

Category	Type	Condition	Description
Blood Chemistry	Cholesterol	Total Cholesterol Low Density Lipoprotein (LDL) High Density Lipoprotein (HDL) Triglycerides	Chromatic chemical test strips or biosensing (such as enzyme-based amperometric. sensing). Results are sensitive to the method of blood collection and fasting prior to testing.
	Ketones	Diabetic ketoacidosis	Enzyme-based colorimetric assay or chromatic chemical test strips for detection of ketones in blood (acetoacetate or beta-hydroxybutyrate) or urine (acetoacetate or acetoacetate and acetone). Ketones can indicate low or lack of insulin (diabetes), or dieting effects (as with Atkins and alcoholism).
	Hormones	Hormone insufficiency Hyper- or hypothyroidism Cushing disease Lack of libido	Chromatographic immunoassay of saliva, urine, and blood samples. Determination of estradiol (E2), progesterone (Pg), testosterone (T), DHEA-S, cortisol levels, thyroid-stimulating hormone (TSH). Serum tests are normally unable to distinguish the protein-bound (inactive form) from its free form (biologically active), thus giving only a rough estimate of hormone levels. Urine testing normally requires repeated testing over 24 hours for accurate results. Saliva tests give a better indication of bio-available or active hormones.
		Menopause	Chromatographic immunoassay measurement of follicle-stimulating hormone (FSH) in the urine. High levels of FSH can signal menopause.
	Anemia	Ferritin	Immunoassay (polyclonal antibody/streptavidin-peroxidase conjugate) determination of ferritin protein levels in blood. Ferritin is an iron storage protein and is a sensitive indicator of iron deficiency anemia.
Food and Drink	Allergies	Egg Wheat Soya Peanuts Seafood Fish Tree nuts Caffeine	Immunoassay measurement of Immunoglobulin E (IgE) antibody.
Environmental	Allergies	Cat dander Dog dander Dust mites Grass Pollen	Immunoassay for qualitative detection of IgE antibodies in whole blood due to airborne allergen response.

(*continued*)

Table 9-3. (*continued*)

Category	Type	Condition	Description
Disease	Celiac disease	Gluten	Immunoassay for IgA and/or IgG antibodies. The presence of gluten in a celiac's diet causes the body's immune system to produce antibodies that attack the lining of the small intestine.
	Colon (gastrointestinal, cancer, Crohn's)	Blood in fecal stools	Guaiac fecal occult/ hemoccult test (FOBTs)—chemical test strips for measurement of peroxidase activity Immunoassay for globins or transferrin proteins.
Fertility	Ovulation detection	Luteinizing hormone (LH)	Immunoassay with color indication for detection of elevated LH hormone in urine or blood during ovulation.
Pregnancy	Pregnancy test	Human chlorionic gonadotropin (HCG) hormone	Tests work by binding the hCG hormone in urine to a monoclonal antibody and an indicator/pigment molecule. Urine-based (HCG) hormone.
	Amniotic Leak Detector	Amniotic fluid	pH sensitivity polymer-coated polyester strip (panty liner) with color indication.
Organ Function	Prostate Disorder	PSA	Immunoenzymometric assay. PSA appears in higher concentrations in the bloodstream when the gland is enlarged or cancerous.
	Adrenal	NaCl	Titration method using with color indication at end to determine salt level in urine.
	Liver	Bilirubin, urobilinogen	Chromatic chemical reagent strip for measurement of bilirubin and urobilinogen in urine.
Drugs	Illegal	Amphetamines (speed) Barbiturates (barbs, downers, reds) Cocaine and crack Methamphetamines (ecstasy) Opiates (heroin) Phencyclidine (angel dust) Cannabis	Drug-specific chromatic chemical test strips with urine sample. Immunoassay screening tests.
	Prescription	Painkillers Antidepressants Benzodiazepines Methadone	Chromatic chemical reagent strips for measurement of Oxycodone, Oxycontin, Vicodin TCA Tricyclics (antidepressants) Tranquillizers such as diazepam, temazepam, nitrazepam, and flunitrazepam
Alcohol	Breath Urine	Ethanol	Fuel cell-based sensor. Metal oxide semiconductor sensor. Test strips—conversion of ethanol by alcohol oxidase (ALOx) in the presence of peroxidase and an indicator such as tetramethylbenzidine (TMB) to produce acetaldehyde and colored TMB (oxidized).
Smoking	Active Passive	Nicotine	Immunoassay for detection of cotinine (metabolite of nicotine) in saliva and urine.

Home Genetic Testing

One area in home diagnostic testing that has received significant attention recently is direct-to-consumer genetic testing. This form of testing currently falls outside the sensing domain, as samples are collected at home and sent to laboratories for testing using techniques such as polymerase chain reactions (PCR). However, it is a growing element of the home testing market.

Efforts to bring this form of testing into the mainstream have met with considerable opposition. For example, the planned partnership between Pathway Genomics and Walgreens to provide testing quickly drew both congressional and FDA scrutiny and resulted in the plans being dropped almost immediately (Wanner, 2012). Many in-home genetic tests lack rigorous scientific validation and fail to capture important contextual information, which is required when building a complete picture of risk (School, 2010).

However, interest among the public still remains, in particular in identifying genetic risks including Alzheimer's, diabetes, and certain forms of cancer such as breast and ovarian (based on the inherited mutation of the BRCA1 and BRCA2 genes). Tests are desired to determine if any genetic risks exist that could be passed on children, such as those causing cystic fibrosis and Tay-Sachs. Recent research has shown that a normal, healthy person has on average about 400 potentially damaging DNA variants, of which two have known disease-trait correlations. Research indicates that the actual possession of these variants is not enough to cause disease in most cases. The catalyst for disease expression remains unknown. (Xue et al., 2012). It is highly likely that factors such as lifestyle and environment are contributory influences. This area will remain hotly debated by doctors, politicians, patient advocacy groups, and individuals with specific family histories. For the moment, we are "opinion rich and information poor" in our understanding of genetic expressions and disease risk. It is likely that it will be a number of decades before we bridge the knowledge gap and realize the value of clinical genomics.

Key Drivers and Challenges

A variety of organizational, technical, and end-user challenges and drivers currently exist for successful sensor utilization in the healthcare domain. Demographic changes, technology innovation, and the cost of reactive healthcare are driving the adoption of in-home and in-community health monitoring. Yet many barriers remain, such as the organizational changes required within healthcare systems to realize the value and utility of sensor technologies. There are also key challenges to be addressed, such as usability of the sensor technology to ensure patient compliance. Despite these challenges, there is growing momentum behind the adoption of sensor technologies based on their ability to provide new and potentially lower-cost models of care. These models of care are also more adaptable to the needs and lifestyle choices of patients. We will now look at the key drivers and challenges in more detail.

Drivers and Challenges in Healthcare Systems

Home monitoring is potentially a less-expensive way to diagnose and watch a patient than intermittent clinical assessment or reacting following a health event—the current model of care. For example, diagnosis of an irregular heart rhythm disorder is more effectively determined through continuous home monitoring rather than with numerous hospital visits or extended in-patient assessment. It is widely agreed that early detection and treatment of most diseases results in lower cost and better outcomes. The adoption of smartphones as health platforms will provide an ability to deliver continuous health monitoring, through body-worn or point-of-care sensors, or sensors integrated into the smartphone itself. This, in turn, will provide early warnings of impending critical health events, such as a heart attack or other significant disease episode. Such capabilities would allow movement toward predictive healthcare rather than the reactive healthcare that dominates the current approach. Political pressure is another key driver toward adopting new, clinically effective monitoring, diagnostic, or treatment strategies, especially if there is a significant projected economic value.

The interface between healthcare systems and technology can be challenging, and this is particularly true when introducing new technologies, new protocols, or new non-clinical settings. Home and community-based sensing promises to deliver all three of these "new" features. The healthcare professions and the healthcare industry are both complex and conservative, however, and are often seen to be slow to embrace innovation and change. They often require expensive longitudinal, randomized control trials to prove efficacy before adopting new treatment protocols and technologies. Their cautious approach may serve to protect patients. But in many ways, preventing patients from accessing new technologies and treatments may put their health at greater risk than the technology or treatment itself.

The regulatory system, discussed in Chapter 6, also provides a barrier to getting technology to patients. While regulation is a costly, bureaucratic, time-consuming activity, it is necessary to protect vulnerable patients. An unregulated system, such as in-home test kits and mobile apps, can mislead patients with dangerous consequences. A streamlined regulation system that keeps pace with rapidly evolving technology is long overdue. Individual clinicians may also resist change as they may feel uncomfortable using and interpreting remote sensing technologies. Or they may fear these technologies could provide increased transparency into their clinical evaluations, protocol utilization, and decision-making on treatment plans.

Technology Drivers and Challenges

Sensors, especially wearable sensor devices, need to be fashionable, unobtrusive, comfortable, and wireless. The emerging range of "band-aid" sensor formats coupled with smartphones are addressing many of these requirements (Kumar et al., 2011, Whitney, 2010, Montalbano, 2013). However, the form factors of some physiological sensors, such as ambulatory blood pressure monitors, remain large and intrusive due to the physical requirements of their sensing method. Body-worn sensing solutions need to adapt to individual requirements, personal preferences, and habits. The biocompatibility of sensor materials is an important consideration. While much progress has been made at a basic material level, much work remains to fully understand the relationship between the sensor interface and the human body and skin during long term monitoring. Epidermal sensors, such as "smart skin," promise sensors that can be worn for weeks or months without any obvious impact on the skin or surrounding tissues of the patient. The implantable devices domain has already led the way with significant progress achieved to date. Most implants have already achieved a normal operational life span of 10-15 years.

There is much work to be done in breaking down the silos within the health technology industry. A lack of interoperability often exists between sensors and devices, resulting in data being transferred to separate back end systems that make it impossible or extremely inconvenient for a consumer or caregiver to manage all the available data. Initiatives such as the Continua Healthcare Alliance are helping to address many of these interoperability issues and will ultimately make remote clinical sensing more affordable and more effective.

Security and privacy issues are pervasive in many aspects of our daily lives, some of which we give higher priority over others. Healthcare is and will most likely always be one of those high-priority areas. Beyond the technical aspects of security, which depend on the weakest link in the chain (the human), attention must be paid to understanding the societal, ethnographic, and demographic impacts of sensing in healthcare. People have concerns about genetic profiling, third-party exploitation, "big brother," and so forth. These concerns must be addressed up front and policies must be developed and agreed upon before the technology becomes pervasive. Personal ownership and informed consent, which maintain the rights of individuals to privacy with respect to their health data, must be protected. However, individuals must also protect themselves. As people use sensing to obtain more and more information about their health, they should know the implications of sharing this data in an open and uncontrolled manner. Privacy must also be maintained as wireless sensor networks become more pervasive.

Consumer Drivers and Challenges

The patient acts as both a driver and inhibitor of sensor technologies. Some patients instinctively resist new technology, particularly if they feel it will result in a loss of personal contact with their clinician. Others embrace technology as they see it as a mechanism to collect the evidence for the symptoms and issues they are experiencing. Some patients may feel a sense of comfort in knowing that their vital signs are normal and someone is watching their data, while others may be motivated by a desire for the latest and coolest technology device. As with most technologies, ease of use is of critical importance. A poor experience with using a sensor, difficulty interpreting a result, or a getting a false reading may negatively impact a patient's view of the technology and prevent subsequent use.

As more technology is integrated into healthcare, the complexity of personal health data management will increase significantly. People have to become more data literate (see Chapter 5) to understand what their sensor measurements mean. They will also have to understand that an individual measurement in isolation may not necessarily reveal any great insight into their health, but can provide substantial insight if combined with other data sources. An integrated view of the data will be critical in providing context for measurements and for proving meaningful consumer benefits. A positive home test result may be misleading without supporting measurements and additional contextual information, for example. It is therefore essential to consider the end user and different contexts when designing such technology.

As new sensor technologies provide greater insights into the parameters of health, we must be careful to develop robust models of cause and effect. This is particularly true of genetic markers, which of themselves do not necessary mean someone will develop a particular disease. This is one of the key weaknesses of genetic home testing kits. Many people will never develop a particular disease, even if they have been identified as having a risk. Therefore, even if no preventive measures are taken, they would not develop the disease or condition anyway. Once identified as having a particular risk, an individual must be treated under a duty of care or they will demand some form of treatment from their doctors. That could result in greater costs and reduce the economic benefits of preventive measures. As the precision of sensor technologies and our understanding of how to piece together the various individual sources of information improve, we will have more precise tools to identify individuals who really need to and can benefit from proactive treatments.

The Future of Sensor-Based Applications for Healthcare

Current trends indicate that the future of health sensing will be a convergence of many areas—health, technology, fashion, clothing and lifestyle. As health consumerism continues to grow, people will expect their medical devices, particularly non-prescribed monitoring devices, to be aesthetically pleasing. Many healthy people want to keep track of their health status on a continuous basis through easy to use, non-intrusive, fashionable devices. This growing group of people ranges from those who proactively manage their health, to the "worried well" who are concerned about the latest health scare in the media. Patients are becoming more aware of the sensors and services that have emerged in the wellness and fitness domain. In the future, they will likely demand similar capabilities for their prescribed healthcare therapies. This will also lead to a rebalancing of the dynamic between patients and healthcare professionals. Many will view this as a positive development as it will empower individuals to have a more active role in the decision making process with respect to their health. People are becoming better educated and, as a result, are questioning and demanding more of their healthcare providers. Patients will want choices and will play a more active role in the decision-making process with respect to their health and issues associated with it.

The next decade will bring acceleration in the use of personalized medicine, as it moves toward becoming standard practice in healthcare. This will be driven by the utilization of "omics" technologies, where genomic information will be used to determine the most effective course of treatment for an individual. It will move us away from population-centered statistics, where we look at the average effect of treatment, and toward tailoring treatments and continuously modifying that treatment base on the biological data of the individual. That approach is commonly known as theranostics, which focuses on targeted drug therapies and companion diagnostic tests to advance personalized medicine. Testing forms an integral part of it, as immediate reactions to taking a new medication must be detected and the patient treatment can then be optimized based on the test results. Sensing will play a central role in this approach, ranging from determining which drug treatment will be most effective for an individual's biology, to monitoring its efficacy.

From a technology perspective, sensing will be heavily influenced by increased integration of devices through the continued evolution of MEMS. The size of sensors will continue to shrink, enabling to them to be used in form factors that match the needs and expectations of patients. New epidermal sensing technologies—such as electronic skin patches, or "smart skin," where the sensor is literally tattooed onto the patient's skin—will enable clinicians to monitor vital size in almost any location without the need for prodding or poking. This technology will form part of the new world of cyber-physical systems, where the physical world and the cyber world are connected in a seamless, natural way. Sensing platforms based on the "smart band-aid" form factor are the first significant step on this journey (Fangmin et al., 2012, Hoi-Jun et al., 2010).

There will also be exciting developments in the use of smartphones as health platforms. Their pervasiveness and familiarity will see smartphones gain greater adoption as healthcare sensing and management devices. There is already growing interest among the major smartphone players, including Samsung and Apple, and Telco providers, in delivering future devices and services. Initial product offerings will be based on a combination of existing sensors, innovative smartphones, and cloud-based software. For example, an Israeli company called LifeWatch has an Android-based smartphone product (shown in Figure 9-9) that has integrated blood glucose monitoring, EKG/ECG, body temperature, percentage body fat, blood oxygen saturation levels, and stress-level sensors. Innovative product offerings will be developed as new discrete sensors emerge and the integrated sensing capabilities of smartphones continue to evolve. These products will include apps and services to provide continuous, always-connected sensing in any location required by the lifestyle of an individual. This will in turn drive the growth of cloud services and features such as security, privacy, configurable access rights, and integrated electronic health records.

Figure 9-9. *The LifeWatch health sensing smartphone (image used with permission from LifeWatch)*

The development of new drugs is slow and costly. Still, our understanding of how diseases affect individuals at a molecular level due to subtle variations in or genetic and biochemical make-up is growing at a significant pace. This knowledge is driving requirements for many new drugs that are designed for specific genetic markers and biochemical pathways. The current models of clinical trials will have to change in order reduce costs, support assembly of cohorts with specific genetic characteristics, and expedite the output of results demonstrating efficacy. Approximately USD 25 billion is spent on trials annually in the US alone, accounting for around 60 percent of the development costs. Sensing will play a greater role in clinical trials by providing extensive quantitative measures of a subject's physiological and biochemical well-being. Data-quality issues, one of the leading issues currently in clinical trials, will be reduced by using sensors to continuously monitor and automatically report data during home monitoring. The data will be stored in electronic health records on cloud infrastructures that enable real-time demonstration of clinical effect and the identification of potential side effects. This will lead to shorter clinical trials, as substantial evidence with respect to efficacy can be demonstrated during the trial, thus expediting the licensing process. Sensor-based physiological monitoring is already an emerging reality in trials of cardiac drugs, where 24-hour continuous EKG/ECG monitoring is becoming normal practice. The increase in sensor adoption for home monitoring during clinical trials should lead the way to faster, better-characterized and a cheaper drug development process.

The use of sensing technologies is already attracting growing interest from insurance and national services providers as a means to prevent serious health events through proactive monitoring programs or for post-discharge monitoring of patients. In the US, over 30 percent of Medicare patients discharged from the hospital are readmitted with 90 days, in what is sometimes referred to as the revolving-door syndrome. There is a reassessment underway of how medical care is reimbursed with a move toward pay-for-performance. Medicare has now modified its reimbursement policy to penalize care providers when a patient with a chronic disease is readmitted within 30 days of discharge (CMS, 2013). Sensing technologies will play a greater role in assessing the physiological and kinematic status of patients to ensure they are fit for discharge. The use of body-worn and ambient sensing to monitor a patient post discharge will become normal clinical practice. This type of monitoring will be further catalyzed as we move towards more stringent and frequent requirements on compliance reporting for patients with various disorders and conditions.

Sensing, coupled with other ICT capabilities, such as smartphones, clouding computing, and healthcare data analytics, can offer many potential benefits to society. However, the adoption of these technologies and what their data can reveal about the current or future health status of an individual will have ethical and societal aspects. These aspects must be addressed in a transparent and balanced manner to ensure trust among the monitored and the data consumer. We are on the cusp of an exciting era, where sensing, combined with other technologies, will make a meaningful impact on the health and well-being of individuals and society at large.

Summary

In this chapter we looked at how sensor technologies play a key role in the continuum of healthcare, ranging from the hospital environment, to the community, to home-based monitoring. A variety of factors—including an aging population, moving to proactive healthcare, personalized healthcare delivery, and greater involvement by patients in their health and well-being—are driving this sensor-based, proactive health monitoring approach. We reviewed how sensing is already playing an important role in chronic disease management, investigative monitoring, home rehabilitation, mobility monitoring and consumer sensing. The integration of sensor and ICT technologies into mobile form factors such as smartphones is leading to the development of a new wave of products and services. This evolution is helping to address patient expectations that technology can adapt as required to their lifestyle choices and needs. Finally, we looked at the future of sensing and how it will help deliver new models of care.

References

Suzman, Richard and John Beard, "Global Health and Aging", World Health Organisation, 2011.

Fodeman, Jason and Robert A. Book. *"Bending the Curve": What Really Drives Health Care Spending*, The Wall Street Journal, New York, http://online.wsj.com/article/SB10001424052748703787304575075843971534082.html, 2010.

Vavilis, Sokratis, Milan Petković, and Nicola Zannone, "Impact of ICT on Home Healthcare," in *ICT Critical Infrastructures and Society: 10th IFIP TC 9 International Conference on Human Choice and Computers (HCC10)*, Amsterdam, The Netherlands, 2012, pp. 111–122.

Colvin, Geoff. *"We're having the wrong debate about rising health care costs"*, Last Update: 2012, http://finance.fortu ne.cnn.com/2012/04/25/health-care-costs-debate/

Corocoto, Genalyn. *"Diabetes and Other Lifestyle Diseases Are Now Leading Causes of Death: Study"*, Last Update: November 16th 2011, http://au.ibtimes.com/articles/250122/20111116/diabetes-lifestyle-diseases-leading-causes-death-study.htm#.UUihoxy-2So

Chase, Dave. *"Health Systems Ignore Patients at Their Own Peril"*, Last Update: April 8th 2012, http://www.forbes.com/sites/davechase/2012/04/08/health-systems-ignore-patients-at-their-own-peril/

Porter, Michael E., "What Is Value in Health Care?," *New England Journal of Medicine,* vol. 363, (26), pp. 2477–2481, 2010.

Scher, David Lee. *"How Outcomes-Based Reimbursement Will Change Healthcare"*, Last Update: October 25th 2011, http://davidleescher.com/2011/10/25/how-outcomes-based-reimbursement-will-change-healthcare/

Stankovic, John A., Anthony D. Wood, and Tian He, "Realistic Applications for Wireless Sensor Networks," in *Theoretical Aspects of Distributed Computing in Sensor Networks*, Nikoletseas, Sotiris and José D.P. Rolim, Eds., Berlin, Springer, 2011, pp. 835–863.

Comstock, Jonah. *"2018: 5 million disposable, mobile medical sensors"*, Last Update: May 3rd 2013, http://mobihealthnews.com/22089/2018-5-million-disposable-mobile-medical-sensors/

Miguel, Kristen De San, Joanna Smith, and Gill Lewin, "Telehealth Remote Monitoring for Community-Dwelling Older Adults with Chronic Obstructive Pulmonary Disease," *Telemedicine and e-Health,* vol. 19, (9), pp. 652–657, 2013.

Cox, Narelle S., Jennifer A. Alison, Tshepo Rasekaba, and Anne E. Holland, "Telehealth in cystic fibrosis: a systematic review," *Journal of Telemedicine and Telecare,* vol. 18, (2), pp. 72–78, 2012.

Cartwright, Martin, *et al.*, "Effect of telehealth on quality of life and psychological outcomes over 12 months (Whole Systems Demonstrator telehealth questionnaire study): nested study of patient reported outcomes in a pragmatic, cluster randomised controlled trial," *BMJ*, vol. 346, 2013.

InMedica. "Telehealth to Reach 1.8 Millio Patients by 2017", http://in-medica.com/press-release/Telehealth_to_Reach_18_Million_Patients_by_2017, 2013.

Versel, Neil. *"Momentum for home monitoring of costly chronic diseases",* Last Update: 23rd August, 2012, http://mobihealthnews.com/18297/momentum-for-home-monitoring-of-costly-chronic-diseases/

NCCDPHP, "Chronic Diseases The Power To Prevent, The Call To Control ", National Centre for Chronic Disease Prevention and Health Promotion Atlanta, GA, http://www.cdc.gov/chronicdisease/resources/publications/aag/pdf/chronic.pdf, 2009.

Mearian, Lucas. *"In-home health monitoring to leap six-fold by 2017",* Last Update: 22nd January, 2013, http://www.computerworld.com/s/article/9236026/In_home_health_monitoring_to_leap_six_fold_by_2017

Pasolini, Antonio. *"Smart T-shirt to remotely monitor chronically ill patients",* Last Update: 26th June, 2012, http://www.gizmag.com/t-shirt-remote-medical-monitoring/23088/

Schwartz, Ariel. *"No More Needles: A Crazy New Patch Will Constantly Monitor Your Blood",* Last Update: 19th June, 2012, http://www.fastcoexist.com/1680025/no-more-needles-a-crazy-new-patch-will-constantly-monitor-your-blood

Gilles, Gary. *"FreeStyle Navigator CGM is Being Phased Out in US",* Last Update: 2011, http://type1diabetes.about.com/b/2011/09/07/freestyle-navigator-cgm-is-being-phased-out-in-us.htm

WebMD. "Diabetes and Continuous Glucose Monitoring", http://diabetes.webmd.com/continuous-glucose-monitoring#, 2012.

SBWire. "Continuous Glucose Monitoring (CGM) Market - Global Industry Analysis, Size and Forecast (2012–2018)", http://www.sbwire.com/press-releases/continuous-glucose-monitoring-cgm-market-global-industry-analysis-size-and-forecast-2012-2018-255983.htm, 2013.

Podimetrics. "Podimetrics - a world with diabetic foot ulcers", http://www.podimetrics.com/press.html, 2013.

Intelesens. "Miniaturised, non invasive wireless monitoring at home with zensor", http://www.intelesens.com/inhomemonitoring/zensor.html, 2013.

Rull, Gurvinder. *"Ambulatory Blood Pressure Monitoring",* Last Update: 25th August, 2010, http://www.patient.co.uk/doctor/Ambulatory-Blood-Pressure-Monitoring.htm

Uen, Sakir, Rolf Fimmers, Miriam Brieger, Georg Nickenig, and Thomas Mengden, "Reproducibility of wrist home blood pressure measurement with position sensor and automatic data storage," *BMC Cardiovascular Disorders,* vol. 9, (20), 2009.

Parati, G., *et al.*, "European Society of Hypertension Practice Guidelines for home blood pressure monitoring," *Journal of Human Hypertension,* vol. 24, pp. 779–785, 2010.

Anderson, Kenny, *"Wrist versus Upper Arm Blood Pressure Measurement",* Blog@SunTech, Last Update: April 14th 2010, http://blog.suntechmed.com/blog/29-bp-cuffs/290-wrist-versus-upper-arm-blood-pressure-measurement-wrist-versus-upper-arm-blood-pressure-measurement

Ning, Huansheng, "Unit Internet of Things," in *Unit and Ubiquitous Internet of Things,* Boca Raton, FL, CRC Press, 2013, pp. 39–40.

Stanley, Kevin G. and Nathaniel D. Osgood, "The Potential of Sensor-Based Monitoring as a Tool for Health Care, Health Promotion, and Research," *Annals of Family Medicine,* vol. 9, (4), pp. 296–298, 2011.

Lisovich, M. A., D. K. Mulligan, and S. B. Wicker, "Inferring Personal Information from Demand-Response Systems," *Security & Privacy, IEEE,* vol. 8, (1), pp. 11–20, 2010.

McKenna, Eoghan, Ian Richardson, and Murray Thomson, "Smart meter data: Balancing consumer privacy concerns with legitimate applications," *Energy Policy,* vol. 41, pp. 807–814, 2012.

Stafford, Nancy. *"Who owns the data in an Electronic Health Record?",* Last Update: June 16th 2010, http://www.ehrinstitute.org/articles.lib/items/who-owns-the-data-in

Alwan, Majd, "Passive In-Home Health and Wellness Monitoring: Overview, Value and Examples," presented at the 31st Annual International Conference of the IEEE EMBS, Minneapolis, Minnesota, USA, 2009.

Atallah, Louis, Omer Aziz, Edward Gray, Benny Lo, and Guang-Zhong Yang, "An Ear-Worn Sensor for the Detection of Gait Impairment After Abdominal Surgery," *Surgical Innovation,* vol. 20, (1), pp. 86–94, 2013.

Taylor, M., R. Goubran, and F. Knoefel, "Patient standing stability measurements using pressure sensitive floor sensors," in *Instrumentation and Measurement Technology Conference (I2MTC), 2012 IEEE International*, 2012, pp. 1275–1279.

Pouliot, M., V. Joshi, J. Chauvin, R. Goubran, and F. Knoefel, "Differentiating assisted and unassisted bed exits using ultrasonic sensor," in *Instrumentation and Measurement Technology Conference (I2MTC), 2012 IEEE International*, 2012, pp. 1104–1108.

Patel, Shyamal, Hyung Park, Paolo Bonato, Leighton Chan, and Mary Rodgers, "A review of wearable sensors and systems with application in rehabilitation," *Journal of NeuroEngineering and Rehabilitation*, vol. 9, (21), 2012.

Smith, Abbie. "*Telefónica launches tele-rehabilitation solution*", Last Update: 20 February, 2012, http://www.healthcareglobal.com/healthcare_technology/telefonica-launches-tele-rehabilitation-solution

MotionHealth. "SmartStep", http://www.motionhealth.com/webpage/1002829/1000572, 2013.

Carlo, Antonio Di, "Human and economic burden of stroke," *Age and Ageing*, vol. 38, (1), pp. 4–5, 2009.

Centers for Disease Control and Prevention. "Stroke", http://www.cdc.gov/stroke/facts.htm, 2013.

Chee Kian, Lim, I. Ming Chen, Luo Zhiqiang, and Yeo Song Huat, "A low cost wearable wireless sensing system for upper limb home rehabilitation," in *Robotics Automation and Mechatronics (RAM), 2010 IEEE Conference on*, 2010, pp. 1–8.

Bin Ambar, R., H. Bin Mhd Poad, A. M. Bin Mohd Ali, M. S. Bin Ahmad, and M. Mahadi bin Abdul Jamil, "Multi-sensor arm rehabilitation monitoring device," in *Biomedical Engineering (ICoBE), 2012 International Conference on*, 2012, pp. 424–429.

Joo, Loh Yong, *et al.*, "A feasibility study using interactive commercial off-the-shelf computer gaming in upper limb rehabilitation in patients after stroke," *Journal of Rehabilitation Medicine*, vol. 42, (5), pp. 437–441, 2010.

Fitchard, Kevin. "*Qualcomm, Verizon promote healthier living without wires*", Last Update: 5th December, 2011, http://gigaom.com/2011/12/05/qualcomm-verizon-promote-healthier-living-without-wires/

Pray, W. Steven. 2010, The Value of Nonprescription Home Test Kits. *US Pharmacist 35(4)*, 3-8. Available: http://www.uspharmacist.com/content/s/121/c/20198/

NHS Choices. "Warning about self-test health kits", http://www.nhs.uk/news/2011/03March/Pages/warning-on-self-test-health-kits.aspx, 2011.

Carrell, Rachel. "*It's Time to Allow Home Testing Kit for HIV in the UK*", Last Update: 26th November, 2012, http://www.huffingtonpost.co.uk/rachel-carrell/hiv-home-testing-in-the-uk_b_2177532.html

BIO-RAD. "An Introduction to ELISA", http://www.abdserotec.com/resources/elisa-technical-resources-and-troubleshooting/an-introduction-to-elisa.html, 2013.

Jordan, William J., "Enzyme-Linked Iummonsorbent Assay," in *Medical BioMethods Handbook*, Walker, John M. and Ralph Rapley, Eds., Totowa, New Jersey, Humana Press Inc, 2005, pp. 419–427.

Chronolab A.G. Switzerland. "Urinanalysis by mean of test strips", http://www.chronolab.com/point-of-care/index.php?option=com_content&view=article&id=472&Itemid=78, 2009.

Kelleher, Kathleen. *Medical testing in your home - Forget the office visit. Home-health exams can save time and money, and give patients some control.*, Los Angeles Times, Los Angeles, 2009.

Wanner, Mark, "*Why doesn't a healthy person's genome sequence reveal more about health and disease*", Genetic and Your Health Blog, Last Update: December 7th 2012, http://community.jax.org/genetics_health/b/weblog/archive/2012/12/07/why-doesn-t-a-healthy-person-s-genome-sequence-reveal-more-about-health-and-disease.aspx

Harvard Medical School. (2010, September). Direct-to-consumer genetic testing kits. You send in a sample and get your results online. But is it worth the price? *Harvard Women's Health Watch 18(1)*, 1–3.

Xue, Yali, *et al.*, "Deleterious- and Disease-Allele Prevalence in Healthy Individuals: Insights from Current Predictions, Mutation Databases, and Population-Scale Resequencing," *American Journal of Human Genetics*, vol. 91, (6), pp. 1022–1032, 2012.

Kumar, Prashanth S., *et al.*, "Design and implementation of a bluetooth-based band-aid pulse rate sensor," 2011, pp. 79800P–79800P-7.

Whitney, Eric. "*High-Tech 'Band-Aids' Call Doctors*", Last Update: June 30th 2010, http://www.npr.org/templates/story/story.php?storyId=128877308

Montalbano, Elizabeth. *"Healthcare You Can Wear"*, Last Update: January 30th 2013, http://www.designnews.com/author.asp?dfpPParams=ind_184%2Cindustry_medical%2Caid_257818&dfpLayout=blog&doc_id=257818&page_number=1

Fangmin, Sun, *et al.*, "A design of a Band-Aid like health monitoring node for body sensor network," in *Measurement, Information and Control (MIC), 2012 International Conference on*, 2012, pp. 34–39.

Hoi-Jun, Yoo, J. Yoo, and Yan Long, "Wireless fabric patch sensors for wearable healthcare," in *Engineering in Medicine and Biology Society (EMBC), 2010 Annual International Conference of the IEEE*, 2010, pp. 5254–5257.

Centers for Medicare & Medicaid Services. "Readmissions Reduction Program", http://www.cms.gov/Medicare/Medicare-Fee-for-Service-Payment/AcuteInpatientPPS/Readmissions-Reduction-Program.html, 2013.

CHAPTER 10

■ ■ ■

Wellness, Fitness, and Lifestyle Sensing Applications

Physical fitness is not only one of the most important keys to a healthy body; it is the basis of dynamic and creative intellectual activity.

—John F. Kennedy, 35th President of the United States

Chapter 9 considered how sensors are playing an increasingly important role in health-related applications, such as chronic disease management. Medically, health is sometimes described as the absence of one or more of the "five Ds": death, disease, discomfort, disability, and dissatisfaction. Consequently, the focus is on determining whether disease is present and, when present, managing that condition (Edlin et al., 2000). Wellness takes a different perspective on health. It looks at the entire person, the manner in which they live their life, and lifestyle influences on their well-being. Wellness encompasses six distinct dimensions of well-being: emotional, intellectual, spiritual, occupational, social, and physical (Hettler, 1976). Collectively, these dimensions are often referred to as the *holistic* model of wellness. Sensors can be applied to quantify all dimensions of wellness to a certain extent. Of these dimensions, only physical wellness is monitored by individuals in the consumer domain. This chapter focuses on physical well-being and how sensing can be used to monitor and maintain physical wellness. Positively influencing physical well-being can also have significant benefits for other aspects of well-being, such as socializing with others during physical activities and helping to reduce emotional stress.

A variety of factors can influence personal wellness, including diet, exercise, poor habits, proactive self-care, and seeking medical intervention when appropriate (Edlin et al., 2014). As such, wellness is a dynamic process that is constantly changing based on the daily decisions we make about what we eat, drink, how much exercise we do, and so on. It is easy to lose track of wellness with the demands of busy, modern lifestyles. Technology is now having a positive effect on individuals by helping them to manage their physical wellness. This trend will continue to grow in the future as sensing and supporting technologies are seamlessly integrated into our daily lives. Discrete sensors and sensors integrated into smartphones are already enabling us to monitor our activity levels, fitness, performance levels, and calorie burn/consumption through smartphone apps and web portals. In a broader context, pervasive sensing in our homes and leisure areas will provide passive monitoring on a long-term basis of our physical activities, interactions with our environment, and other physiological, cognitive, and biochemical parameters of interest without activity restriction and behavior modification. The collected data can be used to notify us of immediate risk or to identify trends in parameters that are outside of normative ranges. Sensing sleep quality, in babies and adults, is a now a common application of pervasive sensing. The consumer does not actively track their sleep in real time but they need to be alerted immediately if sleep apnea is detected. Increasingly, we share this data and information about our activities via social media with friends and family. Doing so adds context to the data and supports continued engagement in physical activities through positive social reinforcement. Monitoring, supporting, and improving wellness through the use of sensor technologies will play an increasingly positive role in maintaining health and well-being.

Drivers and Barriers: Sports and Fitness Sensing

The sports and fitness sensing market has been primarily driven by body-worn sensors, which are often integrated or connected to discrete devices with global positioning system (GPS) receivers. The sports sensing market is expected to be worth circa $975 million by 2017 (PRWEB, 2013). Companies such as Apple, adidas, Nike, Motorola, Reebok, and Under Armour are now entering the growing sports and fitness wearables market. This market also includes sensors that can be attached to sports equipment, such as power meters for bikes to monitor the rider's performance and sensors embedded into textiles.

Drivers for Sports and Fitness Sensing

The use of sensing for sports and fitness applications is driven by a variety of factors, as shown in Figure 10-1. For example, people are becoming more aware of the role physical activity plays in maintaining their health. A variety of social and technology factors are now influencing and supporting engagement in physical and sports activities. The following sections examine some of the key factors in more detail.

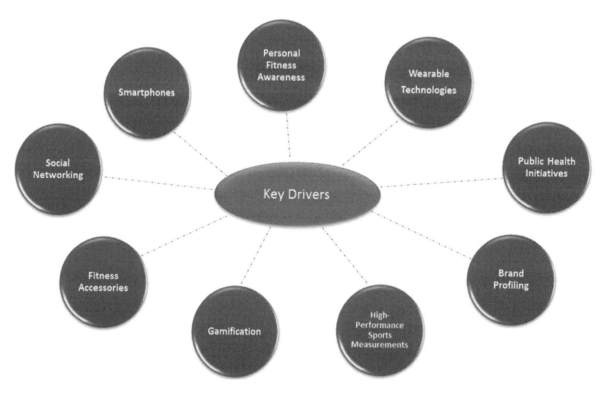

Figure 10-1. *Drivers for fitness sensing adoption*

> **Fitness awareness**: General interest and participation in fitness continues to grow. The increased availability of magazines that focus on generic fitness and specific sports, such as cycling, running, mountain biking, and triathlons, helps to raise awareness and interest. These publications, along with various web sites, are exposing people to information on what types of technologies are available and how to use and interpret fitness statistics.

Public health awareness initiatives: Public health awareness campaigns are making people more aware about the positive influence of sports activities. There is growing awareness among the public about the linkages between being physical inactive and health-related issues, such as obesity and obesity-related conditions, including diabetes and cancer. Activity monitors provide an easy way to track activity levels. Data from these devices can often be shared with peer groups through social networking to gain support and maintain motivation.

Smartphones: The proliferation of smartphones, especially among key fitness demographics, provides essentially a zero-cost sensing and software platform for basic fitness monitoring. This single form factor provides location via GPS, inertial sensing from the built-in accelerometer and gyroscope, mapping software, data analysis apps, large touchscreen display, music players, and connectivity via wireless (Bluetooth, Wi-Fi, ANT, and NFC) and mobile phone networks. From an app developer's perspective, smartphones provide both a development platform and a significant market for innovative apps that allow apps to be rapidly developed and shared with consumers. As a result, the consumer can avail of a large selection of apps for free or for a small one-off fee. As discussed in previous chapters, app developers do not have to be sensor experts, because the smartphone development environment abstracts the functional details of the underlying sensors. This is an advantage to nonsensor experts, but this abstraction can affect the accuracy of sensor measurements. For this reason, smartphones can also connect wirelessly to dedicated external fitness sensors for more accurate sensing.

Availability of wireless fitness accessories: The availability of wireless fitness accessories, such as heart rate monitors (HRMs), step counters, cadence sensors, and power meters, allows consumers to add fitness functionality to their existing smartphones and/or outdoor GPS handhelds. These accessories communicate over standard interfaces, including ANT, Bluetooth, Wi-Fi, and near field communications (NFC) and provide APIs that smartphone developers can use to capture data from the accessories. This removes the need to purchase expensive dedicated fitness data loggers, such as fitness watches. The availability and popularity of fitness accessories is expected to increase as interoperability standards, particularly Bluetooth Smart (a Bluetooth low-energy protocol)(Bluetooth SIG, 2013), are adopted by both smartphone and accessory manufacturers.

Wearable technologies and intelligent textiles: The use of wearable technologies, such as the Fitbit, is becoming increasingly common among the general public. Where once wearing an obvious sensing device, such as a Holter monitor or personal alarm, was seen as a "badge of dependence" or a sign of illness, wearable sensors are now fashion items and "a badge of honor" that indicates the user is actively interested in maintaining their wellness. The form factor of wearables are becoming increasingly small, to the point that they are seamlessly integrating into our normal clothing, such as a sports bra or vest, and lives. The cost of these devices, such as smart wristwear devices like the Nike+ Fuelband, is falling and becoming more accessible to the casual fitness or wellness enthusiast.

High-performance sports: Professional sports teams and athletes are continually seeking methods to gain a competitive advantage over their opposition. The data analytics team and sports scientist team are becoming as important as a coach in the sporting domain. Sports scientists provide insight into the athlete's fitness and well-being and continually monitor the athlete's parameters to optimize their training, nutrition, and rest requirements. Sports "stats" such as team formations, recent results, and real-time status are now an integral part of the television sports viewing experience. Professional sports teams analyze all aspects of their own performance, their opposition's performance, and even the referee's performance to identify weakness, which they can exploit to their own advantage, and strengths, which they must plan to counteract. For example, a study in New Zealand used GPS technology in combination with heart rate to assess the accuracy of the decision-making experience of soccer referees (Mascarenhas et al., 2009).

Brand profiling: Fitness sensing technologies are becoming increasingly visible because of the entry of high-profile brands such as Nike and adidas to the fitness sensing market. These manufacturers have partnered with existing fitness technology manufacturers, such as Polar and Garmin. These partnerships have raised the profile of existing technologies and are giving this previously niche market a desirable lifestyle choice position. High-profile technology brands, including Apple, Motorola, and mobile operators, are also actively monitoring this market for new service opportunities. The presence of these high-profile companies is a clear indication that these companies view significant potential for a technology enabled fitness market.

Social networking: Another important driver of fitness applications is the integration of a social networking dimension. Users can upload their data from integrated or external fitness sensors to the Web/Cloud and share their fitness statistics online with their families, friends, and peer groups. It is also possible to follow each other's activities in real time using Internet-enabled devices. The ability to track and share fitness data online can enable positive reinforcement by peer groups, which encourages people to remain engaged in their physical activity and set new goals. Like magazines, online fitness communities provide a valuable channel for discussing and making people aware about personal fitness sensor technologies and applications. For example, the RunKeeper app allows runners to track their distance, speed, and pace on their smartphone. In addition, it utilizes social networking to allow runners to stay in touch with friends on Facebook, Twitter, Google, and other sites by adding them to their Street Team. The Street Team features enables users to share details of their workouts, including course maps, topography details, and various statistics such as distance covered, pace, and so on (`www.RunKeeper.com`).

Gamification of fitness data: Building on the social networking angle of fitness data sharing, gaming features are becoming a driver for the adoption of fitness technologies. Gaming also allows like-minded users to interact, compare, and compete. Such techniques will be used to encourage usage and create "stickiness" for applications. For example, the "tag it" feature in Nike's iPhone running tracker app enables users to tag each other, bringing multiple friends to a game of tag. Whoever starts the game decides whether the game is based on the distance run, time of run, or being the last to run. Another example of this type of approach is used by the Basis B1 fitness tracker, which monitors heart rate, perspiration, steps taken, and skin temperature. The data is transmitted to a web application that provides analysis of your daily patterns and encourages you to adapt your existing habits or to develop new healthy ones by gamifying your lifestyle (`www.mybasis.com`).

Barriers to Sports and Fitness Sensing

Despite recent advances in the adoption and utilization of technologies for fitness applications, a number of barriers remain in place. These include limitations in smartphone form factors, fitness apps, proprietary wireless protocols, and costs. The following sections now examine some of the key limiting factors in more detail.

App selection: The App Store and Google Play store contain thousands of fitness monitoring and education apps. The most common app categories are body mass index (BMI) and calorie calculators, diet guides, exercise guides, and sport tracking apps. Like health apps, the sheer number and diversity of such apps means that selection of a relevant and high quality app can be a frustrating challenge, unless you use an app designed by the manufacturer of a specific sensor. As discussed in Chapter 6, the quality and accuracy of information provided by fitness apps is generally not regulated, and misleading information may be provided by these apps. It is therefore essential to exercise caution when following advice provided by such apps and to consult with a "gold standard" reference, such as a health/fitness professional or a professional-grade sensor device if you suspect information or data from the app is inaccurate or worrying.

Smartphone design: Although ideal for the casual fitness users who simply want to track time and estimate distance, smartphones may not be appropriate as a fitness sensing device for serious outdoor and fitness users. Most smartphones lack the necessary ruggedization, such as toughened enclosures, waterproofing, and impact protection, required by serious fitness users. Smartphone form factors are relatively large for fitness and running applications and can actually impact performance. GPS is still a relatively new and evolving sensor on mobile devices. GPS performance may not be optimal for fitness applications, especially when compared to dedicated devices. Although battery technology is continually improving, the battery life of a smartphone may not be sufficient for continuous capture of sensors with high power requirements (for example, GPS) and analysis for longer endurance events such as mountaineering.

Proprietary wireless connectivity protocols: Until recently, discrete fitness sensing devices from the major device vendors were based on the proprietary ANT personal wireless protocol. Penetration of the protocol was high among device vendors because it encouraged people to remain with the same vendor in order to exploit their previous investments in sensing devices and aggregators. Nevertheless, apart from a couple of niche offerings, there was almost no adoption of this protocol in mobile phones. Standardization of wireless device communications is now underway with the rollout and adoption of the Bluetooth Smart standard; however, Bluetooth Smart will take a number of years to reach critical mass.

Device costs: The cost of dedicated sensors, particularly those with integrated GPS tracking, remains relatively high. This high cost limits their market potential to professional or serious fitness enthusiasts. However, new entrants into the market and the inclusion of sensors in smartphones are expected to decrease device costs.

Sports and Fitness Applications

It has been estimated by ON World that by 2017 the annual market for mobile sensing health and fitness applications will be in the region of 500 million units (PRWEB, 2013). Large retailers such as Best Buy and Target are providing more and more shelf space to these types of devices to meet the growth in popularity. Sensors can be found in a variety of form factors to support different usage patterns:

Sensors integrated into sports equipment: Fitness sensors are commonly integrated into gym equipment to monitor biomechanical parameters, such as force, torque, cadence, and so on, or physiological parameters, such as heart rate, respiration rate, and more.

Sensors attached to sports equipment: This method of sensing is growing in popularity, particularly as the size of sensor units decreases. Data from these sensors are typically used to analyze the mechanics of performance and to provide insights into how a particular style is positively or negatively impacting performance level.

Personal body-worn sensors: This is probably the most common method of sensing fitness and wellness. Fitness wearables typically capture physiological and kinematic datasets from small lightweight sensors worn on the body during training and everyday living.

Wearable fitness sensors were initially discrete sensors, such as simple pedometers. But these devices are now being replaced by "smart devices" that provide both local computational capabilities and remote connectivity to another device. These devices include both smartphones and sports watches (for example, the Polar sport watch with integrated GPS tracking and heart rate monitoring, at www.polar.com). Data from these sensor devices can be combined with other information sources to create a holistic picture of an individual training session and longer-term trends. The data may also be incorporated into a web-based portal for additional processing, sharing among family and friends, or for comparative purposes among peer groups.

Companies operating in the wearable fitness sensor market include specialist companies that focus exclusively on fitness and wellness devices such as Polar and Fitbit; large sportswear companies like Nike and adidas; and new companies such as Jawbone that develop fitness and wellness peripherals. Wearable sensors come in a variety of form factors, including armbands, wristbands, clip-ons for clothing, and sensors directly integrated into footwear and clothing.

Supporting Wireless Technologies

A key capability of "smart" fitness sensors is their ability to communicate with external devices, such as smartphones. Although some devices feature wired USB connections, the majority support wireless connectivity. Wireless connectivity between sensors and a master device like a smartphone, is a key requirement to avoid movement restrictions during activities. A variety of proprietary protocols have been utilized by vendors, including Polar's proprietary W.I.N.D. wireless protocol, ANT from Garmin's acquisition of Dynastream, Simpliciti from TI, BodyLAN from FitLinxx, and BlueRobin from BM innovations.

Of the proprietary protocols, ANT has the greatest penetration in the fitness sensors market. As outlined in Chapter 3, ANT is a low-cost, low data rate, ultra-low power protocol designed to work on the same batteries for months or years. It is primarily used for heart rate monitors, speed/cadence sensors, and power meters to provide connectivity to devices such as fitness watches. It can also be found in fitness equipment. To support interoperability between devices that use the ANT protocol, the ANT+ standard has been created. ANT+ defines network parameters and the data content for ANT-based communications. This allows ANT-based devices from different manufactures to communicate with others and exchange data. ANT has been estimated that there is over 60 million ANT+ sport, fitness and health devices currently available (www.thisisant.com).

Bluetooth (BT) has made limited inroads into the fitness sensor domain because of its relatively high power requirements. Nevertheless, Bluetooth low energy (BLE) or Bluetooth Smart—a low-cost, low-power, low data rate extension of regular Bluetooth—is predicted to be widely adopted by the market because it has comparable power consumption performance to ANT. Power consumption of Bluetooth Smart is about one-tenth that of Bluetooth, which enables a standard button cell battery to power devices for more than a year. A comparison of ANT and BLE is shown in Table 10-1. IMS Research has estimated that by 2016 the penetration rate of Bluetooth Smart in sports and fitness devices will overtake that of ANT with around 45 percent of devices featuring Bluetooth Smart (IMS Research, 2012).

Table 10-1. *Comparison of Bluetooth Smart and ANT Specifications*

Specification	Bluetooth Smart	ANT
Frequency range	2.4GHz to 2.483GHz	2.4GHz to 2.483GHz
Network standard	IEEE 802.15.1	Proprietary
Software stack	128–256KB	16KB
Security	128-bit AES	128-bit AES
Data rate	1Mps	1Mps
Power consumption	15mA Rx and Tx	15mA Tx and 17mA Rx
Range (free field)	100m (outdoor)	100m (outdoor)
Topology	Simple star topology only	Complex topologies
Network type	WPAN	WPAN

Fitness Sensing

Wireless sensors allow smartphones or bespoke aggregators to capture and process sensor data into parameters of interest, such as speed, cycling cadence, and heart rate. In most fitness applications, sensors cannot be integrated into the master device, because they have to be close to the source of the signal, such as the heart, the cycle wheel, or the foot. In cases where sensors are integrated into the master device, the quality of the resulting data depends on the location of the master device relative to the parameter to be sensed. This is particularly true for any kinematic-related parameter captured. For example, integrated accelerometers often provide poor data quality because of the counter movements of the arms holding the device. Discrete kinematic sensors will continue to provide superior sensor data quality for the foreseeable future.

The ability to wirelessly connect sensors and master devices allows the fitness enthusiast to track their performance in real-time. Friends, peers, and coaches can also track real-time sensor data online, provided the master device has Internet connectivity and the data owner is willing to share the data. From a form-factor perspective, the screen size requirements for the master device are somewhat activity specific. "Black box" sensors, such as bicycle power meters and heart rate monitors, have no screen and therefore depend on a master device to visualize the data in real time. Large screens are advantageous for activities such as cycling, while a small smartwatch screen may be desirable for activities such as running to minimize any impact on the wearer. For many users, the ability to interrogate the data beyond real-time information display is an important requirement. Data can be viewed offline in a number of ways, such as visualizing basic summary data directly on the master device or uploading the data to a tablet/PC or the Internet for complex analysis and visualization. It is important to note that the quality of the supporting software tools is becoming as important to the user who wants to improve and analyze their performance as the quality of the device itself. Sharing fitness data and statistics with friends as well as adding a competitive element to fitness activities can be closely tied to the rising popularity of social networking. Competing with a friend or peer group or exchanging statistics can make fitness a more enjoyable activity and helps maintain engagement over a longer period of time. Sharing data can also enable a degree of flexibility as people move to new locations for varying amounts of time. It allows them to connect with like-minded individuals with similar motivations, independent of geographical location. Converged applications are central to engaging new users by providing them with a real-time dimension, which is important for the instant gratification expected by the current tech-savvy generation. In addition, longitudinal presentation of data with sharing capabilities provides both the motivational and social elements for individuals who live online. Many fitness solutions include interfaces with multimedia features that allow users to listen to their preferred music or take geotagged photos during fitness activities to share with others.

A number of wearable form factors have emerged that provide real-time physiological and/or biomechanical fitness monitoring. Fitness accessories, targeted at consumers, are typically smartphone enabled to reduce the total cost of the system and leverage the connectivity, processing power, and display capabilities of the smartphone. The most common form factors are as follows:

> **Chest straps**: This form factor is placed close to the chest to measure cardiac parameters, including heart rate and R-R interval. Many chest straps also feature inertial sensors to calculate speed, distance, and body position. Associated smartphone apps or wearable display devices, such as smartwatches, provide both real-time and summary data. A fitness enthusiast can monitor in real-time their pace and the cardiac zone that they are training in and can adjust their training intensity accordingly. Chest straps are also used to view summary data after a training session to analyze training intensity, calories burned, and recovery time. In professional team sports, sports scientists can monitor the cardiac parameters of individuals in real time during training sessions by assigning each player a chest strap. A sports scientist can analyze the data after the training session to identify whether any team members are overtraining and adjust their training to prevent injury. In the consumer domain, companies such as Zephyr are providing SDKs with their fitness accessories to allow them to be integrated into third-party applications. For example, the Zephyr BioHarness^T chest strap (Zephyr, 2013) can be interfaced with a number of free and paid third-party fitness apps, including Endomondo (www.endomondo.com) and Fit4Life (www.fit4life.com).

Wristbands: The wristband form factor is portable and quick to access. The simple digital wristwatch with timer functionality was one of the first mainstream consumer fitness accessories. Advances in sensor, processor, and battery technologies have allowed device manufacturers to embed much more intelligence in the wristband form factor. As a result, two new device types, sports watches and smartwatches, have emerged in recent years. Sport watches, such as the Polar RC3 GPS, combine built-in sensing and may also have the ability to communicate with external accessories, such as a chest strap. All processing is performed on the sports watch, and the results are presented to the user on the sports watch's display. Data from the sports watch can often be connected to a tablet/PC or smartphone for long-term data storage and analysis. Smartwatches, such as the Pebble (getpebble.com), allow the fitness enthusiast to leverage the processing power of a smartphone without the challenges of wearing and reading the smartphone device during a training session. The smartphone has the processing, storage, and battery capabilities to integrate data from multiple integrated and body-worn sensors. The smartwatch simply displays the relevant summary data to the user in a manner that can be quickly and easily read by the athlete.

Footpods and insoles: Accelerometer and/or gyroscope-based footpods are attached to running shoes to directly measure pace, speed, and distance from the motion of the foot. These small, lightweight devices are paired to a sports watch or smartphone device, which process the data from the pod. The Nike+ iPod sensor is one of the most popular foot pod devices. It is inserted into the sole of Nike+ running shoes or attached to the laces of incompatible running shoes using a shoe pod holder. Data from the Nike+ sensor is streamed to an iPhone or Nike+ SportWatch GPS. Pressure sensitive insoles were initially only used by podiatrists in a clinical setting to dynamically measure interaction between foot and footwear. This data was applied to identify asymmetry in foot placement and to create corrective orthodontics for health and sporting purposes. Insoles are becoming increasingly common outside of the clinical setting to monitor sporting performance. Nike+ basketball shoes have pressure sensors built into the sole of the shoe. That data can be combined with accelerometer data to calculate movement-related parameters such as vertical jump height (Nike, 2012).

Sensor patches: Small form factor sensors can be attached to the body adhesively (like Band-Aids) and can transmit data wirelessly to a smartphone app. For example, Somaxis MyoLink is a sensor patch, which measures muscle energy output. It can measure how warmed up your leg muscles are as you start to run and provide data on the intensity of the workout, fatigue levels, endurance, and recovery level. Muscle symmetry can be measured by using a MyoFit sensor on each leg. Identification of asymmetry can be an early indication of potential injury onset (Davies, 2012). In professional sport, a Slovenian company called TMG-BMC uses tensiomyography (TMG) to diagnose muscle imbalances associated with athletic injuries. The sensor is designed to measure the muscle contractions, which are induced artificially with an electro stimulator. As the muscle enlarges, a displacement sensor in contact with the skin measures the radial enlargement of the muscle. Results are presented as time/displacement curves. This technology has been used by Olympic sprinters and the FC Barcelona soccer team (TMG-BMC, 2013). ECG/EKG sensor patches that provide continuous heart rate measurements are becoming increasingly popular and may soon replace chest strap devices in the fitness domain. Like chest strap devices, EKG/ECG sensor patches, such as the Somaxis MyoBeat and the Zepher BioPatch, are typically paired with a smartphone and provide continuous heart rate measurements.

Portable devices: An emerging trend is the development of miniature versions of bulky lab equipment that can be used by individuals outside the confines of the lab. For example, this approach has been used by the Breezing Company, an Arizona State spin-off, to develop an innovative portable metabolism tracker, shown in Figure 10-2. The sensor provides accurate estimates of energy expenditure by using the well-established indirect calorimetry technique. The technique, frequently used in sports clinics, measures carbon dioxide production and oxygen consumption during rest and steady-state exercise. The traditional approach is to use a metabolic cart with bulky and expensive equipment resulting in limited mobility and access. The small form factor of Breezing's sensor means it can be easily carried by athletes during training (Coxworth, 2013). Apart from measuring metabolism, the sensor also determines respiratory quotient (RQ), which is the ratio of produced carbon dioxide to consumed oxygen. It can also identify the type of "energy source" the body uses, whether someone is burning carbohydrates, fats, or a mix of both. Data from the sensor is sent via Bluetooth to either an Android or iOS device, where users can view and track their metabolism history, RQ, and weight (either via wireless scale or manual input). It also has an intelligent algorithm to support users in defining their fitness or weight loss plan. A similar indirect calorimetry device called the BodyGEM RMR is available from Microlife. It produces what the company calls a Metabolic Fingerprint (BodyGem, 2013). The device measures resting metabolic rate and is designed for use in fitness programs that target weight loss.

Figure 10-2. *Breezing, a metabolism tracker device, is battery-operated and syncs with a smartphone. It includes an application used as user interface (image used with permission from Breezing Company)*

The use of sensors for sports and fitness applications continues to evolve. Although many of the currently available products have an acceptable performance and form factor for amateurs, they may be less acceptable to elite athletes and sports scientists. In the professional sports arena, specialized sensing capabilities are used to provide highly accurate measurement of specific physiological and metabolic parameters, which cannot be supplied by general consumer sensing devices. But as the capabilities of low-cost body-worn sensors continue to improve, the need for more expensive proprietary solutions will reduce. Performance sensing can often result in what is known as the *observer effect*, where the athlete's awareness of the sensor impacts their performance. The goal for these users is to make the sensors undetectable. Ideally, the sensors should not result in any perceived inertia, and the attachment mechanism should not result in any discernible discomfort (Harle et al., 2012). As fabrication techniques evolve, the reduction in the size of sensors will address some of these issues. Another part of the solution is to integrate sensors directly into sportswear clothing; which is discussed in the next section.

Clothing

The integration of sensors into clothing is driven by a growing convergence between electronics and new forms of fibers and textiles. Clothing provides a natural platform for human subject monitoring during exercise and sporting activities. More recently, intelligent or smart materials that sense and respond to environmental stimuli or that monitor the physiological well-being of the wearer have emerged. This form of sensing is often referred to as *smart clothing* or a *smart clothing system* (Kaur, 2012). These systems can provide insights to vital signs, movement, biopotential, and ambient environment (Jeong et al., 2013). The use of sensors in clothing offers a number of advantages including making sensors invisible to external observers. Using carefully designed clothing as the mechanism to hold the sensors on the body can address tricky issues related to sensor placement and orientation. A well-fitted smart clothing sensor can also greatly simplify data analysis by reducing unwanted motion artifact in the measured signal. Wired connects between sensors and support electronics can be integrated into the fabric of the clothing, which potentially can improve the reliability of communications over wireless sensors.

Various products ranging from T-shirts, tank tops, and even women's sport bras with heart-sensing capabilities from companies such as adidas and Textronics have been demonstrated and are commercially available (Textronics, 2013, Eric, 2012). Emerging products and prototypes provide full end-to-end connectivity based on smartphone compatibility. The availability of Bluetooth Smart could also drive the popularity of smart clothing for sports-related applications. There are several smart clothing applications, including the following:

- **Detection of physical impact**: Physical impacts during contact sports, particularly head impacts, have been an area of concern for many years. Sportswear manufacturer Reebok and device manufacturer mc10 developed the CheckLight head impact indicator, targeted toward American football players. The concept behind the product is to give a visible indicator when a player has taken a dangerous blow to the head. The sensor is worn by the player in a special skullcap. The sensor, in the form of a strip, provides information on directional and rotational acceleration and impact location and duration. Data fed into a microcontroller is processed using a proprietary algorithm to determine the severity of the impact. The output of the algorithm is used to light one of two LEDs in the sensor module. One flashes yellow after moderate impacts, and the other flashes red to indicate a severe blow (Gorman, 2013).

- **Biosignal monitoring**: More than half of the world's heart rate belts are created by Finnish company Clothing+. These textile transmitter belts are found in products created by adidas+, Garmin, and Philips. Researchers at Northeastern University have developed a prototype electromyography (EMG)-based, sensor-based shirt that tracks the electrical activity of muscles during workouts. Data is streamed in real-time to an Android smartphone that reports heart rate and repetition countdown. Data is also sent to a web-based portal for historical data analysis (Belezina, 2012).

- **Biomechanical monitoring**: The Danish company Danfoss PolyPower has developed sensors based on dielectric electroactive polymer (DEAP) technology. As the material stretches, its thickness changes, resulting in a measurable change in capacitance. This change in capacitance can be used to measure biomechanical changes in the body such as joint angles, range of motion, and shoulder alignment. The elastic material's thin, low-profile form factor makes it possible to integrate into clothing, muscle wraps, protective gear, and other sportswear. PolyPower has demonstrated a wireless version of the sensors based on Bluetooth Smart, which can connect to mobile devices. The prototypes also feature integrated inertial sensors (gyroscope, accelerometer, and magnetometer). PolyPower has also demonstrated a prototype golf training sleeve based on the sensing material. In this application, the wireless sensor system is used to measure the angle of the elbow and metrics of the swing. The sensor stretches with elbow movement, measuring changes in joint angle; this data is coupled with data from additional body-worn inertial sensors (acceleration, force, and so on). The combined datasets are sent wirelessly to an iOS device, which then provides feedback, informing the golfer how to improve their swing (Weiss, 2013).

- **Biofeedback**: The Move project is focused on producing clothing with embedded sensors as part of a platform that can help people improve their Pilates technique. The Move project platform consists of a garment with four stretch and bend sensors (*resistance* decreases when bent or flexed in either direction) located in the front, back, and sides, as shown in Figure 10-3(a). The mobile app with cloud service is shown in Figure 10-3(b). The sensors track the specific positioning of back and abdominal muscles. The mobile app assesses whether the position is correct. Real-time haptic feedback is provided through haptic components located in the hips and shoulders to correct inaccurate movements. The cloud service provides historical tracking of performance and a library that can be used to store new custom moves or to access predefined moves (Krakauer, 2012).

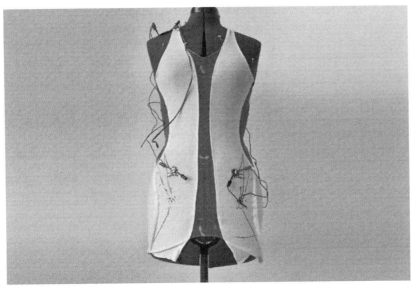

(Credit: fashion photographer Leo Lam)

Figure 10-3(a). *Prototype version of the MOVE sensing garment (image used with permission from* electricfoxy.com*)*

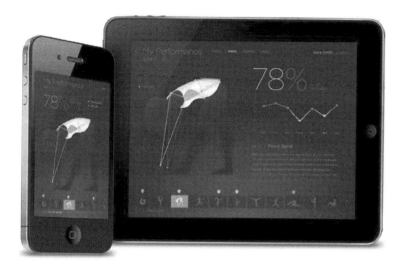

Figure 10-3(b). *MOVE user interface (image used with permission from* `electricfoxy.com`*)*

- ***Environmental monitoring***: Smart clothing is also attracting interest in the outdoor sporting market and in other recreational activities. Sensors and actuators can be used to change response to environmental conditions or other local external stimuli (Bye, 2010). Many of the sensing technologies emerging in this new category have military origins. For example Brenig has embedded wearable technologies in polar-expedition lines of clothing to create a sleeve compass.

The symbiosis of sensors, clothing, and wearable computing and mobile devices will continue to evolve in terms of capabilities, robustness, and applications. From a sensing perspective, applications will continue to be a mixture of direct/near and indirect skin contact. Sensors will be enclosed in layers of fabric or integrated into the fabric itself using sensing modalities such as piezo-resistive yarns, capacitive materials, and optical fibers. The role of fashion will also have an important influence. There is a growing interest in the confluence of fashion and technology in the form of fashion-forward wearables. This will be an area of rapid and exciting innovation over the coming years (Higginbotham, 2013, Darmour, 2013).

Sports Equipment Sensing

The integration of sensors and ICT technologies into sports equipment provides a platform to deliver new insights into athletic performance and the athlete's interaction with sports equipment. Sensors can be attached or integrated into the sports equipment or can be worn by the athlete as they use the equipment. One of the key advantages with the use of modern wireless sensing is that it now frees the athlete from the confines of the laboratory and allows data to be captured in conditions closer to competition settings. The combination of equipment-specific sensing with standard physiological and kinematic sensing can provide a rich multisensor dataset. This dataset can reveal nonobvious relationships between parameters and give a more informed picture of performance improvements and areas to target for further improvement.

Cycling

Sensing requirements for cycling are similar to general-purpose fitness sensing: tracking speed/distance, elevation, energy expenditure (calories), and heart rate. In sports such as cycling, which use some form of equipment, there is an opportunity to capture additional equipment-specific parameters. Two parameters highly useful in cycling are cadence and power. Cadence sensors generally use magnetic-based technology. A magnet is fitted to one of the rear wheel spokes, and a receiver is fitted to the frame of the bike. The receiver detects each revolution of the magnet and streams data from the receiver to a display fitted to the handle bars. The display allows the cyclist to maintain a target cadence normally in the 95 revolutions per minute range (Maker, 2011).

A more recent development in the mainstream sports cycling market has been the availability of power meters (Cycling Weekly, 2013). Digital display units mounted on the bike's handlebars can provide real-time information on a variety of power metrics, such as instantaneous, maximum, and average power. These displays can also connect to other wireless sensors, such as heart rate monitors, to provide a multisensor view of performance. Power meters are useful for providing an objective measurement of the cyclist's real output and are regarded as a better metric of training progress than pure physiological measurements, such as a heart rate. Power meters are available from a variety of manufacturers including Polar, Garmin, Quarq, SRM, and Power2Max. These sensors can be either placed on, or integrated into the crank of the bike or onto the wheel hub. Power meters are normally based on a combination of strain gauges and accelerometers. Strain gauges measure torque applied, and accelerometers measure velocity. This data is combined to calculate power. Power sensors cost in the region of $2,000 to $3,000. Cheaper alternatives include external magnetic sensors mounted on the crank, sensing chain tension and chain speed, or measuring wind speed using a handle-mounted sensor. Each of these approaches has its respective limitations and is less accurate in comparison to strain gauges.

An Irish company, Brim Brothers, has developed an innovative approach to measuring power. Its prototype data collection pod, weighing just 18 grams, clips to the instep of a shoe, as shown in Figure 10-4(a). The pod includes motion sensors to measure the rotational position and velocity of the pedal and the crank and to calculate cadence. As a result, no magnets are required to detect cadence. The motion sensors also have the potential to provide detailed continuous information about a rider's pedaling style and efficiency on the road. This capability can currently be achieved only with static bikes in research laboratories. Power measurements are collected from proprietary sensors based on piezoceramics. This type of sensor is more robust and less temperature sensitive in comparison to strain gauges. They measure force without the need for a mechanical part to bend, and therefore the whole force measurement system can be made extremely small. The force sensors are embedded in the cleat rather than being attached to the cleat, as shown in Figure 10-4(b). That means that there is no increase in cleat size or stack height, and the system is bike independent (Brim-Brothers, 2013).

Figure 10-4. *(a) Data collection pod, (b) strain gauge sensors attached to cleat (image used with permission from Brim Brothers)*

Golf

Because of the technical nature of the sport, golf has a long history of players utilizing various aids and mechanical devices to improve either their swing or their putting accuracy. Golfers are also generally characterized as having higher purchasing power to invest in such aids. Professional golf coaches use IR optical sensing, video analysis, sonic sensing, and Doppler radar as aids in helping to improve a player's golf swing. More recently, the use of inertial sensors has emerged in golf. The sensors can be attached to the golf club, hand, or arm. Some examples include the following:

- The Golfsense product utilizes four MEMS-based inertial sensors, integrated into a small unit. The unit weighs 17 grams and is attached to the back of a golf glove, as shown in Figure 10-5. Data from the sensor unit is streamed via Bluetooth to either an iOS or Android mobile device for analysis and display. Parameters such as club speed, club position, swing tempo, and swing path are calculated and displayed (GolfSense, 2013). A key advantage of this approach is its flexibility. It can be used anywhere and without assistance. An alternative approach to swing sensing is to attach the sensor directly to the shaft of the golf club as used by products such as SwingSmart (www.swingsmart.com) and SwingTIP (www.swingtip.com) and Swingbyte (www.swingbyte.com). These products also use wireless transmission of data to a mobile device for analysis.

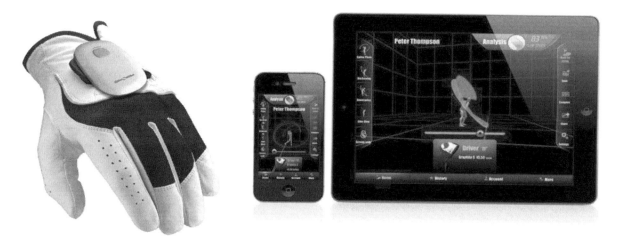

Figure 10-5. *The GolfSense inertial sensor for golf swing analysis (image used with permission from Golfsense)*

- Although the majority of sensor-related products are for golf swing analysis, 3Bays has developed an innovative sensor product called 3BaysGSA Putt. The device, which weighs less than 10 grams, is based on 9-axis inertial sensing. The device attaches to the end of a putter and streams data via Bluetooth to an iOS mobile device. The 3BayGSA PUTT app provides a variety of metrics including face angle at impact, backswing time, downswing time, and so on (3BaysGSA, 2013).

In January 2006, the use of range-finding devices (GPS and laser) were sanctioned for use in competition by the USGA (United States Golf Association) and the R&A (Royal and Ancient – Golf Club of St Andrews), subject to the approval of the local competition committee. Laser range finders can measure the distance to any object on the golf course that can reflect light, including trees, hills, bunkers, and so forth. They can also be used to determine distance to players who are putting on the green ahead to obtain an accurate measurement of distance to the pin. GPS units are used to display distances to preselected points on the course. Many devices can provide a color aerial view of the hole, which can be useful in determining the most appropriate approach shot. Other products, such as the Garmin Approach 1, provide simple distance from the green information in a wristwatch form factor. Some of the more advanced devices provide a virtual fly-over of the entire hole. GPS systems are generally smaller than laser devices, which require sophisticated optics to measure distance.

Sensing in Other Sports

Sensors are now being adopted in a variety of other mainstream and niche sports, particularly those that have a technical element to them or use some sporting equipment. Doppler radar sensors, such as those from Sports Sensors, are used in sports such as archery, baseball, and tennis (Sports Sensors, 2013). These sensors provide real-time velocity feedback, which can be used to improve performance. The sensor may be attached directly to sports equipment, for archery and baseball, or used in a noncontact mode in the case of tennis or golf. The data can be used to improve speed, accuracy, and consistency. In activities, such as mountain climbing, paragliding, hang gliding, and hill walking, barometric pressure sensors are used to determine altitude. They are commonly combined with GPS units or into a variometer (measures rate of descent or climb) for paragliding use. For mountaineering applications, the sensors can be incorporated into wristwatch form factors, such as the Casio PROTREK watch. Apart from altitude data, changes in barometric pressure can be used to indicate impending changes in weather conditions. However, the accuracy of these sensors can vary because of barometric drift and temperature, which may cause large errors in altimeter measurements.

In swimming, the Australian Institute of Sports has used sensors in its elite training program to track the number of laps, the time taken, the stroke rate, and the type of stroke for each lap. This has allowed coaches to replace written training diaries with web-based data portals that are accessible anywhere and at any time (Chaganti et al., 2011). AvidaMetric produces a system that comprises body-worn wireless sensors attached to the wrists, ankles, and head. Data is streamed to a pool-side laptop that can process the data from up to 100 swimmers at a time (Zarda, 2010). Sensors have also been used to measure performance parameters such as approach time, contact time glide, kick time, and stoke time during a swimmer's tumble turn with comparable accuracy to that achieved using digital video analysis (Sage et al., 2012). The system has been adopted by a number swimming programs in U.S. universities. Sensors are also used in martial arts to measure speed and force of impact during a striking motion (Cowie et al., 2008).

Sports and Fitness Statistics

The granularity and sophistication of fitness data analysis and presentation depends on the type of end user. An amateur generally has less complex requirements compared to a professional athlete and coach, who often require a myriad of physiological and biomechanical parameters. As our data literacy improves and we become more attuned data consumers, the gap between the expectations of the amateurs and professionals is diminishing, particularly among more committed amateurs. In fact, access to unlimited amounts of data and information has become almost a basic expectation. As already mentioned, social media is driving the sophistication of fitness statistics as knowledge and analysis can be freely shared among group members.

The raw sensor output can be analyzed using specialized algorithms that provide interesting insights into athletic performance, but this analysis can only be as good as the quality of the data. It is important to consider that sensors, particularly inertial sensors, have limitations that become more pertinent in certain types of sports. For example, many general-purpose MEMS accelerometers are rated in the 2–9g range, which is sufficient for activities such as running. However, the centrifugal acceleration may exceed the range of these sensors in sports such as basketball, baseball, cricket, and golf. For example, fast cricket bowlers generate accelerations in the forearm in excess of 70g (Wixted et al., 2010). Specialist accelerometers rated up to 100g and higher are commercially available but are currently too expensive for use in consumer products.

It is important to consider that the majority of body-worn fitness sensors aren't 100 percent accurate. The performance may be inferior to bench-top systems found in sports clinics, but the differences are likely to be relatively small and may only be noteworthy for consideration by elite athletes. Certainly, the majority of available sensors will deliver superior accuracy over any form of manual estimation such as heart rate (Wixted, 2012).

Data and statistics have been an integral part of professional sports for many years. Performance metrics such as batting average, points scored, yards covered, driving distance off the tee, and goals scored have been routinely tracked. These metrics describe the output of performance. Sensors can be used to provide insight into how that performance was achieved and how it might be improved. Sensing is being applied in both competitive and training scenarios. In team sports, GPS sensors are worn by players in sports such as Rugby Union and Australian Rules Football to track the distance covered on the pitch during the game (Wisbey et al., 2010, Waldron et al., 2011). The sensor can also provide data on the player's proximity to play and their speed throughout the match. During training, team members may also wear heart rate monitors to measure the athlete's heart rate and recovery during a training session. This data, recorded during team sessions, allows the coach to identify a team member who is showing early signs of fatigue and determine whether they need rest or additional training. Identifying early signs of fatigue and intervening can prevent injury, which is also a key concern for highly paid athletes. Both professional and amateur athletes and their coaches are turning toward using rich sensor datasets to find a competitive edge over their opponents. The theory of "marginal gain," in which making slight improvements in numerous aspects of performance results in a cumulatively large improvement, is becoming increasingly important in competitive sports. Sensing and advanced data analytics allows athletes and coaches to identify potential areas of marginal gain and quantify improvements in these areas.

In personal fitness, the Quantified Self movement is going beyond simply tracking the time and distance of our runs or bike rides. Casual athletes are becoming much more data driven. Access to more sophisticated data sets from wearable sensing devices and advanced statistical analysis are taking this to the next level. By using motion sensor subsystems, we now have the data to analyze our activity throughout the day. How much time did I spend sitting, walking, exercising, and sleeping? How does this match to the activity goals I've set for myself? While exercising, did I expend more calories on my 30-minute run or that pickup game of basketball?

A vast array of biomechanical and physiological parameters can be calculated. Some are common across all activities, and some are activity specific. The most common range of fitness statistics includes these:

- Distance covered

- Speed (maximum, average moving, and overall speed)

- Time

- Heart rate

- Cadence

- Number of calories burned

- Total energy expenditure

- Lap measurements

These statistics can be used to provide insight into questions such as these: How much time am I exercising? Am I improving? Which activity resulted in the highest calorie burn? Did I reach my target for today? Movements such as the Quantified Self are increasing our awareness about ourselves through sensing, data, and statistics.

Beyond their use in training and performance improvement, sensor data and statistics are increasingly playing a role in the broadcast media to enhance the viewing experience. For a number of years, motorsports such as Formula One and NASCAR have been providing on-screen real-time telemetry from in-car sensors ranging from acceleration, braking, g forces, and so on. With the availability of low power, small form factor, and wireless-enabled sensors, real-time data from the athlete for broadcast media purposes is now possible. Viewers at home will have access to highly granular statistics on how someone is performing and how their performance compares to others. In the future, there may be no hiding place on the field or track. Sky Sports, which broadcasts Premiership soccer in the United Kingdom, already provides extensive analysis of player performance from video analysis. If sensors were to be placed on the players, viewers may soon be able to obtain data on the speed of each player as they run down the wings, their energy expenditure during the game, their acceleration in chasing a ball, and so on. This could potentially make the game even more engrossing for the soccer fan. A trial has already occurred in the MLS (Major League Soccer - US) all-star game in July 2012. Players were equipped with wearable sensors from adidas that allowed viewers of the game to track individual performance statistics of players via their PC or tablet (Householder, 2012).

Activity and Well-Being

Activity and wellness monitoring devices feature the same motion sensing capabilities as fitness sensors. In many cases, the line between them is blurred. The key difference with activity devices is to encourage movement in sedentary individuals and to maintain a minimum level of activity that will benefit their health and well-being. While activity and calorie balance are an important element of wellness, additional measurements that can be captured by sensors are being added to the base activity-related measurements. These measurements include sleep quality, which is a clinically proven element of personal wellness. Popular devices in this category include the following:

- Fitbit's product range comprises of both clip-on and wrist worn activity and sleep tracker sensors. The Fitbit One, for example, clips to a waist band, weighs only 8 grams and has both accelerometer and altimeter sensors. The sensor tracks steps taken, distance traveled, calories burned, stairs climbed, and recent activity. It also acts as a watch with a time display. It can interface to a free smartphone or tablet app and a web-based portal using Bluetooth Smart. The web portal allows users to track what they eat from a database of products and foods with corresponding calorie content. Although imperfect, it gives a useful indication of calorie intake versus calories burned. The Fitbit Force feature a wristband form factor and an OLED display that provides up-to-the-minute statistics such as steps taken, distance travelled, calories burned and so forth, similar to the Nike+ FuelBand. The Force also incorporates NFC, allowing instant download of data to another NFC-enabled device such as a smartphone by simply bringing it into close proximity of the other device. The sleep monitoring capabilities of the Force are similar to those of clinical actigraphy sensors, which are commonly used in sleep monitoring trials.

- The Jawbone Up has a similar wristband form factor to the Fitbit Force and is designed to be worn continually. It positions itself to take a holistic approach to a healthy lifestyle by providing sleep, 24/7 activity, and food/drink tracking. The Jawbone has no visual display to minimize size and weight (less than 23 grams). It is water resistant and can be worn in the shower. The Up band provides standard pedometer capabilities to detect steps and measure overall activity level. Data is sent from the wristband via a cable to either an iOS or Android mobile device. The supporting app for the mobile devices calculates a variety of statistics including the number of calories burned (based on age, height, and gender), total active time, longest period of activity, longest idle period, hours of sleep, and more. It also provides a means to track calorie consumption via web portal. The device has a configurable idle alert function that vibrates the band if movement is not detected after a specified time limit (Bennett, 2012).

The concept of the smartwatch has been around in various forms for many years. Recently the concept has experienced a resurgence, with new smartwatches, such as the Samsung Galaxy Gear and the Pebble, featuring integrated inertial sensing. Here are two more smartwatch developments:

- The MotoActv smartwatch from Motorola is aimed at the sports and activity tracking market. The MotoActv has the same basic capabilities as many sports GPS watches, including those from Nike, Timex, and Garmin, and offers a number of significant additional capabilities. Android-based, it features a variety of apps including a music player that downloads songs from your PC and wirelessly uploads your fitness data (including GPS tracks) to its web site. The watch can also connect to other fitness sensors, such as heart rate monitors, via either ANT or Bluetooth Smart. Workouts can be synced with `Motoactv.com` using the watch's Wi-Fi radio. The watch can also operate in different modes for different sports and activities such as running, gym workouts, walking, and cycling (Maker, 2011).

- Finnish company Vivago Oy's Vivago Watch is focused on 24-hour wellness monitoring. The watch continuously measures physiological signals, including movement, body temperature, and skin conductivity. During the initial phase of use, the watch and supporting software learn the wearer's normal behavior patterns. After this learning phase, the system sends an automatic alert after a predetermined period if it detects a significant change from normal activity patterns. The watch also measures total activity in real time and tracks it historically. It informs the user if physical activity has increased or decreased in comparison to the previous four weeks' average value. The watch also tracks calorie consumption on a 24-hour basis and sleep quantity and quality. Sleep tracking is coupled with an intelligent alarm capability that is designed to wake up the wearer during the lighter stages of sleep, which improves their feeling of well-being (Vivago, 2013).

Another approach to wellness monitoring is the integration of sensors directly into clothing. These sensors can collect data such as physiological, biochemical and biomechanical measurements directly from the wearer's body. Examples of this approach include the following:

- First Warning Systems is developing a breast tissue screening bra. The sensor-layered bra is designed to measure circadian rhythm-based temperature changes that occur as blood vessels grow and feed tumors. Predictive analytic software, co-developed with Nanyang Technological University and Lytix, Inc., categorizes abnormal patterns in otherwise healthy cellular behavior within the breast. This data can be used by a clinician to make an informed clinical decision. In three clinical trials, the bra correctly identified 92.1 percent of tumors, compared to the 70 percent accuracy of routine mammograms (First Warning, 2012). In a conceptual approach, Electrifoxy has created the Modwells prototype for personal wellness monitoring. The system comprises of input/output objects called *mods*, which are worn as part of your clothing. The mods are sensor modules that collect environmental or biometric data sets. The company has demonstrated a prototype concept for assessing posture. The posture garment consisted of a stretch sensing eTextile to which a "move" mod is attached. The mod is used to power the garment and collect data. The garment's stretch sensing capabilities allows the measurement of body movement in various directions. The mod processes the data and provides haptic feedback that alerts if the posture does not match a defined goal (Electricfoxy, 2013). Though speculative in nature, it provides interesting insight to how sensor technologies can be integrated into daily life to improve health and well-being.

Obesity and Weight Management

Obesity is recognized as a major public health issue in the Western world. In the United States, two-thirds of the population is estimated to be overweight, including 35.7 percent who are classified as being obese. The problem is also growing among children, with an estimated 16.9 percent of kids aged 2 to 19 being obese (CDC, 2012). Sensors and accompanying technologies are increasingly being used to monitor an individual's participation in a weight management program and to provide motivation to maintain engagement. There is a significant overlap with the sensor technologies utilized in the fitness market and weight management market. Early devices were based around standard pedometers, with data being transferred manually or via PC to web-based portals. More recently, MEMS-based inertial sensing devices such as Gruve (`www.gruvetechnologies.com`) are being utilized in the weight-management domain. Data from the sensors are transferred to web portals that are designed specifically to deliver custom weight loss and management programs. These programs are based on a combination of data tracking and visualization, online coaching, and nutrition management. One limitation in this form of sensing approach particularly for weight reduction programs is the accuracy in determining calories burned. Data collected from accelerometers during physical activities that require high-energy expenditure but low levels of movement (such as lifting weights) can underestimate calories burned (Cready et al., 2013). A multisensor approach may be a more accurate method to measure calorie burn. Products such as BodyMedia's armband body monitoring system contain skin temperature, heat flux, and galvanic skin response (GSR) sensors in addition to standard accelerometer-based inertial sensors. GSR provides a mechanism to determine how much you are sweating through changes in the skin's electrical conductivity. Skin temperature is also reflective of activity level. Finally, heat flux determines how much heat is being produced by your muscles and radiated into the ambient environment. Collectively, data from the sensors is claimed to measure calorie burn with less than 10 percent error. In addition, the sensor module also measures sleep quantity and quality. There is growing evidence to show the correlation between weight gain or loss and sleep because of the effect on hormone levels in the body, particularly leptin and ghrelin (Kollias, 2011, Thomson et al., 2012). These hormones are responsible for the stimulation and suppression of appetite. Their production can be affected by both the quality and quantity of sleep. The use of sleep sensors is likely to play an increasing important role in weight-reduction programs. Sleep data will be used to provide insights into the affects that lifestyle choices and behaviors are having on an individual's weight gain or loss. The next section looks in more detail at current sleep-sensing approaches.

Another approach to measuring caloric burn is based on indirect calorimetry. The technique is recommended by the World Health Organization, American Dietetic Association, and the American College of Sports Medicine for the treatment of obesity and the management of weight. As previously described, portable calorimeters are now available that provide accurate metabolism tracking which has utility in weight management applications. Inertial sensing approaches can have some difficulty with determining context, that is, running on a flat surface or running up a 20 percent incline. In-direct calorimetry provides insight to exactly how hard the body is working, or not, as the case may be. The disadvantage of portable calorimeters is that the measurements are not continuous and offer only snapshots in time. However, they do provide a means to accurately establish a baseline of how many calories you burn.

The other side of the equation in weight and obesity management is determining how many calories you are consuming. This is extremely challenging to achieve with any degree of accuracy because of the variety of variables that must be considered. However, most of the products available do provide some form of capability within their web portals to input your food intake. You can generally select the foods from a prepopulated database with accompanying calorie values. Or you can add your own meal information based on ingredient selection and quantity. Although this approach is imperfect, the process can be useful to making people understand how much food they are consuming without their full realization.

Sleep

Increasing evidence shows the impact of sleep on overall health, wellness, and even weight control. The measurement of sleep, and particularly the quality of sleep, is challenging. The gold standard method for measuring sleep is polysomnography (PSG). This method measures variables including EKG/ECG, electroencephalogram, oxygen saturation levels, and breathing patterns. Despite its accuracy, the method has a number of distinct disadvantages. First, it requires a significant number of electrodes to be attached to the subject. This is often uncomfortable for the patient, disturbing their sleep. It also requires the subject to stay overnight in a specialist sleep clinic, which is expensive and takes subjects from their normal environment, which again may influence the data. However, the data collected can be used for sleep staging determination, which is important in calculating the ratio between REM and non-REM sleep. REM sleep should account for about 20–25 percent of total sleep in most adults. Poor sleeping patterns and poor sleep quality have a variety of issues associated with them:

- Impaired memory and thought processes

- Depression

- Decreased immune response

- Fatigue

- Increased pain

- Weight gain

- Loss of creativity

Apart from the impacts on health, sleep disturbances may also be early indicators for poor health and functional deficits, especially in older adults. Sleep complaints are particularly prevalent in the over-65 age group, with more than 50 percent reporting issues including getting less sleep, frequent awakenings, waking up too early, and sleeping and napping during the day (Miles et al., 1980).

Given the significance of sleep in the matrix of health and well-being and the limitations of PSG, there has been a growing interest in the application of sensor technologies for home monitoring of sleep. Early devices used actigraphy, which is comprised of a dual-axis accelerometer worn in a wristwatch-like device. Data from the sensor is stored locally on the device and downloaded to a PC for analysis after each night's sleep. Analysis of the data reports motion over a predefined epoch length, as shown in Figure 10-6. The upper graph shows both the times and the magnitude of any individual activity measured. The lower timeline (in red) shows the cumulative activity for a given period of time. Low levels of activities may be associated with non-REM phases, while periods of high activity may indicate that the subject is awake. Estimates of sleep-to-wake stages are made using regression-based algorithms. The approach is good at identifying patterns of sleep disturbance; the data cannot be used for sleep staging, which is required for the measurement of sleep quality. But this limitation can be addressed in part through the use of either a respiration or EKG/ECG sensor to estimate the REM and non-REM sleep stages.

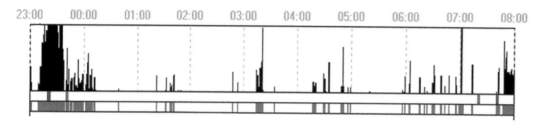

Figure 10-6. *Acitgraphy sensor data from a nine-hour sleeping period*

Although actigraphy sleep data can be useful, it requires the subject to remember to wear the sensor each night. Noncontact methods have the advantage of being able to operate without subject involvement. Sensing approaches include load cells (Austin et al., 2012), radar-based technologies (Vasu et al., 2011), force sensitive resistors (Lokavee et al., 2012), and wireless inertial sensors (McDowell et al., 2012). Walsh et al. has demonstrated the use of an under-mattress pressure sensor, as shown in Figure 10-7, which uses 24 fiber-optic sensors embedded into a mat to detect body position and movement during sleep. A home-based study of elderly subjects demonstrated accurate temporal resolution of activity monitoring in bed that was correlated with activity data captured using an actigraphy watch (Walsh et al., 2008).

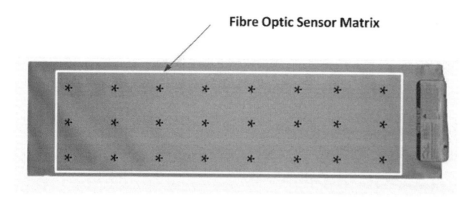

Figure 10-7. *Under-mattress pressure sensor*

The consumer-focused Zeo sleep monitoring system took a PSG-type approach to sleep monitoring by tracking brain activity. The systems comprised a lightweight wireless headband that was worn during sleep. The data from the headband was streamed either to a bedside display or to a smartphone. The aggregated data was sent to a web portal for online analysis. The web portal had a number of other features including a sleep journal that was designed to identify the links between lifestyle influences and sleep quality. The system features a SmartWake capability that looks for a "natural awakening point"—that is, a light point in your sleep to help you wake up without feeling groggy. Unfortunately, the company closed down in early 2013 because of financial difficulties (Dolan, 2013). Apps, such as Sleep Cycle Alarm (Maciek-Drejak-Labs, 2013), use the smartphone's integrated accelerometer as actigraphy to monitor quality of sleep. The smartphone is placed on the person's mattress, and the user calibrates it to detect motion. The app claims to be able to detect REM and non-REM sleep by indirectly measuring how much the person is moving while they sleep. The user can set an alarm to wake them when they enter a period of light sleep rather than waking them from a deep sleep.

Baby Sleep Monitoring

Anxious parents have always worried about the well-being of young babies while they sleep. Incidences of cot deaths reported in the media only heighten those anxieties. As a result, there is significant interest in sensor technologies that can monitor a child when sleeping. The most common approach simply monitors for sounds that indicate whether the child is asleep or not, and monitors the temperature in the child's environment. However, more sophisticated sensors have emerged that can monitor the baby via contact or noncontact modes.

One approach is to place a pressure sensitive mat under the baby's mattress. The AnglecareAC401 sensor system shown in Figure 10-8, for example, has an under-mattress sensor that provides continual monitoring of a baby's movements while they sleep. An alarm sounds to alert parents if no movement is detected for 20 seconds. The system also features sound monitoring to augment the motion sensing capabilities. Additionally, the system has room temperature monitoring with upper and lower temperature alerts. Collectively, these sensing capabilities give parents a degree of reassurance, particularly those who are concerned by sudden infant death syndrome (SIDS).

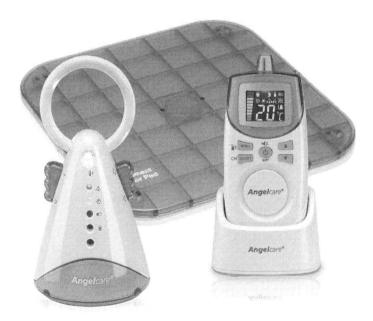

Figure 10-8. *The Anglecare under-mattress movement and sleep sensor for use with babies (image used with permission from ANGELCARE)*

The pressure of the baby lying on the mattress over the sensor is typically measured using either piezoresistance or optical sensing. In a piezoresistance sensor, changes in electrical resistivity relate to applied pressure, which varies during the breathing cycle or as the baby moves. In the fiber-optic approach, a transmission fiber and receiver fiber are enclosed in a cell structure. When pressure is applied to the cell, it is distorted, which affects the amount of light collected by the receiver fiber in proportion to the amount of applied pressure. The sensors in the mat are connected to an aggregation unit, which processes the sensor readings. Lack of detectable respiration in a defined period or a low respiration rate (>10 breaths per minute) triggers an audio alarm alerting the parents.

The second type of sensing is body-worn. These sensors clip onto the baby's clothing or diaper. These sensors use an inertial sensing approach to monitor movement of the chest or stomach area. Many of the available products feature a built-in tactile stimulator that is generally triggered if no movement is detected for 15–20 seconds. If the sensor does not detect movement after use of tactile stimulation, an alert is generated. Correct attachment to the body is important to prevent false positive alerts, which can be challenging with babies. The key advantage of this sensing approach is its mobility in comparison to under-mattress sensing. Under-mattress sensing is often tied to a specific mattress type and thickness for optimal performance.

A number of baby monitoring approaches have been investigated in the research domain, including a sensory vest that features EKG/ECG, respiration, moisture, and temperature sensing integrated into a baby's vest (Linti et al., 2006). A more recent smart clothing approach is the Exmobaby suit, which features a thermometer, heart rate monitor, and movement sensor built into the fabric. The suit also features a moisture sensor that is used to indicate when the baby requires changing. A Zigbee transmitter pod attaches securely to the suit and is used to stream the sensor data to a receiving PC. An application on the PC processes the data and sends information to a web site. Users can connect to the Web via smartphone app. The web site also generates SMS and e-mail alerts as required (Waugh, 2012). Other reported approaches include pulse oximetry monitoring (Rimet et al., 2007), wireless audio sensing (Al-Dasoqi et al., 2010), and UWB radar sensing (Ziganshin et al., 2010).

Sleep Apnea

Sleep-related complaints include insomnia, restless leg syndrome, snoring, parasomnias, and sleep apnea. Incidences of sleep apnea are relatively common and affect men more than women. Studies in the United Kingdom have estimated that about 4 percent of middle-aged men and 2 percent of middle-aged women suffer from the condition. Left untreated, the condition has the potential to cause high blood pressure, heart attacks, stroke, obesity, and type 2 diabetes (NHS, 2012). In addition, sleep apnea causes daytime sleepiness that can result in accidents, lost productivity, and other issues. The condition is commonly associated with being overweight.

Sleep Apnea Syndrome describes the cessation of respiration during sleep. The most common kind of sleep apnea is called Obstructive Sleep Apnea Syndrome (OSA), which is defined as a total blockage of the airway for 10 seconds or more. Polysomnography is the gold standard used as the diagnostic test to identify OSA; however, in 2008, the FDA approved home monitoring as a tool for diagnosing sleep apnea. Home sleep monitoring utilizes a variety of sensors, including the following:

- Airflow (pressure-based)

- Blood oxygen saturation (pulse oximetry, normally at 0.1 percent resolution)

- Heart rate (EKG/ECG)

- Respiration effort (respiratory inductive plethysmography)

In addition, it is strongly recommended that the following parameters are monitored:

- Temperature-based airflow (thermistor)

- Snoring patterns (acoustic microphone)

- Muscle activity (EMG)

- Head movement/position (inertial sensing)

- Body position (inertial sensing, supine or nonsupine sleep positioning)

It has been reported than home sensor platforms can deliver comparable accuracy to PSG. For example, the Ares Unicoder system from Watermark Medical has a reported correlation of 0.96 with PSG when recorded concurrently and 0.88 for home-based monitoring when compared to PSG (Westbrook et al., 2005). Other home monitoring solutions include the Stardust II Sleep Recorder (`www.stardust2.respironics.eu`) and Alice PDx portable sleep diagnostic system (`www.alicepdx.respironics.eu`) from Philips, SleepView from Cleveland Medical Devices (`www.clevemed.com/SleepView/overview.shtml`), and AccuSom from NovaSom (`www.novasom.com`).

When mild sleep apnea is diagnosed, treatment is normally based around lifestyle changes including losing weight, cessation of smoking, and limiting alcohol consumption. In moderate to severe cases, continuous positive airway pressure (CPAP) machines are used to treat sleep apnea. This involves using a mask worn over your nose that delivers a continuous supply of compressed air. The compressed air prevents the airway in the throat from closing. Sensing plays a key role in the operation of these machines. Precision MEMS pressure sensors monitor the instantaneous pressure at the output of the machine and inside the breathing mask. This data is used to dynamically adjust the air pressure in order to maintain a set value required by the prescribed therapy. This increases the accuracy and sensitivity for individual CPAP users. Pressure data can in some cases be used to identify the need for specialized therapy. In addition to pressure measurement, the CPAP machines may also capture data on the duration of the therapeutic episodes each night, leak rate, pressure settings, pauses in breathing, and periods of shallow breathing. This data can be used by clinicians to modify or refine the therapy for each patient.

Posture Monitoring

Back pain is a prevalent problem among adults, with 80 percent of people experiencing lower back pain sometime during their lives and with 20 to 30 percent experiencing it at any given time (Virutal Health Care Team, 2012). The American Academy of Pain Medicine reports that back pain in workers in the 40–65 age bracket costs employers an estimated $7.4 billion a year in the United States alone. There are also indications that the prevalence of back pain is increasing. The reasons for this increase are unclear, but factors such as obesity and increased numbers of people in desk-based jobs may be a factor (UNC School of Medicine). Frequently, back pain can be successfully addressed with a combination of exercise, nonsurgical treatment, and alternative therapies. For some chronic back pain sufferers, implantable neurostimulation devices that deliver mild electrical signals to the epidural space near the spine may also provide a solution. Poor posture has been identified as a significant contributor to back pain issues. It is important to maintain the spine in a strong and stable position through healthy posture. Stooping or slouching deviates the spine from its three natural curves (cervical, thoracic, and lumbar). As a result, the back muscles and ligaments are overextended as they struggle to maintain postural balance which leads to back pain, headaches, and other related problems.

Inertial sensing is also playing a role in intervention, particularly with posture monitoring applications, as shown in Figure 10-9. Already a number of products, such as Lumoback, are available that can monitor and improve posture. The Lumoback sensor is worn around the lower back provides vibro-tactical feedback when the wearer slouches. The sensor connects via Bluetooth Smart, to a smartphone app that delivers real-time posture tracking. The sensors provide tracking of pelvic tilt alignment and slouch due to the lower back position, leaning forward, leaning backward, or incorrect balancing of weight to one side (Lasky, 2013).

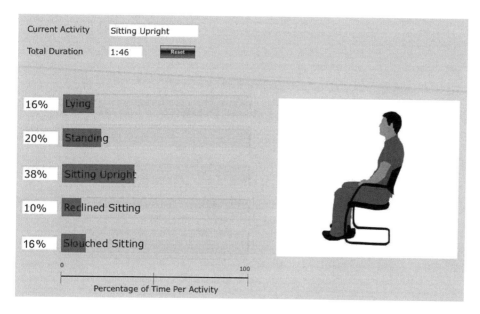

Figure 10-9. *Posture monitoring and classification using inertial sensors*

The Philips ErgoSensor monitor uses an optical CMOS camera to determine distance from the screen and neck angle while sitting. The screen provides a warning when your posture is not ergonomically correct (Chang, 2012). Other approaches to posture monitoring reported in the literature include smart clothing featuring integrated accelerometers and gyroscopes (Wong et al., 2008), force-sensitive resistors (FSRs) embedded into shoes (Sazonov et al., 2011), and piezoelectric eTextile cushions (Wenyao et al., 2011).

Personal Safety

Sensors are being applied to make our lives safer. Sensors can notify us of potentially dangerous conditions in our homes, such as the presence of smoke or carbon monoxide. They can also help to secure our homes and notify us of potential break-ins or intruders. They can even detect when we've experienced an accident. When an accident, such as a fall, occurs sensors can be used to identify that a dangerous event is occurring and trigger preventative measures to protect us from injury. Sensors can also be used proactively to determine whether we are in satisfactory physical condition to engage in routine daily activities. Older adults may test their balance to ensure they are sufficiently stable before leaving the house or walking around their garden. For adults who like to socialize with an alcoholic drink at home or outside the home, testing of your blood-alcohol level before driving may be of enormous benefit for obvious reasons.

Home Safety Monitoring

Home safety monitoring embraces various sensing functions, ranging from traditional home security monitoring to ambient environment monitoring to health-related event detection and response. PIR motion sensors can detect motion in rooms, and magnetic or vibration sensors are attached to windows and doors to detect tampering. These sensors can be augmented with video surveillance to provide continuous monitoring or motion activated monitoring via PIR sensing. Home security systems are now being augmented with "smart" features that allow people to monitor their home remotely. Monitoring can include access to real-time video streams and the ability to receive alerts such as SMS messaging if an issue, such as an intrusion, is detected. The capabilities of these smart security systems are being further enhanced with home automation features or domotics (automated controls for homes), such as light and HVAC (heating, ventilation, and air conditioning) control. Additional sensing capabilities, such as water and flood monitoring, can also be included to increase the home owner's peace of mind when they are away. These systems are natural extensions of the Internet of Things approach (see Chapter 5), where all sensors and devices around us are connected in some manner to deliver intelligent applications. In the United States, AT&T has recently launched its Digital Life home security and automation product, which features sensing capabilities for water and flood monitoring, carbon monoxide and smoke detection, and glass breakage (AT&T, 2013).

The use of smoke alarms as shown in Figure 10-10 in the home has been common practice for many years—their installation is a legal requirement in many countries. As described in Chapter 2, smoke detectors come in two types: ionization detectors and photoelectric detectors. For carbon monoxide detection, semiconductor or electrochemical sensors are normally used for residential applications. They can be either battery powered or powered by the home's electrical mains. Mains-powered devices typically feature a battery backup to ensure that during a mains power outage there is no loss of monitoring.

Figure 10-10. *A home smoke alarm*

Safety Monitoring and Falls Detection

Another key element of wellness is personal safety, which can be of particular concern for older adults, especially in their own homes. Falls-related injuries, which commonly occur in the home, are the single biggest cause of injury-related death in older adults. It is estimated that falls-related injuries cost approximately $30 billion annually in the United States. The use of notifications systems for older adults to alert support services in the case of an emergency such as a fall has been common practice for many years. These systems often take the form of stand-alone units, simple pendants, or wristbands with a help button. Activation of the button notifies a remote monitoring service that there is an issue. Examples of product offerings include AlertOne (`www.alert-1.com`), LifeStation (`www1.lifestation.com`), and Bay Alarm Medical (`www.bayalarmmedical.com`). Emergency monitoring can also form part of an overall home monitoring service, including additional services such as security and ambient sensing as provided by products like Life Alert Classic from Life Alert Emergency Response, Inc. (`www.lifealert.com`).

Falls detection devices are another common home safety application and often build upon an extended medical alert service. This form of product is commonly known as mobile personal emergency response (M-PERS). The detection devices are based on single or multiple inertial sensors (e.g., accelerometers and gyroscopes). Using multiple inertial sensors reduces the false positive rate and improves sensitivity. The sensor modules are worn on the wrist or waist or as a pendant. The modules feature an emergency response button, which is wirelessly connected to a base station in home. Once triggered, the base station can send an alert to a monitoring center. More sophisticated devices have integrated GSM modules, which automatically send an alert when a fall is detected. Alternatively, the sensor can automatically notify the in-home base station that a fall has occurred, which then notifies the call center. The call center contacts the wearer to assess the level of urgency. If an emergency is determined or there is no response, the call center notifies the emergency services and alerts designated caregivers and family. This form of approach has the advantage of being able to operate even when the fall results in the person losing consciousness. Some devices also feature GPS tracking, which is useful if the fall occurs outside the home.

The development of falls detection sensing technology remains an area of active research. Approaches reported in literature include inertial sensors embedded in a custom-designed vest (Bourke et al., 2008) and an inertial sensor embedded into a cane (Lan et al., 2009). Smartphones have also attracted attention as potential falls detection devices because of their integrated inertial sensors. Tacconi et al. report the use of data from a tri-axial accelerometer embedded in an Android smartphone to detect falls and to deliver the Timed Get Up and Go test (Tacconi et al., 2011). This test is a common clinical test to determine falls risk because of gait and balance issues. A key limitation of the approach outlined is the requirement that the smartphone must be worn on the waist, which may not be practical for everyday use as a falls detector, particularly for women. Yavuz et al. also report the use of a smartphone for falls detection. They also utilize the GPS functionality of the smartphone with Google Maps to provide information on the location of the fall. This information is provided together with notification of the fall event to caregivers through various notification mechanisms such as SMS, e-mail, and Twitter (Yavuz et al., 2010). The BuddyGuard from MPOWER Labs is a commercial product that takes a similar approach. The app running on an iPhone provides a number of personal protection services including falls detection. The app automatically senses when a fall followed by a 5G stop occurs using the phone's built-in accelerometer. An emergency alert is triggered within five seconds if users do not respond to a warning notification displayed by the application. The alert transmits the faller's location to friends and family via e-mail, automated phone call, and text message (PR Newswire, 2011).

While there have been various efforts to determine falls risk in older adults (see Chapter 8), other efforts have focused on preventing or reducing the severity of injury when a fall occurs. A common research approach is the use of body-worn air bags such as the jacket system developed by Tamura at Chiba University in Japan. The system comprises both an accelerometer and gyroscope that are used to trigger airbag deployment when acceleration and angular velocity thresholds are exceeded (Tamura et al., 2009). A similar approach using airbags has also been reported in the research literature (Guangyi et al., 2009, Fukaya et al., 2008). There are still considerable practical obstacles that must be addressed before such devices could be considered usable in the general population.

Alcohol Monitoring

We are all aware of the issues associated with driving impairment and the consumption of alcohol (ethanol). In many countries, the legal drink limits are falling. As a result, a single drink may potentially place you over the legal drink/drive limit. Both roadside and bench-top systems have been used by law enforcement agencies for many years. A more recent development has been the use of personal alcohol monitoring sensors, some of which are small enough to attach to car keys. In France, it has been a legal requirement since July 2012 to carry a breathalyzer kit in your car. This is likely to be replicated in many other countries before too long. There are three major types of breath alcohol testing devices commonly available, which are based on different detection principles:

- Chemistry (based on a chemical reaction between alcohol and other chemicals that produces a visible color change)

- Infrared (IR) spectroscopy (intoxilyzer)

- Sensor (fuel cell or semiconductor sensor)

For personal use, semiconductor sensors are the most common because of their low cost and ease of integration into an electronic device. Commercially available personal breathalyzers can cost as little as $20. In a semiconductor alcohol sensor, a bead of metal oxide is heated to around 300 °C. A voltage is applied to produce a small standing current. When alcohol in the breath is exposed to the bead, it changes its resistivity, resulting in a change in the standing current. Semiconductor sensors exhibit a number of problems:

- Nonalcohol specific response. The sensors can react to other volatile organic compounds such as hairspray and breath acetone.

- Relatively short working life.

- Sensor saturation.

- Drift. The sensor can exhibit variation in response that normally increases with age.

- Nonlinear response. Sensors have a narrower and reduced linear range of alcohol measurements in comparison to fuel cells.

Fuel cell devices are generally regarded as the gold standard for field sobriety testing and are used extensively by law enforcement agencies. In fuel-cell devices, the breath sample is exposed to dual platinum electrodes in the cell. Any ethanol in the breath sample is oxidized to acetic acid at the anode, which generates an electrical current. The current generated is proportional to the concentration of ethanol in the breath sample. Fuel cells have a number of key advantages over the semiconductor sensors. They have very high specificity and sensitive for ethanol. The alcohol measurement cannot be influenced by endogenous substances such as acetone (produced by diabetics) or by ambient environmental gases such as carbon monoxide or toluene. The sensors normally have an operational lifespan of more than five years.

Recently fuel cell devices have entered the mainstream consumer market at an affordable price point. As with so many other application domains described in this book, breathalyzer sensors are now being integrated with smartphones. The BACtrak, shown in Figure 10-11, is a fuel cell (Xtend electrochemical fuel cell) breathalyzer that provides accurate blood alcohol content (BAC) measurement in the 0.000–0.400 percent range. (Generally the legal limit in the United States for alcohol intoxication is 0.08 percent, whereas in Europe it is generally 0.05 percent.) The sensor connects to an Android or iOS smartphone via Bluetooth (v4.0). The BACtrak features an internal air pump designed to ensure precise and consistent results. The supporting software offers a number of social media features, including the ability to share results privately via text message or publicly via social media or to simply delete the data. Other features include the ability to share photos, notes, and drink logs. The data provided allows users to gain insight into their drinking habits and to learn how their body processes alcohol (Ferro, 2013). The Alcohoot from an Israeli startup company also utilizes a fuel-cell sensor targeted at the consumer market. It attaches to either an Android or iOS smartphone via the audio port. The supporting software app automatically calls a cab if the reported result is higher than the legal limit (Ferenstein, 2013).

Figure 10-11. *BACtrack Fuel Cell personal breathalyzer (image used with permission from BACtrack)*

The Future of Sensor-Based Wellness, Fitness, and Lifestyle Applications

We are now entering an age where wellness is being embraced as a means to proactively manage health and well-being. As we have seen in this chapter, sensor technologies are playing a pivotal role in enabling us to understand our wellness and the factors influencing it. Sensors can help us identify behaviors such as sedentary lifestyle choices, overeating, poor sleeping patterns, and engaging in unsafe behaviors that will negatively impact on our well-being.

Both discrete and integrated sensors found in mobile devices will continue to be used for wellness-orientated applications. These applications will utilize either active or passive modes, or a combination of both. For active use scenarios, we wear a particular sensor for the duration of a particular activity, such as running or walking. This form of use currently dominates our interactions with fitness and activity sensors. In the future, most interactions with sensors will be passive. We are already seeing this approach starting to emerge with some of the commercial activity sensing products. They are designed to be worn all the time with minimal physical impact on the wearer. This passive approach to sensing will be reflected in opportunistic sensing, which will emerge as we carry our smartphone, wear certain pieces of clothing, or drive to work.

Although the integration of sensing capabilities in smartphones continues to increase, physical limitations in the form factor of smartphones will ensure that discrete sensors will continue to be used for specialized usages. For example, integration into clothing, particularly for sports-related activities, is one such case. We are also likely to see acceleration in the use of smart or eTextiles, where the garment itself acts as the sensor. The evolution of smart clothing will make sensing almost transparent to the user and will move from initial specialist applications for high-performance sport, and so on, to being commonly use in our daily lives.

Pervasive connectivity will be a key enabler. The trend of sensor integration with smartphones is becoming more and more ubiquitous. The vast majority of sensors for fitness and wellness-oriented applications now come with free smartphone apps. These apps provide local aggregation of the sensor data, processing, visualization, and connectivity to web-based portals hosted on the cloud. The future will be very much about a data-driven society. We will increasingly socialize our personal wellness data to achieve a variety of goals: group support to maintain current endeavors, expert analysis and opinion, and affirmation from friends and family. Socializing this data is also likely to have unforeseen consequences in the future. Tracking our levels of food and drink intake on a weekly basis and sharing that data via social media may attract unwanted interest from service providers we might need to engage in the future, such as insurance companies. While many people currently share personal wellness–related data without much thought of privacy concerns, the social norms of the future may change sharing behaviors. The Facebook generation has grown up sharing their personal information with little consideration for the consequences. The sharing of wellness-related data is an unknown quantity for the vast majority of people. Opinions and views are likely to have an age-related perspective in the short term. However, as the wellness domain evolves and matures, people will have to weigh the potential benefits of data sharing against the actual or perceived risks. Technology developments will certainly allow us to enforce better fine-grained control over our data in the future; however, ultimately we will have to make conscious decisions on what we share, with whom, and for what purposes. We are likely to see people's actions and opinions evolve over time as we build our collective social knowledge on best practices relating to personal wellness data sharing.

Sensing will also enable us to actively monitor both the physical and ambient environments in our homes from wherever we may be located at a given time. We already have home security systems and stand-alone smoke and carbon monoxide detectors. The future will bring us smart integrated systems that proactively monitor, manage, enable remote dynamic management, and proactively communicate with us. Our homes will leverage the drive toward the Internet of Things in ways that make meaningful and practical impacts on our lives.

We are also likely to see greater synergies between our personal physiological well-being and the environmental conditions that impact our well-being. Our physical environment will adjust to us, whether it is the temperature in the bedroom to ensure it is optimal for a good night's sleep, whether it is waking us at exactly the right time during our sleep cycle to ensure we wake refreshed, or whether it is turning on the lights automatically at night for trips to the bathroom. The future will be about managing our wellness in a seamless, almost invisible manner, allowing us to remain healthy and active and socializing that fact among friends, family, and peers. Sensors, mobile devices, and ubiquitous connectivity are already playing a vital role in making this future happen.

Summary

This chapter looked at how sensors are being increasingly adopted across a wide range of sporting and physical activities. Many of these sensors utilize the same sensing principles and measure many of the same parameters as healthcare sensors. Adoption of these technologies is increasing as people become more proactive in engaging with physical activities. Users are also increasingly interested in sharing their activity online among peers, friends, and families. We have also seen how sensor technology is being integrated into clothing and how this is advantageous for applications that require a precise location on the body. Sensors that are integrated into or attached to sports equipment, such as bikes or golf clubs, are becoming more widely available. Technologies used in the sports and fitness domains are also being used to support individuals in weight management programs by providing them with constant data on how they are performing. Throughout this chapter we have seen the importance of sensor integration with smartphones to provide processing and visualization of data—and as a platform for remote connectivity to enable sharing of data on the Web. Finally, we looked at how sensors can be used in the home to protect us by identifying hazards or by proactively securing assistance when an accident such as a fall has occurred.

References

Edlin, Gordon, Eric Golanty, and Kelli McCormack Brown, *Essentials for Health and Wellness*, 2nd ed. Sudbury, MA: Jones and Bartlett Publishers, 2000.

Hettler, Bill, "The Six Dimensions of Wellness Model", National Wellness Institute Inc., http://c.ymcdn.com/sites/www.nationalwellness.org/resource/resmgr/docs/sixdimensionsfactsheet.pdf, 1976.

Edlin, Gordon and Eric Golanty, *Health & Wellness*, 11th ed. Burlington, MA: Jone & Bartlett Learning, 2014.

PRWEB. "*$975 Million Sports & Fitness Mobile Sensing App Market in 2017, Says ON World*", Last Update: 23rd May, 2013, http://www.prweb.com/releases/2013/5/prweb10758313.htm.

Bluetooth SIG Inc, "Momentum Builds for Bluetooth Smart Devices", http://www.bluetooth.com/Pages/Bluetooth-Smart-Devices.aspx, 2013.

Mascarenhas, D. R., C. Button, D. O'Hara, and M. Dicks, "Physical performance and decision making in association football referees: A naturalistic study," *Sports and Exercise Sciences*, vol. 2 (9), pp. 1–9, 2009.

IMS Research, "ANT+ to Lead the Way in Sports and Fitness but Bluetooth Smarting is Biting on it Heels", http://www.imsresearch.com/press-release/ANT_to_Lead_the_Way_in_Sports_and_Fitness_but_Bluetooth_Smart_is_Biting_on_its_Heels, 2012.

Zephyr, "*HxM™ Smart Heart Rate Monitor*", Last Update: 2013, http://www.zephyr-technology.com/products/hxm-smart-heart-rate-monitor/

Nike. "*Nike+ Fuelband*", Last Update: 2012, http://nikeplus.nike.com/plus/

Davies, Stephen, "*Amazing muscle sensor from Somaxis*", BIONIC.LY, Last Update: 17th July,2012, http://bionic.ly/2012/07/amazing-muscle-sensor-from-somaxis/

TMG-BMC. "*About Tensiomyography*", Last Update: 2013, http://www.tmg.si/en/products/tmg-products/about-tensiomyography

Coxworth, Ben. "*Breezing device tracks your metabolism and acts as a fitness coach*", Last Update: 4th February 2013, http://www.gizmag.com/breezing-indirect-calorimeter-metabolism/26096/

BodyGem, "*BodyGem RMR – Resting Metabolic Rate Test Device*", Last Update: 2013, http://metabolicratetest.com/

Harle, Robert and Andy Hopper, "Sports Sensing: An Olympic Challenge for Computing", *Computer*, vol. (June), 98-101, 2012.

Kaur, Kal. "*Smart Clothes*", Last Update: 8th November, 2012, http://www.azosensors.com/Article.aspx?ArticleID=84

Jeong, Kee-Sam, Sun K. Yoo, Joohyeon Lee, and Gilsoo Cho, "Smart Clothes for Biometrics and Beyond," in *Biometric from Fiction to Practice*, Du, Eliza Yingzi, Ed., Singapore, Pan Stanford Publishing Ltd, 2013, pp. 165-186.

Textronics. "*The NuMetrex Heart Rate Monitor System*", Last Update: 2013, http://www.numetrex.com/about/the-system

Eric, "*Adidas Performance Bra with HRM sensor*", talk2myshirt, Last Update: 2012, http://www.talk2myshirt.com/blog/archives/5668

Gorman, Michael. "*Reebok and mc10 team up to build CheckLight, a head impact indicator (hands-on)*", Last Update: 11th January 2013, http://www.engadget.com/2013/01/11/mc10-reebok-checklight-hands-on/

Belezina, Jan. "*Squid fitness monitoring shirt keeps track of your gym progress*", Last Update: 8th February, 2012, http://www.gizmag.com/squid-emg-fitness-shirt/21386/

Weiss, Chris C. "*PolyPower electrostatic film measures athletic movements, harvests energy*", Last Update: 28th February, 2013, http://www.gizmag.com/danfoss-polypower-sport-sensors/26324/

Krakauer, Hannah, "Buzzing clothes could teach you to be a better athlete", *New Scientist*, vol. 2877, pp. 19, 2012.

Bye, Elizabeth, "A Look to the Future," in *Fashion Design*, Oxford, UK, Berg, 2010, pp. 145–147.

Higginbotham, Stacey. "*You call Google Glass wearable tech? Heapsylon makes sensor-rich fabric*", Last Update: 16th May, 2013, http://gigaom.com/2013/05/16/you-call-google-glass-wearable-tech-heapsylon-makes-sensor-rich-fabric/

Darmour, Jennifer. "*Work*", Last Update: 2013, http://www.electricfoxy.com/work/

Maker, Ray. "*The ANT+ Bike Speed/Cadence Sensor: Everything you ever wanted to know*", Last Update: 2011, http://www.dcrainmaker.com/2011/07/ant-bike-speedcadence-sensor-everything.html.

Cycling Weekly, "Power meters: Everthing you need to know", http://www.cyclingweekly.co.uk/news/latest/536237/power-meters-everything-you-need-to-know.html, 2013.

Brim Brothers, "Zone - It about you", http://www.brimbrothers.com/, 2013.

GolfSense, "*Product*", Last Update: 2013, http://www.golfsense.me/pages/pro#a1

3BaysGSA. "*3BaysGSA Putt - How it Works*", Last Update: 2013, http://www.3bayslife.com/gsa/product.php?pid=103i#how_it_works

Sport Sensors Inc., "The Leader in Affordable Sports Radars", http://www.sportssensors.com/, 2013.

Chaganti, Vasanta and Leif Hanlen. "*Smart sensor save swimmers seconds*", Last Update: 15th June, 2011, http://theconversation.com/smart-sensors-save-swimmers-seconds-1687

Zarda, Brett. *Stopwatches? Sensor Technology Puts the Laptop in Lap*, The New York Times, New York, http://www.nytimes.com/2010/07/19/sports/19swimming.html?_r=0, 2010.

Sage, Tanya Le, *et al.*, "A Multi-sensor System for Monitoring the Performance of Elite Swimmers," in *e-Business and Telecommunications*, Berlin Heidelberg, Springer 2012, pp. 350–362.

Cowie, J. l., J. A. Flint, and A. R. Harland, "Wireless Impact Measurement for Martial Arts (P43)," in *The Engineering of Sport 7* vol. 1, Estivalet, Margaret and Pierre Brisson, Eds., Paris, Springer, 2008, pp. 231–237.

Wixted, Andrew, Wayne Spratford, Mark Davis, Marc Portus, and Daniel James, "Wearable Sensors for on Field near Real Time Detection of Illegal Bowling Actions," presented at the Conference of Science, Medicine & Coaching in Cricket, Shearton Mirage Gold Coast, Queensland, Australia, 2010.

Wixted, Andrew J., "Healthcare Sensor Networks: Challenges Towards Practical Implementation," in *Healthcare Sensor Networks: Challenges Toward Practical Implementation*, Lai, Daniel T. H., Rezaul Begg, and Marimuthu Palaniswami, Eds., Boca Raton, Florida, CRC Press, 2012, pp. 407–437.

Wisbey, Ben, Paul G. Montgomery, David B. Pyne, and Ben Rattray, "Quantifying movement demands of AFL football using GPS tracking," *Journal of Science and Medicine in Sport,* vol. 13 (5), pp. 531–536, 2010.

Waldron, Mark, Craig Twist, Jamie Highton, Paul Worsfold, and Matthew Daniels, "Movement and physiological match demands of elite rugby league using portable global positioning systems," *Journal of Sports Sciences,* vol. 29 (11), pp. 1223–1230, 2011.

Householder, Mike. "*Wearable sensor devices leverage MEMS motion tracking innovations*", Last Update: 28th September, 2012, http://www.eetimes.com/design/medical-design/4397350/Wearable-sensor-devices-to-leverage-MEMS-motion-tracking-innovations?pageNumber=0

Bennett, Brian. "*Jawbone Up review: An easy-to-wear and insightful fitness pal*", Last Update: 9th May 2013, 2012, http://reviews.cnet.com/wearable-tech/jawbone-up/4505-34900_7-35536649.html

Maker, Ray. "*Motorola MOTOACTV In Depth Review*", Last Update: November 9th 2011, http://www.dcrainmaker.com/2011/11/motorola-motoactv-in-depth-review.html

Vivago. "*Measure Your Wellbeing - Measure your activity and sleep*", Last Update: 2013, http://www.vivago.com/

First Warning Systems Inc., "Core Technology", http://www.firstwarningsystems.com/for-clinicians.html, 2012.

Electricfoxy, "*Modwells: personal modules for wellness*", Last Update: 2013, http://www.electricfoxy.com/projects/modwells/

CDC, "*Adult Overweight and Obesity*", Last Update: 27th April, 2012, http://www.cdc.gov/obesity/adult/index.html

Cready, Gwyn and Ted Kyle. "*Every Move You Make, Every Step You Take: How Activity Monitoring is Changing the World of Fitness and Weight-loss*", Last Update: 2013, http://www.obesityaction.org/educational-resources/resource-articles-2/exercise/every-move-you-make-every-step-you-take-how-activity-monitoring-is-changing-the-world-of-fitness-and-weight-loss

Kollias, Helen. "*Research Review: Leptin, ghrelin, weight loss – it's complicated*", Last Update: 25th February, 2011, http://www.precisionnutrition.com/leptin-ghrelin-weight-loss

Thomson, Cynthia A., *et al.*, "Relationship Between Sleep Quality and Quantity and Weight Loss in Women Participating in a Weight-Loss Intervention Trial," *Obesity,* vol. 20 (7), pp. 1419–1425, 2012.

Miles, Laughton E. and William Charles Dement, *Sleep and Aging*, vol. 3. New York: Raven Press, 1980.

Austin, Daniel, *et al.*, "Unobtrusive classification of sleep and wakefulness using load cells under the bed," in *Engineering in Medicine and Biology Society (EMBC), 2012 Annual International Conference of the IEEE*, 2012, pp. 5254–5257.

Vasu, Vishalini, Conor Heneghan, Sakir Sezer, and Thianantha Arumugam, "Contact-free Estimation of Respiration Rates during Sleep," presented at the Irish Signals and Systems Conference (ISSC), Dublin, 2011.

Lokavee, Shongpun, Theerapom Puntheeranurak, Teerakiat Kerdcharoen, Natthapol Watthanwisuth, and Adisom Tuantranont, "Sensor pillow and bed sheet system: Unconstrained monitoring of respiration rate and posture movements during sleep," in *Systems, Man, and Cybernetics (SMC), 2012 IEEE International Conference on*, 2012, pp. 1564–1568.

McDowell, Andrew, Mark P. Donnelly, Chris D. Nugent, and Michael J. McGrath, "Utilising wireless sensor networks towards establishing a method of sleep profiling," *International Journal of Computers in Healthcare,* vol. 1 (4), pp. 346–363, 2012.

Walsh, Lorcan, Sean McLoone, Julie Behan, and Terry Dishongh, "The deployment of a non-intrusive alternative to sleep/wake wrist actigraphy in a home-based study of the elderly," in *Engineering in Medicine and Biology Society, 2008. EMBS 2008. 30th Annual International Conference of the IEEE*, 2008, pp. 1687–1690.

Dolan, Brian. "*Exclusive: Sleep coach company Zeo is shutting down*", Last Update: March 12th 2013, http://mobihealthnews.com/20772/exclusive-sleep-coach-company-zeo-is-shutting-down/

Maciek Drejak AB, "Sleep Cycle", http://www.sleepcycle.com/, 2013.

Linti, Carsten, Hansjurgen Horter, Peter Osterreicher, and Heinrich Planck, "Sensory baby vest for the monitoring of infants," presented at the Proceedings of the International Workshop on Wearable and Implantable Body Sensor Networks, 2006.

Waugh, Rob. *Peace for parents? New 'smart' baby suit contains sensors that tell you WHY your child is crying,* Daily Mail, http://www.dailymail.co.uk/sciencetech/article-2110999/New-smart-baby-suit-contains-sensors-tell-baby-crying.html, 2012.

Rimet, Yves, *et al.*, "Evaluation of a new, wireless pulse oximetry monitoring system in infants: the BBA bootee," presented at the 4th International Workshop on Wearable and Implantable Body Sensor Networks (BSN 2007), Aachen, Germany, 2007.

Al-Dasoqi, N., A. Mason, A. Shaw, and A. I. Al-Shamma'a, "Preventing cot death for infants in day care," in *Sensors Applications Symposium (SAS), 2010 IEEE*, 2010, pp. 179–182.

Ziganshin, E. G., M. A. Numerov, and S. A. Vygolov, "UWB Baby Monitor," in *Ultrawideband and Ultrashort Impulse Signals (UWBUSIS), 2010 5th International Conference on*, 2010, pp. 159–161.

NHS. *"Sleep apnoea"*, Last Update: 26th June, 2012, http://www.nhs.uk/Conditions/Sleep-apnoea/Pages/Introduction.aspx

Westbrook, Philip R., *et al.*, "Description and Validation of the Apnea Risk Evaluation System: A Novel Method To Diagnose Sleep Apnea-Hypopnea in the Home," *CHEST*, vol. 128 pp. 2166–2175, 2005.

Virtual Health Care Team, School of Health Professions, University of Missouri-Columbia, "Mechanical Low Back Pain - Prevalence and costs", http://shp.missouri.edu/vhct/case1699/preval_costs.htm, 2012.

University of North Carolina, School of Medicine, "Chronic low back pain on the rise: UNC study finds 'alarming increase' in prevalence", http://www.med.unc.edu/www/newsarchive/2009/february/chronic-low-back-pain-on-the-rise-unc-study-finds-alarming-increase-in-prevalence, 2009.

Lasky, Michael S. *"LUMOback"*, Last Update: 15th March, 2013, http://www.wired.com/reviews/2013/03/lumoback/

Chang, Alexandra. *"New Philips Monitor Uses Sensor to Promote Better Posture"*, Last Update: 4th June, 2012, http://www.wired.com/gadgetlab/2012/04/new-philips-monitor-uses-sensor-to-promote-better-posture/

Wong, Wai and Man Wong, "Smart garment for trunk posture monitoring: A preliminary study," *Scoliosis*, vol. 3 (1), pp. 7, 2008.

Sazonov, Edward S., George Fulk, James Hill, Yves Schutz, and Raymond Browning, "Monitoring of Posture Allocations and Activities by a Shoe-Based Wearable Sensor," *Biomedical Engineering, IEEE Transactions on*, vol. 58 (4), pp. 983–990, 2011.

Wenyao, Xu, Li Zhinan, Huang Ming-Chun, N. Amini, and M. Sarrafzadeh, "eCushion: An eTextile Device for Sitting Posture Monitoring," in *Body Sensor Networks (BSN), 2011 International Conference on*, 2011, pp. 194–199.

AT&T, *"Digital Life"*, Last Update: 2013, https://my-digitallife.att.com/support/digitallife

Bourke, Alan K., Pepijn W. J. Van de Ven, Amy E. Chaya, Gearoid M. Olaighin, and John Nelson, "Testing of a long-term fall detection system incorporated into a custom vest for the elderly," in *Engineering in Medicine and Biology Society, 2008. EMBS 2008. 30th Annual International Conference of the IEEE*, 2008, pp. 2844–2847.

Lan, Mars, *et al.*, "SmartFall: an automatic fall detection system based on subsequence matching for the SmartCane," presented at the Proceedings of the Fourth International Conference on Body Area Networks, Los Angeles, California, 2009.

Tacconi, Carlo, Sabato Mellone, and Lorenzo Chiari, "Smartphone-based applications for investigating falls and mobility," in *Pervasive Computing Technologies for Healthcare (PervasiveHealth), 2011 5th International Conference on*, 2011, pp. 258–261.

Yavuz, Gokhan Remzi, *et al.*, "A Smartphone Based Fall Detector with Online Location Support," presented at the International Workshop on Sensing for App Phones (PhoneSense), Zurich, Switzerland, 2010.

The Street, "BuddyGuard Personal Protection Service Debuts In App Store", http://www.thestreet.com/story/11038957/1/buddyguard-personal-protection-service-debuts-in-app-store.html, 2011.

Tamura, Toshiyo, Takumi Yoshimura, Masaki Sekine, Mitsuo Uchida, and Osamu Tanaka, "A Wearable Airbag to Prevent Fall Injuries," *IEEE Transactions on Information Technology in Biomedicine*, vol. 13 (6), pp. 910–914, 2009.

Guangyi, Shi, *et al.*, "Mobile Human Airbag System for Fall Protection Using MEMS Sensors and Embedded SVM Classifier," *Sensors Journal, IEEE*, vol. 9 (5), pp. 495–503, 2009.

Fukaya, Kiyoshi and Mitsuya Uchida, "Protection against Impact with the Ground Using Wearable Airbags," *Industrial Health*, vol. 46 (1), pp. 59–65, 2008.

Ferenstein, Gregory. *"This iPhone Breathalyzer Wants To Call You A Cab"*, Last Update: 3rd March, 2013, http://techcrunch.com/2013/03/03/this-iphone-breathalyzer-wants-to-call-you-a-cab/

CHAPTER 11

■ ■ ■

Environmental Monitoring for Health and Wellness

Our environment plays a pivotal daily role in our health and well-being. The air we breathe, the water we drink, the noise levels we're exposed to, and the weather we experience, all directly affect us in terms of our quality of life, our life expectancy, and the prevalence of certain diseases or other aspects of our personal health.

Poor air quality, for example, has been linked to premature death, cancer, and respiratory conditions such as chronic obstructive pulmonary disease (COPD). Second-hand smoke from cigarettes has been correlated with lung cancers and other respiratory conditions among non-smokers (Barnoya et al., 2005, Sasco et al., 2004). Pesticide contamination in the environment has been linked to a drop in male fertility (Bretveld et al., 2007, Balabanic et al., 2011). Global industrialization, urbanization, transport systems, agriculture, and energy production—all driven by population growth— are putting an enormous strain on our environment.

If current human societal behavior continues unchecked, we will need to consume more resources to drive our energy-hungry lifestyles, resulting in increased levels of pollution— including greenhouse gases, as shown in Figure 11-1. The Global Burden of Disease study estimates that 24 percent of the world's burden of disease can be attributed to environmental factors (IHME, 2013). The report attributes 3.2 million adult deaths globally to ambient air pollution in 2010, up from 2.9 million in 1990. In addition, 3.5 million adult deaths were associated with household air pollution exposure, such as indoor smoke from solid fuels. The report points out that the total number of deaths related to air pollution (6.9 million) exceeded those attributed to cigarette smoking (6.3 million). However, when dealing with such estimates, the contribution of modifiable risks factors also needs to be considered. For example, how many of the individuals were cigarette smokers or had occupations that increased their risks, as opposed to individuals who were unavoidably exposed to air pollution? Personal sensing in the future may offer quantifiable insights at an individual level into the amount of avoidable and unavoidable air pollution we are exposed to.

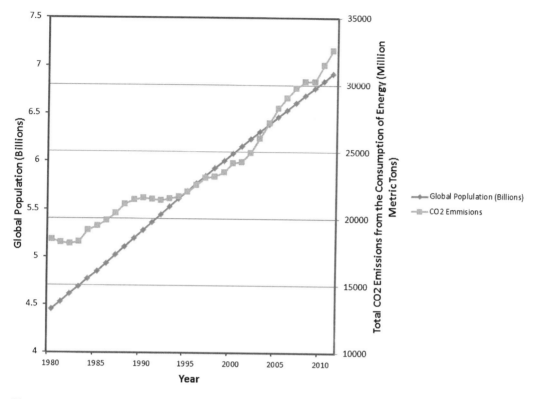

Figure 11-1. *Growth in global population and rise in carbon dioxide (CO$_2$) emissions due to energy consumption (Sources: US Energy Information Administration, US Bureau of the Census)*

Environmental monitoring focuses primarily on the identification and measurement of pollutants in the form of chemical, biological, microbiological, and radiological containments in water, soil, and air. In addition, ambient environmental monitoring targets variables such as temperature, humidity, and noise levels. While monitoring has been used for many decades, approaches to date have relied mainly on in-situ representative sampling (grab sampling), followed by laboratory analysis of samples. While highly accurate, this is slow, laborious, intensive, and not scalable. From a regulatory perspective, there has been significant interest in the use of sensing technologies, which can extend the capabilities of the laboratory to sites of interest. Some successes have been achieved, particularly with air-quality monitoring. However, these sensors cost tens of thousands of dollars, which limits their scalability and restricts their use to a small number of static sites within a given area.

Because of the need for improved, affordable and scalable sensing, there is growing interest in the use of lower-cost wireless sensors for environmental monitoring applications, both in the regulatory and non-regulatory domains. Moreover, individuals who have become increasingly aware of their ambient environment are interested in monitoring the quality of that environment. This is driven in part by extending the concept of the quantified self to embrace environmental influences. The ubiquitous nature of smartphones and tablets is also enabling the development of early-stage crowdsourced sensing capabilities in which citizens become mobile sensors of their own environment.

> ■ **Quantified Self**   A movement of individuals who are interested in using sensors and other computing technologies to track on a daily basis a variety of data about themselves, such as what they eat, the quality of their ambient environment, their physical activities and performance, and other key health metrics in order to better understand their health and well-being (QS, 2012).

Environmental monitoring can generally be categorized into indoor and outdoor applications. Indoor applications typically focus on home, workplace, and office environments. Quantities of interest measured using sensors include temperature, humidity, light levels, air quality, and noise. Other measurands of interest from a safety perspective include smoke and carbon monoxide (CO) (see Chapter 10). Outdoor monitoring involves a wide variety of scenarios, including air pollution, water quality, traffic noise, weather, geological events such as earthquakes and volcanic eruptions, and agricultural applications that monitor, for example, soil moisture levels. In this chapter we focus on environmental sensing as it relates to human health and well-being.

Drivers of Environmental Sensing

A number of technical, social, and economic drivers are influencing the growing interest and adoption of sensors for environmental monitoring applications. As the cost of sensors decreases and their accuracy grows, they are becoming more viable platforms for in-situ monitoring applications. In addition, flexibility in their form factor enables protocol innovation and supports sampling regimes, which would be impossible or prohibitively expensive using traditional approaches.

Cost

The current approaches to environmental monitoring use high-cost analytical instrumentation for either in-situ monitoring or online analysis in laboratories. While these techniques, such as gas chromatography and mass spectroscopy, are accurate and offer appropriate sensitivity, they range in cost from thousands to tens of thousands of dollars. In contrast, sensors costing tens or low hundreds of dollars based on semiconductor, optical, and electrochemical techniques are becoming available. These devices can be incorporated into discrete, autonomous platforms, which can form the basis of distributed wireless sensor networks. With careful calibration strategies, these sensors can serve as low-cost alternatives to centralized instrumental monitoring for certain applications. The increasingly lower price point is enabling a rapidly developing market for personal environmental products, such as AirQualityEgg, which runs between $100 and $200.

Smartphones

The widespread adoption of smartphones is providing both a low-cost environmental sensor-aggregation platform and, in some cases, the actual sensing platform. For example, applications that track ambient noise can use the microphone integrated in every smartphone. The built-in GPS functionality can be used to geotag data, which is particularly important for mobile crowdsourced applications. Data shared via e-mail, SMS, or the Web can be a particularly useful for local environmental monitoring agencies. Smartphones provide a single form factor for all data-related processes, and their use will continue to grow in both professional and citizen-centric applications, particularly as more wireless-enabled environmental sensors become available.

Civic Sensing

As sensor technologies for environmental monitoring become more widely available and affordable, interest among individuals in monitoring their environment will grow. Active involvement in the generation and consumption of environmental data changes perceptions, attitudes, behaviors, and the level of engagement. Concerns are driven by frequent media reports of issues with air quality, drinking water, and food contamination, coupled with visible signs of problems, such as smog in many large cities. Individuals may be worried about exposure to environmental contaminants during outdoor exercise, such as running or jogging, particularly in urban environments. Parents may have concerns about the impact of pollution on a child or other family member, such as an elderly parent whose health makes them sensitive to environmental factors. The data is often seen as being complementary to personal health and wellness initiatives, as outlined in Chapters 9 and 10. Increasingly, society is focusing on creating a better understanding of cause-and-effect relationships between health and the environment, based on sharing data among online communities.

Sampling

Environmental monitoring often relies on the use of in-situ sampling, sometimes referred to as grab sampling. These samples are collected in labeled sample containers or gas bags and then stored under environmentally controlled conditions for transport back to the laboratory for analysis. The approach is slow, costly, and may even be unrepresentative of the quantities of interest, particularly in dynamic environments where pollutants may be transient. Delayed detection of issues can also have public health implications. For example, in epidemics, members of the public inevitably become ill before the problem is identified more broadly. The use of sensor-based approaches can help to address these limitations and facilitate earlier detection of contaminants and pollutants. However, the sensors may need to be coupled with automated sampling systems to ensure that they are exposed to consistent and reproducible samples.

Environmental Sensing and Network and Communications Technologies

Many environmental sensors have wireless capabilities ranging from low-power Zigbee to Wi-Fi or 3G/4G communications. Zigbee-based nodes can be deployed in a mesh network configuration using multihop protocols to cover larger geographical areas than can be covered using a standard star topology. Wi-Fi offers outdoor ranges of 100 to 200 meters (about 300-600 feet), while 3G and 4G both have significantly longer ranges. This allows the sensors to be deployed over larger geographical areas, a frequent requirement for environmental applications. However, it is important to ensure that, from an economical perspective, the density of deployment required for effective communications is appropriate. There is often a trade-off to be made between building a network with a small number of high-power devices, and using a larger number of low-power devices with sufficient overlap in their communication fields to ensure reliable communications (Linear-Technology, 2012, Ghosh et al., 2008). There is growing support for IPv6 on sensor nodes to provide IP end-to-end connectivity (see Chapter 4). Use of this protocol simplifies the process of connecting wireless sensor network (WSN) devices to the Internet and helps to realize the paradigm of the Internet of Things (Mainwaring et al., 2010).

Making the data generally available online will enable environmentally aware hacktivists to easily create web-based applications and mobile apps that can be used to inform and educate the general public. The use of IPv6-based protocols also allows system designers and users to leverage the rich ecosystems of tools that have already been developed for commissioning, configuring, and administering these networks.

■ **Hacktivists** Those who use computers, the Internet, social media, and other digital tools to promote a political or ideological cause. Hacktivism incorporates a broad range of activities that often operate just within the boundaries of legality by exploiting the concept of freedom of speech (Conway, 2012). However, some consider that certain activities cross the threshold of legality. Environmental hacktivists can use sensor technologies to collect data in order to promote a specific cause, or to highlight a specific issue. Their intention is typically to raise public awareness in an effort to put pressure on politicians to implement policy changes that are beneficial to the environment. However, the ability of environmental hacktivists to interpret the data correctly is subject to some debate. Some argue that they may cause unnecessary panic and misinform the public. How we educate the public to deal with such campaigns will grow in importance. In a data-driven society, individuals need to have a greater understanding of scientific data in order to make their own interpretations. Understanding and a skeptical mind are required for stimulating informed criticism, which ensures that suppositions and hypothesis are adequately tested and debated and not simply accepted as fact.

Barriers to Adoption

Despite the potential of sensor-based monitoring, both from a regulatory and a citizen perspective, many barriers remain to be overcome before widespread adoption is truly possible. These include power consumption, robustness and cost, available sensor technologies, security, usability, scalability, and interoperability. Let us examine these factors in more detail.

Power Consumption

Power consumption remains an operational constraint, particularly for remotely deployed applications where it is not possible to provide access to AC power. Even when AC power is an option, the cost of provisioning connections is usually expensive. Energy-harvesting options, such as solar panels, are available; however, they can be expensive relative to the cost of the sensor. The return on investment can be on the order of years, which may be longer than the planned lifetime of the deployment. Maintenance overhead is also a consideration that adds cost to the system deployment (Zervous, 2013). Panel size can be issue in term of power output; that is, panel sizes may have to be large to generate sufficient power for some system configuration, such as embedded computing data aggregators. (See Chapter 4.) Large panel sizes may not be an option, depending on the location of the deployment. Sensor-node deployments with battery-power sources are still the most popular. Sensor-node lifetimes typically exhibit a strong dependency on battery life. Improvements in battery technologies and the use of energy-harvesting techniques, such as solar panels and micro wind turbines, have increased the available energy budget. However, careful design of sensor networks is generally required to minimize compromises in duty cycle and measurement frequencies.

Robustness and Cost

Many environmental applications expose sensors to harsh conditions. The sensors, batteries, and other sensitive electronic equipment need to be protected from rain, ice, dust, and other sources of contaminants. The enclosures will typically have an Ingress Protection Rating (IPR). The IPR specification (see Table 11-1) is published by the International Electrotechnical Commission (IEC) within the IEC 60529 standard. The IPR rating for an electronic device typically consists of the letters IP, followed by a two-digit number, such as IP65, which indicates complete protection, limited ingress permitted. The first digit identifies the protection against intrusion of solid objects, such as human or tool contact or foreign bodies, such as dust. The second digit in the IP rating identifies the level of protection again moisture ingress. For environmental applications, this ranges from 6 to 8. In the United States, the National Electrical Manufacturers Association (NEMA) publishes protection ratings for enclosures that are similar to the IP ratings. It differs from the IPR specification in that it dictates other product features, such as corrosion resistance, gasket aging, and construction practices.

Table 11-1. *Ingress Protection Rating Codes*

First Digit			Second Digit	
Protection against Human/Tool Contact	**Protection against solid objects**		**Protection against water**	**Protection against condition**
0 No special protection	No protection	0	No protection	
1 Back of hand, fist	Protection against a solid object >50mm	1	Protected against vertically dripping water	Condensation, light rain
2 Finger or similar objects	Protection against a solid object >12mm	2	Protected against vertically dripping water when tilted 15 degrees	Light rain with wind
3 Tools and wires etc. with a thickness > 2.5mm	Protection against a solid object >2.5mm	3	Protected against water spraying at an angle up to 60 degrees	Heavy rainstorm
4 Tool and wires etc. with a thickness >1mm	Protection against a solid object >1mm	4	Protected against water splashing from any direction	Splashing
5 Complete protection (limited ingress permitted)	Dust protected	5	Protected against jets of water from any direction	Hose down, residential
6 Complete protection	Dust proof	6	Protected against powerful jets of water from any direction	Hose down, commercial
		7	Protected against immersion between a depth of 150mm and 1000mm	Immersion in tank
		8	Protected against submersion—depth specified by manufacturer.	Immersion > 1M

Sensors can be purchased with casings that have high IPRs or, especially when a deployment requires multiple sensors, they can be mounted in an IPR cabinet enclosure. The cost of enclosures meeting these specifications can be relatively high, often more than the sensors themselves. For example, a small IP-67 all-weather plastic enclosure (150mm x150mm) will cost in the region of $100 to $200. There is growing interest in the use of 3D printers to create low-cost enclosures that can be produced at a fraction of the cost of injection molded plastics (Boisvert, 2013). However, the technology needs to mature further to meet the rigorous demands of environmental applications.

While the cost of some environmental sensors is becoming affordable for use by consumers, the cost of institution-led deployments (by academic and regulatory bodies) remains high if not prohibitive. The actual sensor cost may represent a fraction of the overall deployment cost, which includes enclosures, aggregators, communications installation, as well as ongoing administration and maintenance costs. New system-on-chip (SOC) components are emerging, particularly for M2M (machine-to-machine) applications, which will help to reduce some of these deployment costs. However, it is likely to take a number of years for these components to feed into the sensor ecosystem. Moreover, the ability to produce low-cost, sensitive, and reliable sensors remains a challenge. But the proliferation of smartphones can provide a zero-cost platform for the acquisition, processing, presentation, and archiving of disposable sensor data, which greatly simplifies sensor requirements (Crisostomo, 2013, Sensorcon, 2013).

Technology Limitations

The capabilities and sensitivity of low-cost sensors remain somewhat limited. Currently, environmental monitoring usually uses a restricted range sensors types, such as those for temperature, light, humidity, and atmospheric pressure, which might found in a hobbyist weather station. While low-cost semiconductor and electrochemical gas sensors and particulate matter (PM) monitoring sensors are available, their sensitivity and accuracy are often inferior to current instrumental techniques (Choi et al., 2009); (Romain et al., 2010). Careful and continuous calibration protocols can improve the performance of some sensors, but significant progress remains to be made. The use of sensors to detect bacterial contamination in water is one of many areas of active research (Grossi et al., 2013). Sensors to detect pathogens such as E. coli have been demonstrated (Mannoor et al., 2010). However, the availability of commercial sensor technologies is still extremely limited. It will likely be a number of years before sensor technologies for in-situ detection of bacterial contamination for real-world applications emerge.

Security Concerns

The security of sensors for institutional applications remains a cause for concern. Data that identifies particular threats to public health often results in preventative or remedial actions by public officials, which can have significant social and economic impacts. It is therefore critical that the data used to initiate such actions has appropriate integrity. Highly robust security generally requires significant computational capabilities to implement correctly, which is difficult to achieve on energy-constrained sensors. Progress continues, but the challenges of implementing scalable, robust, security systems for low-computational sensor devices are significant. The emergence of low-cost M2M SOCs with integrated software and hardware security features may offer some relief in the medium term.

Usability and Scalability

The usability of sensors and their supporting software can be challenging, particularly for the hobbyist user who buys them off the shelf. The development of firmware remains outside the technical capabilities of most potential users. It is therefore important that both discrete and wireless sensors become easier to install, maintain, and understand. Ideally, the sensors need to evolve into plug-and-play operability. And they need to be easily discoverable by aggregators such as smartphones, with highly intuitive support apps and simple connectivity to cloud services for sharing, aggregation, and analysis.

WSNs for environmental monitoring, scaled to thousands of nodes over large geographical areas and operating successfully for years, have yet to be achieved. To date, WSNs have been demonstrated for environmental proposes but have been limited to double-digit or low hundreds of sensor nodes (the term node or sensor node is used to describe a sensor that is part of a larger network and is capable of connecting to the other nodes in the network to exchange data and other messages). It remains to be demonstrated that the available theoretical solutions reported in the literature are suited to large WSNs supporting real-world environmental applications.

Interoperability

The interoperability of sensors from different vendors is a major challenge for market participants. Sensors are available with a variety of standards-based or proprietary communications protocols. Even when standards-based radios are used, the firmware usually implements a custom data payload that varies from vendor to vendor. Wireless communication technology can be successful only if the sensors of different vendors can communicate successfully. Such a multivendor interoperability environment is expected to be a long-term challenge.

Data Quality and Ownership

As sensors become more widely available and deployed, the granularity and pervasiveness of monitoring will increase. The concomitant increase in data will most likely generate significant discussion and debate. Key among the questions that will have to be answered are as follows:

- Whose data is it?

- How should it be interpreted?

- How do we ensure data quality?

- Does crowdsourced data have appropriate statistical significance?

These questions and many others will likely fuel debates between environmentally concerned citizens and vested interests in the form of commercial, public, and government entities and environmental activists. The debates will center on the validity and meaning of the data and the potential actions to be taken to improve the health and wellness of citizens.

Environmental Parameters

Environmental monitoring has generally focused on the detection and measurement of contaminant concentrations and identifying when contaminants have dissipated to levels that no longer pose a public health risk. Monitoring approaches assess the chemical, physical, radiological, and biological properties of a medium under test, such as air or water. Longitudinal monitoring in a particular location is used to establish normative ranges and identify results that fall outside these ranges. More recently, the focus area of environmental monitoring has expanded beyond contamination detection to include noise pollution, solar radiation levels, and ambient urban conditions.

Air Quality and Atmospheric Conditions

Air quality receives frequent attention in the media in relation to topics such as the burning of fossil fuels, global urbanization, the proliferation of cars, intensive agriculture and industrial pollution. Human activity is having an impact on air quality in many parts of the world. One of the most visible manifestations of this is photochemical smog, comprising pollutants such as nitrogen oxides and dioxides, volatile organic compounds, ozone, and aldehydes. Smog is a global problem affecting cities such as Los Angeles, Beijing, and Mexico City. Figure 11-2 shows the annual mean of PM_{10} (particles with a diameter of 10 micrometers or less) in cities by region from 2003 to 2010. Clearly, many regions across the globe are exceeding what are considered to be safe limits for various forms of pollutants, including airborne particulate matter.

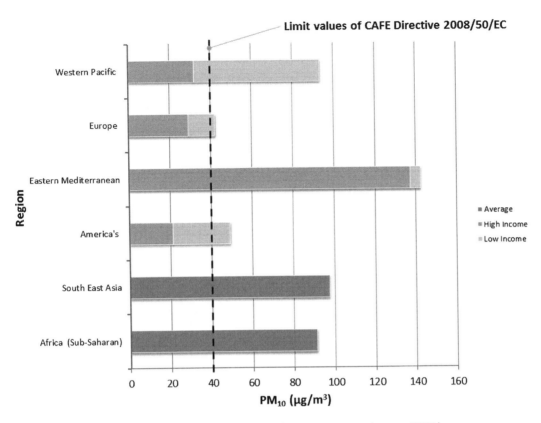

Figure 11-2. *Annual mean of PM₁₀ in cities by region from 2003 to 2010 (source: WHO)*

Air quality and its components are generally defined by national legislation such as the Clean Air Act in the U.S., and in Europe by EU ambient-air legislation, such as the Ambient Air Quality and Cleaner Air for Europe (CAFE) Directive (2008/50/EC); see Chapter 7 for further details. Legislation defines both qualities of interest and their limits, and how they should be assessed and managed by national agencies.

The technique used depends on the pollutant of interest. O_3 (ozone), for example, is measured using ultraviolet (UV) absorption, whereas fluorescence spectroscopy can be used for the detection of inorganic compounds such as SO_2 (sulphur dioxide) (Queensland Government, 2011). In the U.S., fixed monitoring stations are augmented with self-contained mobile laboratories called Trace Atmospheric Gas Analyzers (TAGA). The TAGA bus can be deployed to monitor air quality and other measures of interest during or after exceptional events—such as the BP spill in the Gulf of Mexico—to determine risks to public health. From an air-quality perspective, the EPA focused on measuring concentrations of volatile organic chemicals (VOCs) from the oil spill and chemicals used in the oil-dispersant process, both of which had vaporized into the air (EPA, 2010). All instruments used for institutional air-quality measurements must meet the required standards, such as EN12341, the EU specification for the performance of PM_{10} sampling instruments (Standards, 1998), and 73 FR 66964, the U.S. national ambient air-quality standard (NAAQS) for lead (EPA, 2008). Strict guidelines also cover the calibration of the instrumentation, sampling methodologies, and so on. Collectively, this makes ambient air quality monitoring specialized, inflexible, expensive (with instruments ranging from thousands to tens of thousands of dollars), and not very scalable across large geographical areas. As a result, there is growing interest in the use of lower-cost, discrete, wireless sensor networks to augment regulatory air quality monitoring.

Monitoring air quality entails measuring a wide variety of parameters at different levels of sensitivity across different timeframes, which can be difficult for the public to consume and interpret to their satisfaction. To address this issue, government agencies often use an air-quality index for health (AQIH). This number expresses complex air-quality information in simple terms to inform the public of the current air pollution level and its potential impact on their health. Such indices are particularly important for sensitive groups, such as asthmatics. In Ireland, the AQIH is a ten-point range, divided as follows (EPA, 2013):

- Good (1-3)

- Fair (4-6)

- Poor (7-9)

- Very poor (10)

The index is based on five parameters: the one-hour average of SO_2, NO_2 (nitrogen dioxide), and O_3, combined with a rolling 24-hour average of PM_{10} and $PM_{2.5}$ (particulate matter with a diameter less than 2.5 microns). The overall AQIH is the highest of the five pollutant indices. In the U.S., the air-quality index is defined by the EPA. The AQI comprises six categories correlated with increasing impact on health, as shown in Table 11-2. Values over 300 indicate hazardous air quality, while values below 50 are considered good (EPA, 2013).

Table 11-2. *EPA Air Quality Index Based on Five Pollutants Regulated by the Clean Air Act (ground-level O_3, particulate matter, CO, SO_2, and NO_2); (source: U.S. EPA)*

Air Quality Index (AQI)	Levels of Health Concern	Definition
0-50	Good	Air quality is satisfactory.
51-100	Moderate	Air quality is acceptable. Some pollutants may be at a level to be of moderate concern for a very small number of individuals who are sensitive to air pollution.
101-150	Unhealthy for sensitive groups	Members of sensitive groups may experience health effects. The general public is unlikely to be affected.
151-200	Unhealthy	Most people are likely to experience health effects.
201-300	Very unhealthy	Health warnings to indicate emergency conditions.
301-500	Hazardous	Health alert—everyone is at risk for serious health effects.

In addition to air-quality measurements using sensors and analytical instrumentation, satellite monitoring has been used for many years. A key advantage of a satellite-based approach is its ability to cover a large geographical area, which can be useful in identifying and tracking sources of pollution. A number of instrumental techniques are employed for measuring pollutants. For example, the GOME-2, launched in 2006, is a European instrument carried on the MetOp-A satellite. GOME-2 uses a scanning spectrometer that captures light reflected from the Earth's surface and atmosphere. The spectrometer splits the light into its spectral components to map concentrations of atmospheric O_3 as well as NO_2, SO_2, other trace gases, and ultraviolet radiation (see Figure 11-3). Data from the GOME-2 instrument provides insights into atmospheric composition and levels of pollutants (WDC-RSAT, 2103). Data from NASA's Earth Observatory satellite Terra has recently been used to show $PM_{2.5}$ pollution over Beijing in China. The satellite images were in used in conjunction with ground-level sensing at the U.S. embassy in Beijing, which recorded $PM_{2.5}$ measurements of 291. The World Health Organization specifies that $PM_{2.5}$ levels above 25 are considered unsafe (CBS, 2013). Scientists are becoming interested in combining satellite measurements of $PM_{2.5}$ with ground-based measurements, and there are calls within the scientific community for air-quality and space scientists to work together more closely on $PM_{2.5}$ and other forms of pollution monitoring (Hidy et al., 2009).

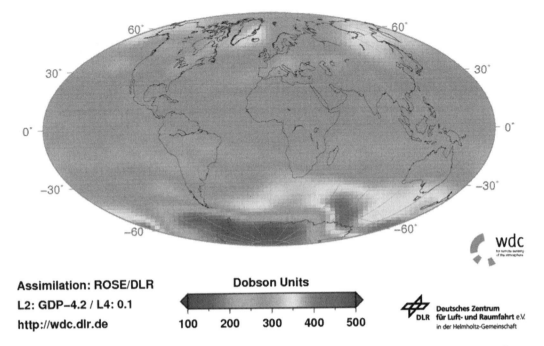

GOME2 METOP–A　　　　　　　　　　　　　　**Sep 13, 2013**

Ozone Vertical Column Density

Assimilation: ROSE/DLR

L2: GDP–4.2 / L4: 0.1

http://wdc.dlr.de

Dobson Units

100　200　300　400　500

Figure 11-3. *Global ozone levels measured by GOME-2 (image source: the ICSU World Data Center for Remote Sensing of the Atmosphere)*

Satellite observations also play an important role in monitoring global temperatures. Temperature measurements are made indirectly by measuring radiances (the quantity of radiation that passes through or is emitted from a surface at a given angle in a specific direction) in various wavelength bands, which are then mathematically converted into temperature measurements. Various methods exist for the conversion of the radiance measurements into temperature. Differences in the results obtained from these methods have led to some debate, especially because the data is an important input into global temperature models. Groups such as the Remote Sensing Systems (RSS) and the University of Alabama in Huntsville (UAH) play an active role in calculating temperature measurements from satellite observation (MedLibrary.org, 2013).

Sensing Air Quality

The use of low-cost sensors to generate air quality data that is then made available online for public consumption has been gaining in popularity. These data sets can be used to support local initiatives, such as driving changes to local government policies. They can also be used for personal applications, for example, to improve asthma management. Keep in mind, however, that these data sets will often have limitations due to data-quality issues. Low-cost sensors, particularly semiconductor-based ones, may not have the required level of sensitivity. They may also exhibit drift without appropriate calibration procedures. The performance of the sensor may be influenced by the ambient conditions such as temperature. It is therefore important to select sensors with an appropriate level of sensitivity and linear range for the given use case. The deployment strategy, enclosures, sampling methodology, and so on must be carefully chosen to minimize any impacts on performance within the required operational envelope.

A variety of wireless sensor deployments to monitor air quality and corresponding weather conditions, particularly in urban locations, have been reported in the literature over recent years. One such deployment in Taipei, Taiwan monitors CO emissions from vehicular traffic. The system consists of sensor nodes, a gateway, and a back-end platform controlled by a LabVIEW program through which sensing data was stored in a database. The deployment consisted of nine sensor installations with Global System for Mobile Communication (GSM) connectivity. Two CO peaks were found, at 7 a.m. and 7 p.m., corresponding to rush-hour traffic. Moreover, high concentrations of pollutants were detected that continued accumulating when motor vehicles waited for red lights. Some sensor nodes detected CO concentrations of up to 9 parts per million (ppm)—above the limit recommended for long-term human exposure (Jen-Hao et al., 2011).

Other efforts include the CitySense platform deployed at Harvard University and the surrounding area to monitor a number of air-quality parameters, including PM_{10}, CO_2, NO (nitrogen oxide), and O_3. These measurements were augmented with weather and ambient-noise data. Visualization of the data was achieved using Microsoft's SensorMap platform (Murty et al., 2008). A similar deployment was carried out in New York City, where mote-based sensors were used to measure humidity, temperature, atmospheric pressure, barometric pressure, and light levels. To add context to the sensor data, a geographic information system (GIS) implementation provided a geographic overlay for understanding the sensor locations. Each node was identified by name, tag, and current measurements at the nodes location (Morreale et al., 2010).

A key enabling feature of wireless sensors is supporting mobile applications, which give them an advantage over static monitoring stations that are tied to a specific location. This capability has been used in air-quality monitoring deployments in cities such as Cape Town, South Africa. In that deployment, Waspmotes (an extensible wireless sensor platform with sensor boards for environmental, agricultural, smart cities, and radiation monitoring), with gas sensor boards from the Spanish company Libelium, were used in a car following predefined routes to map the pollution levels in the city. The data was presented as a proof of concept—a first step in realizing a vision of how cars with cloud connectivity and integrated sensors could act as mobile, real-time air-monitoring stations (Bagula et al., 2012).

Transport-enabled sensing has been effectively demonstrated by researchers from ETH Zurich using the public tram system in Zurich. Their air-quality project, OpenSense, monitors four primary pollutants O_3, CO, NO_2 and particulate matter (Li et al., 2012). All sensors are housed in a self-contained measurement station, as shown in Figure 11-4 (a). The core of the prototype station is a Gumstix embedded computer running Linux. The station supports General Packet Radio Service/Universal Mobile Telecommunications System (GPRS/UMTS) and wireless local area networks (WLANs) for communication and data transfer. A GPS receiver supplies the station with precise geospatial information. The measurement station is equipped with an accelerometer and, once installed on a tram, receives the door release signal to assist in recognizing tram stops to minimize positioning uncertainty. The station is supplied with power from the tram, as shown in Figure 11-4 (b).

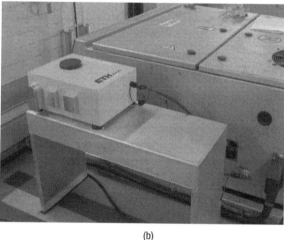

(a)   (b)

Figure 11-4. (a) ETH OpenSense sensor station (b) Installation of an OpenSense measurement station on top of a VBZ cobra tram (image used with permission from Computer Engineering and Networks Laboratory (TIK), ETH Zurich)

There are five stations on top of trams in Zurich and one at the national air pollution monitoring network (NABEL) station in Dübendorf. The performance of ETH's sensors can be compared with the EMPA's (EMPA, 2013) fixed environmental monitoring station. Reference data obtained by this station is used to calibrate the mobile sensors and to evaluate their performance under a wide range of weather conditions. The data is made public and can be accessed online at `http://data.opensense.ethz.ch`. It can be used to model how the various sensor parameters vary over the course of the year. For example, Figure 11-5 shows the variation in ultrafine particulate concentrations between spring and winter (Hasenfratz et al., 2012, Keller et al., 2012).

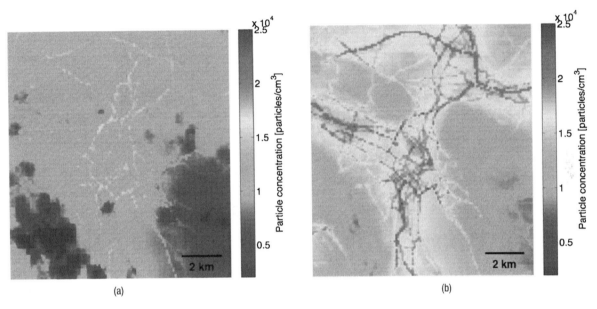

Figure 11-5. *Modeled ultrafine particle concentrations for Zurich during spring (a) and winter (b) (image used with permission from Computer Engineering and Networks Laboratory (TIK), ETH Zurich)*

In the commercial domain, AirBase Systems (`www.myairbase.com`), an Israeli start-up, has developed a low-cost, easy-to-use air quality sensor unit for indoor and outdoor monitoring applications, as shown in Figure 11-6(a) . The system is currently equipped to measure levels of O_3, NO_2, total VOC, total suspended particles (TSP), noise, relative humidity, and temperature. Other sensors can be added to monitor odor, light, and SO_2. The units require external power and feature both Wi-Fi and GSM communications. Once the sensor is powered up, data is available on a 20-second duty cycle. Any deviation from the allowed (or input) exposure standard generates an alert. Data from deployed stations can be made available on Google Maps to provide a live global view of air quality with drill-down into the data from each station, as shown in Figure 11-6(b)

Figure 11-6a. *Outdoor CanarIT air monitoring from AirBase Systems (image used with permission from AirBase Ltd)*

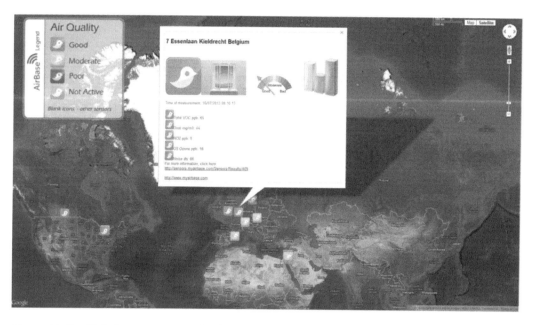

Figure 11-6b. *Global representation of real-time data from CanarIT air quality monitoring stations (image used with permission from AirBase Ltd)*

Sensing Indoor Air Quality

The use of sensors in a home for a variety of applications is well-established. Chapter 9 reviewed how sensors have been used to deliver healthcare applications, and Chapter 10 looked at home safety and security applications. There is now a growing interest in developing applications that monitor the ambient environment in people's homes to enhance their comfort and wellness. One key focus area has been indoor air quality, which can negatively impact well-being. This interest is often driven by concerns about allergies or asthma, or the use of solid fuel heating stoves in a family living area. Poor air quality can result in symptoms often mistaken for colds, flu, or allergies: nausea, dizziness, headaches, breathing problems, eye irritation, and muscle pain. Common sources of indoor air pollution include carpeting and the adhesives used to install it, furniture fabric, and mold.

Kits are available that can collect air samples, which are then sent for laboratory analysis to identify problems, such as the presence of VOCs. The kits can be expensive and they provide only a snapshot in time of air quality. A number of sensors with smartphone connectivity, like the AQM-p from Esensors, are now available. They are aimed at the general public, and can provide continuous measurements of air quality inside or close to homes. One community-based initiative supported by a Kickstarter campaign that has received significant attention is the Air Quality Egg (`airqualityegg.com`). This sensor is designed to allow anyone to collect data on NO_2 and CO concentrations together with temperature and humidity. The sensor is placed outside the home to measure ambient gas concentrations and it streams the data wirelessly to an egg-shaped base station. The base station connects to a home broadband router via an Ethernet connection and sends data to the Xively web application, which visualizes and stores the data.

Another interesting sensor platform currently in beta testing is the AirBoxLab (`www.airboxlab.com`), which is actually a sensor array that measures VOCs, CO_2, CO, particulate matter, temperature, and relative humidity. Data from the sensor can be streamed to any computing device, including smartphones, for data access, and to the cloud for storage and additional processing. AirBoxLab is developing analytics capabilities, including pattern-recognition and machine-learning algorithms, that will enable proactive messaging designed to modify behavior to improve home air quality. That behavior might include air renewal by opening windows and doors in living spaces and locating sources of pollution to eradicate them.

A commercial product receiving significant media attention is Netatmo's personal weather station with air quality sensors, which monitors both indoor and outdoor air quality, weather, acoustic comfort, and other environmental parameters. The aesthetically pleasing aluminum enclosures (separate ones for indoor and outdoor use) are designed to be placed prominently in a living space, as shown in Figure 11-7. A key goal for the product is helping to improve people's wellness in their homes by informing them (via an iOS or Android app) when they should ventilate their living environment.

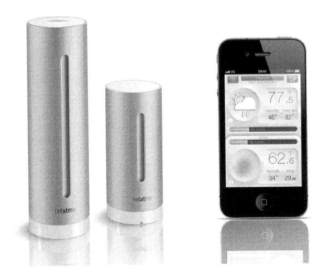

Figure 11-7. *The Netatmo personal weather station with air quality sensors (image used with permission from Netatmo, `www.netatmo.com`)*

This theme of wellness and improved quality of indoor living is also reflected in the recently launched CubeSensors product. These small, wireless sensors (50x50x50mm) continuously measure temperature, humidity, noise, light, air quality, and barometric pressure in any room in which they are deployed, and stream the data via the cloud to any computing device. The cloud service also sends alerts and recommendations to users on how to improve the indoor environment, including ventilation notifications, when to humidify or dehumidify, and so on. Launched in the summer of 2013, the initial batch of sensors sold out immediately.

For technically oriented environment enthusiasts, a number of kits have emerged, many based around the popular Arduinio platform. Arduinio kits based on a Sharp optical dust sensor are available for particle detection, for example. The sensor connects to an Arduinio shield via an Ethernet connection. Data can be sent to Xively for storage and visualization. In addition, Facebook and Twitter alerts can be received when new air quality sensor measurements become available (Nafis, 2012).

Researchers continue to actively develop and evaluate indoor environmental sensing platforms. Unsurprisingly, there is a particular focus on the use of smartphones for sensor data aggregation, processing, and remote transfer to cloud-based storage and processing. One example of this approach is the MAQS/M-Pod system developed by researchers at the University of Colorado at Boulder, which is designed to be body-worn on the upper arm or attached to a backpack. The M-Pods provide sensing for a standard range of air quality parameters. The system features a fan that pulls air through the sensor module. The fan is required to ensure that sensors are exposed sufficiently to the ambient atmosphere as they are housed within a plastic enclosure for protection. Data is streamed to a smartphone via Bluetooth. The system also features room location capabilities. The system leverages the smartphone's accelerometer to monitor the owner's entrance and departure. It triggers room localization via Wi-Fi RSSI (received signal strength indicator) room mappings only when a room entrance event is detected (Jiang et al., 2011).

The BodyTrack project at Carnegie Mellon University expands on smartphone-enabled monitoring by combining indoor air quality parameters with physiological sensing such as EKG/ECG, respiration and ambient parameters such as light and sound levels. The rationale behind this multisensory approach is to enable individuals to explore potential environment/health interactions. The influence of air quality on respiratory issues such as asthma or sleep problems can be investigated based on a cause and effect relationship. These relationships between data can be explored using an open source web service that allows users to aggregate, visualize, and analyze data from a variety of sources (Wright et al., 2012).

Community-Based Outdoor Air Quality Monitoring

For accurate and detailed information about the ambient air quality of a geographical area, covering the whole area with sensors is ideal. In practice, this is not feasible, so sensors are placed at desired locations, and useful information is constructed from the gathered data. With standard approaches, it can take a few years to collect and analyze the data for large-scale air-quality monitoring and generate detailed reports. This can be source of frustration for people dealing with air quality concerns such as odorous emissions from a local factory. To address this issue, community sensing is rapidly gaining attention. In this scheme, standalone mobile sensors or sensors integrated into wireless sensor networks capture data from the environment and share it on the Web. Discrete sensors can be paired with smartphones for data aggregation, processing, and sharing. The collected data can be further augmented by taking advantage of smartphone capabilities—for instance, geotagging the data using the built-in GPS. A key limitation of crowdsourcing is the potential variability in the quality of the sensor data. Issues can arise due to poor calibration of the sensors, unidentified degradation of sensor performance over time, use of poor sampling techniques, and more. As the popularity of this approach grows, initiatives will be required to address issues related to sensor calibration and data reliability, particularly if the data is necessary for informed decision-making.

The Common Sense project, which involved researchers from Carnegie Mellon and Intel Labs, deployed sensors onto a fleet of street sweepers in San Francisco (Aoki et al., 2008). Sensors for measuring CO, NO_x (oxides of nitrogen, for instance, NO and NO_2), O_3, temperature, relative humidity, and motion (using a 3D accelerometer) were connected to a mobile phone via Bluetooth. Location data was provided by the phone's integrated GPS. Data collected was sent to a database server via GSM text messages. The results from preliminary trials suggest the existence of microclimates (localized pockets with different mixtures of CO and NO_2) within sections of the city areas monitored by the Bay Area's air-quality agency. Eric Paulos, a researcher from Carnegie Mellon, argues that maintaining measurement stations across the city would cost millions of dollars and wouldn't deliver the kind of detail researchers can get from citizens' mobile phones with sensors costing as little as $60 each (Westly, 2009).

A similar approach called CitiSense was developed by researchers at the University of San Diego. They conducted a field trial with 30 users, each with a smartphone connected to an Amtel ATMEGA 128-based mobile sensor platform. The platform had sensors for temperature, humidity, barometric pressure, CO, NO_2 and O_3. An application running on the participant's smartphone displayed sensor readings using the EPA's color-coded scale for air quality (see Table 11-2).

Researchers were able to identify pollution hot spots along main roads, at traffic intersections, and at other places, which varied with the time of day. Participants in the study used the data to reduce their exposure to pollutants through personalized online maps. The maps were designed so that participants could visualize and explore their exposure data over the course of the study. People who cycled to the university modified their routes slightly to avoid busy streets with high levels of pollutants. Commuters who took the bus avoided waiting near the buses' exhaust (Zappi et al., 2012).

In Copenhagen, the public Wheel Project transforms ordinary bikes into hybrid e-bikes that function as mobile sensing units. Sensors were installed via a custom wheel hub onto the rear wheels of the bikes. Sensors measure ambient carbon monoxide, NO_x, noise, ambient temperature, and relative humidity as the bikes move through the city. Users place their smartphones on the handle bars, where data from the sensors streams via Bluetooth to the phone, which displays the data, allowing users to plan healthier bike routes. Users also have the option to share the data from their journeys online to build maps of city pollution levels (Wheel, 2013). Other platforms that report enabling community air-quality monitoring in local areas are P-Sense (Mendez et al., 2011) and the Citizen Sensor open source project (Saavedra, 2013).

While most efforts to date have used discrete sensors with smartphones to measure air quality, researchers at the University of Southern California have developed an Android app called Visibility, which uses the smartphone's camera to measure airborne particulate matter. User images of the sky are tagged with metadata such as location, orientation, and time. The data is then sent to a remote server for analysis, where the air quality is estimated by calibrating the images sent and comparing their intensity against an existing model of luminance in the sky. Once processing is complete, the result is sent back to the user. The data is also used to create pollution maps for the local geographical region (Ganapati, 2010).

Commercially available sensors have started to emerge to enable crowd-sourcing of environmental data, such as SensPods (Sensaris, 2013). Their compact wireless environmental measurement unit is designed for participatory sensing. They have sensing capabilities for a variety of parameters, including humidity, CO_2, temperature, CO, radiation, noise, NO_x, luminosity (UVA, UVB, UVC), GPS, O_3, and $PM_{2.5}$ or PM_{10}. The sensor modules can be integrated with either Android or iOS smartphones via Bluetooth. Data can also be sent to the Sensaris Sensdot web back end for intuitive visualization in a variety of graphs over user-defined time periods. The data can also be displayed on a geolocalized map (as shown in Figure 11-8) so users can develop a picture of the air quality in areas where they live or work.

Figure 11-8. *The Senaris SensPods system for mobile ambient environmental monitoring (image used with permission from Sensaris - www.sensaris.com)*

Monitoring Ambient Weather

Although ambient monitoring applications normally focus on air quality measurements, interest is emerging in using sensors to monitor the outdoor influence of weather on physiological well-being. As the manner in which we live becomes more urbanized, the built environment (particularly when combined with weather events such as heat waves) can have a significant influence on health and well-being through thermal stress. The heat-island effect associated with large cities is a well-documented phenomenon: temperatures can range from 1 to 10°C higher than surrounding rural areas. Typically satellite observations coupled with GIS systems have been used to monitor the effect. Previous generations of satellite instruments suffered from granularity constraints; however, the current generation of instruments has significantly improved spatial-resolution capabilities. Sensor deployments, either fixed or mobile, can provide highly granular data, capturing the impact of local influences. This kind of detail at ground level complements satellite observations, particularly in urban environments. Ambient urban sensing platforms are likely to emerge from technology rollouts associated with smart cities initiatives. Citywide sensing is a foundational technology for many of the trials underway in cities such as Santander (SmartSantander, 2013), Barcelona (BarcelonaSmartCity, 2013), and Amsterdam (Amsterdamsmartcity, 2013). These trials aim to monitor meteorological conditions to identify impacts on citizen safety. These sensor systems will also be used by city managers and planners to monitor remedial interventions, such as planting trees and creating green spaces.

Quantifying the influence of meteorological variables in outdoor environments on human comfort and well-being is challenging due to differences in the physical and biological characteristics of human clothing, context, microclimate influences, and so on. (Honjo, 2009). A number of indices have been developed in an effort to quantify these effects. The most broadly used of these indices are the Standard Effective Temperature (SET*), Predicted Mean Vote (PMV), and Physiological Equivalent Temperature (PET). SET represents the thermal strain experienced by a "standard" person in a "standard" environment. PMV represents the "predicted mean vote" of a large population of people exposed to a certain environment. PMV is derived from the physics of heat transfer combined with an empirical fit to sensation, as shown in Table 11-3. PMV establishes a thermal strain based on steady-state heat transfer between the body and the environment and assigns a comfort vote to that amount of strain. PET was developed as an index that takes into account all basic thermoregulatory processes and is based on a thermo-physiological heat balance model, called the Munich Energy-Balance Model for Individuals (MEMI).

Table 11-3. *Ranges of PMV and PET for different grades of thermal perception and physiological stress*

PMV	PET (°C)	Thermal Perception	Grade of Physiological Stress
-3.5	4	Very cold	Extreme cold stress
-2.5	8	Cold	Strong cold stress
-1.5	13	Cool	Moderate cold stress
-0.5	18		
0.5	23	Slight Cool	Slight cold stress
1.5	29	Comfortable	No thermal stress
2.5	35	Slight Warm	Slight heat stress
3.5	41	Warm	Moderate heat stress
		Hot	Strong heat stress
		Very Hot	Extreme heat stress

From a sensing perspective, the measurements of interest are air temperature, radiant temperature, air speed, and relative humidity. Sensor deployments in cities such as Hong Kong (Cheng et al., 2012), Colombo, Sri Lanka (Johansson et al., 2006), and Glasgow (Krüger et al., 2013) have been reported in the literature. These studies show that sensor-based approaches are useful for identifying and quantifying local influences such as wind speed and solar radiation on thermal comfort, and their influence on human biometeorology—the study of the interactions and relationships between human beings and atmospheric conditions (Höppe, 1997). Additional studies using sensors have looked at how green spaces can have a positive influence on ambient environment, comfort, and improved air quality. Reported studies include Hangzhou (Shuo et al., 2010), New York City (Gaffin et al., 2009), and Tel Aviv (Cohen et al., 2010). While a wide variety of weather apps for smartphones already exist, user-centric weather-monitoring capabilities for smartphones have also started to emerge. Sensordrone, funded under a Kickstarter campaign, has developed a multi-sensor platform small enough to attach to a key ring that can stream data via Bluetooth to a smartphone. It supports a variety of applications, including a mobile weather station. Sensors can monitor humidity, temperature, light intensity, O_3 and CO. A number of apps are available for download, including a relative humidity monitor and an air quality index (which displays measurement of CO, CO_2, temperature, humidity and air pressure) (Sensorcon, 2013).

UVA/UVB Monitoring

The link between exposure to UV radiation and skin cancer is well established. Excessive exposure to UV radiation is a global problem due to ozone depletion in the atmosphere, pollution (Gillette, 2011) and unsafe human behaviors. Lack of exposure to sunlight can also have health implications due to Vitamin D deficiencies. Vitamin D levels are determined by the sum of exposure to UV radiation and dietary intake. Sun exposure in moderation is the major source of Vitamin D for most humans (Holick et al., 2011). In northern latitudes, Vitamin D deficiency is now recognized as being medically significant; it causes rickets in children and is a contributing factor in osteoporosis and osteopenia in older adults. It has also been associated with increased risk of common cancers, autoimmune diseases, and hypertension.

UV radiation is typically subdivided into three components based on wavelength:

- UV-A (wavelengths between 315nm and 400nm)

- UV-B (wavelengths between 280nm and 315 nm)

- UV-C (wavelengths between 200 and 280nm)

UV-C is absorbed by the ozone and normally does not reach the earth's surface. But in the southern hemisphere, where ozone holes can appear, it is an issue. Erythema curves that plot UV wavelength (nm) versus irradiance (W/m²) are used to determine the UV exposure levels that may damage human skin as a result of sunburn, as shown in Figure 11-9.

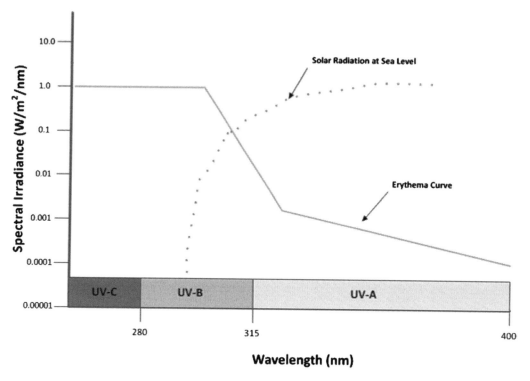

Figure 11-9. *Erythema curve for human skin damage*

UV can be measured in a variety of ways, including instrument radiometers, personal dosimeters, and satellites instruments, such as GOME-2. Sensors in dosimeters generally focus on measuring UV-A/B. In their simplest form, they can be adhesive patches (chemical dosimeters) that stick onto exposed skin (SunSignal, 2013) or wristbands (UVSunSense, 2013). Products are often aimed at parents who want a simple method to monitor their child's exposure. Biological dosimeters measure UV exposure by the rate of mutation induction in microorganisms, for example, Bacillus subtilis (Biosense, 2013). Although they can provide a good estimation of exposure, they can be difficult to manage and analysis can be time-consuming. The most common form of UV-A/B sensing is the electronic dosimeter in various forms, including bodyworn wristwatches such as the Sunsaver, which developed as part of the FP7 ICEPURE project (ICEPURE, 2009).

There are already a variety of UV smartphone apps available, such the EPA UV Index, My UV Check, Sun Safe, and so on. Data used by the apps is generally provided by the local National Weather Service. Converting a smartphone into a personal UV dosimeter has also been demonstrated via the DoCoMo sensor jacket in Japan (Lamkin, 2011). Other initiatives include Sundroid, which is based on a photodiode UV-A/B sensor worn externally on the body and connected to an Android smartphone via Bluetooth. The app running on the phone displays the accumulated UV dose, the current UV index, and the timeline of UV exposure, as shown in Figure 11-10. A detailed view is also available with more comprehensive exposure information. The platform has been applied to a number of use cases, including snowboarding and climbing. (Fahrni et al., 2011). A similar approach has also been reported by MIT's Mobile Experience Lab (Laboratory, 2011).

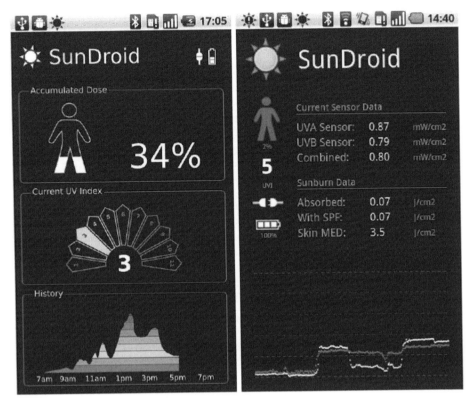

Figure 11-10. *Sundroid activity screens: The Simple View (left) and Advanced View (right) (image used with permission from the Distributed Computing Group, ETH Zurich*

Monitoring UV radiation using a smartphone without a dedicated sensor has been demonstrated by researchers in the University of Southern Queensland. The built-in camera in a smartphone was used to measure UVA irradiance down to 340nm in a feasibility study (Igoe et al., 2013). It is an interesting development, but smartphone camera technology needs to evolve to a point where irradiance can be measured down to 280nm before this approach would be of practical use.

Water Quality Monitoring

The need to accurately monitor water quality continues to grow due to the ever-increasing demand for fresh, clean water all over the world. Urbanization, intensive agriculture methods, food processing, and so forth have increased the demand for water. Meanwhile, these and other human activities have resulted in increased incidences of contaminated water supplies. Concerns about water will only increase as new human activities emerge that impact our environment. New sources of pollutants are emerging that have the potential for significant adverse impact on water quality. For example, shale gas extraction using fracking is causing international controversy. The process uses horizontal drilling with hydraulic fracturing by means of high pressure water and chemicals. There is much heated public debate due to concerns about contamination of water supplies with chemicals used in the fracking process and the release of naturally occurring gases such as methane into underground aquifers. As a result, there is a growing need for water-quality sensing to provide real-time information to complement traditional laboratory analysis. Furthermore, the data from these sensor measurements should be made public to ensure transparency and to keep citizens informed appropriately.

To monitor water quality, a variety of sensor technologies have been utilized. Handheld sensors can be used by scientists to make measurements in situ. Fixed sensing can be integrated into the control systems for public water utilities. Wireless sensor modules can be used to monitor a specific water source, such as the WaterBot project (Carnegie-Mellon, 2013). Some of the key technologies utilized in water-sensing applications to date include electrochemical (Kimmel et al., 2011), biotechnology (Lagarde et al., 2011), MEMS (Jang et al., 2011), nanotechnology (Rassaei et al., 2011), optical (Namour et al., 2010).

Over the past few years, optical sensor and measurement technologies have emerged as a more reliable alternative to electrochemical approaches due to simpler operation. Methods such as optical fluorescence and absorbance are being widely adopted in various applications. The growth of laser and LED technologies are also stimulating the growth of the water-quality monitoring market. For complex analyses that require sample preparation and multi-analyte analysis, lab-on-chip technologies are being developed (Jang et al., 2011). This technology enables miniaturized design and fabrication of laboratory-based techniques on a single chip to deliver the same reliability and efficiency while providing flexibility and portability capabilities.

These types of sensing approaches can be used to measure a wide variety of parameters relevant to the quality of water for human use. The parameters can be classified in three major categories—physical, chemical, and biological. Significant factors that affect water quality include suspended sediments (turbidity); algae (that is, chlorophylls and carotenoids); chemicals (fertilizers, pesticides, and metals); dissolved organic matter (such as sewage); thermal releases (from food processing); aquatic vascular plants; pathogens; and oils. While traditional laboratory methods can provide accurate analysis of these contaminants, they are time-consuming and can only provide delayed results. Laboratory-based quality assurance programs use scheduled sample collection and, therefore, depending on the sampling intervals, anomalous events may go unnoticed. Such undetected changes can be of potential risk to public health. Therefore, there is a growing trend toward real-time analysis capabilities to augment laboratory analysis in an effort to guard public safety.

Companies such as YSI Inc. (`www.ysi.com`), Intellitect Water (`www.intellitect-water.co.uk`), Liqum Oy (`www.liqum.com`), and Optiqua (`www.optiqua.com`) provide real-time quality-sensing systems that can detect key physical and chemical characteristics of water. Real-time sensing capabilities will play a vital role in the evolution of smart water systems. In these systems sensing and management technologies will be used to optimize the availability, delivery, utilization, and quality of water, together with others systems such as water treatment management. Companies like IBM are working with public authorities such as Sonoma County Water Agency in California and the Beacon Institute on the Hudson River in New York to deliver the first generation of these systems (IBM, 2010, Beacon Institute, 2007).

In an approach that is analogous to some of the crowdsourcing efforts in air quality, the Don't Flush Me project in New York City is focused on reducing sewage overspill into the Hudson River by modifying citizen behavior. The initial prototype involves an Arduinio-based proximity sensor and mobile phone that measure the water level in sewers. If the water levels are high enough to result in overflow into the river, various forms of visual feedback are created to encourage citizens to reduce their waste output. This feedback includes a web site with area-specific indicators, SMS messaging, and an Internet-connected light bulb. Later versions of the platform have used temperature and conductivity to detect sewage overflow into the river. (Percifield, 2012).

The Argo project has deployed a global array of more than 3,600 autonomous sensor floats to measure temperature and salinity in the oceans. Each float sinks to a prescribed drifting depth of 1000 to 2000m, (1300–6500 ft.) where it remains for about 10 days. It then rises to the surface, collecting temperature and salinity data. The float remains at the surface while it transmits its position and sensor data to a satellite, then sinks back down to its prescribed drifting depth, completing the collection cycle and starting a new one. Other types of sensors—for pH, oxygen, and nitrate levels—are currently in development or being evaluated. Data from the project is freely available for anyone to use in various research domains, including climate, weather, oceanographic, and fisheries (Kramer, 2013).

Physical Water Sensing

A number of sensors are available for the continuous monitoring of the physical characteristics of water; the most commonly measured characteristics are shown in Table 11-4.

Table 11-4. *Sensor-Based Physical Water Quality Analysis*

Characteristic	Description	Sensor
Temperature	Water temperature influences its density, the solubility of constituents, pH, specific conductance, the rate of chemical reactions, and biological activity.	Thermistor
Conductivity	Measurement of the capacity of water to conduct an electrical current. Conductivity is a function of the concentrations and types of dissolved solids, such as metals, inorganics, and organics. Changes in conductivity can result from discharges into the water. Sewage, for example, raises conductivity due the presence of chloride, phosphate, and nitrate. In contrast, an oil spill may cause a drop in conductivity due to the presence of organic compounds.	Conductivity Electrode
Color	Apparent color is the color of the water sample as a whole, which is affected by both dissolved and suspended compounds. True color is obtained after filtering the water to remove all suspended material. The health impact of color depends on the type of dissolved compounds.	Optical *Colorimeter*
Turbidity	Turbidity is the cloudiness of a water sample, caused by suspended particles or impurities may include clay, silt, vegetable matter, soluble colored organic compounds, algae, and microorganisms. Excessive turbidity in drinking water is aesthetically unappealing and may also represent a health concern, resulting in issues such as gastroenteritis.	Optical *Nephelometer* *Surface Scatter* *Method*

Chemical Water Sensing

Sensors used for chemical analysis of water quality measure a variety of organic and inorganic elements and molecules that are either dissolved or suspended in water. Sensors based on electrochemical or optical techniques can be used to detect pollutants such as nitrates or heavy metals in real-time. Common chemical parameters of interest that can be measured by sensors, include pH, hardness, nitrates, phosphates, and dissolved oxygen, are presented in Table 11-5.

Table 11-5. *Common Sensor Approaches Used for Chemical Water Quality Analysis*

Characteristic	Description	Sensor
Dissolved Oxygen	Adequate dissolved oxygen (O_2) is necessary for good water quality. The main factor contributing to changes in dissolved oxygen levels is the build-up of organic wastes. Low levels of dissolved oxygen maybe indicative of microorganisms in the water consuming oxygen as they decompose sewage, urban and agricultural runoff, and discharge from food-processing plants	Electrochemical *Amperometric* *Galvanic* *Polarography* Gas Optical *Luminescence* Biosensor
pH	The pH of a water sample relates to the concentration of hydrogen ions. Drinking water has a pH range of 6.5 to 9.5. Extreme pH values can indicate chemical spills, treatment plant issues, or problems with the supply pipe network.	Electrometric *Potentiometric* ISFET Optical *Colorimetric*

(continued)

Table 11-5. (*continued*)

Characteristic	Description	Sensor

Chlorine	As ground water percolates underground through bedrock or sand and gravel, it dissolves various minerals and constituents, including chloride. Chloride (Cl^-)levels in wells and reservoirs that are higher than normal may indicate pollution such as sewage, industrial contamination, fertilizers, and so on.	Electrochemical
		  Amperometric
		Optical
		  Colorimetric

ORP	The oxidation-reduction potential (ORP) of a water sample is a key measure of how well a water treatment or sanitization process is working. It is used to monitor drinking water, swimming pools, and spas. ORP targets are expressed in millivolts, which can be determined for each specific application and will result in completely reliable disinfection of pathogens.	Electrochemical *Potentiometric*

Free Chlorine	Free chlorine is formed by the reaction of chlorine gas with water. This molecule and its ion are essential in ensuring that water is safe to drink. They act as oxidizing agents (disinfectants), killing bacteria. Excess chlorine in drinking water has been linked with bladder and rectal cancers.	Electrochemical
		  Polarography
		  Amperometric
		Optical
		  Colorimetric

Heavy Metals	Common heavy metals, such as cadmium (Cd), copper (CU), mercury (Hg), and lead (Pb), in water have been linked to a variety of health risks, including reduced growth and development, cancer, organ damage, nervous system damage, and, in extreme cases, death. Young children are particularly susceptible to the toxic effects of heavy metals.	Electrochemical
		  ISE
		  ISFET
		Optical
		  Photoluminescence
		  Fluorescence

Phosphate	Phosphates (PO^{3-}_4) are naturally absorbed in water from bedrock and other mineral deposits. Human and animal waste, washing powder and detergents, and fertilizers in the water supply can cause an increased level of phosphates. This can lead to water-quality problems, including algal blooms, and impacts to human health, such as kidney damage and osteoporosis.	Optical
		  Colorimetric
		Electrochemical
		  Potentiometric ISE

Nitrate	Nitrate (NO_3^-) is an inorganic compound that is highly soluble in water. Major sources of nitrates in drinking water include fertilizers, sewage and animal manure. When ingested, nitrate is converted to nitrite in the body. Nitrite can result in health issues, particularly for young children. In infants it can cause methemoglobinemia or blue-baby syndrome. It has also been linked to cancers through the formation of nitrosamines, which are known cancer-causing agents.	Electrochemical
		  Potentiometric ISE
		Optical
		  UV Absorption
		  Fluorescence

Biological Pathogen Water Sensing

Biological water sensing focuses on the detection of pathogens or related products that can impact human health. The presence of biological contaminants is normally regulated. For example, in the U.S., the Safe Drinking Water Act (SDWA) and the Clean Water Act (CWA) address microbial contamination in water. The CWA is designed to protect surface water for drinking, aquatic food sources, and recreational use. The SDWA provides a regulatory framework to manage drinking water for human consumption and to protect source waters (EPA, 2012).

Many types of pathogens can be found in contaminated water, such Escherichia coli (E. coli), Cryptosporidium, and Giardia lambilia. Most of the current techniques require overnight culture to produce high cell numbers before visual screening to confirm the presence of a pathogen, which is time-consuming. As a result, significant numbers of individuals may be infected before an issue is detected, the public is informed, and boil notices are put in place. Sensors provide an attractive way to quickly detect microbial contamination. But the development of such technologies is challenging, with few sensors commercially available at present. This continues to be an area of active research, though, with promising developments in DNA-based biosensing for species-specific determination of bacteria starting to emerge. Table 11-6 outlines the sensors currently available for biological water-quality monitoring.

Table 11-6. *Common Sensor Approaches for the Identification of Biological Contamination in Water*

Characteristic	Description	Sensor
Blue-Green Algae (cyanobacteria)	Cyanobacteria (blue-green algae) is a bacteria that has the potential to cause health problems in humans and animals. Cyanobacteria are common and naturally occurring, but water pollution, such as sewage effluent, fertilizer run-off, sediment, and food-processing effluent, can cause some types to form dense blooms. Toxins released by the bacteria can cause nausea, vomiting, abdominal pain and diarrhea.	Optical *fluorescence*
Chlorophyll	Chlorophyll is produced by phytoplankton. It does not negatively impact human health and has been reported to actually have beneficial effects. However, the presence of chlorophyll may indicate high nutrient levels, perhaps from fertilizer runoff, which could impact human health.	Optical *fluorescence*
Cryptosporidium	Cryptosporidium is a protozoan parasite that causes a severe diarrhea disease known as cryptosporidiosis. Both human and animal waste are potential sources of contamination. Outbreaks of the disease are normally associated with poor water treatment. Cryptosporidium oocysts are resistant to chlorine disinfection, so the water treatment process must be tightly controlled. Oocyst removal is achieved with effective clarification and filtration stages during the treatment process.	*Biosensor (research)*
Coliforms E. Coli	Human consumption of water contaminated with E. coli results in nausea, vomiting, abdominal pain, diarrhea, and even death in severe cases. E. coli can result from sewage contamination in water.	Biosensor (research)

Mobile Water-Quality Sensing

As with many other areas of sensing described in this book, water-quality monitoring applications are beginning to emerge for mobile form factors. Smartphones have started to replace the dedicated data loggers that have been used with handheld sensors for in-situ sensing for many years. For example, In-Situ Inc. (www.in-situ.com) recently announced its iSitu smartphone app, which can connect via Bluetooth to its handheld probe that includes an optical dissolved-oxygen sensor, as well as sensors for barometric pressure, air temperature, and water temperature. The phone's GPS can be used to geotag the sensor readings together with photos from the smartphone camera. Data can also be sent in real-time to any required location, giving the field operators flexibility in delivering information to their offices and receiving instructional updates In a related application, Insta-link provides a smartphone app that can be used to scan a test-strip for free chlorine, pH, alkalinity, hardness, and cyanuric acid to determine if water quality in a pool or spa is sufficient for human recreational purposes (Insta-Link, 2012).

The development of smartphone water-quality sensors has also become the focus of community initiatives. The MoboSens campaign, for example, is developing a smartphone-based sensor to provide accurate nitrate measurements. MoboSens hopes the platform will provide citizens with the capability to collect and share water-quality data via social media, with a view to improving public safety by augmenting existing institutional sensing. There are plans to extend the sensing functionality of the platform to include the detection of arsenic, heavy metal ions, bacteria and radioactivity (Edgar, 2013). Another community initiative is the Sensordrone multi-sensor tool. Sensors for pH and dissolved-oxygen measurements are under development to complement their existing ambient environmental sensing platform (Sensorcon, 2013).

The combination of sensing and mobile devices for water-quality measurements, though in the early stages, promises a powerful capability. Discrete water quality readings, together with geographical tagging and temporal information collected and shared by citizens, can be used to generate community water-quality maps. Concerned citizens will be able to test their water supply on a regular basis and upload the data. This will help promote communal knowledge of local water quality and how it varies over time. It will allow citizens to rapidly identify influences impacting water quality. This approach has the potential to become the environmental equivalent of the quantified-self movement (see Chapter 7) in the health domain—that is, the collective identification of early signs that there may be something wrong with the local water quality.

Environmental Noise Pollution

Noise pollution keeps growing, particularly with increased urbanization, industrialization, and air traffic. The EPA describes noise pollution as *"sound that becomes unwanted when it either interferes with normal activities such as sleeping, conversation, or disrupts or diminishes one's quality of life."* The correlation between health and noise has been well-established in a number of studies. Problems connected to noise pollution include stress-related illnesses, high blood pressure, speech interference, hearing loss, sleep disruption, and lost productivity. Individuals and community groups are embracing sensing technologies, and leveraging their smartphones with apps such as Sound Meter. Home environmental sensing platforms such as CubeSensors also have integrated noise-level monitoring capabilities. Such approaches help to improve the spatial and temporal granularity of data, which can be limited in official noise surveys. Data from these surveys is often used to extrapolate dispersed measurements to wider geographical areas without sufficient consideration of influences such as open spaces, building types, green areas, traffic flows, and so forth.

Crowdsourcing as a means to generate noise pollution maps in urban areas has been a focus of the research community, leading to the development of a number of platforms. The NoiseTube project uses a crowdsourcing approach based on smartphones. The app running on the phone collects noise level, GPS coordinates, time, and user input. The application contains a real-time signal-processing algorithm that measures the loudness of the environmental sound recorded via the microphone. A real-time visualization is displayed on the phone, with color-coded values to indicate the health risk of the current exposure level. The application also allows the user to annotate the data to provide context information about the source of the noise. The collected data is used to build noise maps using Google Earth. It is envisaged that these maps and user-generated environment logs or "elogs" can help citizens to make local officials aware of noise pollution issues and their social implications (Maisonneuve et al., 2009). Similar smartphone sensing platforms have been deployed in city environments such as Ear-Phone in Brisbane, Australia (Rana et al., 2010) and NoiseSPY in Cambridge, UK (Kanjo, 2010).

In an effort to quantify the body's response to noise pollution, the SMART-Band was developed to sense skin conductance and temperature. This approach is built on the concept of using humans as sensors in their environment. The sensor is intended to translate subjective feelings and emotions into quantifiable measurements. An 18-person trial was conducted in the city center of Kaiserslautern to examine the effect of noise on emotional well-being. A number of areas in the city with different noise levels were selected, varying from areas of high noise pollution from city traffic to quieter inner-city parks. Standalone sensors were used to measure noise levels. The study generated limited results and findings due to issues with the body-worn sensors (Bergner et al., 2012). The issues reported are not unexpected, due to the difficulties in collecting reliable and reproducible skin conductance sensor data. Problems such as baseline drift, reliable contacts, and the development of robust correlations to various emotional states are challenging. However, the concept gives us insights into how in the future we may use sensing to determine the effects of the environment on our health and wellness, and to influence changes in behavior. Building on the concept of humans as sensors and adding gamification (using principles of game play to boost participation and engagement) into the mix, researchers at University Jaume I in Spain are developing a noise-tracking game, NoiseBattle, for Android smartphones. Game players are required to move around a city, taking noise samples with the goal of completing a noise map for the city (Martí et al., 2012).

Radiation Sensing

Radiation exposure is a topic that strikes fear in the public mind. Accidents, such as those at Chernobyl and Fukushima, have only increased these fears. For most people, exposure to radiation from such incidents is of little real concern. However, a natural radiation threat can exist in some people's homes in the form of dangerous levels of radon gas. Radon gas comes from uranium decay in soil and can enter homes through cracks in foundations, ventilation openings, and so on. Radon is the second leading cause of lung cancer, after cigarette smoking, with an estimated 21,000 lung cancer deaths alone in the U.S. each year (EPA, 2013). Testing for radon normally involves in-home air sampling over a defined period, with the sampling unit then sent to a laboratory for analysis. Sensors are now available that can provide continuous monitoring of the gas, the levels of which can vary significantly. Sensors such as the Safety Siren Pro 3 Radon Gas Detector from Family Safety Products provide continuous monitoring with an audio alarm if the levels of radon exceed safe limits.

The 2011 nuclear power plant disaster at Fukushima in Japan resulted in a huge environmental impact that required the evacuation over 150,000 people from a 20 mile-exclusion zone around the plant. For people near the exclusion zone, access to data on radiation levels was a significant concern. Due to a lack of trust and resolution in the available radiation level data, a community-led initiative using online data platforms such as Xively and citizen-contributed radiation measurements facilitated better access to data among the general public. However, the limited availability of local radiation-measurement capabilities led the Spanish company Libelium to initiate an international community-based project to develop a wireless radiation sensor. A radiation sensor board for Arduinio was quickly built and validated (see Figure 11-11). The design of the board was based on open hardware and the source code was released under a general public license. The sensor platform provided a means for local engineers to collect data in communities around Fukushima and to make that data publically available to concerned citizens (Boyd, 2011). In a similar manner, the problems at Fukushima acted as the catalyst for the formation of Safecast, a global sensor network based on community efforts to collect and share radiation measurements with a view to empowering people with information about the safety of their environment. All data collected by Safecast using mobile, handheld, and fixed sensing is made publicly available under creative commons rights (Safecast, 2013).

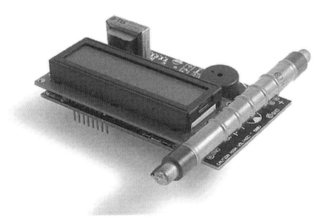

Figure 11-11. *Libelium's Radiation Sensor Board for Arduino (image used with permission from Libelium)*

Environmental Impact on Food

The use of sensor technologies to monitor agricultural production has been an area of research for many years. In recent years, commercial wireless sensor network products have emerged that target commercial agriculture. The use of technology in agricultural production is likely to increase as we become more concerned about food security. For example, Libelium is already targeting this market with its Waspmote Agriculture Board. This board supports the monitoring of multiple environmental parameters, including air and soil temperature and humidity, solar visible radiation, wind speed and direction, rainfall, atmospheric pressure, and leaf wetness.

Such sensing technologies are designed to reduce human-resource requirements during the growing cycle. Optimal growth parameters, such as soil moisture content, can be defined for a crop. When the sensor readings detect that conditions are not optimal, the data can be used to automatically switch on the irrigation system. This helps maintain optimal growing conditions while restricting water use to only what is necessary. The use of sensors in agriculture, food production, and food logistics is an extensive topic and beyond the scope of this chapter. However, sensor technologies that measure environmental impact on quality are starting to emerge for consumers.

The use of intensive agricultural methods, including the pervasive use of fertilizers and pesticides, has been the subject of much public debate over the last decade with regard to their effects on food quality and safety. As a result, many people are turning to organically produced foods. In China, there is significant concern about food safety based on a number of recent scandals. For example, the Sanlu Group was found to have sold milk powder contaminated with melamine, an industrial compound used to create plastic that makes milk appear protein-rich (Lawrence, 2008). As a result, sensor technologies for consumer use targeting food safety concerns are starting to emerge.

One particular sensor platform that is focused on environmental and food sensing is the Lapka personal environmental monitor. This is multisensory platform has an aesthetically appealing form factor, as shown in Figure 11-12 (a). The platform has sensor modules for radiation, electromagnetic field (EMF), humidity, and organic measurements. Data from the sensors is streamed to an iPhone app via a wired connection. The organic sensor module is used to detect significant quantities of nitrates in raw produce, which may originate from the use of synthetic fertilizers, according to Lapka. The stainless steel probe, shown in Figure 11-11 (b), is inserted into any fruit or vegetable included on a preset list, which contains a defined limit for nitrate concentrations. Conductivity that significantly exceeds the limits apparently suggests the use of nonorganic farming practices. The sensor has an operational range of 0-5000 ppm NO_3^-.

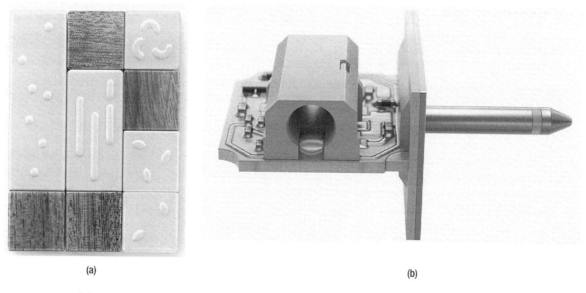

(a)   (b)

Figure 11-12. *(a) Lapka's integrated sensors (b) The organic sensor module (images used with permission from Lapka)*

Such sensing capabilities are likely to appeal to health-conscious consumers. A variety of new sensors that measure various environmental impacts on our food quality and safety are likely to emerge in the near future. But significant challenges are also likely to materialize, in particular, distinguishing between inorganic compounds that occur naturally due to the underlying geology of where food is grown, and those that are introduced artificially through intensive agricultural production methods. Geotagging of food sources is one potential initiative where natural background levels in water and soils can be measured by citizens to create maps of farm regions. These maps can then be used as a reference against parameters measured in food samples. Consumer-oriented sensing in the food domain is still in its infancy. There will certainly be public debate as to the respective merits of various sensor products as they emerge in the marketplace. Ultimately, consumers will determine whether they are successful and offer meaningful data.

Future Directions for Environmental Monitoring

The market for environmental sensing and monitoring is estimated to be growing by 6.5 percent per year and is expected to be valued at $15.6B USD by 2016. A significant portion of this value will be related to institutional and regulatory activities, but there will also be a growing consumer element. Sensors and applications that extend the concept of the quantified self into the living environment will continue to evolve. These technologies will enable interesting new use cases, delivering new insights into the environment around us and how it impacts our health and wellness.

The first wave of these products has already reached the consumer market. The fact that the initial batches of some products sold out, for example, CubeSensors (Isakovic, 2013), illustrates an obvious public appetite for this information, whether it be air quality, noise pollution, or determining whether food is organic. As with the other forms of sensing discussed in this book, mobile devices are the key enabling platform, providing convenient and intuitive data access points through accompanying apps for the sensors. These apps act primarily as simple visualization portals for the data. But elements of intelligent data processing and prediction using cloud-based services are starting to emerge. This is an area likely to see interesting developments in the coming years. Some products are already using pattern-recognition techniques to tell users how to modify their environment. Simple actions, such as increasing the ventilation in a room to raise oxygen levels and decrease CO_2, can be identified. These actions have the simple goal of improving the wellness of people in their homes. In the future, such systems will be able to indicate the best time to exercise based on measurements of the weather, air quality, and physiological status. Or they may suggest an alternative route to work or school if the pollen count is above safe levels on the normal route.

The convergence of health, wellness, and environmental sensing will continue to grow and deliver a more holistic approach to maintaining our health and wellness. Already in the research domain we are seeing the emergence of multi-sensor techniques that look at the impact of environmental parameters on our physiological and psychological well-being. Emerging crowdsourced environmental applications, where humans become mobile sensors in their environments, are utilizing these technologies in interesting ways. Such initiatives are likely to have growing importance in how citizens manage and modify their living environments to ensure the health of all citizens.

In the future, citizen sensors will play a growing role as mobile data sources in an ambient intelligent environment. The role of human sensing will also evolve beyond the current solutions of smartphone and discrete sensors deployed in our homes or other environment to modalities that are both organic and natural. For example, concepts for clothing that can act as environmental pollution monitors are already emerging. A collaboration between diffus.dk, Alexandra Institute, The Danish Design School, and embroidery company Forster Rohner has produced a dress that indicates CO_2 levels by illuminating integrated LED lights (Johannesen, 2009). In a related approach, a dress that contains pH-sensitive dyes that change color in response of the acidity or alkalinity of rain has also been created (Chua, 2012). New materials, including nanomaterials, will emerge that have switchable behaviors, including color, polarity, and porosity, related to environmental stimuli such as pollutants. It will be possible to integrate these materials into wearable fabrics to add ambient intelligence capabilities, such as warning and protecting the wearer from environmental threats, including pollution. This fusion of environmental sensing and clothing, though still experimental, may soon lead to some interesting practical use cases of wearable technologies. Potentially important use cases aside from pollution monitoring may include the detection of hazardous gases, which could greatly help to protect emergency services personnel.

However, many challenges must be overcome before we can truly benefit from advances in environmental sensing. Key among these is improving the quality of sensors at affordable price points. Many of the current consumer products utilize semiconductor sensors, which may have poor sensitivity and may not be particularly selective for the compound of interest. These sensors may also experience drift, and without frequent calibration the data will often contain significant errors. The development of low cost, stable, and sensitive sensors is critical to the future of this domain.

In the biological-sensing domain, the use of sensors to determine species-specific bacterial contamination or the presence of other biological species is still in its infancy. However, the need for these sensor technologies is ever-present, with an estimated 3.4 million people dying each year from water-, sanitation-, and hygiene-related causes (Lees, 2013). Future developments in biotechnology, optics, and packaging technologies will enable these sensing technologies to move from the laboratory into real world use (Banna et al., 2013). In other domains, such as sensing of chemical components in water, a variety of optical sensing technologies have emerged. Optical sensing approaches can provide improvements in performance stability over traditional electrochemical sensing approaches. They are also starting to approach the sensitivity levels of electrochemical sensors in some cases (Namour et al., 2010, Pellerin et al., 2009). As always, translating promising research into reliable and effective real-world applications is challenging. However, successful new innovations will continue to emerge, building on the lessons learned from current deployments of sensing technologies.

Although the use of discrete sensors is gaining steady momentum for individual use, wireless sensor networks for environmental applications still have significant challenges to overcome, and truly scalable deployments of WSNs have yet to be achieved. A review by Corke et al., points out that networks to date are typically small in size (generally <30 nodes) and are deployed for relatively short periods of time (weeks or months). They argue that technical and cost elements of sensors make widespread environmental monitoring with hundreds or thousands of nodes generally not economically feasible. However, a few areas of significant scientific interest, such as improved understanding of greenhouse-gas emissions and innovative water monitoring, have the potential to see increased investment in large-scale, long-term monitoring initiatives (Corke et al., 2010).

What is certain is that independent of the sensing modality, we will have greater access to data about our environment and that we will play an integral and active role in sensing our environment. As the technology evolves and the quality and breadth of sensor data increases, the potential use of the data will be limited only by our insight. At a minimum, we will have a better understanding of the dynamic nature of the relationship between our health and wellness and the environments in which we work, live and play.

Summary

This chapter has looked how sensors can be used to monitor key aspects of our environment, such as air and water quality, exposure to solar and radioisotope radiation, and noise pollution. Global stressors, such as urbanization, industrialization, and a variety of human activities are increasing the pressure on our environmental integrity, resulting in an ever-growing need to monitor environmental resources. New sensing technologies and applications are emerging that are designed to empower individuals with data and knowledge about their ambient environment. This data can be used by individuals to better understand the relationship between their environment and their health and wellness. Sensors designed for personal use are also catalyzing community-led initiatives. Citizens can participate in the collection and sharing of data on key environmental parameters, such as air quality. Such approaches have the potential to provide scalable sensing capabilities that are not possible with traditional institutional monitoring regimes.

References

Barnoya, Joaquin and Stanton A. Glantz, "Cardiovascular Effects of Secondhand Smoke Nearly as Large as Smoking," *Circulation,* vol. 111 pp. 2684–2698, 2005.

Sasco, A. J., M. B. Secretan, and K. Straif, "Tobacco smoking and cancer: a brief review of recent epidemiological evidence," *Lung Cancer,* vol. 45, Supplement 2 (0), pp. S3–S9, 2004.

Bretveld, Reini, Marijn Brouwers, Inge Ebisch, and Nel Roeleveld, "Influence of pesticides on male fertility," *Scandinavian Journal of Work, Environment & Health,* vol. 33 (1), pp. 13–28, 2007.

Balabanic, Damjan, Marjan Rupnik, and Aleksandra Krivograd Klemencic, "Negative impact of endocrine-disrupting compounds on human reproductive health," *Reproduction, Fertility and Development,* vol. 23 (3), pp. 403–416, 2011.

IHME, "The Global Burden of Disease: Generating Evidence, Guiding Policy", Institute for Health Metrics and Evaluation, Seattle, Washington, 2013.

Quantified Self Labs, "Quantified Self - self knowledge through number ", http://quantifiedself.com/, 2012.

Linear-Technology, "Wireless Sensor Network Challenges and Solutions", http://cds.linear.com/docs/en/white-paper/wp001fa.pdf, 2012.

Ghosh, Amitabha and Sajal K. Das, "Coverage and connectivity issues in wireless sensor networks: A survey," *Pervasive and Mobile Computing,* vol. 4 (3), pp. 303–334, 2008.

Mainwaring, Keith and Lara Srivastava, "The Internet of Things - Setting the Standards," in *The Internet of Things: Connecting Objects,* Chaouchi, Hakima, Ed., Hoboken, New Jersey, Wiley, 2010, pp. 208–2010.

Conway, Maura, "What is Cyberterrorism and How Real is the Threat?," in *Law, Policy, and Technology,* Reich, Pauline C. and Eduardo Gelbstein, Eds., Hershey PA, IGI Global, 2012, pp. 279–307.

Zervous, Barry. "*Q&A on energy harvesting, wireless sensors, wireless sensor networks,*" Last Update: April 4th 2013, http://www.energyharvestingjournal.com/articles/q-amp-a-on-energy-harvesting-wireless-sensors-wireless-sensor-networks-00005316.asp

Boisvert, Sarah. "*3D printing enclosures for micro wireless sensors and circuits inexpensive and practical solution for company,*" Last Update: 2013, http://www.3dprinter.net/3d-printing-enclosures-for-micro-wireless-sensors-and-circuits

Crisostomo, Christian, "*Monitor Air Pollution with Smartphone Accessed Portable Sensors*", The Environmental Blog. org, Last Update: January 20th 2013, http://www.theenvironmentalblog.org/2013/01/monitor-air-pollution-smartphone-accessed-portable-sensors/

Sensorcon. "*Make Sensordrone Do Even More,*" Last Update: 2013, http://www.sensorcon.com/sensordrone-extensions/

Choi, Sukwon, Nakyoung Kim, Hojung Cha, and Rhan Ha, "Micro Sensor Node for Air Pollutant Monitoring: Hardware and Software Issues," *Sensors,* vol. 9 pp. 7970–7987, 2009.

Romain, A. C. and J. Nicolas, "Long term stability of metal oxide-based gas sensors for e-nose environmental applications: An overview," *Sensors and Actuators B: Chemical,* vol. 146 (2), pp. 502–506, 2010.

Grossi, M., *et al.,* "A Portable Sensor With Disposable Electrodes for Water Bacterial Quality Assessment," *Sensors Journal, IEEE,* vol. 13 (5), pp. 1775–1782, 2013.

Mannoor, Manu S., Siyan Zhang, A. James Link, and Michael C. McAlpine, "Electrical detection of pathogenic bacteria via immobilized antimicrobial peptides," *Proceedings of the National Academy of Sciences,* vol. 107 (45), pp. 19207–19212, 2010.

Department of Environment and Heritage Protection - Queensland Government, "Sulfur Dioxide", http://www.ehp.qld.gov.au/air/pollution/pollutants/sulfur-dioxide.html, 2011.

EPA. "*Mobile Air Monitoring on the Gulf Coast: TAGA Buses,*" Last Update: 2010, http://www.epa.gov/bpspill/taga.html

Standards, European, "http://www.en-standard.eu/csn-en-12341-air-quality-determination-of-the-pm10-fraction-of-suspended-particulate-matter-reference-method-and-field-test-procedure-to-demonstrate-reference-equivalence-of-measurement-methods/Air " vol. CSN EN 12341, ed: European Standards, 1998.

EPA, "National Ambient Air Quality Standards for Lead; Final Rule," vol. 73 FR 66964 ed. United US Environmental Protection Agency 2008.

Evironemental Protection Agency-Ireland, "What is the Air Quality Index for Health", http://www.epa.ie/air/quality/index/#d.en.51765, 2013.

EPA. "*Air Quality Index (AQI) - A Guide to Air Quality and Your Health,*" Last Update: May 17th 2013, http://www.airnow.gov/index.cfm?action=aqibasics.aqi#good

The World Data Centre for Remote Sensing of the Atmosphere (WDC-RSAT), "GOME-2 Global Ozone Monitoring Experiment", http://wdc.dlr.de/sensors/gome2/, 2103.

CBS. "*NASA releases images of Beijing air pollution,*" Last Update: January 15th 2013, http://www.cbsnews.com/8301-205_162-57564051/nasa-releases-images-of-beijing-air-pollution/

Hidy, George, *et al.,* "Remote Sensing of Particulate Pollution from Space: Have We Reached the Promised Land?," *Journal of the Air & Waste Management Association,* vol. 59 (6), pp. 645–675, 2009.

MedLibrary.org. "*Satellite temperature measurements,*" Last Update: 2013, http://medlibrary.org/medwiki/Satellite_temperature_measurements

Jen-Hao, Liu, *et al.,* "Developed urban air quality monitoring system based on wireless sensor networks," in *Sensing Technology (ICST), 2011 Fifth International Conference on,* 2011, pp. 549–554.

Murty, R., *et al.*, "Citysense: An urban-scale wireless sensor network and testbed," presented at the IEEE International Conference on Technologies for Homeland Security, Boston, MA, 2008.

Morreale, P., *et al.*, "Real-Time Environmental Monitoring and Notification for Public Safety," *MultiMedia, IEEE,* vol. 17 (2), pp. 4–11, 2010.

Bagula, Antoine, Marco Zennaro, Gordon Inggs, Simon Scott, and David Gascon, "Ubiquitous Sensor Networking for Development (USN4D): An Application to Pollution Monitoring," *Sensors,* vol. 12 (1), pp. 391–414, 2012.

Li, Jason Jingshi, Boi Faltings, Olga Saukh, David Hasenfratz, and Jan Beutel, "Sensing the Air We Breathe — The OpenSense Zurich Dataset," in *Proceedings of the Twenty-Sixth AAAI on Artificial Intelligence,* Toronto, Ontario, Canada, 2012, pp. 323–325.

Swiss Federal Laboratories for Materials Science and Technology "Empa - a Research Institute of the ETH Domain," `http://www.empa.ch/plugin/template/empa/4/*/---/l=2`, 2013.

Hasenfratz, David, Olga Saukh, and Lothar Thiele, "On-the-Fly Calibration of Low-Cost Gas Sensors," in *Wireless Sensor Networks.* vol. 7158, Picco, GianPietro and Wendi Heinzelman, Eds., Springer Berlin Heidelberg, 2012, pp. 228–244.

Keller, M., J. Beutel, O. Saukh, and L. Thiele, "Visualizing large sensor network data sets in space and time with vizzly," in *Local Computer Networks Workshops (LCN Workshops), 2012 IEEE 37th Conference on,* 2012, pp. 925–933.

Nafis, Chris. "*Air Quality Monitoring,*" Last Update: 2012, `http://www.howmuchsnow.com/arduino/airquality/`

Jiang, Yifei, *et al.*, "MAQS: a personalized mobile sensing system for indoor air quality monitoring," presented at the Proceedings of the 13th international conference on Ubiquitous computing, Beijing, China, 2011.

Wright, Anne, Candide Kemmler, and Rich Gibson. "*BodyTrack: Open Source Tools for Health Empowerment through Self-Tracking,*" Last Update: July 18th 2012, `http://www.oscon.com/oscon2012/public/schedule/detail/24733`

Aoki, Paul M., *et al.*, "Common Sense: Mobile Environmental Sensing Platforms to Support Community Action and Citizen Science," Computer Interaction Institute `http://www.paulos.net/papers/2008/CommonSense%20UbiComp2008Demo.pdf`, 2008.

Westly, Erica. "*Citizen Science: How Smartphones Can Aid Scientific Research,*" Last Update: 2009, `http://www.popularmechanics.com/science/4308375`

Zappi, Piero, Elizabeth Bales, Jing Hong Park, William Griswold, and Tajana Šimunić Rosing, "The CitiSense Air Quality Monitoring Mobile Sensor Node," presented at the 2nd International Workshop on Mobile Sensing (ISPN'12), Beijing, China, 2012.

The Copenhagen Wheel, "The Copenhagen Wheel," `http://senseable.mit.edu/copenhagenwheel/index.html`, 2013.

Mendez, D., A. J. Perez, M. A. Labrador, and J. J. Marron, "P-Sense: A participatory sensing system for air pollution monitoring and control," in *Pervasive Computing and Communications Workshops (PERCOM Workshops), 2011 IEEE International Conference on,* 2011, pp. 344–347.

Saavedra, Joe. "*Citizen Sensor - DIY Environmental Monitoring - Development Blog,*" Last Update: 2013, `http://thesis.jmsaavedra.com/concept/`

Ganapati, Priya. "*Android App Uses Cellphone Camera to Measure Air Pollution,*" Last Update: September 24th 2010, `http://www.wired.com/gadgetlab/2010/09/cellphone-camera-air-pollution/`

Sensaris. "*Discover of SensPods,*" Last Update: 2013, `http://www.sensaris.com/products/senspod/`

SmartSantander. "*Smart Santander,*" Last Update: 2013, `http://www.smartsantander.eu/`

BarcelonaSmartCity. "*Barcelona Ciutat Intel·ligent,*" Last Update: 2013, `http://smartbarcelona.cat/en/`

Amsterdamsmartcity. "*Amsterdam Smart City,*" Last Update: 2013, `http://amsterdamsmartcity.com/`

Honjo, Tsuyoshi, "Thermal Comfort in Outdoor Environment," *Global Environmental Research,* vol. 13 pp. 43–47, 2009.

Cheng, Vicky, Edward Ng, Cecilia Chan, and Baruch Givoni, "Outdoor thermal comfort study in a sub-tropical climate: a longitudinal study based in Hong Kong," *International Journal of Biometeorology,* vol. 56 (1), pp. 43–56, 2012.

Johansson, Erik and Rohinton Emmanuel, "The influence of urban design on outdoor thermal comfort in the hot, humid city of Colombo, Sri Lanka," *International Journal of Biometeorology,* vol. 51 (2), pp. 119–133, 2006.

Krüger, Eduardo, Patricia Drach, Rohinton Emmanuel, and Oscar Corbella, "Urban heat island and differences in outdoor comfort levels in Glasgow, UK," *Theoretical and Applied Climatology,* vol. 112 (1–2), pp. 127–141, 2013.

Höppe, Peter, "Aspects of human biometerology in past, present and future," *International Journal of Biometeorology,* vol. 40 (1), pp. 19–23, 1997.

Shuo, Liu, Zhou Guomo, and Mo Lufeng, "The green space monitoring system based on Wireless Sensor Network," in *Education Technology and Computer (ICETC), 2010 2nd International Conference on,* 2010, pp. V5-180–V5-183.

Gaffin, Stuart R., Reza Khanbilvardi, and Cynthia Rosenzweig, "Development of a Green Roof Environmental Monitoring and Meteorological Network in New York City," *Sensors,* vol. 9 pp. 2647–2660, 2009.

Cohen, Pninit and Oded Potchter, "Daily and Seasonal Air Quality Characteristics of Urban Parks in the Mediterranean City of Tel Aviv," presented at the CLIMAQS Workshop, Antwerp, Belgium, 2010.

Gillette, Bill, *"Pollution and UV Damage"*, The Centre for Dermatologic Surgery, Last Update: 2011, `http://blogs.cooperhealth.org/drlawrence/2011/03/pollution-and-uv-damage/`

Holick, Michael F., *et al.*, "Evaluation, Treatment, and Prevention of Vitamin D Deficiency: an Endocrine Society Clinical Practice Guideline," *Journal of Clinical Endocrinology & Metabolism,* vol. 96 (7), pp. 1911–1930, 2011.

SunSignal Sensors, "How It Works", `http://sunsignals.com/how-it-works/`, 2013.

UVSunSense. *"UVSense Wristbands,"* Last Update: 2013, `http://www.uvsunsense.com/uvss/`

Biosense. *"High quality personal dosimetry,"* Last Update: 2013, `http://www.biosense.de/home-e.html`

ICEPURE. *"ICEPURE: The impact of climatic and environmental factors on personal ultraviolet radiation exposure and human health,"* Last Update: 2009, `http://icepure.eu/WP_descriptions.html`

Lamkin, Paul. *"DoCoMo breath testing smart jacket pictures and hands-on,"* Last Update: October 7th 2011, `http://www.pocket-lint.com/news/112373-docomo-breath-testing-hands-on`

Fahrni, Thomas, Michael Kuhn, Philipp Sommer, Roger Wattenhofer, and Samuel Welten, "Sundroid: Solar Radiation Awareness with Smartphones," in *13th International Conference on Ubiquitous Computing (Ubicomp '11)*, Beijing, China, 2011, pp. 365–374.

MIT Mobile Experience Laboratory, "Mobile UV Monitor", `http://mobile.mit.edu/portfolio/mobile-uv-monitor/`, 2011.

Igoe, Damien, Alfio Parisi, and Brad Carter, "Characterization of a Smartphone Camera's Response to Ultraviolet A Radiation," *Photochemistry and Photobiology,* vol. 89 (1), pp. 215–218, 2013.

Carnegie-Mellon. *"WaterBot,"* Last Update: 2013, `http://waterbot.org/`

Kimmel, Danielle W., Gabriel LeBlanc, Mika E. Meschievitz, and David E. Cliffel, "Electrochemical Sensors and Biosensors," *Analytical Chemistry,* vol. 84 pp. 685–707, 2011.

Lagarde, Florence and Nicole Jaffrezic-Renault, "Cell-based electrochemical biosensors for water quality assessment," *Analytical and Bioanalytical Chemistry,* vol. 400 (4), pp. 947–964, 2011.

Jang, Am, Zhiwei Zou, Kang Kug Lee, Chong H Ahn, and Paul L Bishop, "State-of-the-art lab chip sensors for environmental water monitoring," *Measurement Science and Technology,* vol. 22 (3), 2011.

Rassaei, Liza, *et al.*, "Nanoparticles in electrochemical sensors for environmental monitoring," *TrAC Trends in Analytical Chemistry,* vol. 30 (11), pp. 1704–1715, 2011.

Namour, Philippe, Mathieu Lepot, and Nicole Jaffrezic-Renault, "Recent Trends in Monitoring of European Water Framework Directive Priority Substances Using Micro-Sensors: A 2007–2009 Review," *Sensors,* vol. 10 pp. 7947–7978, 2010.

IBM. *"IBM Aims to Help Alleviate Water Shortages in Northern California's Wine Country,"* Last Update: June 25th 2010, `http://www-03.ibm.com/press/us/en/pressrelease/31995.wss`

Becaon Institute, "Beacon Institute and IBM Team to Pioneer River Observatory Network", `http://bire.org/institute/ibm.php`, 2007.

Percifield, Leif. *"dontflush.me,"* Last Update: 30th October, 2012, `http://dontflush.me/about`

Kramer, Herbert J. *"Argo (Data Collection in the Global Oceans),"* Last Update: 2013, `http://www.eoportal.org/directory/pres_ArgoDataCollectionintheGlobalOceans.html`

EPA. *"Microbial (Pathogen),"* Last Update: November 2nd 2012, `http://water.epa.gov/scitech/swguidance/standards/criteria/health/microbial/index.cfm`

Insta-Link, "Get Started with an Advanced SmartScan™ Kit", `http://insta-link.com/poolspa/learn_morehome.html?tab=2#tabbedpanels1`, 2012.

Edgar, Tricia. *"Smartphones to Determine Water Quality,"* Last Update: June 4th 2013, `http://www.kalev.com/clean-water-from-the-cloud-mobosens-uses-smartphone-technology-to-determine-water-quality/`

Maisonneuve, Nicolas, Matthias Stevens, Maria E. Niessen, Peter Hanappe, and Luc Steels, "Citizen noise pollution monitoring," presented at the Proceedings of the 10th Annual International Conference on Digital Government Research: Social Networks: Making Connections between Citizens, Data and Government, 2009.

Rana, Rajib Kumar, Chun Tung Chou, Salil S. Kanhere, Nirupama Bulusu, and Wen Hu, "Ear-phone: an end-to-end participatory urban noise mapping system," presented at the Proceedings of the 9th ACM/IEEE International Conference on Information Processing in Sensor Networks, Stockholm, Sweden, 2010.

Kanjo, Eiman, "NoiseSPY: A Real-Time Mobile Phone Platform for Urban Noise Monitoring and Mapping," *Mob. Netw. Appl.,* vol. 15 (4), pp. 562–574, 2010.

Bergner, Benjamin, Jan-Philipp Exner, Peter Zeile, and Martin Rumberg, "Sensing the City – How to identify Recreational Benefits of Urban Green Areas with the Help of Sensor Technology," presented at the RealCORP, Vienna, 2012.

Martí, IreneGarcia, *et al.*, "Mobile Application for Noise Pollution Monitoring through Gamification Techniques," in *Entertainment Computing - ICEC 2012.* vol. 7522, Herrlich, Marc, Rainer Malaka, and Maic Masuch, Eds., Springer Berlin Heidelberg, 2012, pp. 562–571.

EPA. *"Radon - Health Risks,"* Last Update: March 19th, 2013, `http://www.epa.gov/radon/healthrisks.html`

Boyd, Mark. "*Sensors Monitor Radiation in Japan - Engineers give data to the people*," Last Update: May 1st 2011, http://www.deskeng.com/articles/aabawh.html

Safecast, "*Safevcast - A Global Sensor Network Collecting and Sharing Radiation Measurements*", Last Update: 2013, http://blog.safecast.org/about/

Lawrence, Dune. "*China Says Sanlu Milk Likely Contaminated by Melamin*," Last Update: September 12th 2008, http://www.bloomberg.com/apps/news?pid=newsarchive&sid=at6LcKJB6YA8

Isakovic, Alja, "*An important milestone for CubeSensors: the Summer batch sold out in just a month!*", CUBESENSORSBLOG, Last Update: April 16th 2013, http://blog.cubesensors.com/2013/04/an-important-milestone-for-cubesensors-the-summer-batch-sold-out-in-a-month/

Johannesen, Hanne-Louise. "*Pollution sensoring and visualizing garment (CO2-dress)*," Last Update: December 15th 2009, http://www.fashioningtech.com/photo/album/show?id=2095467%3AAlbum%3A12419

Chua, Jasmin Malik. "*Dahea Sun's Cabbage-Dyed Dresses Change Color to Indicate Rain's pH*," Last Update: June 27th 2012, http://www.ecouterre.com/dahea-suns-cabbage-dyed-dresses-change-color-to-indicate-rains-ph/

Lees, Kathleen. "*World Water Day: 3.4 Million People Die Each Year from Water, Sanitation, and Hygiene-Related Causes*," Last Update: March 23rd 2013, http://www.scienceworldreport.com/articles/5756/20130323/world-water-day-3-4-million-people-die-each-year.html

Banna, Muinul H., *et al.*, "Online drinking water quality monitoring: review on available and emerging technologies," *Critical Reviews in Environmental Science and Technology*, pp. null-null, 2013.

Pellerin, Brian A., *et al.*, "Assessing the sources and magnitude of diurnal nitrate variability in the San Joaquin River (California) with an in situ optical nitrate sensor and dual nitrate isotopes," *Freshwater Biology*, vol. 54 (2), pp. 376–387, 2009.

Corke, P., *et al.*, "Environmental Wireless Sensor Networks," *Proceedings of the IEEE*, vol. 98 (11), pp. 1903–1917, 2010.

■ ■ ■

CHAPTER 12

Summary and Future Trends

In this chapter, we present a summary of the subject matter covered in previous chapters. We revisit the key influences that currently drive the development of sensor-based applications in the health, wellness and health-related environmental monitoring. We also look toward the future of sensing by examining some emerging trends, including those that suggest how sensors will become integral to many aspects of our daily lives. We discuss how the evolution of technology brought pervasive connectivity and computing, and how it will impact future sensor applications. We also examine how crowdsourcing empowers citizens, adding an innovative element to future sensor applications. Finally, we explore the sensing nexus that stems from the way sensors interconnect with information and communications technologies. New and innovative sensing solutions will enable us to develop fresh insights at a personalized level into how our behaviors, lifestyle choices, and other factors influence our health and wellbeing.

So Far

In this book we looked at many of the key drivers that are influencing sensor-based applications for monitoring health, wellness, and the environment. Global challenges such as aging, water constraints, and environmental pollution require innovative solutions. Sensors already play a key role in enabling innovation as we endeavor to make the world around us smarter—to improve our quality of lives, to better utilize our natural resources, and to reduce our impact on the planet. The role of sensors in enabling innovative solutions will continue to grow in the coming decades. The falling cost of sensor technologies is playing a key role in the rapid growth of their utilization. For example, the cost of MEMs accelerometers has fallen by 80-90 percent over the last five years (Manyika et al., 2013). Advances in sensor technologies will also be closely interleaved with progress in infrastructural technologies that support the aggregation, processing, transport, storage, and visualization of sensor data, as outlined in Chapters 4 and 5. The evolution of machine-to-machine (M2M) technologies and the Internet of Things (IOT) are examples of application domains where infrastructural technologies are utilizing sensors to advance the current state of the art. New revenue streams will emerge by fitting sensors to existing products and to new product ranges. The data can then be used to support improved client services and enhanced product development (Economist, 2013).

We have described a variety of sensing approaches that are commonly utilized. New approaches to sensing over the past 30 years, such as the development of biosensors and microelectromechanical systems (MEMS) technology, have significantly increased the breadth of available applications. We have witnessed a significant reduction in device costs and an increased prevalence of sensor-based solutions. These developments have coincided with the integration of information and communications technology (ICT) capabilities into sensors. The addition of computation, memory, and communications features to sensors ushered in the era of the smart sensor. And support for wireless communications set the stage for the development of wireless sensor networks with their promise of ubiquitous ambient sensing. More recently, the utilization of smartphones and tablets as sensor aggregators significantly influenced their adoption by the general public. Since the launch of the iPhone in 2007, growth in the sales of smartphones and tablets has increased sixfold (Manyika et al., 2013). IDC estimated that sales of smartphones will reach 1.7 billion units by 2017 (Llamas et al., 2013). Some 56 percent of people in the US already use smartphones for Internet access, while 31 percent use smartphones to collect and access health and medical information. This represents a 50-percent increase since 2008 (Jones, 2012). Similarly, growth in the adoption of tablets has seen current ownership rates among adults in the US reach 34 percent (Zickuhr, 2013) with global sales of tablets projected to reach 400 million units by 2017 (Mainelli, 2013). Smartphones and tablets provide an intuitive platform for users to digest and interact with sensor data and to collect data as the user requires. A technology that was relatively abstract or considered by many to be the preserve of specialized users can now deliver real meaning and have context for ordinary individuals.

Movements such as the quantified self have embraced ICT-based sensing capabilities—to track, to share, and to build knowledge about health and well-being. This form of sensing also underpins new thinking in medicine. This model moves away from reactive treatment toward proactive management of health. Sensors are used to identify the early warning signs of health issues so intervention can occur before a significant problem arises. Sensors also support the goals of personalized medicine, where treatments are tailored to our own unique biochemistry and DNA. This desire for personal understanding has now permeated our social and recreational activities. We have seen how many sensing technologies commonly used in healthcare are being utilized in sports and wellness applications to monitor performance. Interest is also growing in how the environment influences our health and well-being, leading to commercial products and platforms that let concerned citizens and technical enthusiasts monitor the air, water, ambient noise, and more.

Socializing data is a constant theme across our application domains, driven by our increasingly connected lifestyles. Mobile devices with ubiquitous connectivity, coupled with cloud-based, scalable computational and storage capabilities, enable sharing of data in real-time at the point of origin. The collective power of online communities is being applied to these data sources in order to make sense of them, to generate context, and to trigger actions as required. People will increasingly become mobile sensors, driving growth in crowd-sourced data sets. Initial applications have been focused on participatory sensing, where individuals actively participate in the sensing process. In the future, opportunistic sensing may become common, where individuals may not be aware of active sensing applications running on personal devices like smartphones. Changes in state, such as location, activity, and so forth, are automatically detected, which triggers the collection of sensor data based on the new context. The device owner is not required to play an active role in the sensing process beyond the initial setup (Lane et al., 2008). Of course, privacy must be carefully managed to protect participants. Urban sensing, particularly environmental applications, may utilize these approaches as the potential scale and density of sensing that can be delivered would be impossible to achieve otherwise. Both approaches leverage people-centric sensing to avoid the deployment of an expensive static infrastructure to create this new sensing paradigm (Kapadia et al., 2009). Similarly, as sensors are built into more and more devices, there is potentially an infinite number of "things" that can be sensed with a corresponding growth in data. The age of "big sensor data" has arrived, with huge opportunities for exciting innovations, but also with significant challenges. As frequency, volume, and diversity of sensor data increases, so does the importance of data visualization. Data visualization allows people to makes sense of the information by enabling knowledge discovery. Visualization also adds vibrancy to the data—a key element in stimulating and maintaining user engagement. Visualization will be a critical element in making the data actionable. Big data analytics will enable people to connect with their own data in meaningful ways, and will allow them to see how they can change their behaviors and lifestyles. As individuals, we ultimately want the sensor data to foster concrete, actionable suggestions.

Throughout the book we have been careful to ground the expectations of sensors in reality. Sensors are not a silver bullet for every problem that needs to be fixed. They can, however, enable innovative solutions if their operation characteristics are matched appropriately to the required use case. Some sensor technologies—particularly wireless sensors networks—have been overhyped to a certain extent. Networks comprising thousands or tens of thousands of nodes have yet to be realized. There are many technical and logistical barriers to achieving this goal. If we set aside the hype promoting pervasive wireless sensor networks as the solution to all of our problems, we find that they are being successfully utilized in small-scale, focused deployments, such as wellness monitoring of older adults. The reality may not live up to the hype for some time. For the foreseeable future, the value of these networks will be realized in more micro-level deployments with very targeted and specific use cases.

The potential to quantify our health and well-being on a continuous basis has significant implications at personal and societal levels. We have to be careful not to generate nations of "worried well" individuals who are paranoid about every decimal-place variation in their measurements. It is counterproductive for individuals to engage in self-stigmatization just because a sensor reading indicates that a particular health metric is not in the desired region. When used correctly and in the appropriate context, sensors can have an enormously positive impact on our lives that will grow into the future. So, what does the future of sensors hold for us?

Into the Future

To glimpse the future, sometimes it is useful to recall what has happened in the past. For example, the measurement of temperature can be traced back to ancient times. The works of Philo of Byzantium and Hero of Alexandria demonstrated an early thermoscope based on a closed tube that was partially filled with air. One end of the tube was placed into a vessel containing water. Expansion and contraction of the air due to temperature changes altered the position of the water and air interface along the tube. A number of European scientists in the 16th and 17th centuries, including Galileo, are credited with further developing the thermoscope. Sanctorio Sanctorius and/or Gianfrancesco Sagredo are said to have put a scale to the thermoscope, producing the first rudimentary air thermometer (Chew, 2008). The German physicist Daniel Gabriel Fahrenheit invented an alcohol thermometer in 1709, followed by the mercury thermometer in 1714. In 1724, he introduced the standardized Fahrenheit scale. In 1742, the Celsius scale was invented by the Swedish astronomer Anders Celsius. This scale is divided into 100 degrees between the freezing point (0°C) and boiling point (100°C) of water at sea-level air pressure. The Kelvin scale was invented by Lord Kelvin in 1848 and incorporates extremes of hot and cold. The Kelvin scales starts with 0K at absolute zero or –273°C degrees Celsius. In 1866, Sir Thomas Clifford Allbutt invented a clinical thermometer that could take a temperature reading in 5 minutes (Prater, 2008). This allowed clinicians to correlate the relationship between body temperature and a patient's state of health. From a rather slow beginning, then, the past few decades have seen a vast explosion in the variety of temperature sensors based on a diverse range of sensing modalities. Modern temperature sensors are now based on principles such as thermistors, thermocouples, non-contact sensors, and fiber optics with accuracies to 0.001 degrees Celsius, with highly integrated ICT capabilities. Significant progress has indeed been made from the early thermoscope. The same is true for many of the common sensing principles utilized in sensors today, which are based on decades or centuries of careful work to establish and validate their scientific operation. These painstaking efforts have laid a strong scientific foundation that is now being exploited, together with other technology developments, to deliver significant benefits across a wide range of application domains. Sensor technologies have now matured to a point where we are at the cusp of an explosion in the diversity of applications and their adoption.

There is significant momentum behind sensors and their application in healthcare, wellness, and environmental monitoring, as technology and the innovative solutions they can enable are growing steadily. Couple this momentum with advances in mobile and cloud computing and pervasive communications, and a clear inflection point is at hand. This inflection point represents a change in direction based on adoption of sensing and ICT that will allow us to start moving from the current reactive healthcare model to a wellness-preservation model. The next section examines some of the key areas that will influence the future of sensors in application domains of interest.

Pervasiveness

We are entering an era where sensors are becoming an integral feature in daily life. New types of sensors are emerging that can be distributed into the public environment, worn on the body, or integrated into the next generation of intelligent devices. Applications built using advanced sensing capabilities focus on improving the health and well-being of billions of people around the globe, and they are already distributed into ambient environments to passively monitor actions, behaviors, environmental conditions, and even vital signs unobtrusively. While technical challenges remain, the general trajectory of adoption and proliferation has been set. Environments will become smarter by initially announcing when they need adjustment to improve, for example, air quality, lighting levels, ambient noise levels, and so forth. In the longer term, as smart home technologies with integrated sensing become more prevalent, living environments will automatically adjust to maximize the health and well-being of the occupants. Research over the last decade, particularly with living laboratory experiments, has already demonstrated how this kind of sensing can be used in domestic environments. In the future, these environments will become more sophisticated in their ability to model normal patterns of behavior and to identify changes in these patterns that could indicate a potential health concern.

Sensors will be designed into objects people already use or carry on a daily basis. The reality of the sensor as an "everyday technology" has already emerged, with people routinely wearing activity monitors, fitness monitors, and so forth as outlined in Chapter 10. Sensors will reside in new devices that will become everyday objects in the near future, such as multisensing, health-monitoring smartphones or environmental-sensing smart clothing. These devices will increasingly feature desirable design aesthetics (Sarasohn-Kahn, 2013). This trend is already reflected in home environmental sensing products, such as the Netamo wireless weather station, which are designed to be seen and to become desirable lifestyle choices. Sensors will also be integrated into more and more everyday devices. In many cases, they will be invisible to users apart from the utility they deliver. A modern car, for example, may feature over 100 different sensor types. The car's owner doesn't necessarily know they are there, but the sensors enhance the driving experience and enable safer driving, with better fuel efficiency and less impact on the environment. Imagine a future where this is the case for health and wellness, with data collected actively and passively by sensors throughout the day. We will be able to access this data as we want or to be proactively notified of issues that need to be addressed at the earliest possible juncture, through a variety of personal devices. For example, visualize a world where you have a weekly health review on a windscreen heads-up display as you drive to work in a cloud-connected car.

Proliferation and adoption of sensors will also be accelerated by the growing commercial availability of sensor solutions aimed at the consumer market. We are already witnessing how activity monitors and fitness devices have entered into public consciousness. All projections point toward a market that will witness significant growth in the coming decade. Already, established multinational brands have entered the fitness-sensing market as they recognize the growth opportunities. Expect to see more established technology players enter the market in the coming years with their own product offerings or in partnership with niche companies. In the short term, we will likely see a wave of new product offerings, but just as in most markets, this initial influx will see various winners and losers emerge as the market matures and consumer buying decisions adjudicate which products are the most compelling. As the concept of technology development through crowdsourced funding becomes more mainstream, new sensor solutions will emerge to address specific problems identified and funded by communities. These communities will also act as trusted advocates for the solutions that will positively influence adoption rates. The AirQuality Egg sensor described in Chapter 11 is one such community effort by designers, technologists, developers, architects, students, and artists. This community, devoid of vested interests, has the single goal of developing a sensor technology that allows the general public to participate and contribute to the conversation about air quality. Smartphones and tablets will continue to be enablers for personal sensor applications. The number of built-in sensors in these devices will grow and enable new usage models. The integration of dedicated sensor hubs in mobile platforms will also act as a key enabler by offering better performance, predictability, and extensibility.

The next stage of computing innovation is starting to take advantage of the various sensors packed into current and future handsets. Sensor technologies such as accelerometers, magnetometers, and ambient light sensors, together with supporting technologies such as GPS, wireless communications, and bandwidth awareness, are already common in modern mobile devices. The future will see even more types of sensors being integrated into smartphones, such as those for electrocardiography (ECG) monitoring. Opportunistic sensing with these devices will become more prevalent to reduce the requirement for conscious human action in the sensing process. The manner in which people interact with these devices will also provide rich data that can be used to gain insights into such areas as cognitive well-being and cognitive psychology (Lee et al., 2012) (Miller, 2012) Researchers are also looking at ways to use the data from smartphone sensors to provide context when modeling human behavior using classification techniques (Pei et al., 2013). While these types of applications are still in the research domain, their potential to scale, coupled with minimal infrastructural requirements, may well see their exploitation for mainstream clinical wellness monitoring in the near future.

Technology

Sensor technologies will continue to advance, both in terms of improvements to existing approaches and the development of new sensing modalities. That rate of advancement is likely to accelerate, driven in part by growing commercial demand. New consumer markets are emerging, driven by individuals' desires to proactively understand and manage personal health and well-being. The crossover from health sensing into sports and wellness sensing is growing—and generating new demands for sensor technologies.

New sensors will reach lower detection limits, have higher selectivity and sensitivity, and will have enhanced stability. Biosensors in particular have the potential to identify the early biochemical markers of disease. They can also rapidly identify both chemical and biological contaminants. In this regard, they have the potential to play a key role in environmental applications where there is a need, for example, to rapidly identify bacterial contamination of drinking water. A key step in realizing this goal will be the further development of lab-on-chip technologies. These nanoscale systems provide automated laboratory capabilities, such as sample preparation, fluid handling, analysis, and sensing/detection within the confines of a single microchip. Continued advances in MEMS technology and the rapid pace of evolution in semiconductor manufacturing techniques will enable production of these devices in large quantities, cost-effectively, and with the required reliability and stability. MEMs advancements will also undoubtedly enable the development of a new generation of sensors based on electrochemical, semiconductor, optical, and kinematic sensing principles.

We are also likely to see advances in chemo-optical sensors in environmental applications, with improved reliability over existing methods. Water sensing and environmental sensing will feature greater autonomy for long-term independent operations in order to lower support costs. The sensor platforms will be smarter and form smart sensor networks. These smart sensor networks will have features such as automated and remote troubleshooting capabilities, with real-time telemetry, to ensure the fastest possible response times to issues as they arise. Data from various sources such as water quality monitors, geographic information systems, satellite imaging, and so forth will be used with data analytics to build predictive environmental models in order to facilitate real-time decision support. Sensing will play an increasing role in maintaining the stability, reliability, and predictability of environmental resources.

A key area for future sensor technology is non-contact physiological sensing. Any form of longitudinal sensing that requires direct human body contact is challenging. There are obvious issues with this kind of sensing, such as usability, biocompatibility, and behavior modification. Non-contact sensing offers a means to capture the necessary signal—for example, EKG/ECG—through integration with everyday devices such as laptops, smartphones, and tablets. Applications are now appearing that can use a smartphone's camera to measure heart rate. Another useful effort relates to driver drowsiness, a long-standing safety concern. First-generation systems are already emerging from companies such as Mercedes-Benz that use sensors to monitor driving style, and researchers are investigating next-generation non-contact sensing systems based on physiological signal monitoring, such as ECG, EEG, and respiration, to detect drowsiness. Smart clothing is another area where non-contact sensing will grow over the years, ranging from garments that monitor physiological processes to clothing that adapts its properties based on ambient environmental conditions. The development and success of non-contact sensing will be very much use case-specific and will target specific usability constraints.

As this book has shown, smartphones and tablets have already had a significant impact on sensing and related application utilization. The future is likely to see accelerated use of these platforms, and more sensing capabilities are likely to be built into these devices. They will also feature discrete sensor hubs that will overcome current limitations, such as non-deterministic sampling rates. Discrete consumer sensor applications will continue to be available, but they are likely to become specialized when integrating them into a smartphone or tablet is not possible because of limitations that include usability, sampling, and hygiene factors. Software interfaces—and in some cases physical interfaces, particularly with disposable sensors—will become more standardized. This integration will support greater interoperability between sensors and aggregation devices. Standardization of interfaces will ensure that users are no longer tied to a particular end-to-end solution from a manufacturer, but can select the sensor and software components that best fit their needs. The healthcare domain has already seen progress being made by the Continua Alliance, but much work remains. Data security on smartphones, particularly as they hold more personal health information, will become an increasing concern. This is particularly true of regulated healthcare applications. Solutions such as dual-profile smartphones are likely to emerge, with a healthcare profile featuring strong security features, such as local data encryption. Smartphone apps that make health claims will be under increased scrutiny by the FDA, following the publication of their mHealth regulations. A recent IMS report suggested that too many mobile health apps in the market appear to be of limited usefulness or have a questionable link to health and healthcare (Versel, 2013). Regulation will inevitably delay the release of future mHealth applications into the market. However, it will provide a level of quality and accountability lacking in mHealth applications until now.

From a systems perspective, the future will focus on tighter integration between the sensor and the ICT components in system on chip (SOC) designs. The systems will have improved computational power with lower energy usage and on-chip memory. More processing will take place locally, reducing the amount of network traffic. These systems also have a smaller physical footprint, which will enable smaller form factors. The Internet of Things will accelerate development of IP-addressable radio protocols, remote sensor manageability, and light-weight messaging protocols. Connecting sensors to cloud-based storage and services will become as intuitive as pairing a

Bluetooth headset to a smartphone. Such services will allow people to remotely manage how and when the services work. Low-power machine-to-machine devices and services will be a key enabler to manage the relationship between individual sensors and the cloud.

The speed and accuracy of sensor systems will evolve to deliver improved reliability, sensitivity, and selectivity. Calibration of sensors will become a more standardized feature that exists for the lifetime of a sensor, in a manner that is highly automated and, ideally, with little or no human interaction required. Many of the current consumer-oriented sensors have limited calibration (such as a single factory calibration) before shipping. As reliance on sensor data in daily life grows, poor-quality data as a result of inadequate calibration will not be acceptable. Ultimately, the goal is to have sensors that do not require calibration. Approaches such as coulometric sensing (see Chapter 2), which in principle does not require calibration, offers an interesting glimpse of what the future might hold for at least some applications.

Current manufacturing approaches to sensor production have limitations in terms of cost, integration, and scalability. Printable sensors are an area of growing research activity to address these limitations. Existing printable technologies coupled with new materials based on advances in nanotechnology have the potential to deliver large-scale sensor production at ultra-low costs. The flexibility of the technology also has the potential to allow the printing of sensors on everyday items such as clothing. For example, the EU project 3PLAST (an acronym for printable pyroelectrical and piezoelectrical large area sensor technology) is researching methods to produce pressure and temperature sensors that can be printed onto a plastic film. The film can then be affixed to objects such as electronic equipment. The approach is based on pyroelectrical and piezoelectrical polymers that can be screen-printed in large volumes. The sensor is also combined with an organic transistor to improve its signal quality (Printed Electronics World, 2010). Similarly researchers at the University of California have successfully demonstrated printing electrochemical sensors directly onto neoprene wetsuit material (Phys.org, 2011). The sensor features two LEDs: A green LED is illuminated when the water is safe, and a red LED is illuminated when phenols are detected in water. For safety-critical applications, researchers are investigating the potential use of heat flux sensors and motion sensors that can be printed directly onto the protective clothing worn by firefighter to detect when they are in danger (Navone et al., 2013, Wei et al., 2012). We are likely to see many more applications emerge over the coming years that initially focus on specialized use cases. However, given the potential opportunities for innovative product offerings, rapid adoption of these sensing technologies in the consumer market is likely to follow.

The application of screen printing to the fabrication of disposable biosensors is an area of active research. Sensors have been produced via screen-printing for the detection of a variety of analytes, including organophosphates (pesticides) (Crew et al., 2011), Ochratoxin A (a mycotoxin produced by *Aspergillus ochraceus* and a number of other molds) (Alonso-Lomillo et al., 2010), and uric acid (elevated levels associated with gout, diabetes, and kidney stones) in human blood serum (Piermarini et al., 2013). Bio-tattoos (or biostamps) are a form of printable sensor that, while at an early stage of development, is already generating significant interest. For example, MC10 has demonstrated a bio-tattoo that stretches with the skin and monitors temperature, hydration, and strain. These tattoos are protected using a spray-on bandage to make them more durable and waterproof. The sensors can lasts up to two weeks before natural skin exfoliation results in their removal. The next phase of development will focus on the integration of wireless power and communications to enable connectivity to a smartphone (Etherington, 2013). The scalability and cost-effectiveness of such an approach will enable the greater proliferation of disposable sensors, making them accessible for in-situ use to mass markets in the future.

Wireless sensor networks—and their potential for application innovation—have received significant attention and interest over the last 20 years. What is unclear is whether large-scale WSNs can live up to the hype that has surrounded them. Small-scale networks with low numbers of sensors have successfully moved beyond the research domain into the commercial reality. Although some technical challenges remain, commercial exploitation will continue to accelerate. However, for applications that require hundreds or thousands of sensor nodes, the path forward is unclear. The largest deployments achieved to date are in the low hundreds. No one has demonstrated truly large-scale deployments over large geographical areas in either urban or rural environments. Without such deployments, the "practical issues around scale are yet to be fully explored" (Corke et al., 2010). Therefore, questions around the true cost of deployments and whether they are economically viable remain unanswered. Other technical issues, such as reliable outdoor communications in variable environmental conditions, require further research (Zhu et al., 2012). Sensor nodes in WSNs, such as those used for environmental applications, are also likely to feature more sophisticated sensors and multiple sensors on the node. This will generate new challenges, such as multisensor data fusion, multiple calibration strategies, and so on. However, the ability to fuse sensor streams will enable situational awareness—a key element in providing a context for sensor measurements. This information is critical, particularly for remotely deployed sensors nodes, as it helps us to really understand what the data is telling us. The concept of the multi-purpose sensor platform may also emerge, where the sensors and their data from one deployment can be shared among a number of applications. This can decouple the sensing infrastructure from the application (Leontiadis et al., 2012). This approach is analogous in many ways to the development of cloud computing in the IT domain, where applications are decoupled from their computing, storage and networking requirements.

Personal Health

There will be a gradual transformation of healthcare into the digital domain through digital medical records and the widescale adoption of biomedical sensing devices beyond the confines of hospitals. This will help facilitate the realization of Leroy Hood's vision of predictive, preventive, personalized, and participatory (P4) medicine (P4 Medicine Institute, 2012). Members of the current quantified-self movement (individuals who are interested in using technologies such as sensors and mobile computing to collect data about aspects of their own daily life, including physical and mental performance levels, health, food intake, personal environment, and so on), are the first early adopters of this vision. How this form of monitoring translates to the general public is a topic of debate. While members of the quantified-self movement are highly motivated individuals with a real interest in viewing and trying to understand what the data is telling them, many will argue that the general public will be less motivated, if not apathetic. Clearly, engendering a desire among citizens to view their data is going to be important. Providing the public with the necessary motivations and incentives is full of potential minefields. People might argue that it has connotations of the "nanny state," which provokes a strong negative reaction in many. However, possible changes in how insurance companies price premiums, or monitoring of adherence to therapeutic regimes or general lifestyle risk assessments, may provide the necessary impetus to motivate individuals. For example, Professor Larry Smarr at the University of California, San Diego, has been a devotee of the quantified-self practice for many years. He has been tracking over 150 variables related to his health for the last ten years using sensors, self-test kits, and laboratory analysis. Using the data on a longitudinal basis, he was able to identify changes in his levels of complex reactive protein (a biomarker for detecting the presence of inflammation) in his blood that peaked at 27 times above normal levels. Subsequently he identified that lactoferrin (a multifunctional protein that, among other functions, is a sensitive and specific biomarker for inflammatory bowel disease (IDB)) in his stool samples peaked at 124 times above normal levels. Smarr then used the data, along with research in the scientific literature, to self-diagnose Crohn's disease. Smarr also makes extensive use of body-worn sensing as part of his continuous monitoring program. He uses a FitBit to track his activity levels, and at night he uses a Zeo sensor to monitor his sleep quality. He also uses smartphones apps such as Instant Heart Rate to measure his pulse rate via the phone's camera and another app to monitor his stress levels (Landau, 2012).

Although current self-monitoring activities are still in their infancy and are a little cumbersome, they provide insight into the future of self-sensing that over time will undoubtedly lead to a shift within healthcare. This transition is not without significant challenges that extend beyond sensing. Firing data at your doctor from a home-sensing regime that wasn't prescribed by him or her in the first place may receive a frosty reception or be completely ignored. It will take time, as physicians and other healthcare professionals wrestle with these new sources of data. Making sense of the data will be critical and challenging for individuals and their physicians and will require behavioral changes across the clinical ecosystem to fully exploit the value of the data.

Establishing the relationship between sensor measurements, coupled with their variation over time and their relationship to disease state, will be enormously challenging. However, tools such as high performance computing (HPC), cloud computing, big data analytics, and so on are providing key tools to make those breakthroughs possible. Medicine is slowly moving into the digital age. Eric Topol, an evangelist for the use of technology in healthcare, has said: "Medicine today is all about averages, medians, population, and mass screenings … unacceptable and antiquated!" Topol has been a long-standing proponent of a future in which doctors will prescribe sensors and apps running on smartphones to achieve an effective diagnosis, as opposed to prescribing a collection of pills and seeing how the patient responds (Robbins, 2012). Clearly, this vision for the future of healthcare will take time to materialize. Early pioneers such as Topol are forging new territories that will act over time as catalysts to advance sensors and associated technologies in healthcare. Speculating how long these changes will take is challenging. But it is fair to say that change will occur at a slower pace than many predict or would like it to happen at. Ultimately, the magnitude of the problems facing healthcare systems will force radical change, but not before teetering at the brink for a while.

Crowdsourcing

Crowdsourcing, or "participatory sensing" applications, are becoming increasingly common. There is the obvious attraction of using citizens as sensors due to their mobility and their ability to react dynamically to situations or their environment. The growth in crowdsourcing's popularity has been driven by access to low-cost sensors and the availability of Internet-enabled mobile devices such as smartphones. As Chapter 11 shows, environmental sensing among individuals is emerging as an application domain. It is likely that these types of applications will continue to grow in popularity, particularly as more commercial sensor platforms appear to meet demand and interest.

A number of questions will need to be addressed once the initial enthusiasm abates. The quality of the sensing is often problematic. Low-cost sensors are often used to deliver a product within a certain price range, to the detriment of data quality. Therefore, the sensitivity and selectivity of sensors for the targets of interest may not be sufficient. Moreover, the sensors may not have field-calibration features, resulting in drift and erroneous data. Collectively, these limitations can result in data-quality issues for any crowdsourced observations. These issues create a considerable challenge: how do we differentiate between readings from sensors that are accurate and inaccurate? Other issues that need to be addressed in the future include information overload, "noise," malicious misinformation, bias, and trust. These will be areas of significant research in the future as the crowdsourcing domain matures.

As various technology-driven paradigms continue to evolve, such as Web 2.0, cloud computing, mobile computing, and so on, they will enable crowdsourced sensing to play a greater role in creating collective intelligence models. Building these models will require generating shared insights into issues that affect health, such as air and water quality. Crowdsourced sensing will be able to quickly establish the geographic boundaries of issues and to follow these boundaries dynamically. The ability of crowdsourced sensing to empower individuals and to provide a form of data democratization will continue to make it attractive, despite the concerns about data quality and the ability to interpret the data correctly. Finding robust solutions to issues such as data integrity, quality, and reliability will be critical to its success and determine how extensively crowdsourced sensing is ultimately adopted.

In addition to participatory sensing, opportunistic sensing may have a key role to play, particularly in the environmental domain, in future sensor applications such as those that monitor ambient noise pollution, urban air quality, and so forth. Opportunistic sensing has the potential to provide data on a much larger scale in comparison with participatory sensing, which currently predominates. However, as we have discussed previously, there are serious concerns with respect to privacy and security that require adequate protections being in place before such applications can be rolled out on a large scale.

The Sensing Nexus

Many of the factors that influence health and well-being have been well established. As individuals, though, we haven't had the necessary tools to measure, track, visualize, and interpret this data. The sensing nexus that is now emerging, supported by developments in ICT technologies, is giving us the tools for the first time to better understand and take control of our health and well-being, and to understand the environment around us. We are on the cusp of a major paradigm shift where sensors, for the reasons discussed throughout this book, will become more pervasively distributed into our lives. They will allow us to detect health issues earlier, when intervention can be more effective. Even more important, they will enable insight into how behaviors, lifestyle choices, environments, and even emotional states influence health and well-being. The future will be about making informed, proactive choices that focus on us being well and maintaining that state for as long as possible. Sensing and ICT technologies are making this a more accessible goal that will be within the reach of most individuals. These technologies give us tools and capabilities to think about and take ownership of our own health destinies. As the renowned Irish writer Oscar Wilde once said, "A man who does not think for himself does not think at all."

References

Manyika, James, *et al.*, "Disruptive technologies: Advances that will transform life, business, and the global economy. ", McKinsey Global Institute, `http://www.mckinsey.com/insights/business_technology/disruptive_technologies`, 2013.

The Economist Intelligence Unit, "The Internet of Things Business Index - A Quiet Revolution Gathers Pace", 2013.

Llamas, Ramon T. and William Stofega, "Worldwide Smartphone 2013-2017 Forecast", IDC, 2013.

Jones, Chuck. *"What Do People Use Their Cell Phones For Beside Phone Calls?"*, Last Update: November 29th 2012, `http://www.forbes.com/sites/chuckjones/2012/11/29/what-do-people-use-their-cell-phones-for-beside-phone-calls/`

Zickuhr, Kathryn, "One-third of adults (and half of parents) now own a tablet computer," Pew Reseach Centre, `http://libraries.pewinternet.org/2013/06/11/one-third-of-adults-and-half-of-parents-now-own-a-tablet-computer/`, 2013.

Mainelli, Tom, "Worldwide and US Tablet 2013-2017 Forecast Updated: May 2013", IDC, 2013.

Lane, Nicholas D., Shane B. Eisenman, Mirco Musolesi, Emiliano Miluzzo, and Andrew T. Campbell, "Urban Sensing Systems: Opportunistic or Participatory," in *ACM 9th Workshop on Mobile Computing Systems and Applications (HOTMOBILE '08)*, Napa Valley, CA, USA, 2008, pp. 11–16.

Kapadia, Apu, David Kotz, and Nikos Triandopoulos, "Opportunistic Sensing: Security Challenges for the New Paradigm," presented at the The First International Conference on Communication Systems and Networks (COMSNETS), Bangalore, India, 2009.

Chew, Norma. *"The History of the Body Temperature Thermometer"*, Last Update: Oct 7th 2008, `http://voices.yahoo.com/the-history-body-temperature-thermometer-2026933.html?cat=37`

Prater, Alicia M. *"The history of the body temperature thermometer"*, Last Update: December 10th, 2008, `http://www.helium.com/items/828424-the-history-of-the-body-temperature-thermometer`

Sarasohn-Kahn, Jane. *"The future of sensors in health care - passive, designed, integrated"*, Last Update: March 4th 2013, `http://www.thedoctorweighsin.com/the-future-of-sensors-in-health-care-passive-designed-integrated/`

Lee, Hyunkyu, *et al.*, "Examining cognitive function across the lifespan using a mobile application," *Computers in Human Behavior,* vol. 28 (5), pp. 1934–1946, 2012.

Miller, Geoffrey, "The Smartphone Psychology Manifesto," *Perspectives on Psychological Science,* vol. 7 (3), pp. 221–237, 2012.

Pei, Ling, *et al.*, "Human Behavior Cognition Using Smartphone Sensors," *Sensors,* vol. 13, pp. 1402–1424, 2013.

Versel, Neil. *"IMS report heralds the trough of disillusionment for mobile health apps"*, Last Update: November 5th 2013, `http://mobihealthnews.com/27054/ims-report-heralds-the-trough-of-disillusionment-for-mobile-health-apps/`

Printed Electronics World. *"Printable Sensors"*, Last Update: April 27th 2010, `http://www.printedelectronicsworld.com/articles/printable-sensors-00002218.asp`

Phys.org. *"Flexible, printable sensors detect underwater hazards"*, Last Update: July 8th 2011, `http://phys.org/news/2011-07-flexible-printable-sensors-underwater-hazards.html`

Navone, Christelle, *et al.*, "Flexible Heat Flux Sensor for Firefighters Garment Integration," IGI Global, 2013, pp. 36–45.

Wei, Yang, Russel Torah, Kai Yang, Steve Beeby, and John Tudor, "Screen Printed Capacitive Free-standing Cantilever Beams used as a Motion Detector for Wearable Sensors," *Procedia Engineering,* vol. 47, pp. 165–169, 2012.

Crew, A., D. Lonsdale, N. Byrd, R. Pittson, and J. P. Hart, "A screen-printed, amperometric biosensor array incorporated into a novel automated system for the simultaneous determination of organophosphate pesticides," *Biosensors and Bioelectronics,* vol. 26 (6), pp. 2847–2851, 2011.

Alonso-Lomillo, M. Asunción, Olga Domínguez-Renedo, Liliana Ferreira-Gonçalves, and M. Julia Arcos-Martínez, "Sensitive enzyme-biosensor based on screen-printed electrodes for Ochratoxin A," *Biosensors and Bioelectronics,* vol. 25 (6), pp. 1333–1337, 2010.

Piermarini, Silvia, *et al.*, "Uricase biosensor based on a screen-printed electrode modified with Prussian blue for detection of uric acid in human blood serum," *Sensors and Actuators B: Chemical,* vol. 179, pp. 170–174, 2013.

Etherington, Rose. *"Biostamp temporary tattoo electronic circuits by MC10"*, Last Update: March 28th 2013, `http://www.dezeen.com/2013/03/28/biostamp-temporary-tattoo-wearable-electronic-circuits-john-rogers-mc10/`

Corke, P., *et al.*, "Environmental Wireless Sensor Networks," *Proceedings of the IEEE,* vol. 98 (11), pp. 1903–1917, 2010.

Zhu, Chuan, Chunlin Zheng, Lei Shu, and Guangjie Han, "A survey on coverage and connectivity issues in wireless sensor networks," *Journal of Network and Computer Applications,* vol. 35 (2), pp. 619–632, 2012.

Leontiadls, Ilias, Christos Efstratiou, Cecilia Mascolo, and Jon Crowcroft, "SenShare: Transforming Sensor Networks into Multi-application Sensing Infrastructures," in *Wireless Sensor Networks.* vol. 7158, Picco, Gian Pietro and Wendi Heinzelman, Eds., Springer Berlin Heidelberg, 2012, pp. 65–81.

P4 Medicine Institute, "Quantifying Wellness. Demystifying Disease," http://p4mi.org/, 2012.

Landau, Elizabeth. "*Tracking your body with technology,*" Last Update: September 22nd 2012, http://www.cnn.com/2012/09/21/health/quantified-self-data.

Index

Get the eBook for only $10!

Now you can take the weightless companion with you anywhere, anytime. Your purchase of this book entitles you to 3 electronic versions for only $10.

This Apress title will prove so indispensible that you'll want to carry it with you everywhere, which is why we are offering the eBook in 3 formats for only $10 if you have already purchased the print book.

Convenient and fully searchable, the PDF version enables you to easily find and copy code—or perform examples by quickly toggling between instructions and applications. The MOBI format is ideal for your Kindle, while the ePUB can be utilized on a variety of mobile devices.

Go to www.apress.com/promo/tendollars to purchase your companion eBook.

Apress®
THE EXPERT'S VOICE™